Loving the Body

BLACK RELIGION / WOMANIST THOUGHT / SOCIAL JUSTICE

Series Editors Dwight N. Hopkins and Linda E. Thomas
Published by Palgrave:

"How Long this Road": Race, Religion, and the Legacy of C. Eric Lincoln
Edited by Alton B. Pollard, III and Love Henry Whelchel, Jr.

A White Theology of Solidarity: Signified upon and Sounded out
By James Perkinson

The Myth of Ham in Nineteenth-Century American Christianity: Race, Heathens and the People of God
By Sylvester A. Johnson

African American Humanist Principles: Living and Thinking Like the Children of Nimrod
By Anthony B. Pinn

Loving the Body: Black Religious Studies and the Erotic
Edited by Anthony B. Pinn and Dwight N. Hopkins

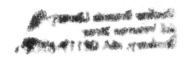

Loving the Body
Black Religious
Studies and the Erotic

Edited By

Anthony B. Pinn and Dwight N. Hopkins

LOVING THE BODY
© Anthony B. Pinn and Dwight N. Hopkins 2004.

First published in 2004 by
PALGRAVE MACMILLAN™
175 Fifth Avenue, New York, N.Y. 10010 and
Houndmills, Basingstoke, Hampshire, England RG21 6XS
Companies and representatives throughout the world.

PALGRAVE MACMILLAN is the global academic imprint of the Palgrave Macmillan division of St. Martin's Press, LLC and of Palgrave Macmillan Ltd. Macmillan® is a registered trademark in the United States, United Kingdom and other countries. Palgrave is a registered trademark in the European Union and other countries.

ISBN 1–4039–6325–8

Library of Congress Cataloging-in-Publication Data

Loving the body : Black religious studies and the erotic / edited by Dwight N. Hopkins and Anthony B. Pinn.
        p. cm.—(Black religion, womanist thought, social justice)
    Includes bibliographical references.
    ISBN 1–4039–6325–8
        1. African Americans—Religion. 2. Sex—Religious aspects—Christianity. I. Hopkins, Dwight N. II. Pinn, Anthony B. III. Series.
BR563.N4L68 2004
270'.089'96—dc22   2004052348

A catalogue record for this book is available from the British Library.

Design by Newgen Imaging Systems (P) Ltd., Chennai, India.

First edition: December 2004

10 9 8 7 6 5 4 3 2 1

To the Ancestors

Contents

IV. Theology

V. Musical Studies

VI. Hermeneutics and Cultural Criticism

VII. Sociology of Religion

About the Contributors

Victor Anderson, Associate Professor of Christian Ethics at Vanderbilt University Divinity School, has authored *Beyond Ontological Blackness: An Essay on African American Religious and Cultural Criticism; Divine Grotesquery: An African American Philosophical Theology;* and *Pragmatic Theology.*

Edward P. Antonio is Associate Professor of Theology and Social Theory at the Iliff School of Theology. With a Ph.D. from the University of Cambridge (England), his research areas consist of historical and contemporary theology, African philosophy, and the history of European thought.

Karen Baker-Fletcher, Associate Professor of Systematic Theology at Southern Methodist University Perkins School of Theology, has authored *Sisters of Dust, Sisters of Spirit: Womanist Wordings on God and Creation* and (with Garth Baker-Fletcher) *My Sister, My Brother: Womanist and Xodus God-Talk.*

Michael Joseph Brown is Assistant Professor of New Testament and Christian Origins at Candler School of Theology (Emory University) and has authored *What They Don't Tell You: A Survivor's Guide to Biblical Studies* and *The Lord's Prayer through North African Eyes.*

Lee H. Butler, Jr. is the author of *A Loving Home: Caring for African American Marriage and Family.* He is Associate Professor of Theology and Psychology at Chicago Theological Seminary.

Allen Dwight Callahan is Professor of New Testament at the Seminário Teolgico Batista do Nordeste in Bahia, Brazil. He holds a B A in Religion from Princeton University and MA and Ph.D. degrees from Harvard University in the Study of Religion specializing in New Testament and the history and literature of early Christianity.

Katie Geneva Cannon, Annie Scales Rogers Professor of Christian Ethics at Union Theological Seminary and Presbyterian School of Christian Education, is the author of *Teaching Preaching: Isaac Rufus Clark and Black Sacred Rhetoric*; *Katie's Canon: Womanism and the Soul of the Black Community*; and *Black Womanist Ethics*.

Kelly Brown Douglas is Professor of Religion in the Philosophy and Religion Department at Goucher College. Her publications consist of *The Black Christ* and *Sexuality and the Black Church: A Womanist Perspective*.

Riggins R. Earl, Jr. has authored *Dark Salutations: Ritual, God and Greetings in the African-American Community* and *Dark Symbols, Obscure Signs: God, Self, and Community in the Slave Mind.* He is Professor of Ethics and Theology at the Interdenominational Theological Seminary.

Horace L. Griffin is Assistant Professor of Pastoral Theology, directs the Chicago Collegiate Seminarians Program, and is Associate Dean for External Relations at Seabury-Western Theological Seminary. Among other pastoral care and counseling concerns, he especially does research in the areas of race, sexuality, and gender issues.

Dwight N. Hopkins is Professor of Theology at the University of Chicago Divinity School. Among his many works are *Heart and Head: black theology past, present, and future* and *On Being Human: black theology looks at culture, self, and race.*

Arthur C. Jones is Senior Clinical Professor of Psychology at the University of Denver and Founder and Chair of *The Spirituals Project* (www.spiritualsproject.org), a nonprofit organization concerned with keeping alive the African American spirituals tradition. He is the author of the award-winning book *Wade in the Water: The Wisdom of the Spirituals.* As an accomplished singer, he maintains an active schedule of lecture-concert programs focused on the spirituals.

Cheryl A. Kirk-Duggan, Ph.D., Professor of Theology and Women's Studies, and Director of Women's Studies, Shaw University Divinity School, is an ordained minister in the Christian Methodist Episcopal Church, and the author of 15 books, and numerous articles.

Irene Monroe is a Ford Fellow and doctoral candidate in the Religion, Gender, Culture program at Harvard Divinity School. Monore is a religion columnist who writes "Queer Take," for the online publication

THE WITNESS, a progressive Episcopal magazine, and "The Religion Thang," for In Newsweekly, the largest lesbian, gay, bisexual and transgender newspaper in New England.

Anthony B. Pinn is the Agnes Cullen Arnold Professor of Humanities and Professor of Religious Studies at Rice University. His interests include Black religious thought, liberation theologies, religion and popular culture, and Black humanism. He is the author/editor of thirteen books, including *Terror and Triumph: The Nature of Black Religion* (2003) and *Noise and Spirit: The Religious and Spiritual Sensibilities of Rap Music* (2003).

Alton B. Pollard III is Director of the Black Church Studies Program and Associate Professor of Religion and Culture at Candler School of Theology (Emory University). Some of his published works include *Mysticism and Social Change: The Social Witness of Howard Thurman* and *"How Long This Road: Race, Religion, and the Legacy of C. Eric Lincoln.*

Abraham Smith, Southern Methodist University Perkins School of Theology, is Associate Professor of New Testament. Among his works are *Introducing the New Testament: Literary, Theological, and Multicultural Perspectives*. He is currently completing a major work on African American biblical hermeneutics (Routledge Press).

Traci West is the author of *Wounds of the Spirit: Black Women, Violence, and Resistance Ethics*. She is also Professor of Ethics and African American Studies at Drew University Theological School.

Introduction

Anthony B. Pinn

Depicting a Problem

While scholars engaged in the study of Black religion have labelled literature a valuable resource, one that provides glimpses into the cultural and historical memory of Black America, not all the lessons this literature provides have been absorbed or even acknowledged. What we are pointing to is the manner in which African American literature has given graphic attention to the uneasy presence of sexuality and the erotic within the context of religious life. The secrets, the unspoken and unaddressed realities of human existence are not bracketed within the environs of religious community, according to the genius of African American literature. Physical needs and desires remain ever present, although an effort is made to drown them underneath a flood of theological rhetoric and ritualized distrust of the body. In this regard, the Apostle Paul's suspicion of the human body is played out in African American religiosity

> For they that are after the flesh do mind the things of the flesh; but they that are after the Spirit the things of the Spirit. For to be carnally minded is death; but to be spiritually minded is life and peace. Because the carnal mind is enmity against God for it is not subject to the law of God, neither indeed can be. So then they that are in the flesh cannot please God.[1]

Or, these words

> Let not sin therefore reign in your mortal body, that ye should obey it in the lusts thereof. Neither yield ye your members as instruments of unrighteousness unto sin but yield yourselves unto God, as those that are alive from the dead, and your members as instruments of righteousness unto God.[2]

Paul's pronouncements and suspicions are played out by means of a disregard, if not outright hatred, for the manner in which we must carry our bodies through the world—responding however reluctantly to its needs and desires. The Apostle Paul's sentiment is hauntingly familiar to those, say, in James Baldwin's *Go Tell It on the Mountain*.

Near the end of the book, the protagonist, John Grimes, finds himself on the floor of the small Pentecostal church his family attends wrestling with the will of God in/through his body. It is as if conversion requires a ripping apart of body and spirit, the former denounced and despised, and the latter renewed and freed. Those in the field of literary studies who have given attention to Baldwin's novel, note with great insight the manner in which John's "wrestling with God is also a wrestling against his own flesh and its unspeakable desires—those yearnings John has but cannot express."[3]

A similar tension is expressed in more recent literature, such as Alice Walker's *The Color Purple*. Celie, in the form of letters written to God, articulates the discomfort with flesh encouraged by social perceptions of black women. In one such letter, Celie notes that "Mr._____ come git me to take care his rotten children. He never ast me nothing bout myself. He clam on top of me and fuck and fuck, even when my head bandaged. Nobody ever love me, I say." Walker makes the tension between spiritual "matters" and flesh more explicit when Shug talks to Squeak (Mary Agnes), encouraging her to sing in public irrespective of what Squeak thinks about her voice and ability to sing well. In making her point that Squeak should sing, Shug says

> I tell you something else, Shug say to Mary Agnes, listening to you sing, folks git to thinking bout a good screw. Aw, Miss Shug, say Mary Agnes, changing color. Shug say, What, too shamefaced to put singing and dancing and fucking together? She laugh. That's the reason they call what us sing the devil's music. Devils love to fuck.[4]

What is so odd, and so brilliantly presented in African American literature (and biblical literature, if one reads carefully) is the stated purpose of religiosity as a buttress against misery and injustice over the manner in which religious thought and activity often attempt to achieve liberative ends through a negation of the flesh. Put differently, some of the same folks who sang Marvin Gayes' 1980s anthem of sensuality, desire, and sexual celebration—"Sexual Healing"—also sat in religious services marked by a perception of sexual pleasure as dangerous. Saturday night and Sunday morning were epistemologically opposed and existentially tense. (Readers will recall Shug's words provided above.) That is to say, black religion often promotes an illogical disembodied (or body despising) formulation of the "fullness" of life.

Black Religion, Sex, and Sexuality

Most forms of Black Christianity, for example, a tradition premised on the presence of divinity in flesh, are philosophically constipated in that the sacred story of embodiment does little to affect an embrace of the worshipper's physical body and the full range of pleasures this body can give and receive. Although the story of embodiment might encourage an appreciation for the cosmic significance within flesh—If the divine finds a "home" in flesh, why should humans find the body so uncomfortable?—it becomes a parable of escape, of struggle to get out of the body. Flesh becomes a burden to lament, a weight the righteous seek to overcome at least momentarily through rituals of purification (e.g., baptism).

It is widely argued that black religion develops in the context of the United States, as elsewhere, as a creative response to the human desire for a greater sense of "being," a fuller sense of self in relationship to the world and perhaps a transcendent reality. Mindful of this, modalities of black religion such as the Black Church have received praise for strides made concerning the "wholistic" liberation of African Americans, conceived in theological-religious, sociopolitical, economic, cultural, and psychological terms. And these institutions have been critiqued (and at times denounced) when they fail to promote the betterment of life for African Americans. When, however, one analyzes the engagement of black churches with the development of black "being," there is a glaring lack of attention to the bodies of African Americans. "Realness" is desired, but this quality of existence entails a rejection of the body's historical presence and suspicion toward the culturally contrived reminders of its tenacity and ever-present yearnings.

Black religion seeks to enhance the subjectivity of African Americans by securing more complex spaces of identity and creativity. Yet, this is often done in ways that ignore, if not deny, the manner in which African Americans are embodied and the way they are often defined by and reduced to popular perceptions of Black flesh. Put differently, there is still a tendency in Black churches, for example, to privilege the "spiritual" over the physical in ways that actually do damage to subjectivity by encouraging suspicion toward the needs, wants, and desires expressed by the physical body.

There remains a tension within Black religious institutions such as the Black Church with respect to sex and sexuality. Although the Black Church has traditionally avoided discussion, it has not meant that sex and sexuality were not an issue. If this were not the case, many pastors could spend less time in counseling sessions with church members, and fewer pastors would lose the moral and ethical authority of their pulpits due to "indiscretions." Defining an acceptable and working standard of Black sexual identity has been difficult, so difficult that few even venture an attempt.

All too often the Black Church has attempted to cover the issue with religious platitudes. According to cultural critic and Baptist minister Michael Dyson, "To a large extent, the black church has aimed to rid the black body of lascivious desires and to purge its erotic imagination with 'clean' thoughts."[5] The uselessness of such efforts is clear when one considers the manner in which it simply attacks aesthetics within Black religion, failing to address the more basic recognition that human bodies are sexual, represented in part by the libido as well as by a fuller sense of relationship that is properly understood in terms of a broad definition of eros. Religious doctrine and ritual structures become epistemological and existential prisons—houses of detention—where those seeking redemption do their time, distanced from themselves and what could be meaningful relationships with others. Cornel West points out and critiques the problematic posture of major black organizations, the church not excluded " . . . these grand yet flawed Black institutions refused to engage one fundamental issue Black sexuality. Instead, they ran from it like the plague. And they obsessively condemned those places where Black sexuality was flaunted: the streets, the clubs, and the dance-halls."[6]

In large part relative silence on this issue stems from the connection between sexuality and sexual activity. The Black Church by and large operates in accordance with an interpretation of scripture that makes sex outside marriage sin. Hence, addressing sexuality without entertaining this problematic dimension has been extremely difficult. When the Church has addressed this issue, it has typically revolved around the development of proper notions of manhood and womanhood. And sex (and the erotic) itself is discussed in less than helpful ways. The Black Church has faced many challenging issues over the course of its two centuries and it has handled some better than others. And many of these issues revolve around the needs and wants of the body—food, shelter, medical care, and so on. Few issues, across the various denominations, however, have been handled as badly as that of sexuality, the sexual dimension of the human body.

Sexuality and the physical expression of this have fueled tremendous and serious debate over the centuries, but with some glaring absences including the Black Church. While churches have played a role—albeit uneven—that is creative at times in the sociopolitical and economic development of African American communities, their response to libidinal issues has been rather provincial and antiquated—an assumption that prayer trumps passion. An early version of the now somewhat popular "What would Jesus do?" mantra pervaded Black churches as ministers argued, often with great style, that we were free to do what we will, recognizing that Jesus is in the room with us. That is to say, a proper relationship with Jesus meant stifled and strained relationship with other humans (and ourselves). More millenialistic churches attempted to solve the problem of sex by arguing the impending return of Christ should mean a willingness to forego all questionable activities. Act as if the second coming of Christ is about to occur served as a common response to questions of sexual desire and activity.

Black Theology, Sex, and Sexuality

Ritual practices and theology are meant to work through the tension between religiosity and the body (and its needs and desires). Religiosity is here understood as the total attitude or posture toward one's ulti-mate concern. It includes ritual practices but is not limited to these in that they represent the manifestation of this attitude. The tension between religiosity and the body stems from the manner in which various forms of Black religion, such as the Black Church, understand the body as representing desires and needs that harm one's ability to maintain a proper attitude or posture toward the divine. And this working through is most intense regarding groups who have for a variety of reasons (whether self-imposed or externally enforced) the most discomfort with their flesh—such as women and people of color.

Black flesh was doubly damned or at least more deeply stained, but open to a certain type of freedom. Black theology has wrestled against this duality, but the liberative content of this wrestling has often been questionable. Think for instance of Black theology's early preoccupa-tion with the presence of the Black male body and its need for libera-tion against racism. Only some bodies, then, were worthy of concern and only if these male bodies expressed themselves in ways that did not challenge long-established sexual norms. This of necessity meant little attention to Black female bodies and the sexism implicitly excepted by many Black male theologians. Furthermore, on both fronts, Black male and female theologians have often observed the pleasures of the body strictly in terms of heterosexual orientation and in this way buttressed a long history of homophobia within Black religious institutions and communities. Such a twist is only one example of the strain present in black religious thought and practice.

As it currently stands, Black theology is incomplete (a natural consequence of theology's apologetic posture) to the extent it fails to recognize and respond to erotic realities and relationships that comprise an important component of desired complex subjectivity, or human fulfillment. Over the course of better than thirty years, first generation, second generation, and womanist theologians have articulated a Christian vision of liberated life. The benefits of Black and womanist theologies are clear, and we are indebted to those who have fostered their birth and growth. Through the work of early figures such as James H. Cone and J. Deotis Roberts, the racism found within American churches and their theology was exposed and an agenda of liberation in keeping with the Gospel of Christ was articulated. Second generation theologians have pointed to the importance of African American cultural memory as a source of liberative discourse that informs the religious experience of African Americans. And womanist thinkers have challenged the sexism found within Black churches and theological discourse, and in this way they have enlarged our understanding of the necessary scope of liberation. This work is vital, but it has not meant sustained attention to the full ramifications of embodiment—the manner in which embodiment means an inescapable connection to sex, sexuality—eros. Are there not ways in which the pleasuring of the body as a free exercise of our humanity is a precious but ignored dimension of the liberation Black theologians have preached for better than thirty years?

Rethinking a Problem

In this book we argue that scholars involved in the study of Black religion must wrestle with sex and sexuality—and the erotic—if they are to actually present liberation as a mode of existence that frees the body and fully appreciates the body. We believe such a study is the next logical step within Black religious studies. This is because liberation must not only involve the restructuring of socioeconomic, political, and cultural space, it must also involve an appreciation of the body and the pleasuring of the body. Because the Black theological sensibilities that guide much of what takes place in Black religious studies involve a sense of embodiment, we raise a few questions. What might Black religious studies look like if this idea of embodiment involved a creative and constructive discussion of physical pleasure? How might we develop a theological/religious language for talking about Black sexuality (and the erotic/pleasure)? How might other methods in Black religious studies wrestle with embodiment and its ramifications for notions of pleasure and the erotic? How might religious life and theological discourse be expanded and intensified in ways that recognize the manner in which our most important relationships, including with the divine for theists, are earthbound, grounded in the reality of historical functions and substances?

There has been very little work done on issues of sex and sexuality within Black religious thought, and nothing that involves such a wide range of disciplinary perspectives. We have invited a group of scholars in Black religious studies to address questions such as these in light of their subfields, particular intellectual inclinations, vocational and avocational commitments and responsibilities. The essays that comprise this volume involve an honest and straightforward wrestling with an issue of tremendous importance. And what connects these essays is a general concern with the development of a much more mature and beneficial Black religious studies discourse on sex and sexuality.

There are certainly areas uncovered in this volume, angles of exploration that go unnoticed, and assumptions unchallenged. However, we make no claims to have provided the only possible course of development, of theological and religious renewal. It is our hope that these essays will stimulate and challenge, and in the process lay the groundwork for healthier notions of the sexual self within the context of Black religious experience and thought.

The discussion presented here is typically framed in terms of the Black churches—Black christianity—yet we hope that this project will encourage an ongoing and hard-hitting discourse that will grow to become comparative in nature, bringing into consideration the nature of sexuality discourse within a fuller range of Black religious traditions. We, however, leave it to readers to determine the success of this venture and the future developments it might simulate.

Notes

1. *Romans* 8:5–8 (King James Version).
2. *Romans* 6:12–13 (King James Version).

3. Vivian M. May, "Ambivalent Narratives, Fragmented Selves Performative Identities and the Mutability of Roles in James Baldwin's Go Tell It On the Mountain," in *New Essays on Go Tell It On the Mountain*, ed. Trudier Harris (New York: Cambridge University Press, 1996).
4. Alice Walker, *The Color Purple* (New York: Washington Square Press, 1982), 109, 111.
5. Michael Eric Dyson, *Race RulesNavigating the Color Line* (New York: Addision-Wesley Publishing Company, Inc., 1996), 91.
6. Cornel West, *Race Matters* (Boston: Beacon Press, 1993), 86.

I
Ethics

Sexing Black Women: Liberation from the Prisonhouse of Anatomical Authority[1]

Katie G. Cannon

The vast majority of Black churchwomen live in the midst of two competing sexual realities. Either sex is a positive blessing for procreative purposes only, or sex is a negative curse that lays claim to bodily pleasure, contaminating the mind. This moralizing hegemonic construct of irreconcilable opposites insists that normal sexual activity should only occur between female and male inside of reproductive contexts. Given the specificity of the African American ecclesial backdrop,[2] the very talk about the pleasures of genital-sexual eroticism[3] locks women between rigidly disembodied hetero/homo binaries. Far too many African American women struggle, says Susan Newman, with the deep division between the two fundamental pillars of their identity—spirituality and sexuality.

> The church tells them that to live "holy and sanctified" lives that they must give up sexual activity outside the institution of marriage, and yet their bodies and souls cry out for a way to express and fulfill their natural passion.[4]

In her assessment of this type of antisensual ambivalence, Beverly W. Harrison, writes:

> The religious dictum that the only moral expression of sexuality is that which is at least open to the possibility of procreation has been a source of many women's inability to achieve a self-defining role in relation to their bodies. Many women have been denied their own needs for bodily pleasuring at the cost of being "good" women. Conversely, when women have been sexually active or self-initiating, society has defined them as " 'whores' or 'deviants.' "[5]

Perceived through the lens of hetero-patriarchal imagination, Black women's bodies have been degraded, demeaned, demonized—locked

꿈o an oppressive gaze of beauty created in opposition to us.[6] So, in a collective struggle to counter more than four hundred years of dehumanizing, racist stereotypes of the Black-body-as-ugly, while simultaneously being an object-of-sexual-desire, the Black Church tends to confine sexual ethics to abstract, Puritanical condemnations.[7] The underpinning of anti-body dualism, compounded by chattel slavery and racial segregation, signify Black bodies, female and male, as inferior, mere performers of brute drudgery; white male bodies as unmarked, normative, full humanity, signifying superior individuality; while white female bodies represent the apex of "genteel" femininity, the prized possession in a privileged masculinist culture.

Therefore, in order to inscript our skin that is "too dark," our hair that is "too nappy," our facial features that are "too broad," and our buttocks that are "too wide" as definitive loci of positive human beingness, Black churchwomen are taught that we must suppress the sexual aspect of our humanity, by reinforcing norms and practices that proclaim procreational sex as a gift from God and relational/recreational sex as the devil's handiwork. Harrison goes on to say that "we are conditioned by religious and philosophical orthodoxy, or the official doctrines of the elites, to view the body and bodily needs as 'lower,' 'animal' modalities of existence that have to be tamed or in some way overcome and transcended by a higher and loftier power that is 'really' rational and spiritual."[8]

Living between the razor-blade tensions of heteronormativity and hypersexuality, Evelyn Brooks Higgenbotham contends that the politics of respectability caused some women to promote the ill-fitting Victorian cult of true womanhood as the proper way to eradicate distorted images of the sexually immoral Black woman.[9] Darlene Clarke Hines agrees that by embracing the socially conservative, circumscribed notions of super-morality, as a defensive survivalist strategy, Black women hoped to put an end to negative stereotypes, garnering greater social respectability for all African Americans.[10]

This deferential, Victorian strategy of lady-like, super-morality, result in churchwomen assuming the supplicant-position, renouncing their own erotic pleasures in the name of procreation, and, in turn, engaging in sexual activities as part of one's wifely duty; quieting the needs of husbands, while laboriously compressing, depressing, repressing their own desires. Beverly Harrison observes that "many of us are at our moral worst in our closest relationships, we frequently use sexual exchange, or it's withholding, as a weapon to wound, punish or reward. . . . Why do we, in fact, usually 'hurt the ones we love' "?[11]

We must ask what norms of justice can church members appropriate in erotic practices when intimate relationships, which supposedly facilitate domestic tranquility, require many women to accept unfulfilling sex lives as dependant appendages. One of the more detailed descriptions of the considerable cost of sex-role counterproductivity in the Black community goes like this:

> I know a woman who lives in Harlem who has reared her biological children and her husband's illegitimate children in poverty, suffered his mistress under her roof, had to ask for money to buy sanitary napkins, been sent out to work when he needed money, been forced to quit when it looked as if she was saving some money for herself on the side, been forced to steal from the house money to buy a bottle of toilet water from the Avon Lady. She has endured indignities beyond measure; beyond sadness, beyond bitterness and redress. Now this much abused, long suffering lady is said to be crazy.[12]

In sharp contrast to a firmly fixed life of domesticated resignation, other women pay homage to an excessive lifestyle of self-abnegation, misusing and abusing their bodies in cruel, exploitative and wasteful ways, because their capacity for sensual-sexual pleasure operates as an end unto itself. In the Introduction to her recently published book, *Longing to Tell: Black Women Talk about Sexuality and Intimacy*, Tricia Rose sums up the dilemma of "living as we do in a culture both fearful of the body and of sex and, at the same time, nearly preoccupied with these concerns,"[13] in this way:

> Black women's sexual lives are pinned between the powerful uses of distorted myths about black sexuality to fuel racist, demeaning stories about black men and women and the sexuality myths used to maintain the subordination of women as a whole.[14]

Individually and collectively, far too many African American Christian women restrict their sexual agency, by binding them with all kinds of biblical cords and ecclesiastical strings, in order to counter the age-old, pervasive stereotypes of being either sexually insatiable wenches—virile, promiscuous, and lusty, or fat, jolly, neutered mammies. Within this value-laden matrix of moral interpretations, that moves back and forth between past and present, churchwomen feel overwhelmed by contradicting socialization, and in turn they deny the gift of sexuality. As Blanche Richardson, the editor of *Best Black Women's Erotica* explains:

> As women, so many of us are deprived of a healthy respect of and connection to our sexuality. For some, it is shrouded in so much shame,

by so many convoluted messages, that we actually become detached from our sexual identities. We like sex, but we can't talk about it. We engage in sex, but we are, at times, afraid to enjoy it. When we do enjoy the act, and our partners, we are often subjected to ridicule and heartbreak. It can get confusing and tiring. How something so good, can be bad for you? How can something that feels so good, cause so much pain?[15]

Lest we forget, there are significant resemblances as well as differences oscillating between the sexed-body imprisonment of men-identified-women and women-identified-women. If the statistical ratios regarding the variance of sexual orientation among members of the dominant society also ring true in the African American context, then this spectrum of sexual equation indicates that at least one out of every ten Black women is a woman-identified-woman.[16] The basic assessment is that lesbians in the Black Church community are confined to a mode of closeted exclusion that can be compared to isolation in solitary confinement.

Evelyn Hammonds suggests that the operating assumption is that Black lesbian women hide the truth of their lives because their desire for women is considered deviant sexuality existing within an already preexisting deviant sexuality.[17] Moreover, Renee L. Hill speaks disapprovingly of how the subordination of lesbian women as "other" licensed their invisibility.

Her otherness has been such a powerful source of fear that she has had to be made invisible, her liberation and well-being made non-issues. But in looking directly into the eyes of the "other" and by listening to her voice, womanists may find the tools to re-examine and do away with not only lesbian stereotypes, but also other negative images of Black women (the "Mammy," the "whore," and the baby maker for example). . . . In listening to the lesbian voice womanists, heterosexual and lesbian, can learn the importance of self-naming.[18]

To begin with, powerbrokers in the Black Church, all too often, subject women to a litany of verbal abuse, known as lezzy-baiting. To a large degree, anti-lesbian hysteria consists of assaultive speech, wherein the word lesbian is used as a weapon, as a defiant verbal punch, teetering on the edge of physical violence, in order to terrorize women who refuse to acquiesce to the so-called supremacy of the mama–papa, missionary position as the solo, dominant pattern for love making.

Second, bulldagger-phobia is deployed so as to indoctrinate African American women to eschew any allegiance except to men, because a straight-laced, male gaze is the all-important prize that supposedly legitimizes women's existence.[19] In order to understand the death-dealing insinuations operative in this scare tactic, we have to begin from the premise that bulldagger-phobia is an unfounded aversion to female homosexualities, wherein imaginary anatomical body parts are grafted onto the genitalia of women who desire and engage in same-sexual lovemaking activity, because the arrogant presumption is that some form of the male penis is essential for sexual gratification. In *Outlaw Culture*, bell hooks explains that patriarchal pornography has always appropriated and exploited homoeroticism, while simultaneously fanning the flames of homophobia, by consistently reinforcing the stereotypical notion that gay folks are predators, eager to feast upon the innocent.[20] In essence, pervasive, overt lezzy-baiting and anxiety inducing bulldagger-phobia exacerbate the lockdown of genital-sexual eroticism for women of faith.

Renita Weems' essay, "Just Friends," captures a vivid portrait of a common dynamic that often reaches obsessional fervor whenever the story of Sodom and Gomorrah is discussed in Bible classes. On this occasion a deacon argued vehemently against homosexuality on the grounds that it is not *natural*. In turn, in an effort to demystify the rights and wrongs of *natural* sex acts, Weems poses the following questions to parishioners:

> . . . will you also want to legislate what *type* of sex between consenting adult men and women is natural? Must it be one woman and one man, or can it be one woman and two men? The man on top or the woman on top? The Sixty-Nine position or the elusive Venus Butterfly? Vaginal only, or will you permit oral sex, too? Must there be love for sex to be normal? Or is the presence of a marriage certificate enough?[21]

When we consider the warped theological teachings that threaten the withdrawal of male approval and economic support under the auspices of sexual abnormality, and the jack-leg preaching that vilifies and condemns Christian lesbians to eternal damnation, we must stay mindful that there are increasing numbers of Black churchwomen who refuse to remain docilely confined inside the walls of compulsory heterosexism. Most significantly, the fact is that due to the persisting legacies of slavery, including racial segregation and its pernicious regimes, the African American church community has not been able to liberate lovemaking from this dichotomous entrapment of normalized procreative economy in order talk about "good sex"[22] for Black women.

Keith Boykin claims that much of the homophobia and heterosexism manifested in the Black Church community has nothing to do with prejudiced fear and irrational hatred of those who sexually love members of their own gender, but these uncharitable attitudes are merely survival strategies for African American people living in a white supremacist society.[23] However, my data reveal that women who love other women, sexually and/or non-sexually, face a greater risk of physical violence even in the churchhouse, because too often the climate of worship is one of warlike hostility.

Audre Lorde combines her intimate knowledge of African American culture with existential evidence as a lesbian-woman-mother-activist-poet in order to disentangle the social environment in which this rule of terror reigns:

> The black lesbian has come under increasing attack from both black men and heterosexual women. In the same way that the existence of the self-defined black woman is no threat to the self-defined black man, the black lesbian is an emotional threat only to those black women who are unsure of, or unable to, express their feelings of kinship and love for other black women, in any meaningful way. For so long, we have been encouraged to view each other with suspicion, as eternal competitors, or as the visible face of our own self-rejection.[24]

However, in taking survivalist cues from Jewelle L.Gomez and Barbara Smith, in order to move in the direction of right-relating in the household of faith, women-identified-women must deal not only with external manifestations of disembodiment, but must also attend to internalized distortions. Smith contends that being homophobic is not a healthy state for people to be in. Gomez points out that she thinks that it is despicable and a desecration that spiritual beliefs are perverted and used against Black gay people. "Anyone who understands what the spirit of Christianity is supposed to be would never use it against gays."[25] Both Gomez and Smith argue in favor of the intellectual, political, and moral character of lesbian women:

> The black lesbian must recreate our home, unadulterated, unsanitized, specific and not isolated from the generations that have nurtured us . . . so that we, who have been lost in the shadows of the past, can be revealed and appreciated for the powerful legacy that we bear.[26]

As a consequence, the significant contributions of Christian lesbians to the Black Church community will no longer be ignored, marginalized, and excluded from the larger tapestry of theological discourse. As heterosexual, lesbian, bisexual women, Audre Lorde argues that we are raised to fear the yes within ourselves, to run from our deepest yearnings. In turn, Church traditions keep the vast majority of women living in a dichotomous state of binary opposites, a mind–body split of conflicted fluctuation. And yet, Lorde maintains that within each of us, there are reservoirs of erotic power that know no boundaries.[27]

In this essay, *Sexing Black Women*, the generosity of my students' interrogation regarding the multiplicity of sexual identities and subjective experiences provide me with data relevant to the erotic desires and embodied beauty of Black femaleness. In order to liberate Black women's bodies from the ideological prisonhouse of male supremacist power, students enrolled in *Resources for a Constructive Ethics*, a course that focuses on Black women's literature as an ethical source for justice-making moral agency, navigate the complex terrain of racialized sexuality. A graduate student puts it this way: "All of us must take personal risks associated with growth and change if we are going to be our best erotic selves. Be forewarned, the risks of embodiment can range from being considered crazy, to being ridiculed, to actually experiencing physical hurt and harm."[28]

Undaunted by historical constructions of propriety and perversion,[29] Womanist ethicists must make available to the contemporary church community counter-hegemonic strategies that debunk and unmask normalizing structures of compulsive heterosexual acceptability. In other words, the Black women's literary tradition acknowledges the discomfort with our bodies in a world where white supremacy associates black bodies with hyper-sexuality and licentiousness, and yet, such discomfort no longer justifies the church's lack of attention to sexuality as a good gift from a gracious God. The objective of this study is to introduce the problem of genital-sexual eroticism in the lived-world experiences of African American women and establish a continuity between our movement from slavery to freedom, so that the Black Church community can begin to envision an ethics of "erotic justice"[30] for African American women in the twenty-first century that embraces the well being of us all.

Invisible Visiblility in Slavery

In attempting to grasp the relation between African American Christian women and the pleasures of genital-sexual eroticism, Womanists begin our analyses writing about women's experiences of New World slavery. Either we assess the usable truth in Black women's narratives that tell stories of rape, battering, compulsory childbearing, medical butchering, sex-motivated murder, forced prostitution, and physical mutilation as verifiable data with lasting cultural meaning and enduring social consequences;[31] or, we reconstruct bits and pieces of fragmented reflections that expose "the attendant invisibility of black women as the unvoiced, unseen, everything that is not white."[32]

In her novel, Free Enterprise, Michelle Cliff[33] contends that as women of African descent we carry within us the haunting presence of our ancestors who empower us to act in the present. Cliff's narrative strategy is predicated on the notion that if our lips, hips, skin color, and bone structure are passed on from our foreparents, then why, why not memory? "In resuscitating the lives of the dead," writes Jenny Sharpe, "by raising the painful memory of slavery,"[34] we make visible not only the sexual abuse that was done to Black woman, but according to Deborah E. McDowell, female-gendered subjectivity in slave novels dramatize "what they did with what was done to them."[35]

While helping us rethink a liberating balancing act between what was done to us sexually and what we can do with those memories, a graduate student says that the twists and tweaks of moral logic used by powerbrokers, professing to be Christians, result in contradictory messages. In Incidents in the Life of a Slave Girl by Harriet Jacobs, the enslaved African supposedly has no soul, just an inferior body that enslavers can do with as they pleased. White-skin privilege indicates "transparent skin," a so-called inner self symbolizing reason, while Black-skin is labeled as an inscrutable, blank page.

Overall, sorrow was the lot of Black women who were at the mercy of white men's lascivious desires and sexual violence. Either as soulless bodies or bodiless souls, women bore the constant torture of never knowing when their children would be torn from them.[36] Linda Brent could not tend to her daughter at all once she was assigned major housekeeping duties on the plantation. Even someone with a lighter workload, like her grandmother, was forced to stop nursing her own baby to take care of the white baby's needs.

For most enslaved women, children—instead of being a joyful blessing—were used as hostages. The constant threats from slaveholders, both spoken and unspoken, meant that if Black women did not do what white men wanted, they were whipped, had food withheld from them, or their children were sold down the river. Everywhere the enslaved woman turned, with few exceptions, she was controlled by institutionalized patterns of rape.[37] Several students wrestled with the questions, "how can we heal from hurting memories that we carry in our bodies when we only see God's back? How can God guide us in acts of self survival, when God always walks in front of us, never turning or looking back to see whether or not we are able to follow?"

Slavocracy was the rude transformation of African people into marketable chattel.[38] Enslaved women were answerable with their bodies to the sexual casualness of "stock breeding" with Black men and to the sexual whims and advances of white men. Being slave and female, the Black woman survived wanton misuse and abuse.

> [T]he systems of slavery and caste encouraged white and black males sexually and socially to exploit black women. Thinking of profits or believing in the inferiority of Afro-Americans, some slave masters encouraged or ignored black male advances to black females, regarding the mating of slaves much in the same way they did their livestock.[39]

Virtually all the slave narratives as well as slave novels contain accounts of the high incidence of rape and sexual coercion.[40] White men, by virtue of their economic position, had unlimited access to Black women's bodies. Sexual victimization of Black women was accepted as inevitable almost as soon as African women were introduced into America. At the crux of the ideology that African American women are an inferior species was the belief that Black women, unlike white women, craved sex inordinately.

La Frances Rodgers-Rose in *The Black Woman* describes the sexual exploitation of the Black slave woman in this manner:

> [T]he Black woman had to withstand the sexual abuse of the white master, his sons and the overseer. A young woman was not safe. Before reaching maturity, many a Black woman had suffered the sexual advances of the white male. If she refused to succumb to his advances, she was beaten and in some cases tortured to death.[41]

Womanist ethics requires that we excavate the rich trove of oral testimonies, recovering lost stories of freed women and their descendents in order to craft stories that reveal hidden meanings of complicated, survival strategies. In order to challenge white supremacist narratives that present slavery as benign, tranquil, and benevolent, wherein Black females are stereotyped as docile, servile automatons, Black women novelists uncover lingering memories of painful degradation.[42]

The body politic of auction-block visibility makes every woman of African descent a member of the collective social-self. At slave auctions, Black people were stripped naked, exposed to public view, and humiliated with pokes, probes, and crude physical examinations. Often traders made slaves run, leap, and perform acts of agility to demonstrate their value as chattel.[43] It is virtually impossible to discuss the enslaved Black woman's sexual-self as solo-singleness, apart from the collective, corporeal scarredness of communal realities.

Conditions of slavocracy forced women into an embattled status; both objects-of-exploitation (those who are violated by others), and agents-of-exploitation (those who are forced to do the reproductive work, producing those who will be violated). For instance, as "brood-sow" the Black woman

> . . . was forced to give birth as often as once a year. Her body was misused, and quite often she was old before her time. Not only was she forced to have children rapidly, but she was given very little time to regain her own strength and only two weeks to care for her children. After that time, the slave woman had to return to work.[44]

Jacqueline Jones' article, "My Mother Was Much of a Woman: Black Women, Work, and the Family Under Slavery," describes the Black woman as reproducer-producer in this way:

> One North Carolina slave woman, the mother of fifteen children, used to carry her youngest with her to the field each day and "when it get hungry she just slip it around in front and feed it and go right on picking and hoeing . . . " symbolizing in one deft motion the equal significance of the productive and reproductive functions to her owner.[45]

Neither pregnant women nor new mothers were exempt from hard labor. The slave narratives of Moses Gandy include the stories of women who were reproducer-producers and the pain they endured because they were unable to nurse their infants regularly.

> On the estate I am speaking of, those women who had sucking children suffered much from their breasts becoming full of milk, the infant being left at home. They therefore could not keep up with the other hands: I have seen the overseer beat them with raw hide, so that the blood and milk flow mingled from their breasts.[46]

Black bondswomen were supposedly impervious to the onslaught of sadomasochistic torture and the pervasive experiences of sexual brutality. Thomas Thistlewood, who assumed the duties of overseer in 1751 on a Jamaican sugar estate, called Egypt, meticulously records in his diary the date, time, and place—the cane field, the curing house, the boiling house, the parlor—of his 1,774 separate sexual acts with 109 different enslaved women during a 13-year period. Jenny Sharpe goes on to say that if the slave women complied, Thistlewood gave them a small sum of money, if they resisted, he raped them.[47]

As a "work-ox" the Black woman was subjected to hard, steady, often-strenuous labor. Slave women worked as common laborers in mines extracting coal, lead, and gold, as well as in pine forests, turpentine, tar, pitch, and rosin plantations. From sunup to sundown Black women either worked alongside enslaved males in the cotton, tobacco, rice, and sugarcane fields or catered as a domestic, from before dawn to late at night, to the demands made by the mistress and other members of the enslaver's family. This compulsory labor forced Black women into anomalous marginal positions in relation to the evolving ideology of femininity. Angela Y. Davis contends, "Where work was concerned, strength and productivity under the threat of the whip outweighed consideration of sex."[48]

Invisible Visibility in Freedom

The second aspect of Womanist analyses related to African American Christian women and the pleasures of genital-sexual eroticism describes the various ways that Black women sustain dignity in the most inhumane of circumstances. The Civil War, from 1861 to 1865, destroyed the institution of chattel slavery. Emancipation removed the legal and political slave status from approximately four million African Americans in the United States, which meant that, in principle, Blacks own their embodied selves and their labor for the first time.

During the post-emancipation period, racism and male supremacy continued to intersect patriarchal and capitalist structures in definitive ways. Black women, young and old, were basically freedwomen on their own. Perhaps deserted or perhaps never married, hundreds of thousands of Black women walked from plantation to plantation searching for lost and stolen children. Due to the more than 38,000 deaths of Black soldiers who fought in, serviced, and led guerrilla actions for the Union Army and Navy during the Civil War and the estimated 5,000 Black men killed during the 10 years following the war, large numbers of African American women found themselves widowed. Hordes of ex-slaves fled as aimless refugees when the Union Military Armies penetrated the South. Other women were fortunate enough to cross the greatest chasm one can imagine, from slavery to freedom, with their families intact. Whether a Black woman began her career as a free woman, as an autonomous family supporter or as a copartner with her spouse, the African American woman began her life of freedom with no vote, no protection, and no equity of any sort.

The Black woman continued to experience the traditional White–Black, master–servant relationship via the sharecropping system that replaced slavery. The relationship of power dynamics remained much as it had before the war. The standardized land-tenure contract was structured so as to maintain the hegemony of the antebellum slave-owning aristocracy. As a result of the crop lien laws passed in 1865, African American people were financially unable or not allowed to purchase land. The Black woman and her family's legal emancipation trapped them in grossly unequal poverty cycle of debt peonage. Every year the white landowners and commissary merchants provided Black sharecroppers with high rates of interest for credit in order to purchase seeds, tools, food, fuel, and other necessities. At the end of the harvest season, the sharecroppers were compelled to accept a settlement of their share of the crop minus charges according to the landlord's rendition of the farm accounts.

Even with newly won civil rights, the economic opportunities for African Americans tottered between dependency and despair. A full complement of Black people soon found themselves legally bound to labor for payment on trumped-up charges that accrued in excessive amounts from year to year. This type of perpetual indebtedness resulted in involuntary servitude for an overwhelming majority of African American families.

The patterns of exploitation of the African American woman as reproducer-producer were only shaken by the Civil War. By no means were they destroyed. Throughout the nineteenth and early twentieth century, Black women were severely restricted to the most unskilled, poorly paid, menial jobs. Virtually no Black woman held a job beyond those of field hand or domestic servant. Farming land, keeping house, bearing and rearing children continued to dominate all aspects of the Black woman's life. This systematic exclusion and routinized oppression of Black females from other areas of employment served as confirmations for the continuation of the servile status of Black women.

It is estimated that three out of every four farmhands were Black females put to work at a very young age, between six and eight. Back women sharecroppers who worked the land, with or without husbands, chopped, hoed, planted, plowed, primed, and picked crops as well as completed those tasks usually defined as within the male domain such as the care and feeding of livestock. The urgency of trying to survive as sharecroppers demanded every hand—female and male—from the youngest to the oldest.

The theme of sexual objectification inherent in the domestic servitude of the Black woman continued to permeate her life. Bereft of formal education and advanced skills, the Black woman as a domestic worker was usually at the white employer's mercy. Her employment arrangements had few, if any demands that white people were obligated to meet. In lieu of salary she was often paid with used clothing, discarded household items, and leftover food. The low and no pay, precariousness of job security and irregular work hours caused many domestic workers to situate their families in the back-yards of white households. Sexual harassment became the lineal descendant of the institutionalization of rape of Black women under slavery. As a vestige of slavery, white male heads of households assumed the sexual accessibility of the Black female domestic worker.

African Americans believed that education made one less susceptible to the indignities and proscriptions of an oppressive white South. From the outset, the education of the Black woman differed from her white counterpart, in that Black women were taught that their education was not an ornament, meant to "uplift" her alone, but that formal education prepared her for a life of service in the "uplifting" of the entire community. Thus, teaching, nursing, and social work represented the pinnacle of professional achievement for the Black woman.

The accelerated movement of African Americans out of the South, to northern and western cities, that began in 1910 and gained momentum after each of the world wars, impinged on the Black woman's moral situation in very definite ways. Tens of thousands of African American females were members of the mass exodus seeking social democracy and economic opportunities. Black females soon found that their situation as women was much more difficult than that of migrant men.

Economic necessity dictated that most Black women who migrated to northern urban centers find work immediately. As a wife and mother, the Black migrant woman was responsible for transmitting the culture, customs, and values of the African American community to her children. At the same time that she was trying to organize family life according to her traditional roles, the male-dominated industrial society required that she serve as a catalyst in the transition process from the rural South to the urban North. Her own unfamiliarity and adaptation difficulties had to be repressed because she was responsible for making a home in crowded, substandard housing, finding inner-city schools that propagated literacy for her children while earning enough income to cover the most elementary needs. Many landlords refused housing to Black women with children. They preferred to provide room and board at excessive rates to single Black men who were thought to be at the height of their wealth-producing capacity.

In order to survive themselves and to provide for their families, African American women once again found only drudge work available to them. Black men worked as porters, janitors, chauffeurs, window cleaners, elevator operators, and as menial laborers in industry, while Black women were restricted to domestic jobs that northern white women scorned or considered demeaning. Racist and male supremacist constraints forced Black women into a status of live-in domestic servants, wherein Black women tried to earn a living as cooks, cleaners, washerwomen, and wet nurses under very hard and exhausting conditions. Barbara Ransby assesses the overall situation in this way:

> Although poor black women were sexually exploited as women, there was no magical, raceless, classless sisterhood between them and the white female employers, who were just as eager to exploit them for their muscle as their husbands were to use them for their sexual services. The economic rigors of the depression had intensified all forms of oppression, pushing black women from the lower rungs of the wage labor force back to day work and even into occasional prostitution.[49]

World Wars I and II brought about the most visible changes in the Black woman's moral situation. As a result of widespread racial animosity of white factory employers and employees, African Americans found scant acceptance in northern communities. Small numbers of Black women were allowed inside of the industrial manufacturing system but were confined to the most tedious, strenuous, and degrading occupations. White manufacturers alleged that undeniable hostility by white labor and the lack of separate entrances, doorways, drinking water buckets and cups, pay windows, and lavatories forced them to exclude Black women from skilled jobs and craft positions. In conjunction with racist stereotypes of Black women's lewdness and immorality that emanated from sexual exploitation of enslaved persons by white masters, northern Black women were subjected to discrimination and pettiness of all kinds. Hazel V. Carby makes the point this way:

> The need to police and discipline the behavior of black women in cities, however, was not only a premise of white agencies and institutions but also a perception of black institutions and organizations, and the black middle class. The moral panic about the urban presence of apparently uncontrolled black women was symptomatic of and referenced aspects of the more general crises of social displacement and dislocation that were caused by migration . . . . Thus, the migrating black woman could be variously situated as a threat to the progress of the race; as a threat to the establishment of a respectable urban black middle class; as a threat to congenial black and white middle-class relations; and as a threat to the formation of black masculinity in an urban environment.[50]

During the 1950s postwar period, a number of African American women became heads of households. Marital instability, low remarriage rates and an increase in out-of-wedlock births resulted in large numbers of Black women becoming dependent on the social welfare system. The persistent obstacles of poverty, sexual apartheid, and white supremacy continue to enslave the Black woman and her family to hunger, disease, and the highest rate of unemployment since the Korean and Vietnam wars. Education, housing, and other necessities which were gained during the mid-1970s and early 1980s are deteriorating faster now than ever before. This overarching sociocultural context renders visibility to Black women's invisible legacy of hard work, perseverance, and tenacity as we spell out new standards for intimate relations that embody mutuality.

Conclusion

Liberating Black churchwomen who live in the midst of two competing sexual realities is a moral imperative. The unjust, oppressive dualism that either sex is a positive blessing for procreative purposes only or sex is a negative curse that lays claim to bodily pleasure, contaminating the mind, must be eradicated. More choices and greater understanding regarding genital-sexual eroticism as a gift from God is the way we must go. To be sure, the issue is not procreative choice for some and no choice for others, but, under the mandate of Christian social solidarity, we must create conditions in which choices of bodily integrity are consistent with our understanding of right-relating that affirms equal discipleship in the household of God.

I believe wholeheartedly that it is time for African American churchwomen who believe in the healing power of sexual touch, to engage in dialogue about the various dimensions of human intimacy. Those of us who see the constraints of anatomical authority as death-dealing, must initiate critical conversations with women, men, and children throughout the Black Church community, so that together we can examine and remove impediments to erotic justice.

The impediments to giving and receiving pleasure are legions, especially among those of us whose ecclesial histories bear witness to our embodiment being rendered hyper/in/visible. Therefore, it is time for clergywomen in particular to speak out, to articulate nothing short of a revolutionary agenda that enables Black females to resist enforced sex role socialization. There is no such thing as neutral, color-blank, value-free space. In these troubled times, acquiescence, indifference, and conformity to oppressive value systems are out of order. As Audre Lorde insists in her remarkable wisdom, "Our silence will not save us."

Notes

1. Major credit is due to my bestest friend, the Reverend Angelin Jones Simmons, for her prophetic accuracy in naming this essay.
2. Kelly Brown Douglas, *Sexuality and the Black Church: A Womanist Perspective* (Maryknoll, N Y: Orbis Books, 1999); and Samuel K. Roberts, *African American Christian Ethics* (Cleveland: Pilgrim Pr., 2001) provide historical frameworks for analyzing religious conventions that substantiate antisexual bias in African American Christianity.
3. For a fuller discussion of sexual eroticism from Black women's perspective, see Gail Elizabeth Wyatt, *Stolen Women: Reclaiming Our Sexuality, Taking Back Our Lives* (New York: John Wiley & Sons, 1997); Miriam Decosta-Willis, Roseann P. Bell, and Reginald Martin, eds. *Erotique Noire: Black Erotica* (New York: Doubleday, 1992); Maxine Leeds Craig, *Ain't I a Beauty Queen? Black Women, Beauty and the Politics of Race* (New York: Oxford University Press, 2002); Hortense Spillers, "Interstices: A Small Drama of Words," in *Pleasure and Danger: Exploring Female Sexuality*, ed. Carole S. Vance (New York: Routledge, 1984).
4. Susan Newman, *Oh God! A Black Woman's Guide to Sex and Spirituality* (New York: Old World/Ballantine Books, 2002). See also, Hilda Hutchison, *What Your Mother Never Told You About S. E. X.* (New York: Putnam, 2002) and Dorothy Roberts, *Killing the Black Body: Race, Reproduction and the Meaning of Liberty* (New York: Pantheon, 1997).
5. Beverly W. Harrison, "Sexuality and Social Policy," in *Making the Connections: Essays in Feminist Social Ethics*, ed. Carol S. Robb (Boston: Beacon Pr., 1985), 87. My indebtedness to Beverly W. Harrison and Audre Lorde for their theoretical sensibilities to the erotic as a source for embodied creativity, which guide this essay, should be obvious to all who know their work.
6. Farah J. Griffin, "Textual Healing: Claiming Black Women's Bodies, the Erotic and Resistance in Contemporary Novels of Slavery." *Callaloo* 19, no. 2 (1996): 519–536; Scholars who devote special attention to this topic are Brenda Dixon Gottchild, *The Black Dancing Body: A Geography from Coon to Cool* (New York: Palgrave Macmillan, 2003); Deborah Willis and Carla Williams, *The Black Female Body: A Photographic History* (Philadelphia: Temple University Press, 2002); Sander Gillman, "Black Bodies, White Bodies: Toward an Iconography of Female Sexuality in Late Nineteenth-Century Art, Medicine, and Literature," in *"Race," Writing, and Difference*, ed. Henry L. Gates, Jr., (Chicago: University of Chicago Press, 1985), 223–261; Michael Bennett and Vanessa D. Dickerson, eds. *Recovering the Black Female Body: Self-Representation by African American Women* (New Brunswick: Rutgers University Press, 2001).
7. Cornel West, "Black Sexuality: The Taboo Subject," in *Race Matters* (Boston: Beacon Pr., 1993), 81–91.

8. Harrison, op. cit., 135–136

9. Evelyn Brooks Higgenbotham, "African American Women's History and the Metalanguage of Race," *Signs* 17:2 (1992): 251–274. One of the best available discussions of the sexual virtues of Black churchwomen, is Higgenbotham's *Righteous Discontent: The Women's Movement in the Black Baptist Church, 1880–1920* (Cambridge: Harvard University Press, 1993). See also, E. Frances White, *Dark Continent of Our Bodies: Black Feminism and the Politics of Respectability* (Philadelphia: Temple University Press, 2001).

10. Darlene Clarke Hines, "Rape and the Inner Lives of Black Female Sexuality in the Middle West: Preliminary Thoughts on the Culture of Dissemblance," *Signs* 14.4 (1989): 915–920. A very important study, which disentangles this history in specific details is Kathleen Thompson and Hilary MacAustin, eds. *The Face of Our Past: Images of Black Women from Colonial America to the Present* (Bloomington: University of Indiana Press, 1999)

11. Harrison, op. cit., 150. Also, Carter Heyward, *Our Passion for Justice: Images of Power, Sexuality, and Liberation* (New York: Pilgrim Press, 1984).

12. Barbara Walker's article in *Redbook* (March 1976): 33; See especially Carolyn M. West, ed. *Violence in the Lives of Black Women: Battered, Black and Blue* (New York: Haworth Press, 2002); Traci West, *Wounds of the Spirit: Black Women, Violence and Resistance Ethics* (New York: New York University Press, 1999).

13. *Presbyterians and Human Sexuality 1991* (Louisville: Office of the General Assembly, Presbyterian Church (U S A) 1991), 1. Recognition of human sexuality as a contestable issue is receiving attention in the works of Christian ethicists James B. Nelson, *Embodiment An Approach to Sexuality and Christian Theology* (Minn: Augsburg, 1978) and Susan E. Davies and Eleanor Haney, eds. *Redefining Sexual Ethics* (Cleveland: Pilgrim Pr., 1991); and in anthologies such as, *Sexuality and the Sacred,* ed. James B. Nelson and Sandra P. Longfellow (Louisville: Westminster John Knox Pr., 1994) and Delroy Constantine-Simms, ed. *The Greatest Taboo: Homosexuality in Black Communities* (Los Angeles: Alyson Books, 2000).

14. Tricia Rose, *Longing to Tell: Black Women Talk About Sexuality and Intimacy* (New York: Farrar, Straus and Giroux, 2003), 5.

15. Blanche Richardson, *Best Black Women's Erotica* (San Francisco: Cleis Press, 2001).

16. For excellent interdisciplinary critiques of sexuality, read Bryan Strong, Christine Devault, Barbara Werner Sayad, and William L. Yarber, eds. *Human Sexuality: Diversity in Contemporary America* (Mountain View, CA: Mayfield Publishers, 1997); Kathleen Kennedy and Sharon Ullman, eds. *Sexual Borderland: Constructing an American Sexual Past* (Columbus: Ohio State University Press, 2003); Eugene Kennedy, *The Unhealed Wound: The Church and Human Sexuality* (New York: St. Martin's Press, 2001).

17. Evelyn Hammonds, "Black (W)holes and the Geometry of Black Female Sexuality," in *Differences* 6 (1994): 125–145. See also, Leanne McCall Tigert, *Coming Through the Fire: Surviving the Trauma of Homophobia* (Cleveland: United Church Press, 1999); Cheryl Clarke, *Living as a Lesbian* (Ithaca, N Y: Firebrand, 1986); Anita Cornwell, *Black Lesbian in America*

(Minneapolis: Naiad Press, 1983); and S. E. Wieringa and E. Blackwood, eds. *Female Desire: Same Sex Relations and Transgender Practices Across Cultures* (New York: Columbia University Press, 1999).

18. Renee L. Hill, "Who Are We for Each Other: Sexism, Sexuality and Womanist Theology," in *Black Theology: A Documentary History, Vol. II: 1980–1992* ed. James H. Cone and Gayraud S. Wilmore (Maryknoll, N Y: Orbis Books, 1993), 350. See also, Lisa C. Moore, ed. *Does Your Mama Know? An Anthology of Black Lesbian Coming Out Stories* (Decatur: Red Bone Press, 1997); Catherine E. McKinley and L. Joyce DeLaney, eds. *Afrekete: An Anthology of Black Lesbian Writing* (New York: Anchor Books, 1995).

19. Audre Lorde, *The Black Scholar* (April 1978), 34.

20. bell hooks, *Outlaw Culture: Resisting Representations* (New York: Routledge, 1994), 15.

21. Renita J. Weems, "Just Friends," in *Que(e)rying Religion: A Critical Anthology*, ed. Gary David Comstock and Susan E. Henking (New York: Continuum, 1997), 353. See Irene Monroe's monthly religion column online, *Queer Take*, for *The Witness Magazine* (www.thewitness.org/agw/agw-monroe.html); Roderick A. Ferguson, *Aberrations in Black: Toward a Queer of Color Critique* (Minneapolis: University of Minne Press, 2003); and G. Winston James, ed. *Voices Rising: An Anthology of Black Lesbian, Gay, Bisexual and Tansgender Writing* (New York: Other Countries Press, 2002).

22. By using the phrase "good sex" I join the conversation of the international, inter-religious feminist scholars whose anthology, *Good Sex: Feminist Perspectives from the World's Religions* ed. Patricia Beattie Jung, Mary E. Hunt, and Radhika Balakrishnan (New Brunswick: Rutgers University Press, 2001) is evoking sexual justice discussions in theoethic classrooms.

23. Keith Boykin, *One More River to Cross: Black and Gay in America* (New York: Anchor Books/Doubleday, 1996), 167. To understand open and affirming congregations, see Gary David Comstock, *A Whosoever Church: Welcoming Lesbians and Gays Men into African American Congregations* (Louisville: Westminster/John Knox Press, 2001).

24. Audre Lorde, "Scratching the Surface: Some Notes on Barriers to Women and Loving," in *The Black Scholar* (April 1978): 31–35. Also Lorde's, *Zami: A New Spelling of My Name* (Freedom, C A: Crossing Press, 1982).

25. Jewelle L. Gomez and Barbara Smith, "Taking the Home Out of Homophobia: Black Lesbian Health," in *The Black Women's Health Book: Speaking for Ourselves*, ed. Evelyn C. White (Seattle: Seal Press, 1990) 198–213. Barbara Smith, *The Truth that Never Hurts: Writings on Race, Gender and Freedom* (New Brunswick: Rutgers University Press, 1998).

26. Jewelle Gomez, "A Cultural Legacy Denied and Discovered: Black Lesbians in Fiction by Women," in *Home Girls: A Black Feminist Anthology*, ed. Barbara Smith (New York: Kitchen Table Press, 1983), 110–123.

27. Audre Lorde, *Sister Outsider: Essays and Speeches* (Trumansburg, New York: Crossing Press, 1984).

28. I thank the students who allow me to quote from their work.

29. Marcia Y. Riggs, *Plenty Good Room: Women Versus Male Power in the Black Church* (Cleveland, Ohio: Pilgrim Press, 2003); and Marita Golden, ed.

Wild Women Don't Wear No Blues: Black Women Writers on Love, Men and Sex (New York: Anchor Books, 1994) are important sources in transforming African American women's self-understanding regarding bodily integrity.

30. A comprehensive understanding of this concept is elaborated in Marvin Ellison, *Erotic Justice: A Liberating Ethic of Sexuality* (Louisville: Westminster John Knox Press, 1996).

31. My notion of embodied-memories-as-reincarnation is dependent on the work of Toni Morrison, *Beloved* (New York: Knopf, 1987); Charlotte Pierce-Baker, *Surviving the Silence: Black Women's Stories of Rape* (New York: W. W. Norton, 1998); Patricia Hill Collins, *Black Sexual Politics: African Americans, Gender, and the New Racism* (New York: Routledge, 2004).

32. Evelyn Hammonds, op. cit., 132.

33. Michelle Cliff, *Free Enterprise: A Novel* (New York: Penguin Books, 1993).

34. Jenny Sharpe, *Ghost of Slavery: A Literary Archaeology of Black Women's Lives* (Minneapolis: University of Minnesota Press, 2003), xi.

35. Deborah E. McDowell, "Witnessing Slavery after Freedom—Dessa Rose," in *Slavery and the Literary Imagination*, ed. Deborah E. McDowell and Arnold Rampersad (Baltimore: Johns Hopkins University Press, 1989), 146.

36. Among novelists who deal with this theme, read Lorene Cary, *The Price of a Child* (New York: Vintage, 1995); Gayl Jones, *Corregidora* (New York: Random House, 1975; rpt. Boston: Beacon, 1990).

37. Of special importance, read Margaret Walker, *Jubilee* (Boston: Houghton Mifflin, 1966; rpt. New York: Mariner Books, 1999); Sherley A. Williams, *Dessa Rose* (New York: W. Morrow, 1986; rpt. New York: Quill, 1999); Hilda Gurley-Highgate, *Sapphire's Grave* (New York: Doubleday, 2003); Austin Clark, *The Polished Hoe* (New York: Amistad, 2002); Ishmael Reid, *Flight to Canada* (New York: Scribner, 1998).

38. Katie G. Cannon, "The Back Woman's Moral Situation, 1619–1900," in *Black Womanist Ethics* (Atlanta: Scholars Press, 1988), 31–57.

39. W. Augustus Low, ed., and Virgil A. Clift, asst. ed., *Encyclopedia of Black America* (New York: McGraw Hill Book Co., 1981), 862.

40. See especially Harriet Jacobs, *Incidents in the Life of A Slave Girl, Written by Herself* (1861; rpt. New York: Penguin, 1987); and Beryl Gilroy, *Stedman and Joanna—A Love in Bondage* (New York: Vantage, 1991).

41. La Frances Rodgers-Rose, ed., *The Black Woman* (Beverly Hills, C A: Sage Publications, 1980), 20.

42. For examples, see J. California Cooper, *The Wake of the Wind* (New York: Doubleday, 1998); Octavia Butler, *Kindred* (New York: Doubleday, 1979; rpt. Boston: Beacon Press, 1988); and Caryl Phillips, *Cambridge* (New York: Knopf, 1992).

43. Katie G. Cannon, "Surviving the Blight," in *Katie's Canon: Womanism and the Soul of the Black Community* (New York: Continuum, 1995), 27–37. See Walter Johnson, *Soul to Soul: Life Inside the Antebellum Slave Market* (Cambridge: Harvard University Press, 2000).

44. Ibid., 8.

45. Jacquelyn Jones, "My Mother was Much of a Woman: Black Women, Work, and the Family Under Slavery," *Feminist Studies* 8 (Summer 1982): 238.

46. Moses Grandy, in E. Franklin Frazier, *The Negro Family in the United States* (Chicago: University of Chicago Press, 1939), chap. IV.

47. Cited by Jenny Sharpe, *Ghost of Slavery: A Literary Archaeology of Black Women's Lives* (Minneapolis: University of Minnesota Press, 2003), 63, based on Thistlewood's sexual practices in Hilary Beckles, *Centering Women: Gender Discourses in Caribbean Slave Society* (Princeton: Marcus Weiner, 1999) 38–58. Such atrocities are clearly depicted in Eddie Donoghue, *Black Women/White Men: The Sexual Exploitation of Female Slaves in the West Indies* (Trenton: Africa World Press, 2002).

48. Angela Y. Davis, *Women, Race and Class* (New York: Random House, 1981), 6.

49. Barbara Ransby, *Ella Baker & the Black Freedom Movement: A Radical Democratic Vision* (Chapel Hill: University of North Carolina Press, 2003) 76–77.

50. Hazel V. Carby, "Policing the Black Woman's Body in an Urban Context," in *Critical Inquiry* (Summer 1992): 738–755. See also, Frances A. Kellor, "Southern Colored Girls in the North: The Problem of Their Protection." *Charities* (March 18, 1905): 584–585.

2

A Space for Faith, Sexual Desire, and Ethical Black Ministerial Practices

Traci C. West

From the first time that I read it many years ago I have been intrigued by the relationship between spirituality and sexuality presented in Ann Allen Shockley's 1980s feminist novel about a Black minister. In *Say Jesus and Come to Me* the main character makes her living as an evangelist preaching at black church revivals. The novel tells the story of how this minister falls in love and how she successfully builds her own church in Nashville, Tennessee. This fictional account has a somewhat startling yet, refreshingly open depiction of sexual dynamics in black church and community life. In one early scene, Rev. Myrtle Black, the lesbian main character, thinks about how much her voice and good looks resemble those of her father. He, too, was a black preacher. The author explains that Myrtle "soon discovered that her voice, coupled with her inherent facility for words, could play havoc in the ears and hearts of people. It served her well, too, in bed as an incitement to lovemaking. Also, just as women were attracted to her father, they were to her. But because she was a woman, too, they blinded themselves to the true nature of the magnetism, preferring to place it in the category of the spiritual."[1] The rest of the story offers a very romantic description of the development of Myrtle's intimate relationship with a celebrity in the music business who attends her revival. It includes some highly erotic moments between them during the altar calls.

I find this story, particularly the passage quoted above, to be wonderfully thought provoking because it elicits pivotal questions about church practices. Within Christian worship experience, what is authentic spirituality and how is it intertwined with sexual desire? For ministers, how is their power and authority linked to sexuality when performing some of the duties of ministry, like preaching or counseling? How *should* it be? What assumptions about gender roles and sexual orientation (their own and their members') inform the spiritual leadership and message of ministers? What assumptions *should* inform their leadership?

By investigating questions like these, churches could perhaps gain clarity on what actually occurs within their church practices as well as what they would want to occur. More discussion of the relationship between sexuality and spirituality is needed in African American churches (as well as in every other church setting, among all racial/ethnic groups). The sexual dynamics in churches should be acknowledged and named in a process allowing for thoughtful reflection that places these dynamics within a theological framework. In my view, sexuality should be understood as an intrinsic, ongoing human quality that is a good gift from God. This divine gift of human sexuality is an ever-present part of our very being, and should not be mistakenly understood as certain acts that one may choose to practice or not.

Historically rooted, white racist distortions of black sexuality also need to be acknowledged as a part of the social context that shapes the relationship between sexuality and spirituality within black church life. The link between these distorting cultural dynamics and the Christian theology of Black Christians has to be sorted out.[2] White racist projections of Black sexuality that saturate U.S. culture can have a damaging impact on black self-perceptions as well as their expressions of Christian faith. Fears about stoking those racist images can halt any effort to openly engage in critical dialogue about sexuality and spirituality in black churches. Therefore, it is all the more essential to find a way to openly affirm black sexuality as an intentional and good element of God's creation. Delineating the specifics of this theological affirmation of sexuality enables black Christians to create healthy self-images and relationships that are authentically rooted in their faith.

However, this strategy is still insufficient. A theological and social vision addressing the abuse of power by clergy within black churches also has to be included. A theological vision of human sexuality will be quite inadequate and perhaps even irrelevant for churches without an accompanying liberatory Christian social ethic. Attention must be paid to the use of power within the organizational structuring of churches that Black Christians create and support. Unlike the sanguine portrayal in the Shockley novel, in actuality, ministers have rampantly abused their power in relation to sexuality. Also unlike that novel, this abuse of power has most often been exhibited by male clergy and featured heterosexuality. We cannot appreciate the blessedness of black sexuality and sexual desire without having conversations about how to shift these patterns of abuse of power, repeated over and over again within certain black churches (not in all of them).[3]

Of course, a considerable amount of discussion about sexuality already occurs in black congregations. It may take place informally among laity in their comments about who is "going with" whom, and in condemnations from the pulpit about certain expressions of sexuality and sexual identity. But the kind of organized, critical dialogue about spirituality and sexuality that I am suggesting is guided by liberatory ethical goals. A liberatory Christian social ethic insists upon building just institutional relationships, ferreting out any practice, especially by leaders, that reproduces the use and abuse of persons (so often done by reinforcing common social patterns of male and heterosexual domination). Thoughtful dialogue should, therefore, be seen as only one part of a process that is advantageous for black churches. This process must also include changes in clergy behavior and church practices. It has to involve the elimination of the clergy's: sexual shaming of certain people from the pulpit; hypocritical private/public sexual mores; and sexual exploitation of parishioners.

Affirming the "already" blessed black sexuality that is part of our God-created humanity is essential for holistic Christian theology and for repairing enduring racist cultural distortions. However, for Christians, this affirmation should be accompanied by a theological vision that also seeks out the unfulfilled potential for honoring varied expressions of black sexual identity. It is a vision of the "not yet" that we are called to realize in our commitment to the kin-dom of God, a vision of retreating from shaming, manipulative, and exploitative Christian practices related to sexuality. Realization of this vision will necessitate a transformation of certain theological and cultural understandings of heterosexuality and of clerical power.

Sexual Desire and Moral Conduct

Creating consensus on what constitutes moral conduct is one of the most fundamental and difficult issues we encounter when trying to affirm sexuality in the church. In the common perceptions of most people, sexual behavior, especially the desire for sexual pleasure seems antithetical to how one honors Christian spiritual commitments.

Historical traditions in Christian theology as well as concrete experiences or knowledge of sexual scandals in the church have helped to shape this common perception. I want to focus mainly on hetero-sexuality because it is so formative and dominant in western Christian notions of sexuality and in most (openly acknowledged) black Protestant clergy lifestyles. A better understanding of some of the dis-torted notions of heterosexuality constructed in Christian theology and regularized in Black church practices suggests key starting points for creating an affirming approach to black sexuality across differing sexual orientations and Black community settings.

For the ancient African "church father" Augustine of Hippo, human desire for anything but the will of God, especially desire for sexual pleasure illustrates a sinful aspect of humanity. According to this African Bishop, and many other Christian leaders of the ancient and early church (including Paul), virginity or celibacy was the prefer-able sexual status for Christians. Entering into Christian marriage was for Augustine, as historical theologian Mark Jordan describes, "a con-cession to uncontrolled or uncontrollable desire."[4] Even within Christian marriage, Augustine advised couples to limit sexual inter-course to what is necessary for procreation and to look forward to a cessation of sexual activities as quickly as possible.[5]

Based on Christian traditions such as this one, sexual desire has been understood as a source of moral corruption. And, being rendered "out of control" is seen as the most dangerous aspect of sexual desire that incites moral corruption and disobedience to God. As womanist theologian Kelly Brown Douglas points out, ". . . Augustine was disturbed by the problem of sexual lust and passion and was most con-cerned about the 'genital aspects' of human sexuality . . . [in Adam] the involuntary movements of sexual organs (such as male erections) were the first sign of this loss of control over his body and body parts, hence disobedience to God."[6] Douglas is referring to Augustine's description of the human condition after original sin where "the law in the members makes war on the law in their minds."[7] The experience of male genital reactions that dominates Augustinian thought and so much of Christian theology (mainly authored by males) dwells on the idea of a dangerous loss of control caused by sexual desire.

This Augustinian perspective represents a typical expression of many ancient Christian writings about the dangers of sexual expres-sion. If one is unable to live at the highest levels of Christian spiritual commitment, which means abstaining from any sexual activity, het-erosexual sexual expression is allowed when placed in the restraining container of Christian marriage. Even within this social container, the sexual activity should be entered into on a very restricted basis. This basic theological teaching about heterosexual sexual activity is constructed out of a kind of begrudging admission about human sexual desire as a problem that needs to be controlled. Heterosexual sexual desire is seen as shameful. It is a pitiable, unavoidable problem in human nature that highlights one's spiritual inadequacy. But we can be reassured by the stipulation that this flawed nature can be managed within Christian marriage.

A primary ecclesiological principle passed down by this tradition is that the only way to produce not only moral conduct, but spiritually faithful and committed conduct in ordinary Christians, is for the ecclesial leader (in this instance, the Bishop of Hippo) to lay out rules about how to restrict sexual urges. Meanwhile the leader, the "Father" of the church, chooses a life of sexual abstinence for himself, which he pronounces as the ideal Christian lifestyle. The centrality of rejected heterosexuality is even maintained in the title of "father" for Christian priests. This title is a constant reminder of male participation in heterosexual sexual activity resulting in procreation—the typical meaning of fatherhood everywhere else except for clerics of the church. It constantly reminds us that the most important church leaders refuse to engage in heterosexual sexuality for sacred reasons. Thus, interrelated notions of maleness (manliness? e.g. real Christian men don't have sex), sexuality, and power are woven into the core meaning of Christian church leadership from as early a point in Christian history as its first few hundred years.

We receive an ecclesiological model of church order where the Christian clerical leader has an obligation to play a role that holds up his own sexual choices as ideal and restricts the sexual choices of the members of his congregation that differ from his own. Though the ideal of celibacy is rejected, this conceptualization of church order is still predominant in many contemporary Protestant Black churches. The sexual conduct of the clergy is usually supposed to offer a model for the church, for example, as the heterosexually married "head" of the "first family" of the church. Clergy then use their power and authority to protect this model as a representation of normative, ideal sexuality and make attempts to regulate the sexual practices of church members accordingly.

I can think of no better (or should I say worse?) expression of this authoritarian ecclesiology and shaming formula for trying to regulate heterosexuality than the treatment of "unwed mothers" in some black churches. For these churches, women and girls who are not married and become pregnant literally *embody* heterosexual sexuality that is not under control (of men??). A particularly harsh tradition for the church's treatment of pregnant teenagers was established in the 1940s and 1950s by Elder Michaux. Elder Lightfoot Solomon Michaux was the influential religious leader and founder of a black Holiness movement in the United States, the Church of God.

As their clerical leader, Michaux ordered his members to put any unwed pregnant daughters out of their churches. Moreover, parents who were members of his churches, were ordered to immediately put their unwed daughters out of their homes. All church members, including their parents, were then forbidden to associate with them. This practice was, of course, quite traumatizing for the girls. The males who shared responsibility for this pregnancy were punished with a period of silencing within the church. Judging from how much worse the punishment was for the girls than for the boys, it seems that heterosexual sexual activity outside of marriage by girls was deemed to be a more egregious form of sin than the same behavior by boys. Moreover, as religious scholar Lillian A. Webb describes, "mothers of unmarried, pregnant girls were punished severely also, while fathers were not. Michaux's thinking was that mothers are responsible for their daughter's moral training, and where a girl 'strayed,' her mother had been careless."[8]

These practices, ordered by the male clerical leader of this movement, cultivate a social culture within the churches of assigning less responsibility to heterosexual males for sinful heterosexual sexual behavior. Church members learn that a certain exemption from social stigma and spiritual culpability appropriately comes with heterosexual maleness. In addition, the church mimics the crass power relations that dominate the broader society. The male, heterosexually married religious leader creates rules that protect and privilege male heterosexual behavior. The extreme suffering and hardship visited upon the pregnant girls taught these lessons on gender, sexuality, and Christianity in dramatic terms.

In certain black churches, unwed mothers have been forced to come before the congregation and admit that they have been sinful. "Karen," a woman that I interviewed, told the story of what happened to her best friend when they were teenagers growing up during the 1970s in a Baptist church in the state of New York.

> . . . my best girlfriend . . . fifteen years old, got pregnant. I later found out she was raped by one of her brother's friends, but wouldn't tell. We

were in the choir together and they asked her to step down off the choir, which I did not understand. So the politics of the church have always been a problem for me . . . They asked her to stop being in the choir because she brought disgrace . . . She was actually protecting someone but nobody ever asked her. They just immediately assumed that, you know, she's a bad girl . . . Now her father was a deacon in the church. He was known to be a womanizer, known to cheat on his wife, known for all of these negative things. You would think that he would have been able to show compassion seeing that compassion was shown to his raggedy behind. But what was asked of her was something that I never understood. She was asked to stand up before the whole congregation on a Sunday morning and ask for their forgiveness . . . And, that was something I didn't understand. I remember talking to her in the bathroom at church, and oh, she was crying. I mean the thought of standing up before hundreds of people and asking for forgiveness for something that she knew wasn't her fault. (I didn't even know at that point that it wasn't her fault.) There was just something about that particular component that I didn't like. And I said, "you don't have to do that." And she said: "well my Dad says that I have to do this." I said to her, "you don't have to do it." I had enough of an understanding of what was going on to know that you don't have to stand up in front of a bunch of hypocrites and ask them for anything. I don't know how, but I knew that there was something wrong with that picture![9]

Incidents like this once again exemplify specifically how gender matters within church practices related to heterosexual sexuality. The problem to be addressed is not merely bringing heterosexual sexual desire under control. It seems that what is most important is to bring the heterosexual sexual activity of *women and girls* under control. The pregnant girls, not the impregnating boys, are the ones that some male clergy find quite useful as objects for public sexual shaming. (As mentioned above in the case of the holiness tradition of Michaux, even the mothers of the pregnant girls are to be blamed and corrected, rather than the fathers of the girls.) For Karen, the spiritual and moral message about heterosexual sexual activity seems to be that, in church, men who engage in this activity outside of wedlock get to insure the public denouncement of girls who do so. The lesson for her friend appears to have been that when something awful happens to you, like being raped and becoming pregnant as a result, the black church will try to shame and blame you.

Note, however, that in that moment of caring and support between the teenagers in the women's bathroom, an empowering rejection of the church's shaming and blaming attempts was asserted by Karen.

Later in her interview she described how she got in trouble with the pastor for initiating that rebellious attitude. (Apparently her friend told her own father what Karen suggested about refusing to apologize to the church, and the father told the pastor.) The pastor called Karen and her mother into his office to chastise them. But Karen's mother defended her daughter's viewpoint and told the minister that if the church was going to use this shaming ritual, they should start with the adults who were involved in extramarital sexual relationships and began naming some of the known offenders. Though there may be abusive, sexually shaming practices in some black churches, sometimes within those same settings, there is also resistance to those practices. In her defiant reaction, Karen (and even her mother) understood that standards of sexual moral conduct should be applied on a more equal basis.

If the expression of heterosexual sexuality were not so thoroughly linked to notions of shame and sin in Christian tradition, might it be less useful as a tool for black male clergy to perpetuate such sexist and demeaning practices? Sexuality could, instead, be understood as a precious dimension of each human person that is not just related to our genitals and the acts we perform with our genitals. Sexuality should be recognized as a key ingredient of our sensory perceptions, our emotional life, our affect (the impact one's presence has on others), our minds (ability to imagine, fantasize, delay, and interrupt sensory responses) and our physicality (our body's shape, texture, stamina, flexibility, capacities, movement). Furthermore, sexuality should not be understood as merely an individualistic quality because it also includes the inherent social dimensions of vulnerability and accountability to others. For Christians who believe that human beings are part of God's creation, sexuality might be seen as utterly precious and wonderful because it reflects the amazing complexity, mystery, and creativity of what our God can do. Thus, sexuality reflects God's presence in our life.

This precious dimension of our humanity could also be understood as a reminder of both our equality and uniqueness before God. If sexuality was appreciated in this way, it could inspire practices of equality in church and society, rather than those autocratic ministerial practices that strengthen hierarchical relations. For instance, recalling some of the ideas in the body theology of 1 Corinthians 12, the preacher/pastor might be seen as one interdependent part of the body of Christ, who performs a particular, needed, function, but does not have a superior relationship to God or to other Christians. Instead of providing another opportunity for male clergy to reinforce the privileges of maleness, recognition of God's gift of sexuality should inspire church leaders to reinforce human equality across gender, race/ethnicity, socioeconomic class, and sexual orientation.

In stressing that the gift of sexuality each person has received from God signals our equality before God, we could invoke an understanding of equal participation in the creation of babies when they result from heterosexual sexual intercourse. This emphasis on equal participation could lead to a notion of equal responsibility for nurturing that new human being. Rather than shaming and blaming pregnant girls, there could be a celebration of our equality before God. This would entail a theo-ethical understanding that human beings coexist as equals even as we participate in God's gift of sexuality. This includes heterosexual sexual intercourse and the responsibility to care for the new human that may result from it. (Highlighting the need to honor God's creative involvement within the very expression of sexuality, such as heterosexual sexual desire could even be a deterrent to teenage sexual intercourse and pregnancy for which they are not emotionally prepared. I don't know.)

An emphasis on equality should not supplant recognition of uniqueness. Especially in Black churches, the God-given beauty of Black bodies and Black sexual desire should be treated as precious, never shameful. Guidance about moral conduct should be based upon assertions of the intrinsic moral worth of each person, and the unique gift of sexuality God has given to each of us. Instead of adding betrayal by trusted Black religious leaders to the stigmatizing and objectifying racist associations already prevalent the culture's treatment of Black bodies, especially Black women's bodies, clergy might make a different choice. Ministers might use their power to lift up the complexity of human sexual desire that God has created and the extraordinary, unlimited opportunities to explore the depths of that gift in covenantal relationships with each other. This could be linked with asserting heterosexual covenantal (marital) relationships as one, among other monogamous, covenantal unions (and marital relationships) to be supported, such as between gay and lesbian intimate partners.

Again, the idea of human (bodily) equality and uniqueness before God prompts a rejection of social hierarchies. Just as God has created a beautiful array of Black bodies including skin tones ranging from ebony black, to reddish brown, to light ivory, so too God has created a beautiful array of sex/gender identities (e.g. bisexuals, transgendered persons, heterosexuals). Just as we must constantly resist the social stigmas and hierarchies invented to value the beauty of certain Black people's features and skin tones over others, we must resist ranking the beauty and complexity of the sexual identities that exist among us. We have the opportunity to joyfully appreciate such beauty and complexity as a dynamic gift that only God could have created.

But this dynamic gift of sexuality that can infuse one's senses, emotions, affect, mind, and physical self, must create powerful needs, right? Does my emphasis on sexuality as a good gift from God, in which God is manifest, side step the issue of the needs sexual desire can arouse? For Black Christians, especially for their clergy in predominantly black churches, how are those sexual needs met in a manner that truly honors the fact that these needs are a gift from God?

Sexual Needs and Clergy Conduct

In many black churches the overwhelming majority of the congregation is comprised of women while the clergy are predominantly men (most often married men). In the broader Black community as well as the church, single women tend to outnumber married women. How do these dynamics of gender/marital status affect the way that sexuality and spirituality interact in the church? When a majority of Black churches are comprised of single women and the only expression of sexuality, identified by the pastor as Godly, is to take place within heterosexual marriage, what about the sexual needs of the majority of people in the church? Also, how does sexual orientation matter for the way that sexuality and spirituality interact—for lesbian parishioners, or single bisexual male clergy, or married heterosexual laity and clergy?

We can assume that clergy and laity enter all church settings with both spiritual and sexual needs, and that one of the major roles of the church is to provide guidance about, and responses to, such personal needs. But, what is an appropriate way for the church to do so? In many Black worship settings, there can be a heightened emotional climate that combines with a strong emphasis on the spiritual appreciation of music. This combination can produce a certain emotional vulnerability and openness deeply engaging one's feelings and senses, awakening one's sensuality and perhaps even sexual aspects of one's self, as well.

When taking into account all of these issues related to sex/gender, marital status, and worship style, we must acknowledge the abuses of power by some ministers as well as the sustaining, constructive dimensions of the interaction between sexuality and spirituality that can occur in Black churches.

The development of criteria for assessing appropriate and inappropriate sexual conduct by Black clergy as well as a method for church response to clergy misconduct, is beyond the scope of what I can adequately cover here. I will however suggest a few of the ethical issues that have to be attended to when defining an appropriate and inappropriate expression of sexual desire by ministers, and offer examples of conduct by clergy that definitely needs redress. My concern with sexual orientation remains focused primarily on the practice of heterosexuality, especially by married ministers. Heterosexual relationships, certainly heterosexual marriages, are often treated as a template in church and society (by anti-gay rights and pro-gay rights activists). Taking into consideration the damaging ways that heterosexual marriage is practiced by certain Black church leaders (not all of them), may help to deter the reproduction of exploitative behavior, across all sexual orientations in the church. Besides, the church too often ignores (and thus protects) the most rampant destructive sexual practices by the majority—heterosexuals—in favor of condemnations of all rights to sexual expression by those in the minority, such as lesbians and gay men. An adequate Christian sexual ethic for Black churches has to consider the realities of distorted practices of heterosexuality, as well as the needs those distorted practices exploit, in order to envision relevant and constructive alternatives for sexual pleasure.

There have been many incidents of widely known sexual liaisons between black women church members and Black male ministers. Some have been broadly publicized and dramatically illustrate the dynamics of clergy abuse of power. The infamous sexual episode involving Rev. Ralph Abernathy in Montgomery Alabama in 1958 is an example of a public scandal that apparently was not damaging to Abernathy's credibility as a leader. It is described in the first volume of Taylor Branch's epic chronicling of the civil rights movement, *Parting the Waters*.[10] Abernathy was involved in a sexual relationship with one of his parishioners, Vivian Davis. When her husband, Edward Davis, found out, he came to the office at their First Baptist church and threatened to kill Abernathy, their pastor. Davis produced a gun and a hatchet. A struggle with Abernathy ensued. Davis chased Abernathy down the street, brandishing the hatchet, and was arrested by the police. The sensationalism of the Edward Davis trial was heightened when Vivian Davis testified to her "natural and unnatural" sexual acts with Rev. Abernathy.[11] At the Negro civil rights mass meetings taking place at that time in Montgomery, Ralph Abernathy was forgiven and embraced, with the assistance of his friend Martin Luther King, Jr. who led the meeting. Edward Davis was acquitted and the case was soon forgotten in most annals of the civil rights movement. (Abernathy himself fails to mention the incident in his autobiography, where, ironically, he became the only movement "insider" to discuss Martin Luther King, Jr.'s extramarital sexual relationships.)[12]

If we assume, as I do, that possessing sexual desire is not, in and of itself, inappropriate for ministers, we still need guidance about how and when it is appropriate to try to fulfill that desire within church relationships. Is this Abernathy episode an example of a pastor–parishioner sexual relationship that is inappropriate conduct because Rev. Abernathy and Vivian Davis were both married, or because he was her pastor, or because of the enjoyment of sexual pleasure that apparently took place, or some combination of these factors?

More recently, in 1997, there were troubling revelations about Rev. Henry Lyons, pastor of St. Petersburg's Bethel Metropolitan Baptist Church and president of the National Baptist Convention (NBC).[13] It was reported that he engaged in extramarital relationships with Bernice Edwards and Brenda Harris. They were both hired to work for the Baptist Convention in differing capacities. It was also reported that he engaged in an extramarital sexual relationship with another devout Baptist churchgoer, Earlene Battle. The sexual relationship with Battle reportedly began after she met him at a church revival and then accepted his invitation to enter into "one on one spiritual counseling."[14] Lyons' activities received considerable national press because of the financial embezzlement (totaling millions of dollars) from the black Baptist denomination that was entangled with his relationships to these women. When the wife of Henry Lyons learned of her husband's relationship with Brenda Edwards, she tried to burn down the $700,000 house that her husband and Ms. Edwards had purchased together, apparently using church funds. The arson occurred while Rev. Lyons and Ms. Edwards were traveling together in Nigeria.[15] Lyons faced some opposition within the National Baptist Convention as a result of the news coverage about his financial misdeeds and extramarital relationships. After tearful pleadings for forgiveness at the National Baptist Convention annual meetings, Lyons was repeatedly retained as their leader.[16] Though they had both previously denied it, in 1998, Rev. Lyons and Harris finally admitted their relationship of several years and apologized to his wife at a board meeting of the National Baptist Convention in Kansas City.[17] Again, Lyons was not asked to step down from his post as head of one of the largest Black denominations. In fact, after this apology, a love offering was collected on the convention floor for his legal expenses and he boldly announced that he would seek another five-year term.[18]

We need to develop criteria for how black churches hold their clergy accountable for sexual misconduct. To set the context for this task, there is a need to question a seemingly general consensus in black communities about separating sexual misdeeds by ministerial leaders from their legitimacy as community leaders, (as would appear to be the case for national leaders like Martin Luther King, Jr., Adam Clayton Powell, or Jesse Jackson). Within the church, are a humble apology and a sincere plea for forgiveness the only demands that the faith community should make of their clergy leaders who are involved in sexual misconduct? Should Christian forgiveness of the misconduct mean exoneration from being held accountable for the harm they have caused? This last question highlights the need for clarity about how sexual misconduct by clergy is harmful. Too often this kind of behavior is excused as merely instances of men "getting carried away" by their needs for sexual pleasure.

In Hartford, Connecticut (2000), it was reported that Rev. Henry Price used his role as a prison chaplain and drug counselor to engage in sex with, and act as a pimp for women newly released from prison and drug-treatment programs.[19] Price was criminally prosecuted. In another case, a woman from the Bethel AME Church in Madison New Jersey filed a lawsuit (1998) because of what happened when she went to her minister for counseling. She reported that she sought counseling because she was experiencing confusion about her feelings of sexual attraction to another woman at church. She said that Rev. Donald Brown told her she "needed an older man" and he would help her, explaining to her: "You need to be in a triangle, because I am married and I would be with my wife and you can be with me . . ."[20] In yet another case, in Oakland, California (2002), after what was allegedly years of sexual harassment that included unwelcome touching and being "physically grabbed" in a "sexually provocative manner" several black women, including the youth minister and the church secretary filed civil charges against Rev. Gilette O. James of the Eden Baptist Church.[21]

Individuals like the women who went to Rev. Price and Rev. Brown, most likely seek out ministers because they believe they can trust them.

Usually they trust them because they assume that ministers have an especially strong commitment and connection to God, the trustworthy center of their own Christian faith. People who work as staff in churches or church organizations, like the women who worked with Rev. James, also often assume that ministers are trustworthy because of their connection to God. Vulnerability always accompanies trust. When this trust is placed in the minister, it represents a significant degree of power that ministers are given based upon the faith related nature of their role as minister. At the same time, sexuality also involves degrees of trust and vulnerability. Spirituality and sexuality have these elements in common. Therefore those who are willingly trusting and vulnerable in an intimate counseling or close working relationship with ministers can sometimes be manipulated by the ministers into being *sexually* trusting and vulnerable as well. Sexual behavior of the clergy with counselees and sexual harassment of church staff demonstrates an abuse of their power by violating the trust that has been placed in them. For ministers like those mentioned above, what are the needs for power and status related to ego, being Black, being male, and being a Black male, that can fuel a sense of entitlement to violate trust given to them?

Sometimes this sense of entitlement can come from the minister's self-assessment of the burdens of ministerial work. Cultural studies scholar Michael Dyson describes the "ministerial Casanova" who "believes he merits sexual pleasure because of his sacrificial leadership of the church community. Ironically, he sees the erotic realm as an area of fulfillment because it is forbidden, a forbiddance that he makes a living preaching to others."[22] Dyson also adds a discussion of women parishioners to his analysis of the confusion about sexuality in Black churches. Some women make it all too clear to Black male ministers that they are sexually available. Dyson illustrates this point with one of the few confessions of sexual misconduct by a Black minister that is in print. He offers graphic details about how difficult it was to yank himself away from a woman parishioner's "luscious lip-lock" and magnificent breasts.[23] She confessed her love for him and "descended on" him after calling him to her home for an emergency counseling session.[24] When Dyson is finally able to stop himself from having sexual intercourse with her, he leaves this pastoral call feeling ashamed and disappointed in himself. As this example points out, in certain instances, women parishioners may not only be victims of ministerial sexual misconduct, they may, at the same time, have sexual desires and needs that they "invite" their ministers to fulfill. If such situations arise, isn't it the minister's responsibility to let parishioners know that servicing the parishioner's need for sexual pleasure is not a part of his or her pastoral role and duties?

Many explanations of sexual misconduct by male ministers that stress the sexual desires of women parishioners as a problem blatantly blame the women in order to excuse male clergy for their abuse of power through sexual misconduct. "Rev. S." offered an example of this type of woman-blaming when I interviewed her.[25] She told me about how the senior minister preached a sermon called "Sleeping With the Enemy" on David and Bathsheba (2 Samuel), where the major point was that "great men are tempted by beautiful women."[26] "Rev. S." was a fledgling staff member at an AME church in New Jersey where this occurred. After finding out that this minister, though married, had fathered a child with another member of the church, her reactions to this sermon shifted a bit. Before these revelations she was bothered by the degree to which the sermon was "male centered" as well as its harsh message about women. "But now, looking back," she explained that she saw "he was justifying his own actions, also."[27] This same senior minister discouraged "Rev. S." from taking any action against a Presiding Elder in the denomination who was sexually harassing her, telling her that she needed to understand that "men have needs."

Merely possessing a desire for sexual pleasure is not the problem. Exploitation occurs when sexuality is reductively regarded like an itch that has to be scratched, and other people are used as a means to scratch that itch. The senior minister seemed to be indicating in the example above that "beautiful women" arouse "great men's" needs for sexual pleasure. And, the assumption made here is that men are then powerless to control "their member" (as Augustine would say). Not only does this understanding of sexuality absolve ministers from assuming responsibility for their own behavior, it treats women as objects that male ministers are forced to sexually use to meet the sexual needs that women have aroused in them.

Women are not the only ones who are treated in a sexually objectifying manner by ministers. In my interview with Christian ethicist and church activist, Randy Miller, he described two such experiences that were certainly "not appreciated."[28] At one point, he was home from college for the summer and visiting his grandmother in rural South Carolina. Miller had a burgeoning sense of confidence about being an openly gay young man. He met the pastor of his grandmother's church, an independent Black Baptist church with about 60–100 worshippers on Sunday mornings. Miller explained that as he stood next to his grandmother and they were surrounded by other members of the church prior to the worship service, the pastor "made it clear that he wanted me to come visit him. He kept emphasizing how lonely he was . . . there was no doubt in my mind that he was a closeted gay man, and that it was a sexual invitation."[29] Miller did not feel exploited because he never took the invitation seriously but he was shocked and offended. Even though "this man [the pastor] was inviting me to come out and have sex with him in the woods," Miller said "I felt a little bit of pity for him, I have no doubt that what he was telling me was true,—[that] he was terribly lonely man."[30]

He had a similar reaction to a prominent, heterosexually married, black United Methodist pastor of a large church in Georgia who also made inappropriate sexual remarks to him. Miller was talking with this pastor, seeking mentoring advice as part of his ministerial candidacy studies when the pastor asked Miller about his penis size and how effectively he used it, ostensibly as a metaphor about ministry, "but it was clearly a crude sexual come-on." Miller compassionately remarks that although he was offended, he still felt a sense of pity because it seemed that this minister was "trapped in a culture that demanded that he play the heterosexual role and have a female spouse" in order "to advance to being a prominent minister."[31]

In a risky, self-centered kind of game, both these ministers treated this Christian young adult as if he was prey to be lured into sexual activity or at least verbally toyed with, and their pastoral authority was the vehicle that allowed them access to him. Having a need for sexual pleasure is not intrinsically self-centered. The use of someone else merely to meet that need for pleasure, however, inappropriately makes them into an object and an instrument that devalues their human worth and dignity. The desire to use someone in this way should be distinguished from a desire for sexual pleasure, which is a wonderfully precious creation of God. Even the act of *satisfying* one's desire for sexual pleasure with another is not synonymous with selfishness. As Christian ethicist Christine Gudorf writes, "Sex is perhaps one of the best life arenas for demonstrating that self and other are not naturally hostile . . . In sex it becomes apparent that the interests of self and the interests of the partner are largely linked . . . within sexual activity it becomes clear that exercising my ability to arouse and please my partner excites me."[32] The opportunity for this expression of mutuality, concern for another, connection to another is indeed blessed activity.

Unlike sexual relationships, pastoral relationships are not mutual. Parishioners do not have responsibility for offering guidance and leadership to ministers. Clergy disrespect God's gift of sexuality when they abuse their power through sexual manipulation or harassment. They demean its blessedness with sexual conduct that assumes a right to violate trust and exploit vulnerability. They thwart opportunities to realize that the gift of sexuality signifies human equality and uniqueness before God.

Heterosexual sexuality ought not be used as an instrument to harm people, to take something from somebody to "scratch your itch." Nor should it be used as an instrument to beat people up because it is seen as a mark of one's human superiority over gay and lesbian people, encouraging emotional and spiritual assaults as well as sanctioning physical brutality against them. If we listen to the actions, rather than the preaching, of pastors like those cited above, heterosexual marriage is practiced with multiple sexual partners, at a very painful cost to the spouses who have usually not agreed to this arrangement. In too many instances, heterosexual marriage is an institution of hypocrisy and duplicity largely due to this predatory expression of heterosexual sexuality.

Besides clearly enforced consequences for sexual abuses of power by clergy, we need a Christian sexual ethic that promotes the exploration of mutual sexual pleasure within covenantal relationships such as heterosexual marriage and gay covenantal unions and marriages. A Christian sexual ethic should also encourage exploration of gentle self-pleasuring, and besides this, for adult singles, guidance for sexual expression in the context of mutual, emotionally supportive, mature relationships that do not violate existing covenantal commitments to others. God's blessedness can be known through creative, erotic, and playful explorations of sexual desire in all such relationships.

If the climate of heterosexist shaming, humiliation, and discrimination prevails, these ideas will only be a partial response for nurturing appropriate power relations by gay, bisexual, and transgendered black ministers. Neither consequences for abuse of power or encouragement of sexual pleasure in covenantal relationships and mutual ones, will be sufficient without an open and affirming church sexual ethic eschewing the notion of shameful, closeted, secret sexual orientations. Therefore, for example, *openly* black gay and lesbian clergy leadership should be sought after and appreciated for their gifts and graces in ministry by many more black congregations, across all denominations and Christian faith traditions.

For Christians, sexuality, like other gifts from God that are available to us, involves choice. It should not be seen as inherently out of control, and thus something that one is forced to control or it would control us. Sexuality is an aspect of self that one can choose to faithfully nurture and respectfully enjoy, or one can choose to use it coercively, manipulatively, and harmfully. What if the sensuality respectfully enjoyed in so many black churches was viewed as a building block for expanding discussions of the relationship between sexuality and spirituality? In worship, whether with an Afro-Latino beat, Carribbean steel drums, crooning gospel choir, Negro spirituals, or vibrant African stepping, there already exists an openness to the joining of sensuality and spirituality in the nurturance of Christian faith. In the emotion of the deacon's prayer, the preacher's cadence, the mourner's wail, the silent testimony of waving hands, the oral testimony paying homage to the elderly "mother of the church," there is already an openness to turning over the raw, stripped-down self to the spirit of God. These are rich starting points for a discussion of how to expand and shift church practices toward creative, enlivening, and respectful sexual–spiritual dynamics in Black churches.

Fears about reinforcing racist stereotypes of blacks will surface to derail this effort. That omnipresent concern about what "white people might think" can discourage open confrontations of the extent of black ministerial sexual misconduct that exists in Black churches as well as openly holding them accountable for it. Anxiety about staying committed to disproving racist notions of Black moral inferiority may erode a desire for alternative strategies to shaming Black teens that are sexually active, or for rejecting heterosexual normativity for clergy as well as laity. Worries about reproducing yet another form of racist sexual objectification of Blacks will be pushed to the forefront and quell enthusiasm for embracing sexual/erotic/sensual dimensions that are already a part of Black church spirituality. Yet, if such explorations are allowed they can be a springboard for developing pleasure-affirming notions of Christian sexual ethics. Remaining hostage to these internalized racist messages will not only mean missing out on some amazing opportunities to uphold Black sexual desire as good, but missing out on honoring God's presence within Black sexual desire.

Notes

1. Ann Allen Shockley, *Say Jesus and Come to Me* (Talahassee, FL: Naiad Press, 1987), 11.

2. See Kelly Brown Douglas, *Sexuality and the Black Church: A Womanist Perspective* (NY: Orbis, 1999).

3. I want to emphatically state that the abuses I discuss in this article do not occur in all black churches. I offer anecdotal examples that suggest a widespread phenomena, but by no means indicate a problem of every black minister in every church with a predominantly black congregation.

4. Mark D. Jordan, *The Ethics of Sex* (Malden, MA: Blackwell, 2002), 110.

5. Roy J. Deferrari, *Saint Augustine: Treatises on Marriage and Other Subjects*, Fathers of the Church: A New Translation (New York: Fathers of the Church, 1955), 3.3, 11.12.

6. Brown Douglas, *Sexuality and the Black Church*, 26.

7. Augustine, *City of God*, ed. David Knowles, trans. Henry Bettenson (NY: Viking Penguin, 1984), Book 14, chapter 17. See discussion of this quotation and translation issues related to this passage by Rosemary Radford Ruether, "Misogynism and Virginal Feminism in the Fathers of the Church," in *Religion and Sexism: Images of Woman in the Jewish and Christian Traditions*, ed. Rosemary Radford Ruether (NY: Simon and Schuster, 1974), 162.

8. Lillian Ashcroft Webb, *About My Father's Business: The Life of Elder Michaux* (Westport, CT: Greenwod Press, 1981), 121.

9. Karen (Pseud.), interview by author, tape recording, June 18, 2003, Hartford, CT.

10. Taylor Branch, *Parting the Waters: America in the King Years 1954–63* (NY: Simon and Schuster, 1988).

11. Taylor Branch, 246. Through further questioning it was revealed that for Davis, unnatural acts referred to oral sex.

12. With regard to his time serving as a pastor in Montgomery, he describes his closeness with his wife Juanita and concern for their children, and how hard he worked to rebuild it after it was bombed. *And the Walls Came Tumbling Down: Ralph David Abernathy: An Autobiography* (New York: Harper and Row, 1989); regarding King's affairs, see 434ff, 471–472ff.

13. For a summary of the news coverage of these incidents see: Jerry G. Watts, "Race and Disgrace" *Religion in the News*, vol. 1; no. 2 (Fall 1998), 4–5, 22.

14. Monica Davey and David Barstow, "Lyons Paid Another Woman," August 22, 1997; Monica Davey, "Jacksonville Woman is Upset by Attention" *St. Petersburg Times*, August 23, 1997. Ms. Battle sought legal help after Lyons became physically abusive to her in their intimate relationship. Lyons reportedly made several payments to her after she threatened him with legal action.

15. Craig Pittman, Tim Roche, "Deborah Lyons Charged with Arson," *St. Petersburg Times*, August 9, 1997. Tim Roche, "Baptist Leader Says He's Been Persecuted," *St. Petersburg Times* July 12, 1997. Even though the house had been ransacked and fires set in several places in the home, and when picked up immediately after setting the fire when she crashed her car into a tree, she admitted the crime and her anger at her husband for having a relationship with that woman, Mrs. Lyons later stated in denials that she had accidentally dropped a match in the house. Finally she pled guilty to Arson, was sentenced to five years probation, and a psychological evaluation for alcohol addiction was ordered by the court.

16. Waveney Ann Moore, David Bartsow, Mike Wilson, and Monica Davey, "Ouster Attempt Fails; Lyons Wins," *St. Petersburg Times*, September 4, 1997.

17. Teresa E. Harris, "Confessions of a Changed Woman," *Gospel Today*, February 1999, 28–33.

18. Monica Davey, David Bartsow, Waveney Ann Moore, and Mike Wilson, "Lyons Admits Affair with Church Aide," *St. Petersburg Times*, September 18, 1998"; Monica Davey, David Barstow, Waveny Ann Moore, and Mike Wilson, "Lyons Asks, and He Receives," *St. Petersburg Times*, September 11, 1998; Michael A. Fletcher, "A House Torn Asunder; Accusations of Wrongdoing Against Baptist Leader Henry Lyons Have Caused a Bitter Schism," *Washington Post*, June 11, 1998, Final Edition, p. C01.

19. Tina Brown, "Community Split on Minister, Price Evokes Feelings of Support, Betrayal," *Hartford Courant*, August 4, 2000, A3; Tina Brown, Eric M. Weiss, and Lizabeth Hall, contributions by Josh Kovner and Jack Dolan, "Affidavits Tie Price to Sex, Money, Judge Orders Documents Released; Allegations Show Pattern of Women Lured to Prostitution; Accusations Against City Minister," *Hartford Courant*, August 3, 2000, A1.

20. Bill Swayze, "Woman Sues Saying Pastor Offered Her Sex, Parishioner Alleges Church Shielded Minister," *Star Ledger* July 7, 1998, 30, Morris Edition Section; Bill Swayze, "Clergyman Accused in Sex Suit," *Star Ledger* July 7, 1998, 30, Morris Edition Section.

21. "Black Pastor Hit with Sex Charges," *The Sun Reporter* December 12, 2002, vol. 58, no. 49.

22. Michael Eric Dyson, *Race Rules: Navigating the Color Line* (New York: Vintage Books, 1997 [1996]), 103.

23. Ibid., 98–99.

24. Ibid., 96–100.

25. Rev. S. (pseud.), interview by author, tape recording, June 23, 2003, Madison, New Jersey.

26. Rev. S., interview.

27. Ibid.

28. Randy Miller, interview by author, telephone interview from Madison, New Jersey to Oakland California, tape recording, June 25, 2003.

29. Miller, interview.

30. Ibid.

31. Ibid.

32. Christine E. Gudorf, *Body, Sex and Pleasure: Reconstructing Christian Sexual Ethics* (Cleveland Ohio: Pilgrim Press, 1994), 94.

II

Biblical Studies

3

Constructing a Doctrine for the *Ecclesia Militans*

Michael Joseph Brown

Living in the Context of Already and Not Yet

Given that modern American society contains a plurality of religious and secular views of the meaning and purpose of human existence, together with various ethical norms that are appended to those conceptions, it seems inappropriate to enforce on all persons in our society any one comprehensive set of values. Indeed, the works of scholars like Michel Foucault, have suggested that all presumably universal sexual ethical norms are inherently tyrannical. To be sure, the "voices that speak loudest across the ages are usually the voices of the most powerful groups or classes."[1] With this in mind, this essay serves as an analysis of how one influential early Christian, Clement of Alexandria, constructed his doctrine of human sexuality within the context of second-century Roman Egypt. It becomes apparent quite quickly that later Christians used Clement's contextualized understanding of human sexuality as a basis for making universal theological claims. Such a strategy is scrutinized in light of the apparent discontinuities in historical contexts. By contrast, I offer programmatic suggestions toward the construction of an African American doctrine of sexuality that are appropriate to our modern context, even as we continue to live in the framework of what Pauline scholars call "already and not yet."

Sex and Sexuality in the New Testament: The Precursor to a Doctrine

The New Testament is characterized by an unconditional repudiation of all extramarital and so-called unnatural intercourse, generally characterized as *porneia* in these texts.[2] In many respects the New Testament *appears* to follow the pattern and judgments regarding sexuality found in the Hebrew Bible and later Jewish teaching. And yet, in reality sexual relations occupy very little of Jesus' direct teaching in the gospels.

While the question of sexuality is only tangentially broached in the canonically recorded ministry of Jesus, it does arise more frequently and centrally in Paul's writings. The apostle consistently advocates to his followers the incompatibility of *porneia* and the kingdom of God. No participant in *porneia* is to have any part in the kingdom (1 Cor. 6.9; Eph. 5.5). In fact, in 1 Cor. 6.9 unacceptable sexual interactions (*porneia*) are placed alongside the fundamental and disgraceful sin of idolatry. Paul demands that an impenitent member be expelled, and that the community cease to engage with anyone who indulges in *porneia* (1 Cor. 5.9, 13). Paul intends to present "pure" communities to Christ (2 Cor. 11.2). This means that each member of the community must understand herself as a temple of the Holy Spirit (1 Cor. 6.19). A man is not free to act as he likes with his body.[3]

The intensity of the New Testament's rhetoric on sexual activity must be understood within the context of an imminent expectation of the *parousia*. This eschatological orientation, more than anything else, governed the earliest Christian paraenesis on sex. As a matter of course, such advice is *ad hoc* because of the community's overriding preoccupation with the eschaton. For example, Paul says,

> I mean, brothers and sisters, the appointed time has grown short; from now on, let even those who have wives be as though they had none . . . I say this for your own benefit, not to put any restraint upon you, but to promote good order and unhindered devotion to the Lord. (1 Cor. 7.29, 35 NRSV)

This doctrine is tempered in later canonical writings, such as 1 and 2 Timothy, although many scholars have pointed out that the governing concern for the author at this point is the acceptability of the community and the reinscription of gender roles.[4] Again, this exhortation appears to be *ad hoc* rather than comprehensive.[5]

An Egyptian Christian View of Sex and Sexuality

As we look over the biblical corpus, it does not fully explain the development of the Christian doctrine of sexuality. For that one must look at the second century C.E. Christian writers. As the apocalyptic fervor Christianity once possessed began to wane, Christians had to develop an understanding of human sexuality that would last in the period between the ascension and the *parousia*.[6] In this case, the interpretation of biblical texts became a central concern. Early Christians argued as to the precise meaning and application of scriptural statements, especially those contained in the Hebrew Bible. Fitting Israelite conceptions of sex and sexuality into a Greco-Roman framework was not as simple as it may appear to the modern reader.

Efforts to make the biblical passages relevant meant disagreements. These interpretive conflicts fostered rhetoric such as this statement made by Clement of Alexandria:

> [There are] people, who, when they read, twist the Scriptures by their tone of voice to serve their own pleasures. They alter some of the accents and punctuation marks in order to force wise and constructive precepts to support their taste for luxury. (*Strom.* 3.4.39.2 [Ferguson])[7]

Needless to say, other Christian thinkers would have made similar statements regarding Clement. Nevertheless, what makes Clement's statement relevant to our discussion is that he is one of the first so-called orthodox Christian writers to pen a treatise on sexuality. Further, Clement purposely attempts to integrate a biblical notion of sex with Greco-Roman philosophical anthropology.

Three salient contextual factors also contributed to the construction of Clement's doctrine of sexuality. Although rarely mentioned in academic discourse, mortality, marriage patterns, and the advocacy of asceticism influenced early Christianity just as much as Greco-Roman philosophy. Clement lived in an environment where very few ever experienced old age, as we know it. General life expectancy at birth was approximately 23.9 years.[8] And because males were valued over females in society, they outnumbered them at a rate of twelve to ten on average.[9] The high mortality rate also forced some people to marry at much earlier ages than in modern societies. According to census data, women began to marry around the age of twelve.[10] Men, by contrast, generally waited until their twenties before they married.[11] Over 25 percent of these marriages ended because of the death of one spouse, more often the wife. Thus, multiple marriages and blended families were common.[12]

As a result of the discrepancies between men and women with respect to life expectancy and representation in the general population, the social dynamics of Roman Egypt fostered fierce competition among men for wives. And not only did men wait longer to get married, but they were also often forced to consider life options other than matrimony.[13] Among the philosophically minded, asceticism functioned as an appealing life regime. "The true philosophers practice dying," Socrates once proclaimed (Plato, *Phaed.* 673 [Fowler]).[14] Such an existential orientation generally required that an individual isolate and control those aspects of daily life that aroused desire, especially when those experiences have been deemed superfluous (see e.g., Plutarch, *Os.* 352d). In this view, that which is superfluous is unnecessary and potentially dangerous to the individual. In practice, this meant abstaining from such things as eating certain foods, drinking wine, and engaging in sexual intercourse.

The ability to distinguish between that which is necessary and that which is not, according to Epictetus, is the task of moral reasoning (see e.g., *Ench.* 5). In order to cultivate virtue, which includes the capacity for choice, the individual must purge her reasoning process of the influences of desire and fear. One of the ways she can reach this goal is through the training of the body. For example, in sexual matters Epictetus advises continence (*egkrateia*), which can mean either the practice of moderation, or abstinence (10). In other words, Epictetus advocates an orientation toward existence that underscores indifference to external matters, including sex and sexual attraction, as a means of cultivating virtue and self-sufficiency. Or, to put it another way, "For where our interest is, there, too, is piety directed" (31 [Higginson]).[15]

In short, the social context of Roman Egypt was one in which death came early and often. As a result of this and other factors, individuals and groups were forced to develop customs and practices appropriate to their social environment. Among these were the promotion of procreation as a response to mortality and permanent celibacy for men as a response to the inequity between the number of men and women in the general populace. And so, in his development of a Christian doctrine of sexuality, Clement had to accommodate social factors as well as address the general philosophical climate.

One of the intellectual elements any early Christian writer in the second century had to contend with was the influence of Platonism on

Greco-Roman philosophical discourse. Clement even makes reference to its importance in his own intellectual environment (see *Strom.* 3.13.93.3). Associated with Platonism was a dualistic metaphysical orientation. Posidonius, although not a Platonist, clearly adopted essential elements of Platonic dualism for his own metaphysics. He posited a distinction between two worlds: the celestial or intellectual world and the sublunar or material world. The material world was transitory and subject to constant change. The intellectual world was imperishable and immutable. The whole, as a result, was a compound.

The compounded nature of reality also meant that there were "male" and "female" principles present in the cosmos. As with most Greco-Roman thinkers, Clement perceived the so-called female principle to be inferior to its masculine counterpart. It was by means of the female principle that the negative predicates of existence came into being. In a couple of key statements, Clement defines these negative existential predicates. He says, " 'Female' refers to sexual desire (*epithumias*), and its works are birth and decay" (3.9.63.2). He goes on to say, "This is what is meant by 'female' lack of self-control (*akrasia*)" (3.9.63.3). And yet, Clement argues that the existence of the female principle should not be seen as entirely negative. It is rather part of the providential plan of God. The providential purpose behind this compounded existence can also be seen in the activity of God, especially the incarnation. Clement says, "[Christ] came in the flesh but without beauty of form, teaching us to fix our gaze on the formless incorporeality of the divine cause" (3.17.103.3). Corporeal existence is the training ground for true existence; that is, life in the incorporeal realm.

Clement's Platonic cosmology sets the functional parameters for his anthropology and, subsequently, his doctrine of human sexuality. This adherence to Platonism, at least as understood in the second-century Alexandrian context, creates two programmatic difficulties with regard to human sexuality. First, there is the problem of corporeal material existence—in short, the body. Clement acknowledges that the body is alien to true existence. And yet, he insists that embodiedness has a providential purpose. It allows for the education of the individual. Also, it allows for the education and salvation of others. As he says, "The object of birth is learning and knowledge" (3.9.64.3). Although it should never be seen as other than subordinate to a spiritual existence, corporeal material existence is not innately evil. Commenting on Phil. 1.20-24, Clement gives corporeal material existence an evangelistic context (possibly analogous to the evangelistic purpose behind the incarnation). He says, "In these words [Paul] showed clearly that love of God is the crowning reason for leaving the body, whereas to remain behind graciously for those in need of salvation is the reason for being in the flesh" (3.9.65.3). A crucial part of this corporeal material existence involves the proper use of one's sexuality.

Sex involves desire (*epithumia*). Desire is the source of pleasure, but it is also indicative of a deficiency on the part of the individual (3.5.42.1). Clement believes that our common positive experience of desire is an illusion. In truth it is a lure that derives from the evil power. As he says, "[Desire] does not come from the body, even though it expresses itself through the body" (3.4.34.2). He goes on to say that "weakness of will and [*porneia*] are passions inspired by the devil" (3.12.81.4). Sexual desire changes a human being into "a wild beast" (3.17.102.3; see also 2.23.139.4). The control of desire and the proper use of one's sexuality leads Clement to distinguish two categories in the created order. He says, "The human condition involves some things which are natural (*physika*) and necessary (*anagkaia*), other things which are merely natural" (3.1.3.2).[16] This culminates in his judgment that "all this business of sexual intercourse is natural but not necessary" (3.1.3.2). It is only perceived as necessary because of the presence of desire in the existential realm, a product of the evil influence of Satan.

The means of counteracting the influence of desire are self-discipline and self-control (3.1.4.1-2). Clement complains that the majority live by the body and not by the spirit, which means they know nothing of self-control (3.6.46.3). Self-control naturally determines how one lives one's life (3.7.57.1). It is finding release from the snares of human existence (3.7.57.1-2). In actual practice, self-control means indifference to all the things that may attract us, including sexual intercourse (3.7.59.2). It is a matter of distinguishing between what is natural and necessary and what is only natural, and acting upon that distinction.

Clement also takes up the discussion of *porneia* in this treatise on sexual relations.[17] In a clarification of his understanding of the term, Clement relies heavily on Pauline texts (see e.g., 3.8.62.2; 3.11.73.4; 3.12.82.1; 3.15.96.1; 3.18.107.4; 3.18.109.2). In 3.12.82.1-90.5, a key portion of *Stromateis* 3, Clement lays out his central argument that marriage is a proper social state for Christians and not, as some ascetics argue, another form of *porneia*. Drawing upon Paul's concessionary statement in 1 Cor. 7.5, Clement says that sex in marriage is a prophylactic against the influences of the devil (3.12.82.1). He goes on to justify marital sex as a practice condoned by the Hebrew Bible for the purpose of "the breeding of children" (3.12.81.5). As such, it is an option available to the Christian as an expression of the will of God. The same is true in the case of a second marriage. It is acceptable as a concession to the Christian who lacks sufficient self-control, although it clearly falls short of "the highest pitch of the gospel ethic" (3.12.82.4). At any rate, to Clement marriage is a proper and legal social arrangement intended by God for procreation. He defines marriage in *Strom.* 2.23.137.1 as follows: "Marriage is a union between a man and a woman; it is the primary union; it is a legal transaction; it exists for the procreation of legitimate children."[18] And so, he says, "If anyone goes so far as to call marriage *porneia*, he is once more reverting to blasphemous slander upon the Law and the Lord" (3.12.89.1).

Clement believes *porneia* to be analogous to covetousness (*pleonexia*) and idolatry. It is covetous in that *porneia* is an indication of an absence of the virtue of self-sufficiency (*autarkeia*). As a central philosophical goal, self-sufficiency is a psychosomatic condition (*hexis*) that allows individuals to govern themselves ([Plato], *Def.*412b6).[19] And this is why sex in marriage is an acceptable social situation. It demonstrates a certain degree of self-sufficiency in that it fulfills a desire that is natural, although not necessary, and easily procured. It further demonstrates self-sufficiency in that it constitutes a severe limitation on the acceptable number of one's sexual partners. Thus, *porneia* is idolatrous in that it forsakes singularity for multiplicity, although polytheism is not a necessary component of idolatry. He goes on to say that *porneia* has a threefold sense. First, it is a defilement of one's body through partnership with an alien body (3.12.89.2). Second, it is the establishment of a union, whether legal or not, for purposes other than the procreation of children (3.12.90.1). Third, it is a misunderstanding of the Hebrew Bible and a rejection of the will of God (3.12.90.2-4).

Clement's advocacy of marriage should not be understood as an absolute moral obligation incumbent upon all Christians. As I indicated, his social context would not allow for such a claim. On the contrary, the Alexandrian provides alternative models of Christian existence for his readers that do no include marriage. In fact, he raises the question of whether marriage is actually appropriate for every Christian. "We ask the question," he says, "whether it is right to marry" (2.23.137.3). Clement sees marriage as acceptable only within certain parameters:

> It is not right for everyone to marry; it is not right at all times. There is a time when it is appropriate; there is a person for whom it is appropriate; there is an age up to which it is appropriate. It is not right for every man to marry every woman, on every occasion, in absolutely all

circumstances. It depends on the circumstances of the man, the character of the woman, the right time, the prospect of children, the total compatibility of the woman and the absence of any violence or compulsion to drive her to look after the man who loves her. (3.23.137.3-4)[20]

As an example of a union that lies outside the parameters of Christian acceptability, Clement rejects endogamy among maternally related siblings, a practice that was still common in second century-Roman Egypt (see 2.23.138.1). For Clement marriage is the proper social arrangement for the procreation of children. The absence of progeny renders the union potentially theologically illegitimate. He says, "Marriage makes a man a *father*, a husband makes a woman a *mother*" (2.23.142.3 emphasis mine).[21] Although Clement mentions mutual support as one of the benefits of marriage, it pales in comparison to the requirement that marriage produce offspring (see 2.23.141.2; 2.23.143.1-3).

As an alternative to marriage, Clement proposes celibacy as an appropriate mode of Christian existence. He defines celibacy as simply an unmarried state, and calls it a form of existence equal to that of marriage (see 3.15.97.4; 3.12.79.3). He goes on to say that it is not particularly "praiseworthy unless it arises through [a] love of God" (3.6.51.1). Although celibacy does not involve the generation of children, Clement argues that it is a state of life appointed by God for a particular purpose: "It is proper to choose celibacy in accordance with the norm of health and to combine it with piety, in gratitude for God's gift of grace, without hatred of creation or denigration of married people" (3.18.105.1). In fact, he reasons that celibacy offers a distinctive form of divine service (3.12.79.5).

In relation to his promotion of celibacy, Clement advocates that celibate men consider themselves eunuchs in obedience to the Lord's command (see 3.6.50.1-2). He understands it to be a reasoned or principled life choice that seeks to avoid the particular obligations that apply to married individuals (3.1.1.4). By contrast to common understandings of eunuchism, Clement maintains that the term eunuch "does not mean the man who has been physically emasculated, still less the unmarried man, but the man who is sterile in relation to truth" (3.15.99.1). In his Christian conception, Clement sees the eunuch as one who is sterile in relation to worldly things; and so, is blessed by God for his lifestyle (see 3.15.99.1-4). And although most modern conceptions of eunuchism would focus on the absence of male genitalia and a consequent absence of sexual desire, the same was not true in antiquity.

Castration served various functions in antiquity, including political, sexual, and religious ones. Most scholars are familiar with the castration of males for political purposes. Eunuchs were trusted political officials because they could not set up rival dynasties (or familial power structures) to that of the reigning monarch. Males were also castrated as a means of prolonging "the androgynous beauty of youth" (e.g., Nero's paramour Sporus).[22] This was also true of male prostitutes, who were castrated because they were then assumed to be more passive sexual partners.[23] Likewise, males who naturally preferred the passive or "feminine" role in sexual relations with other men were regarded as eunuchs. As Theodore Jennings says, "In the highly gender-conscious atmosphere of much of late antiquity, persons could be described as eunuchs who preferred the passive (or "feminine") role in sexual intercourse with other males. In this case, being a eunuch could be as much symbolic as literal."[24] In the religious sphere, the famous *galli* (devotees of the goddess Cybele) castrated themselves for ritual purposes. And yet, the absence of the ability to procreate did not mean that eunuchs did not engage in sexual practices. Scholars have consistently pointed out that the absence of the production of sperm did not otherwise impair male sexual activity.[25] A famous example from the Hebrew Bible illustrating this point would be Potiphar, a eunuch of the Egyptian Pharaoh, whose wife tried to seduce Joseph (Gen. 39.1, 6-20). The Alexandrian's argument for celibacy then does not mean the "natural" absence of sexual desire, rather it is the controlling of desire through its mortification. And so, Clement's understanding and promotion of an Egyptian Christian perspective on human sexuality owes a great deal to his social context, including the prevalence of Platonism as a metaphysical resource. Prompted primarily by the delay of the second coming, Clement moves Christian teaching on sexuality beyond the *ad hoc* formulations of the New Testament and the anachronistic teachings of the Hebrew Bible.

The Unexpunged Remnants of Platonism

Throughout the ensuing centuries Christian concern for the *parousia* would erupt at pivotal times and during critical events (e.g., the year 999 C.E. and the Reformation). And although marriage became the paradigmatic social arrangement for the majority of believers, celibacy continued as an acceptable life option, especially in the hierarchy of Roman Catholicism. In the United States, apocalyptic expectation governed (and still governs) certain groups, subgroups, and sects within the pluralism that characterizes American Christianity.

The Reformation changed some clerical perceptions of marriage, and yet sex still carried a negative stigma. Throughout the Western church sex was seen as a necessary evil, an acquiescence to the powers of desire and carnality. Such an attitude was expressed succinctly in the Westminster Confession of 1646: "Marriage was ordained for the mutual help of husband and wife; for the increase of mankind with a legitimate issue, and of the church with an holy seed; and for preventing of uncleanness."[26] In an almost perverse manner, sexual activity was validated as a means for providing new Christians and for avoiding *porneia* without any real critical engagement with the philosophical model that informed such a doctrine.

In the American colonies, such a view of human sexuality influenced early religious groups like the Puritans. As the recent book edited by Kathy Peiss, *Major Problems in the History of American Sexuality*, illustrates, the influence of Platonic conceptions of material existence and desire continued to govern early popular American understandings of human sexuality.[27] In fact, it would be fair to say that such ideas perdure and exercise undue influence over American attitudes regarding sex and sexuality. This is expressly true in American religious organizations. Under the influence of religious institutions, African Americans, for example, were subjected to the projection of negative European and Euro-American understandings of the body and desire.

Consistently characterized as animalistic in their sexual practices, enslaved African Americans and their descendants have labored under the burden of these negative projections for centuries. African American bodies have become a focal point for residual American disdain for corporeal material existence. Popular American culture, while rewarding its participants, also does so at the expense of African American bodies particularly. Hip-hop culture markedly exploits and degrades African American bodies into instruments of an unrestrained sexuality. When desire is added to this equation, African American sexual practices are perceived as the negative counterpart of acceptable Christian practices of continence. Of course, African Americans have also attempted to fulfill such Platonically influenced understandings of the body and desire. And yet, no serious critical engagement with the philosophical paradigm that continually informs such a negative perception of human sexuality has been advanced in mainstream popular American culture. In fact, the subject of African American sexuality is only explored rarely with any reflective seriousness. Images of African American sexual prowess abound in music videos, movies, and pornography. In fact, even latent sexual desire is often exploited in the popular media. It is rare, for example, to see African Americans on television as having sexual difficulties. Popular culture frequently portrays African Americans as having problems with intimacy rather than potency. African American men are portrayed as and taught to be sexual predators, and women are taught to use sex as a manipulative tool. Even members of our judicial system, that once vaunted component of government that remained aloof from popular influence, have joined in the general promotion of sexual titillation.

Courtrooms have become the modern daytime talk shows. Through the venue of small claims court, countless numbers of people parade their moral failures. And judges entertain extended discussions of moral misadventures. Far too often, the actors in these dramas of sexual indiscretion are African Americans. Even a casual observer of the phenomenon cannot fail to notice that the more sexually laden cases involve young African Americans who appear incapable of initiating and sustaining positive long-term relationships. Such portrayals capture our popular attention because they represent the antithesis of the Platonic sexual paradigm. And while moralists may cast aspersions on their activities, what is needed is not a strengthening of the Platonic model. Radical reevaluation of the paradigm itself is needed. Modern sexual theorists must focus on the root.

In constructing a contemporary doctrine of human sexuality, the designer must confront the residue of ancient Platonism and its programmatic difficulties. For example, negative perceptions of corporeal material existence, or the body, are not biblical in that they are not found in the Hebrew Bible. The scriptures of the Hebrew Bible are not burdened with a perverse Greco-Roman philosophical fascination with the body, although they are certainly burdened with a fascination with procreation among other things. In order to counteract the negative Greco-Roman assessment of corporeal material existence, a renewed Christian doctrine of human sexuality must embrace the central biblical notion of the goodness of creation. Acceptance of embodiedness, especially in light of the incarnation, as a central Christian metaphysical (or existential) claim will go a long way toward renewing Christianity's understanding of human sexuality.

In addition to a renewed appreciation for material existence, contemporary Christianity must negotiate the negative Platonic appraisal of desire. According to Gen. 3.16, the desire of one human being for the other is part of God's providential plan. The erotic, the desire to unite with the other, is at the heart of this plan. God's desire to unite with humanity becomes then paradigmatic of our own *eros*. Already exploited in media and literature, African Americans are poised between the tensions that structure the debate. As the literal and symbolic representation of the other in American society, African Americans were not expected to accept the predominant cultural view in its entirety. As such the African American community can harness its otherness for the benefit of those chaffing under the continued threat of total Platonic hegemony. A renewed appreciation for human sexual desire would begin with the proposal that it is both human and normal. The negative stigma that has been attached to human desire has had the most debilitating effect of undermining the fundamental social nature of human existence as such. An appropriate and contemporary doctrine of human sexuality would incorporate desire as a necessary component of human social interaction generally.

Ancient Social Conceptions versus Contemporary Society

At the dawn of the twentieth century, the average life expectancy at birth in the United States was 47.3 years.[28] On the eve of World War II, average life expectancy at birth had jumped to 62.9 years. For African Americans, the year 1900 brought an average life expectancy at birth of 33 years with a jump to 54.5 years by 1939. In the twenty-first century, average life expectancy at birth has reached 77.1 years for all Americans, and 72.4 years for African Americans. Projections for the year 2010 will add another year to overall American life expectancy and two years for African Americans. The purpose behind this recitation of statistics is to highlight the vast difference between the world in which Clement's doctrine of sexuality was constructed and our own. Even for African Americans, who have lagged behind Euro-Americans in life expectancy consistently, the differences are dramatic. Part of the power of the old sexual paradigm involved the perception among African Americans that our lives ended much earlier than our Euro-American counterparts. And while it was true in 1900 that an African American died on average more than fourteen years earlier than his Caucasian counterpart, a modern African American can expect to precede a Euro-American in death by approximately four years. The point here is not to raise a debate over the equity of life expectations among racial groups. Rather it is to challenge the entrenched idea in many African American churches that the main purpose for sexual activity is the procreation of children, an idea that finds partial justification in a perceived substantial difference in life expectancy.

The continuing orientation among African American religious institutions is to view sex instrumentally. Modern African American congregations affirm consistently the idea that the only appropriate purpose for sex is the procreation of children. Although the unquestionable majority of African Americans intentionally have sex for purposes other than the propagation of offspring, the pretense of adhering to the Platonic paradigm remains. In this paradigm women are reduced to little more than breeding machines. Of course, many in the community will argue that this orientation finds its justification in scripture as well as contemporary social concerns. Unfortunately, as I indicated earlier, the New Testament does not present a coherent understanding of human sexuality. It is far more concerned with the imminent return of Christ than it is with developing a comprehensive understanding of human sexual activity. Furthermore, the social context that prevailed in antiquity is not analogous to that of our modern liberal society. In other words, justifying modern sexual practices on the basis of ancient sexual practices is fatally anachronistic. To reduce men and women to procreative agency is to say that sex serves no other purpose than as an instrument for governmental or religious policy. The differences between the ancient social context of Roman Egypt and that of modern America are such that any attempt to maintain this paradigm would be like putting new wine into old wineskins (see Math. 9.17 and par.). Modern cultural practices indicate that African Americans are either rejecting the Platonic model or paying lip service to it while ignoring its clear ethical demands. Either reality is unacceptable and represents the impotence of the church and other social institutions when it comes to cultivating allegiances that are sustained and enhanced by transparent activity. Either the advocates for the construction of a contemporary doctrine of sexuality need to address the social issue in a manner that will translate into other than hypocritical action, or the subject should be avoided altogether.

It would be a mistake for a religion whose core message is one of love to be silent on the subject of human sexual interaction. In fact, since early Christians already developed a doctrine of sexuality it is too late for modern Christians to think they can put the genie back in the bottle. The modern debate that rages among various Christian communions concerning human sexuality is a welcome reappraisal of this most ancient of doctrines. African Americans in particular must participate in this conversation. Far too often African Americans have lived under the negative perceptions of human sexuality that have abounded since antiquity.

Liberating the Erotic

Cain Hope Felder once wrote, "[The ambiguity of race in the New Testament] confronts us with a challenge to search for more adequate modes of hermeneutics by which the New Testament can be demonstrated as relevant to Blacks and other people of the Third World, even as it stands locked into the socioreligious framework of the Greco-Roman world."[29] And I agree that African Americans need a new hermeneutic (or set of hermeneutics) to make the Bible relevant to them in the contemporary environment. I here offer four programmatic suggestions related to such a constructive enterprise. First, human sexuality must be seen as an integral part of human creation. The Hebrew Bible and early Christianity both agree that change and desire are the proper characteristics of human existence. Of course, under the influence of certain Greco-Roman philosophical beliefs, early Christians understood desire as a negative predicate of that existence. Modern Christians must reevaluate such a thoroughgoing negative assessment of desire. Negative conceptions of human desire must be qualified. For example, if one of the goals of the gospel is to lead individuals into living morally acceptable and accountable lives, then limits must be placed on actions stemming from human desire. In other words, African American Christian understandings of human sexuality must retain a strong ethical component. Serious thought must be given to the Christian ideal of self-control as a means of proscribing and cultivating a set of acceptable sexual norms (e.g., addressing the proper limits to be placed on the number of one's sexual partners). And yet, is self-control even the appropriate ethical category with which to address African American sexual behavior? Must desire be continually linked with procreation when it comes to accepted sexual practice? These are among the questions that need to be addressed in a contemporary formulation of a doctrine. If self-control (*autarkeia*) as traditionally conceived is no longer an appropriate category through which to address African American sexual practice, then is there another norm or category capable of replacing it? If desire and procreation are uncoupled as well, then the grounding of Christian sexual ethics will transform from Clement's vision of the breeding of children to the advocacy of intimate relationships between morally accountable people. In addition, African American Christians should abandon their advocacy of marriage as an absolute social norm. We must posit ways in which individuals can be responsible sexual actors that do not limit them to the categories of married (the acceptable) and unmarried (the unacceptable). Early Christians realized that marriage was not appropriate for all human beings, and African American Christians should recognize and sanction alternative modes of social existence as well. This would represent a recapturing of early Christian tradition, in reality. As we saw in Clement's theology, members of the early church considered celibacy an appropriate moral existence. Of course, given our modern environment I would advocate a reevaluation of sexual mores that would include the viability of modes of existence other than celibacy, such as same sex unions, blended families, and heretofore-untraditional family structures.

Second, early Christians understood, although often inconsistently, that the body was not innately evil. The development of an African American Christian doctrine of human sexuality must begin by advocating the unequivocal acceptance of bodily existence. The Hebrew Bible affirms the goodness of human creation as an intentional act of God (see Gen. 1.26-28; 2.23). Indeed, the notion of the *imago Dei*, whether it is understood formally or substantively, is a peculiar theological expression of the Christian belief that bodily existence is the proper locus for human relationship with God. Likewise, the doctrine of the incarnation functions as a symbolic referent of God's endorsement of the materiality of human existence. As a consequence, in this contemporary discourse on human sexuality African American Christians must affirm the importance and integrity of physical embodiedness. Rather than continuing to denigrate our bodies as a source of animal-like behavior, our unfortunate inheritance of an Euro-American Christian paradigm, African Americans should develop a theological anthropology that posits human corporeal existence as the foundation for our experiences of joy and pain, intimacy and alienation, finitude and transcendence. Part of such a transformation would include by necessity a reappraisal of certain eschatological norms, specifically the orientation toward an imminent *parousia* that dominated the New Testament canon. If I am correct that eschatology continues to lurk behind traditional African American conceptions of sex, then it must be exposed and addressed directly. Unqualified acceptance of embodiedness would not only overturn the prevalent

Platonic model, it would also reconnect African American Christian doctrine to its Hebrew Bible patrimony and reintroduce the possibility of the erotic as a valuable ethical category in the overall discourse.

Third, as a means of constructing a more comprehensive understanding of human sexuality, African Americans would benefit from a recapturing of the importance of *eros* as a component of humanity's idealized relationship with God, as well as the relationship human beings should have with each other. I believe Hugh Montefiore to be correct when he says, "[*Eros*], the passionate desire to be united with the beloved, is part of God's gift to humanity, provided that it is combined with *agape*, the determination of the lover to cherish the beloved with tenderness and affection, and to provide support, help and comfort."[30] A reintroduction of *eros* adds by implication the recognition of intimacy, mutual sharing, generosity, and fulfillment as honorable human experiences. As a complement to the rather disconnected notion of *agape*, the intensity that characterizes most understandings of *eros* balances and humanizes the Christian appreciation for, and appropriation of, love. For example, the idea of sex as an expression of generosity, rarely arises in African American religious discourse. As a consequence, predatory or mercenary orientations dominate popular African American discourse on sex. Love, as a balanced transcendent experience that encompasses sex, is frequently diminished to a relationship that functions primarily as an exchange for sexual and material goods (e.g., the song "Bills, bills, bills" by Destiny's Child). *Eros*, if deeply appreciated, can expand and complexify the representation of human relationships in African American culture. Although still an exchange, a deeply appreciated erotic understanding of this exchange would transcend the acts or goods themselves and embrace them as expressions of a divinely ingrained desire for union. Such an affirmation will assist in the development of a doctrine of sexuality that transcends the unfortunate view that sex should be understood primarily as an instrument for procreation.

Finally, those participating in the construction of this modern doctrine of sexuality should practice a hermeneutic of suspicion when reading and appropriating early Christian documents regarding human sexual behavior. As with antebellum rhetoric that promoted slavery, we must realize that as a whole these documents represent the concerns and interests of the Christian elite, including documents in the New Testament for which authorship cannot be conclusively affirmed. The production of texts was a means used by Christian leaders and intellectuals to organize and impose particular theological opinions.[31] Robin Lane Fox highlights such an interest on the part of Christian leaders when he says,

> Literacy also allowed bishops to outmanoeuvre opponents, display a solid front of opinion, abjure or curse mistaken Christians or "sign up" lists of names for creeds and disciplinary rulings, texts which allowed yet more power to be mobilized. As for sacred literacy, it allowed bishops to cite impersonal sources for their own authority: like visionaries, bishops profited from texts in which God's word, not their own, was made public.[32]

I would not limit such a statement regarding the use of texts to episcopal leadership, as Fox does; rather I would expand it to include all Christian intellectual production as such. As a consequence, modern organizers of Christian public opinion should be careful not to reinscribe uncritically attitudes and norms regarding human sexuality that serve the interests of the few at the expense of the many. If African Americans are going to be successful in their endeavor to construct an appropriate contemporary understanding of human sexuality, then such a doctrine must account for and incorporate shared human sexual experience as well as idealized norms derived from Christian tradition.

Notes

1. Wendy Doniger O'Flaherty et al., "The Dean's Forum on *the Sleep of Reason: Erotic Experience and Sexual Ethics in Ancient Greece and Rome*," *Criterion* 42, no. 1 (2003): 30.
2. I am reticent to offer a definition for *porneia* because of its wide-ranging character. In addition, I believe Martha Nussbaum to be correct in her analysis of the usefulness of lexica. She says, "[Lexica] are simply the record of what some scholars, usually not the best, have thought about the same texts that we can all read. So, in general, I would prefer not to be guided by them, except in the sense that they remind us of pertinent texts, and offer conjectures about them that have the status of any other scholar's conjectures" (Ibid.: 34).
3. On the Pauline notion of freedom, see Hans Dieter Betz, *Paulinische Studien,* vol. 3; Gesammelte Aufsatze, Tubingen: Mohr, 1994, 110–125.
4. See Jennings, *The Man Jesus Loved*, 145.
5. For another perspective, see Peter Robert Lamont Brown, *The Body and Society: Men, Women and Sexual Renunciation in Early Christianity,* vol. 13 *Lectures on the History of Religions* (New York: Columbia University Press, 1988), 33–64.
6. See Elaine H. Pagels, *Adam, Eve, and the Serpent* 1st Vintage Books edn. (New York: Vintage Books, 1989), passim.

7. Unless otherwise indicated, all translations are from Titus Flavius Clemens, "*Stromateis Books One to Three*" in The Fathers of the Church ed. Thomas P. Halton; trans. John Ferguson (Washington, D.C.: The Catholic University of America Press, 1991).

8. Roger S. Bagnall and Bruce W. Frier, *The Demography of Roman Egypt* Cambridge Studies in Population, Economy and Society in Past Time 23 (New York: Cambridge University Press, 1994), 104.

9. Ibid., 104.

10. Ibid., 112.

11. Ibid., 116.

12. Ibid., 123.

13. By celibacy I mean simply the state of living unmarried. Whether or not persons are engaging in sexuality activity is not my concern here.

14. See Plato, *Plato with an English Translation* trans. Harold North Fowler et al., 12 vols., LCL Loep Classic Library (Cambridge: Harvard University Press, 1914).

15. Epictetus, *The Enchiridion* trans. Thomas W. Higginson, Library of Liberal Arts (New York: Macmillan, 1948), 30.

16. In making this distinction between those things that are "natural and necessary" and those things that are just "natural," Clement appears to be in agreement with the Epicureans, who believed, "We must also reflect that of desires some are natural (*physikai*), others are groundless; and that of the natural some are necessary as well as natural, and some natural only" (Diogenes Laertius, *Vitae philosophorum* 10.127.7 [LCL]). See Diogenes Laertius *Lives of Eminent Philosophers* trans. Robert Drew Hicks; 2 vols., Loeb Classical Library (Cambridge: Harvard University Press, 1979), 653.

17. *Porneia* appears in *Strom.* 3 more frequently than it does in any of Clement's other works. The term arises at least twenty-two times, compared to the two or three times it appears in almost all his other writings. The one exception is the *Paedagogus* where *porneia* appears eighteen times. In *Strom.* 3, it appears most frequently in quotations from scripture or Clement's commentary upon them. Nearly 70 percent of the term's usage is conducted in this manner.

18. Clemens, *Strom.*, 249.

19. *Autarkeia* is a form of apotheosis in Stoic thought, and a form of rejection of traditional communal values in Cynic thought.

20. Clemens, *Strom.*, 249–50.

21. Ibid., 253.

22. Jennings, *The Man Jesus Loved*, 148.

23. See Ibid., 149.

24. Ibid., 149.

25. See Ibid., 149–150; Rouselle, *Porneia*, 122.

26. John H. Leith, ed., *Creeds of the Churches: A Reader in Christian Doctrine from the Bible to the Present* 3rd edn. (Atlanta: John Knox, 1982), 221.

27. See Kathy Lee Peiss, ed., *Major Problems in the History of American Sexuality: Documents and Essays* Major Problems in American History Series (Boston: Houghton Mifflin, 2002).

28. For this and the following statistics, please consult, *World Population Profile*, passim, as well as www.census.gov (the official website for the Bureau of the Census).
29. Felder, *Troubling Biblical Waters*, 48.
30. Jack Dominian and Hugh Montefiore, *God, Sex & Love: An Exercise in Ecumenical Ethics* (Philadelphia: Trinity, 1989), 5.
31. See Robin Lane Fox, "Literacy and Power in Early Christianity," in *Literacy and Power in the Ancient World*, ed. Alan K. Bowman and Greg Woolf (Cambridge: Cambridge University Press, 1994), 137.
32. Ibid., 134.

Selected Chapter Bibliography

Armstrong, A. H. "The Self-Definition of Christianity in Relation to Later Platonism." In *Jewish and Christian Self-Definition: The Shaping of Christianity in the Second and Third Centuries*. Edited by E. P. Sanders. Philadelphia: Fortress, 1980.

Bagnall, Roger S. and Bruce W. Frier. *The Demography of Roman Egypt*. Cambridge Studies in Population, Economy, and Society in Past Time 23. New York: Cambridge University Press, 1994.

Betz, Hans Dieter. *Galatians : A Commentary on Paul's Letter to the Churches in Galatia*. Hermeneia—a Critical and Historical Commentary on the Bible. Philadelphia: Fortress, 1979.

———. *Paulinische Studien*. vol. 3. Gesammelte Aufsatze. Tubingen: Mohr, 1994.

Bowman, Alan K. *Egypt after the Pharaohs: 332 BC–AD 642 from Alexander to the Arab Conquest*. Los Angeles: University of California Press, 1986.

Brown, Michael Joseph. "Paul's Use of Doulos Xristou Iesou in Romans 1:1." *JBL* 120, no. 4 (2001): 723-37.

Brown, Peter Robert Lamont. *The Body and Society: Men, Women and Sexual Renunciation in Early Christianity*. Vol. new ser. 13. Lectures on the History of Religions. New York: Columbia University Press, 1988.

Clemens, Titus Flavius. *Stromateis Books One to Three*. Edited by Thomas P. Halton. Translated by John Ferguson. The Fathers of the Church. Washington, D.C.: The Catholic University of America Press, 1991.

Dominian, Jack, and Hugh Montefiore. *God, Sex & Love: An Exercise in Ecumenical Ethics*. Philadelphia: Trinity, 1989.

Epictetus. *The Enchiridion*. Translated by Thomas W. Higginson. Library of Liberal Arts. New York: Macmillan, 1948.

Felder, Cain Hope. *Troubling Biblical Waters: Race, Class, and Family*. Edited by James H. Cone. vol. 3. The Bishop Henry McNeal Turner Studies in North American Black Religion. Maryknoll: Orbis, 1989.

Fox, Robin Lane. "Literacy and Power in Early Christianity." In *Literacy and Power in the Ancient World*. Edited by Alan K. Bowman and Greg Woolf. 126–148. Cambridge: Cambridge University Press, 1994.

Garnsey, Peter. *Food and Society in Classical Antiquity*. Key Themes in Ancient History. Cambridge: Cambridge University Press, 1999.

Jennings, Jr., Theodore W. *The Man Jesus Loved: Homoerotic Narratives from the New Testament*. Cleveland: Pilgrim, 2003.

Koester, Helmut. *History, Culture and Religion of the Hellenistic Age*. 1st edn. 2 vols. vol. 1 of *Introduction to the New Testament*. New York: Walter de Gruyter, 1982.

Laertius , Diogenes. *Lives of Eminent Philosophers*. Translated by Robert Drew Hicks. 2 vols. Loeb Classical Library. Cambridge: Harvard University Press, 1979.

Leith, John H., ed. *Creeds of the Churches: A Reader in Christian Doctrine from the Bible to the Present*. 3rd edn. Atlanta: John Knox, 1982.

Malina, Bruce J. and Richard L. Rohrbaugh. *Social-Science Commentary on the Synoptic Gospels*. Minneapolis: Fortress, 1992.

O'Flaherty, Wendy Doniger et al. "The Dean's Forum on *the Sleep of Reason: Erotic Experience and Sexual Ethics in Ancient Greece and Rome*." *Criterion*, 42, no. 1 (2003): 18–35.

Ogden, Schubert M. *The Reality of God and Other Essays*. Dallas: Southern Methodist University Press, 1992.

Pagels, Elaine H. *Adam, Eve, and the Serpent*. 1st Vintage Books edn. New York: Vintage Books, 1989.

Peiss, Kathy Lee, ed. *Major Problems in the History of American Sexuality: Documents and Essays*. Major Problems in American History Series. Boston: Houghton Mifflin, 2002.

Plato. *Plato, with an English Translation*. Translated by Harold North Fowler et al. 12 vols. Loeb Classical Library. Cambridge: Harvard University Press, 1914.

Plutarch. *Plutarch's Moralia*. Translated by Frank Cole Babbitt. 15 vols. Loeb Classical Library. New York: Putnam, 1927.

Rouselle, Aline. *Porneia: On Desire and the Body in Late Antiquity*. Translated by Felicia Pheasant. Oxford: Blackwell, 1988.

Shelton, Jo-Ann, ed. *As the Romans Did: A Sourcebook in Roman Social History*. New York: Oxford University Press, 1998.

Washington, James M., ed. *A Testament of Hope: The Essential Writings and Speeches of Martin Luther King, Jr.* New York: Harper San Francisco, 1986.

White, L. Michael. "Scholars and Patrons: Christianity and High Society in Alexandria." In *Christian Teaching: Studies in Honor of Lemoine G. Lewis*. Edited by Everett Ferguson. 328–32. Abilene, Tex.: Abilene Christian University Bookstore, 1981.

4

The Bible, the Body and a Black Sexual Discourse of Resistance

Abraham Smith

Sex . . . is a difficult subject to treat in the black church, or for that matter, in any church. This is indeed ironic. After all, Christian faith is grounded in the incarnation, the belief that God took on flesh to redeem human beings. That belief is constantly being trumped by Christianity's quarrels with the body. Its needs. Its desires. Its sheer materiality. But especially its sexual identity.[1]

Introduction

Among recent works on Black sexuality, Cornel West's "Black Sexuality: The Taboo Subject" and Kelly Brown Douglas's *Sexuality and the Black Church* are exemplary in examining the "sexual politics of race" in the United States.[2] Both works decry the dehumanization of Black bodies, the demonization of sexual variation, and the deafening silence of Black institutions on the subject of Black sexuality.[3] Key to both works, moreover, are *deconstructive* and *constructive* modes of resistance.[4] On the one hand, both works demystify Black sexuality by exposing the "dominant myths" that decree "whiteness" as a norm and Blackness (including Black sexuality) as deviant.[5] The works expose these myths—in which Blacks are viewed as oversexed (e.g., with Jezebel or the Black stud images) or desexed (e.g., the mammy or the Sambo images)—for the psychic scarring they engender on Black souls, the stunning silence they effect in Black support structures, and the ideological role they play in the psychocultural theater of White supremacy.[6] On the other hand, both works proffer a proactive and

programmatic sexual discourse of resistance.[7] Brown-Douglas posits
the need "to cultivate a life-enhancing approach to Black sexuality
within the Black community";[8] and West advocates the forging of
"new stylistic options of self-image and resistance" that are not tied to
the "dominant myths" or the "network of white supremacist lies" to
which the myths are tied.[9]

With an eye toward the bible, I wish to use this essay to join West
and Brown Douglas in developing a Black sexual discourse of
resistance.[10] In a *deconstructive* mode, the first part of the essay
exposes the role to which biblical discourse (the discursive nexus of
biblical diction, biblical worldviews, and interpretations of the bible)
has been put in supporting Black dehumanization in general and Black
sexual devaluation in particular. That is, in alignment with ancient
(binary) prejudices, asymmetrical color dualisms in the Middle Ages,
and modern hegemonic discourse,[11] biblical discourse has provided
much of the "rhetorical scaffolding" for the construction of Black
bodies and Black sexuality as "deviant." Then, in a *constructive* mode,
the second part of the essay considers the extent to which the Bible can
be used critically and responsibly in the development of a "liberating
sexual ethic."[12]

Deconstructive Mode of Resistance

From antiquity to today, biblical discourse has played a role in
promoting the hierarchy of oppositions though color signification
took a radically exploitative turn in the so-called voyages of discovery
period.[13] Though many scholars once supported Frank Snowden's thesis that blacks were overwhelmingly idealized in Christian literature
and in the larger worlds of Greek and Roman writings, recent explorations of antiquity call attention to the extant vituperative depictions
of Egyptians, Ethiopians, and Blacks.[14] That is, long before the pre-
Enlightenment and the Enlightenment, the binarism of black and
white[15] and the concomitant association of blackness with evil were
products of Christian symbolism and iconography.[16]

The depiction of the devil as "the Black One" (*ho melas*) in *Epistle
of Barnabas* (70–115 CE) and the typological "blackening" of those
believers "influenced by evil" in *Shepherd of Hermas* (second century
CE) are clear examples of a negative Black aesthetic in early Christian
writing.[17] In his Greek *Commentarium and Homiliae in Canticum
Canticorum*, Origen presents an allegorical interpretation of the Black
bride in Song of Songs 1:5–6. The bride represents the Gentile church,

which is Black by virtue of its ignoble birth (or obscure origins) and yet possessing a beauty based on reception and penitence.[18] Speaking of Ham (based on Genesis 9:20–27), Origen avers that by " 'quickly sink[ing] to slavery of the vices,' Ham's 'discolored posterity imitate the ignobility of the race' he fathered."[19]

Jerome's translation of Song of Songs 1:5 as "I am black but beautiful" also reflects the binary of Black and white. In Hebrew the conjunction between the two expressions is a *waw* (meaning "and") and even the Septuagint's translation uses *kai* (again meaning "and"). Jerome translates the Hebrew *waw* as the Latin *sed* (meaning "but"), however, rather than *et* (meaning "and"), as if the second clause of the sentence compensates for an acknowledged deformity expressed in the first clause.[20] In a letter commending "virginity and abstinence," moreover, Jerome also describes the devil as "black like the night, in which the 'beasts of the woods go about' " (cf. Ps. 104: 21) and he describes the devil as one whose "force against women" lies in his navel (cf. Job 40:16).[21] This binary then becomes the basis for the color prejudice that was present in Christian discourse long before the first use of the term "race" in the fifteenth century or the rise of racialist pseudo-science in the late nineteenth century.[22]

In the medieval period, the color Black signified Christian anxiety in the face of internal and external threats. Internally, the color Black played a role in Christianity's distinctions between insiders and outsiders (or so-called heretics). For example, Gerontius' *Vita Melaniae Junioris* 54 depicts the devil as a Black man in a polemic directed against the so-called heretical teachings of Nestorius.[23] When Christian communities in Roman Egypt faced political or military threats, connections were also made between sexuality and blackness, as for example in the ethnopolitical discourse of the monastic fathers (e.g., the *Life of Antony 6, Apophthgmata patrum* 5.4 and 579).[24] When Christianity encountered the Religion of Islam, however, the idea of the " 'black demon' was transferred to Muslims—in early medieval paintings black Saracens [Arabs], Black tormentors and black henchmen torture Christ during the Passion."[25]

Biblical "Cain" also became Black in the medieval period. From the days of Augustine, Christians had already linked Cain to the Jews.[26] In 1146, however, this "othering" of the Jews permitted the "expropriation of Jewish property;" and in 1215, papal decree assigned the "Jew-badge" that caused immeasurable degradation to the Jews for centuries.[27] The similar "othering" of Blacks as "Cain" can be seen in a twelfth-century German poem in which the progeny of Cain's descendants are declared both "black" and lacking in beauty.[28] In one of the folios of a thirteenth century CE English psalter, moreover, Cain has "predominantly negroid features."[29] The so-called curse on Ham or Canaan was also associated with Cain perhaps because of an orthographic error, that is, the similarity between the word Cain and Cham, the spelling of Ham in the Middle Ages.[30]

Given the asymmetrical color dualism of antiquity and the middle ages, color prejudice was already in place for the arrival of racism and the cultural discourses of modernity that supported it. Modern hegemonic discourse, however, foregrounded phenotypes; regulated black bodies through mythological structures, pseudo-science and legal prescriptions; and proffered sustained biblical support to justify the disparity between the ideals of natural rights and the degradation of slavery.

According to Cornel West, the foregrounding of phenotypes was possible because three earlier historical processes fused, namely, "the scientific revolution, the Cartesian transformation of philosophy and the classical revival."[31] The scientific revolution (in the work of Copernicus, Kepler, Galileo, Newton, Descartes, and Leibniz) "signified the authority of science"; the Cartesian transformation gave the important "gaze" of the value-free subject; and the classical revival furnished an ideal or standard against which to judge contemporary values.[32] The fusion gave authority or a "normative gaze" to those disciplines (phrenology and physiognomy) that used skin color to support an essentialist and hierarchic distinction between European people (based on classical ideals of beauty) and non-European others.[33] The consequence for such Enlightenment writers as Montesquieu, Hume, Jefferson, and Kant, then, was the ready assumption that their racist views needed no proof.[34]

When Europeans first traveled to Africa, they "interpreted African women's sparse dress—dress appropriate to the climate of Africa—as a sign of their lewdness and lack of chastity."[35] Slavocracy needed the mythical Jezebel image for at least two reasons. First, it provided a foil for white women of Victorian ideals.[36] Second, it justified white male rape of black women with the notion that the white males were the victims of enslaved women's sexual aggressiveness.[37] Likewise, the mythic idea of Black men as bucks likely "predate[d] the settlement of America and possibly even the Portuguese explorations of the West African coast."[38] Even if not, pseudo-science advanced ideas about the superiority of Black male genitalia compared to Whites. The ideas in place produced three implications: (1) that the Black male was as powerful as an animal; (2) that the Black male was a good breeder; and (3) that the Black man "posed a potential threat to the peace and security of the White world."[39]

With transatlantic slave-trading, Africans were fully reduced to the status of property; tightly packed in the hulls of ships; and classified as insurable goods on voyages threatened by dangerous winds and epidemic outbreaks. For those Africans who actually survived the "watery, rocking tombs" of the Middle Passage and the concomitant social death or natal alienation, the legal codes brought a fresh torrent of abuses: assigning children born of an enslaved woman to the same status; granting masters the power to maim, sexually abuse, or otherwise torture their "chattel" real estate; and limiting the traveling, educating and corporate assembling of the African captives.[40]

As before, biblical discourse played a role in the assault on Black life. To justify slavery's regime, the Anglican Bishop of London (1727) sanctioned slavery with his reading of 1 Cor. 7:20–24;[41] and many slaveholders in North America appealed to the Bible as well (e.g., Gen. 9; 14:14; 14:18–20; 17:13; Exod. 12:43–45; 20:17; 21:2–6; 21:20–21; Lev. 25:44–46; Deut. 23:15–16; Eph. 6:5–9).[42] Among the aforementioned texts, Gen. 9 deserves special notice, for it played and continues to play a significant role in the discursive logic of hegemony's formation of Black subjectivity.[43] Many of the other Biblical texts supported slavery without (necessarily) associating servitude with a specific color. To support an association between servitude and color, however, proponents of the claim of Negro inferiority turned to the Hamite hypothesis based on Gen. 9. The hypothesis first gained prominence in the sixteenth century (e.g., in the work of George Best) but its roots apparently lie in rabbinical literature from the Babylonian Talmud and in the Middle Ages.[44] Though the text of Genesis 9 speaks of a curse of Canaan without ascribing a specific color, the rabbinic material assigns the color black either to Canaan or to all of Ham's descendants.[45] This association thus provided the basic rationale for later interpreters of Genesis 9 to justify the enslavement of Black persons.

Of course, the "curse of Ham" thesis is riddled with problems. For one, it is not a curse by God—only by Noah. Second, the curse is against Canaan, not Ham, but proponents of Negro inferiority tidied up this little discrepancy with the additional claim that Ham was also cursed because the word Ham meant "burnt black," as if Noah anticipated the curse and so named his son.[46] Third, the whole episode about Noah and Ham only covers fifty-one verses; thus, the verses hardly seem to be salient enough to condemn an entire race of people to servitude.[47] Fourth, if the racists assumed that Noah was not Black but Ham was indeed Black, when did Ham become Black?[48]

In addition to these problems, one must reckon with the New Hamite hypothesis that developed in the wake of Napoleon's 1798 expedition to Egypt.[49] When Napoleon's explorers discovered that the beginnings of civilization were in Egypt as opposed to Rome and Greece, a flurry of scholarship was created with the purpose of distinguishing the Egyptians and other "culture-rich" Africans from the Negroes who were presumed to have been inferior and thus incapable of making a contribution to world civilization.[50] Some scholars thus declared that Ham was not Black for the same reason that some had declared that Ham was indeed Black—to assert a notion of Black cultural inferiority.

Still, the racists used the so-called curse of Ham thesis to support their claim of Negro inferiority. Before the Civil War, Joseph Priestly and Matthew Estes (the former more assiduously) asserted that the enslavement of Blacks was supported by the so-called curse on Ham.[51] Others, like Samuel A. Cartwright and Jefferson Davis (before he assumed the presidency of the Confederacy), linked the Hamite hypothesis to a thesis about Cain. Cartwright actually proposed two theories. The first was the simple Hamite hypothesis but the second, a pre-Adamite thesis, suggested that the first Blacks were created before Adam and Eve and that the serpent was actually a Negro gardener. As well he argued that Cain found his wife among the pre-Adamite Negroes (in the land of Nod), the descendants of which were destroyed in the flood because of the mixing of races. Finally, he argued that a pure race of the Negro continued through Canaan for whom Ham (Noah's son) was the headmaster, not the father. Davis accepted Cartwright's second thesis but he contended that both Ham and Cain were miscegenists.[52]

After the Civil War, Governor Benjamin F. Perry of South Carolina, Buckner Payne, and Charles Carroll advocated Cartwright's pre-Adamite theory,[53] the last of whom called the Negro the "tempter of Eve."[54] Others revived Priest's simple Hamite hypothesis and agreed with him that the "descendants of Ham had overdeveloped sexual organs and were the original Sodomites of the Old Testament, guilty in ancient times of all conceivable forms of lewdness."[55]

Thus, different forms of the Hamite hypothesis incorporated several Genesis traditions—not exclusively Genesis 9. In whatever form the hypothesis took, however, other Biblical arguments about servitude and the so-called scientific arguments were all used to support the ideology of the Negro's inferiority. So, with the aid of biblical discourse, the dominant myths about Blacks found reiteration, the very process by which they came to take on a "natural" semblance. As Rosello has noted, stereotype "is above all defined by a high degree of iterativity. . . . ; it is a strong element of iterativity that insinuates itself like some sort of bacteria to a general statement about a group or a community. The stereotypical infection then turns this nondemonstrable statement into an instantly memorable formula that parades as common sense, truth, and wisdom."[56]

Deconstructing the myths, however, reveals that they are not "natural" but are simply the reiterations of views that take on the semblance of reality. And, in the case of the Black body and Black sexuality, the myths must be constructed because the view of Blacks as hypersexualized continued beyond slavery and the post-Reconstruction period and persists to this day. Much of the politics of respectability advocated in the writings of late nineteenth and twentieth century African Americans was profferred as a reaction to the racist "technologies of power" that viewed Blacks as hypersexual.[57] As Brown-Douglas has asserted, moreover, the image of the Black woman as a Jezebel now appears in the castigation of the Black welfare woman: "The black woman as welfare mother remains essential to White hegemony because the White culture blames the woman for her impoverished condition and again deflects attention away from White, racist, patriarchal structures."[58] Brown Douglas also shows the continuation of the view of the Black male as the Black buck: e.g., in the accusations of Black rapists as a prelude to lynchings, in the Emmitt Till lynching, in the Charles Stewart case, and in the darkened photo of "Willie Horton used in the 1988 presidential campaign."[59]

Constructive Mode of Resistance

Given the negative role that Biblical discourse has played in the history of Black subjectivity, many would advocate a complete dismissal of the Bible from any consideration in the development of a liberating sexual ethic. So mired in structures of exclusion are the Bible and the history of its interpretation that indeed a facile conclusion might be simply to start afresh without biblical discourse at all. In truth, however, that position is virtually impossible not only because the Black church (to whom this essay is addressed) appeals to biblical discourse in its considerations about Black subjectivity but also because Western society's ability to critique structures of exclusion is in part based on biblical discourse. That is, the cultural matrices through which most Westerners categorize reality have already been shaped through biblical discourse.[60]

What then is to be done? Proposed here are three interrelated stances toward Biblical discourse in the shaping of a liberating sexual ethic: (1) recognition of the Bible's social formation; (2) reformulation of the Bible's function; and (3) recovery of the Bible's resistance practices.[61]

Recognition of the Bible's Social Formation

Pleasuring the body, say, through self-arousal, has not always received the press it receives now in some Black circles.[62] In part, perhaps Blacks once spoke little about it because of the influence of pseudo-scentific teachings about continence. These teachings, now debunked, were advanced in the early sex education movement (1890–1920) in the United States to maintain middle class values.[63] In part, perhaps Blacks rarely spoke about autoeroticism because of a politics of respectability. Recent work on Black women's history, for example, has shown that the seeming *preoccupation* of Black women on propriety of dress and sexual behavior in their writings in the late nineteenth and early twentieth centuries was a reaction to the negative stereotypes about Black hypersexuality for which the first part of this essay gives adequate witness. Given such regulatory discipline on Black women's bodies, perhaps the *absence* of frequent comments on autoerotic pleasure by Black women is not a testament to a lack of interest in the subject but rather to the "capitulatory politics of inclusion and respectability."[64]

Looking at the social formation of the Bible, from which most present views of autoeroticism purportedly were drawn, could therefore provide clearer insight about the perceptions of autoeroticism in ancient society—a society known to most readers today as replete with patriarchal values. In turn, the clarity about antiquity's views could help the Black church to rethink its own feelings about autoeroticism today. That is, most serious students of the Bible now recognize how deeply the biblical traditions were shaped by patriarchal cultures. Thus, the goal of a liberative sexual ethic is not merely hindered by poor biblical interpretation that demeans Black subjectivity. Equally problematic are the Biblical traditions themselves because they were formed out of deeply ethnocentric, mysogynistic, and sexually repressive cultures. And, such is the case with autoeroticism.

Most serious readers of the Bible are not blind to its ethnocentrism. The post-exilic "P" traditions use sexual slander to ridicule Africans.[65] Biblical texts justify "Israel's despoliation of Jericho and Ai."[66] And, a post-exilic survivalist mentality precipitates the annulment of marriages to foreigners (Ezra 9–10; Neh. 13:23–31; Mal. 2:11–12).

Likewise, few readers of the Bible would doubt the general misogynistic character of the Biblical traditions. Rape scenes suggest that women are nothing more than the property of another (cf. the rape of Dinah in Gen. 33:18–34:31; the rape of the Levite's concubine in Judges 19:22–30; and the rape of Tamar in II Samuel 13:1–22).[67] Domestic violence is used as a metaphor for divine punishment in prophetic texts (Hosea 2; Jeremiah 13; and Ezekiel 16). Paul insists on the "Fatherhood" of God; and some of the Pastorals (1 Timothy and Titus) include household tabulations that support both women's subordination and slavery.

With respect to the issue of autoeroticism, however, perhaps more light is needed to show the androcentric character of this Biblical tradition about self-arousal. In general, Biblical traditions have a procreational orientation.[68] Pleasure hardly is seen as a factor of sex in the Hebrew Bible except in the Song of Songs. Paul and other New Testament writers virtually refrain from using the word "desire" (Gr: *epithumia*) except in a negative way. More specifically, with respect to masturbation, the *single explicit* biblical tradition about masturbation, in consonance with the bible's androcentric focus, does not mention the autoeroticism of women.[69] In the Hebrew Bible, Onan's "spilling of the seed" (Gen 38:9–10) is generally attributed as an act of masturbation.[70] Yet, neither Genesis nor several translations or commentaries on the Hebrew text (e.g., the LXX, the Targumim, or the Palestinian rabbinic sources) condemn him for his non-procreative seminal emission. Rather, he is condemned for his failure to comply with his Levirate responsibilities.[71] When non-canonical Jewish (e.g., Philo), Greek (Xenophon), or Roman (Philostratus) sources discussed autoeroticism, moreover, they largely read it either as non-procreative or as an indicator of the loss of self-mastery, the most fundamental "masculine" characteristic in Greek and Roman antiquity.[72]

If there is only *one explicit* biblical text about self-eroticism and this text and subsequent ones in antiquity appear uninterested in the issue of autoeroticism for women, one should ask why the Black church would give serious consideration to Biblical discourse on this subject at all. That is, not only are opinions and public policies—in this and other instances—shaped on the basis of limited biblical witnesses, but those witnesses themselves are riddled with antidemocratic values.

Reformulation of the Bible's Function

Notwithstanding impressive analyses of the distinctive perspectives on the Bible in Afro-America and in Black churches, the view of the Bible's function for most denominational bodies is based on the doctrine of biblical authority, a doctrine of recent historical origin but remarkable discursive force.[73] The doctrine attributes authority to the Bible as a normative source for making "beliefs, activities or positions credible."[74] The doctrine, in varying formulations, is a post-Reformation production. For the Reformed tradition, for example, the support for the doctrine emanates out of the seventeenth century Westminster Confession.[75] Though its use can be wide-ranging, in modern social debates, the doctrine has repeatedly fostered structures of exclusion.[76] For example, in the North American slavery debate, biblical authority gave ideological support to slavery. In the debates on women's suffrage, the doctrine sanctioned the subordination of women to men. And, in the recent debates about homosexuality, the doctrine is the basis for denying ordination to "those persons who are openly homosexual."[77]

Mere acknowledgment of the psychological, social, and physical death dealt on the basis of the doctrine should be enough to deny it any continuing force in today's world. Still, there are additional critiques that should give credence to a shift in the Bible's function. First, various types of indeterminacy plague the biblical "text." Aside from the obvious anthological character of the biblical texts or the centuries-long contestation about the "books" that should appear in the canon, the absence of a single autograph (original document) ought to summon caution against any strict idea of textual unity, which is often a hidden assumption behind the doctrine of biblical authority.[78] This assumption explains—though it does not justify—the crude prooftexting or scriptural gerrymandering that is mounted to espouse social views that lack ample biblical attestation. Second, advocates of the doctrine must endure heightened mental gymnastics—not to mention serious ridicule (as with the Scopes "Monkey Trial")—to harmonize post-Enlightenment astronomy with the bible's geocentric assumptions.[79]

Hence, a different approach to the bible's function is to view it as a source of inspiration—not a source of authority. As a source of inspiration, the Bible is not without faults but it "allows us to witness the successes and failures of those before us in the struggle to be faithful doers of the will of God."[80] As a source of inspiration, moreover, the Bible does not become the authoritarian trump card used to dismiss serious debate on complex social issues. Given the pluralistic spheres in which we live, one must not assume that the bible is the lone moral authority, as is often the case in the so-called Word churches though the net could be cast more broadly.[81] Such a view is a "species of bibliolatry," a blatant form of imperialism, and an obviation of the need for public debate, for a wide range of expert analysis, and for a grave consideration of the geopolitical spheres of power that impose norms on sexual valuation and conduct.[82]

Recovery of Resistance Practices

On the one hand, one cannot find much that is life-affirming and life-enhancing for Black bodies and Black sexuality in the *explicit* comments the biblical traditions make about sexuality. Moreover, despite the coming of Jesus in the flesh (what later is called his Incarnation), much of the Christian tradition has created a great divide between the mind and body, with the result that the former is lauded while the latter is rejected. On the other hand, it is possible to find in the biblical traditions some practices that affirm Black bodies and all the bodies of God's creation. Three examples—all from the Gospel of Mark—must suffice, though the examples reflect a pattern visible in the Elijah/Elisha traditions of the Hebrew Bible as well. *First*, the comprehensive health of bodies was a critical concern for the movement to which Jesus belonged. Whatever one's take on the miracles, one can hardly deny that the frequency of the miracles of Jesus' movement suggests a concern for the physical and psychological health of bodies. Jesus' assaults on the evil powers that subjugated these bodies may also be seen as attempts not simply to focus on an individual need here or there (though any act of mercy should not be dismissed). Rather, the healings bespeak Jesus' concern about the larger structural forces that weaken bodies through invasion, neglect, stigmatization, and the creation of despair. Announcements of salvation to persons (Mark 5:34; 10:52) then is never *exclusively* about the healed but they are announcements of the ever-growing reign of God in bringing liberation to *all* of God's creation.

Second, the inclusion of bodily diversity was critical for Jesus' movement. Social outcasts like Levi the tax collector (Mark 1), cripples like the paralytic (Mark 2), victims of failed policies of containment like the Gerasene (and Gentile) demoniac (Mark 5), stricken women like the woman in the crowd (Mark 5), the deaf, the mute, and many others who simply went under the banner of anonymity—all found a cure or a caring heart in that movement. This resistance practice speaks volumes against a notion of *racial authenticity* that would leave anyone behind—any gay, lesbian, bisexual, or transgendered person behind—as if there were a hierarchy of oppressions or a "privileged victim syndrome" (such as the so-called endangered Black male) that must be considered before any and all others.[83]

Third, the touching of bodies was critical for Jesus' movement. Jesus touched or laid his hands on others and others touched him (Mark 1:41; 3:10; 5:27,28,30,31; 6:5,56; 7:33; 8:22; 9:27; 10:13).

The touch of bodies, in cultures regulated by purity discourses, likely generated conflict. Stigma was attached to bodies of the physically diseased—then—as it is now, and for some diseases more than for others. Perhaps this resistance discourse of touching the bodies of others—including the diseased—is the most altruistic act of loving resistance we can offer now at a time when the pandemic of HIV/AIDS has ravaged so many bodies in the "black community." Like the Jesus movement, however, we must fight the structural forces and the epistemic irresponsibility of those who use HIV/AIDS to scapegoat others.

Conclusion

Ultimately, as I have attempted to show, the creation of a liberating sexual ethic involves *deconstructing* or demystifying the Biblical discourses that have demeaned the Black body and Black sexuality and *constructing* a discourse of resistance that is neither exclusively dependent on the Bible nor totally ignorant of some resistance practices that it commends. I acknowledge, however, that the second of these two modes will likely provide the greatest challenges for the Black church, especially the monumental challenge to shift the Bible's function away from that of an authoritative document to one of inspiration. Still, if we are to usher in a new and redemptive day of total love for all of our bodies and for all expressions of Black sexuality, that monumental challenge cannot be escaped.

Notes

1. Michael E. Dyson, *Race Rules: Navigating the Color Line* (Reading, MA: Addison-Wesley Publishing, 1996), 80.
2. Cornel West, *Race Matters* (Boston: Beacon, 1993), 83; Kelly Brown-Douglas, *Sexuality and the Black Church* (Maryknoll, N Y: Orbis, 1999), 34. Like others, I do not see race as biologically determined but as a social construct, and "Black" as a "floating signifier," though I think it is politically expedient to take into account the historical experiences of Black people because of what "blackness" has signified. See Michael Michael Eric Dyson, *Open Mike: Reflections on Philosophy, Race, Sex, Culture and Religion* (New York: Basic Civitas Books, 2003). On the "floating signifier," see Dwight A. McBride, "Can the Queen Speak? Racial Essentialism, Sexuality and the Problem of Authority," *Callaloo* 21 (1998), 366.
3. West *Race Matters* 83–91; Brown-Douglas, *Sexuality and the Black Church* 1–8.

4. The terms are explicitly cited in Brown-Douglas, *Sexuality and the Black Church* 72.

5. West, *Race Matters* 83; Brown-Douglas, *Sexuality and the Black Church* 7.

6. West *Race Matters*, 83–87 cf. Brown-Douglas, *Sexuality and the Black Church* 33–58.

7. Brown-Douglas, *Sexuality and the Black Church* 68–72; West, *Race Matters* 89–90. Stuart Hall provides a practical definition of *discourses*: "Discourses are ways of referring to our constructing knowledge about a particular topic of practice: a cluster (or formation) of ideas, images and practices, which provide ways of talking about, forms of knowledge and conduct associated with a particular topic, social activity or institutional site in society. These discursive formations of, and our practices in relation to, a particular subject or site of social activity; what knowledge is considered useful, relevant and 'true' in that context; and what sorts of persons or 'subjects' embody its characteristics." Stuart Hall, *Representation: Cultural Representations and Signifying Practices* (London: Sage Publications, 1997), 6. David Theo Goldberg *Racist Culture: Philosophy and the Politics of meaning* (Oxford: Blackwell, 1993), 9. (9) avers that *dominant discourses* are the discursive webs "that in the social relations of power at some moment come to assume authority and confer status."

8. Ibid., 69.

9. West, *Race Matters* 90–91.

10. I readily acknowledge that a limitation of this essay is its orientation to the Black Christian church in the United States. Neither experience nor expertise prepares me to speak for Christian Blacks who are outside of the United States or for Blacks who are a part of non-Christian religious traditions.

11. On "rhetorical scaffolding," see Dyson, *Open Mike*, 108.

12. Dyson, *Pass the Mike*, 362.

13. Shawn Kelley, *Racializing Jesus: Race, Ideology and the Formation of Modern Biblical Scholarship* (New York: Routledge, 2002), 25. On asymmetrical dualism as a binary in which "one side is [presented] as inherently superior to the other," see Moyo Okeediji, "Foreword" in Michael D. Harris, *Colored Pictures: Race and Visual Representation* (Chapel Hill, NC: University of North Carolina, 2003), vii.

14. For the recent challenge to Snowden's thesis, see Gay Byron, *Symbolic Blackness and Ethnic Difference in Early Christian Literature* (New York: Routledge, 2002), 4–5; Christian Delacampagne, "Racism and the West: From Praxis to Logos" in *Anatomy of Racism*, ed. David Theo Goldberg (Minneapolis: University of Minnesota, 1990) 83; Allison Blakely, *Blacks in the Dutch World: The Evolution of Racial Imagery in a Modern Society* (Bloomington, I N: Indiana University, 1993), 289–290. One must be careful here not to distort Snowden. Snowden recognizes the presence of color symbolism in antiquity. Where some recent critics part company with Snowden is in his insistence that the extant majority of positive statements about Ethiopians bears witness to antiquity's capacity to "overcome whatever potential for serious anti-black sentiment there may be in color symbolism." See Frank Snowden, *Before Color Prejudice: The Ancient View of Blacks* (Cambridge: Harvard University, 1983), 101. Before any judgment can be

made one way or another, a careful assessment of all the evidence must be weighed with particular emphasis directed to the subtexts of the extant evidence. In truth, one must also avoid homogenization of the evidence either across the entire chronology or geopolitical spheres of the period.

15. According to Stuart Hall, "the binary system of representation constantly marks and attempts to fix and naturalize the difference between belongingness and otherness." Stuart Hall, "New Ethnicities," in *Black Film, British Cinema*, ed. Kobena Mercer (London: Institute of Contemporary Arts, 1988), 28. One can see the binary at work for example, in the *Oxford English Dictionary* of the sixteenth century: "the word [black] is used as a synonym for, among other things, malignant, sinister, foul, dismal, etc." Adam Lively, *Masks: Blackness and the Imagination* (Oxford: Oxford University Press, 2000), 14.

16. Kim F. Hall, *Things of Darkness: Economies of Race and Gender in Early Modern England* (Ithaca: Cornel University, 1995), 4; Jerome, PS.50[51]:9. On sin or evil as a "basic moral concept" for "medieval Christianity from Augustine to Aquinas," see David Theo Goldberg, *Racist Culture: Philosophy and the Politics of Meaning* (Oxford: Blackwell, 1993), 15. As Robert Hood avers, the early Christians themselves inherited a Black aesthetic that was shaped in the ethnocentric cauldrons of Greek and Roman thought. Robert E. Hood, *Begrimed and Black: Christian Traditions on Blacks and Blackness* (Minneapolis: Fortress, 1994), 42.

17. Cf. *Epistle of Barnabas*, 4:9; 20:1–2. On this reading of the Christian work *The Epistle of Barnabas*, see Hood, *Begrimed and Black* 76; Byron *Symbolic Blackness*, 63. On this reading of the Christian work *The Shepherd of Hermas*, see Byron Symbolic Blackness, 67.

18. Origen's view of blackness appears to be positive because he accepts the logic of Song of Songs 1:5 ("I am black and beautiful") but Origen also sees black as a "stain" on the "whole of the Egyptian race." Origen, *The Song of Songs: Commentary and Homilies*, trans. R. P. Lawson (London: Green and Co., 1957), 107. On Origen's "ambivalent [views] about the moral significance of blackness," see Hood, *Begrimed and Black* 81; Byron, *Symbolic Blackness* 71–72.

19. Cited in Haynes, 7. Stephen R. Haynes, *Noah's Curse: The Biblical Justification of American Slavery* (Oxford: Oxford University Press, 2002), 7.

20. The Authorized translation (1611) of Song of Songs 1:5 is based on Jerome's Latin Vulgate translation: "*Nigra sum, sed formosa.*" In the late nineteenth century, the Black Baptist historian Rufus Perry noted Jerome's mistake. See Rufus L. Perry, *The Cushite or the Descendants of Ham as found in the Sacred Scriptures and in the Writings of Ancient Historians and Poets from Noah to the Christian Era* (Springfield, MA: Willey & Co., 1893), 52–53.

21. Scriptural citations in Jerome are quoted in Hood, 83–84 cf. Athanasius, *Life of Antony*, 5.3.

22. The term "race" first appears in the fifteenth century. Goldberg *Racist Culture* (21) warns about the danger of modern mistranslations that anachronistically read "race" into texts that reflect ethnocentricism or xenophobia. The term "racialist" is drawn from Kwame Anthony Appiah. See his "Race," in *Critical*

Terms for Literary Study, ed. Frank Lentricchia and Thomas McLaughlin (Chicago: University of Chicago, 1990), 274–287.

23. Byron, *Symbolic Blackness* 106–108. cf. the example of the exorcized devil in the sixth-century CE Syriac Rabulla Gospels, as cited by Hood, *Begrimed and Black 96*. Also, cf. Albert Biome, *The Art of Exclusion: Representing Blacks in the Nineteenth Century* (Washington: Smithsonian Institution, 1990), 6.

24. Byron, *Symbolic Blackness* 77–103. For connections between blackness and sexuality in the larger culture, one need only consider the Roman beliefs about the large phalluses of Ethiopian males or their representations of Ethiopian females with large breasts. See Dyan Elliott, *Fallen Bodies: Pollution, Sexuality, and Demonology in the Middle Ages* (Philadelphia: University of Pennsylvania, 1999), 37–40; John Clarke, "Hypersexual Black Men in Augustan Baths: Ideal Somatotypes and Apotropaic Magic" in *Sexuality in Ancient Art: Near East, Egypt, Greece, and Italy*, ed. Natalie B. Kampen (Cambridge: Cambridge University, 1996), 184–198; John Clarke, *Looking at Lovemaking: Constructions of Sexuality in Roman Art, 100 B.C.–A.D. 250* (Berkeley, C A: University of California, 1998), 119–142.

25. Jan N. Pieterse, *White on Black: Images of Africa and Blacks in Western Popular Culture* (New Haven: Yale University, 1992) 24.

26. Ruth Mellinkoff, *The Mark of Cain* (Berkeley and Los Angeles: University of California, 1981), 93.

27. Quinones, *The Changes of Cain: Violence and the Lost Brother in Cain and Abel Literature* (Princeton: Princeton University Press, 1991), 52. Though the papal decree was annulled in 1781, Hitler restored it in the twentieth century.

28. Mellinkoff, *The Mart of Cain* 77–78.

29. Ibid., 76.

30. Ricardo Quinones, *The Changes of Cain: Violence and the Lost Brother in Cain and Abel Literature* (Princeton: Princeton University, 1991), 53.

31. Cornel West, *Prophesy Deliverance: An Afro-Revolutionary Christianity* (Philadelphia: Westminster, 1982), 50.

32. West, *Prophesy Deliverance*, 50–53.

33. Ibid., 57–59.

34. Ibid., 61.

35. Brown-Douglas, *Sexuality and the Black Church* 36.

36. Brown-Douglas, *Sexuality and the Black Church* 39.

37. Ibid., 40.

38. Ibid., 45.

39. Ibid., 46.

40. Charles Johnson, Patricia Smith and the WGBH Series Research Team, *Africans in America: America's Journey through Slavery* (New York: Harcourt Brace and Co., 1998), 60–76, esp. 74. On social death or natal alienation, see Orlando Patterson,

41. See Peter G. Mode, *Source Book and Bibliographical Guide for American History* (Menasha, W I: George Banta Publishing Co., 1921), 551.

42. On this list, see Robert Allen Dunne, "Protestant Backlash: The American Dream Myth and Marginalized Groups, 1820–1860" (Ph.d. diss., Lehigh University, 1992), 191, n.5.

43. On the lingering effects of the hypothesis, see Cornel West, "Marxist Theory and the Specificity of Afro-American Oppression," in *Marxism and the Interpretation of Culture* (Urbana, IL: University of Illinois, 1988), 22.

44. See Adam Lively, 21. On the ambiguity of the Jewish sources, see Benjamin Braude, "The Sons of Noah and the Construction of Ethnic and Geographical Identities in the Medieval and Early Modern Periods," *William and Mary Quarterly* 54 (1997), 103–142.

45. Charles Copher avers that rabbinic material-in the Midrash Rabbah-Genesis (200–400 CE) and the Babylonian Talmud (500 CE)–made the first link between slavery and a specific color. In Rabbah-Genesis (36:7–8), Ham receives the curse, "not directly but through Ham's fourth son, Canaan, who will be ugly and dark-skinned (the degree of color being dependent upon the translator of the original)." In the Babylonian Talmud (Tractate Sanhedrin, 108b), Ham comes "from the Ark black, having been turned that color because, contrary to prohibitions, he, along with the dog and the raven, had copulated while aboard the Ark." For both citations, see Charles Copher, "Three Thousand Years of Biblical Interpretation with Reference to Black Peoples," in *African American Religious Studies: An Interdisciplinary Anthology*, ed. Gayraud S. Wilmore (Durham: Duke University, 1989), 111.

46. Forrest G. Wood, *Christianity and Race in America from the Colonial Era to the Twentieth Century* (New York: A. A. Knopf, 1990), 92.

47. Ibid., 87.

48. Ibid., 89.

49. Edith R. Sanders, "The Hamitic Hypothesis; Its Origin and Function in Time Perspective," *Journal of African History* 10 (1969), 521–532.

50. Sanders, "*The Hamitic Hypothesis*" 524–532. Thus, the American School of ethnology could fuse their polygenesis thesis to the story of Ham because they claimed that the story about Ham did not apply to Blacks at all.

51. George M. Fredrickson, *The Black Image in the White Mind: The Debate on Afro-American Character and Destiny, 1817–1914* (New York: Harper & Row, 1971), 61.

52. Fredrickson, *The Black Image in the White Mind* 89.

53. Ibid., 188, 277.

54. Ibid., 277.

55. Ibid., 276. For more on the genesis traditions, see Mason Stokes, "Someone's in the Garden with Eve: Race, Religion, and the American Fall," *American Quarterly* 50 (1998), 718–744.

56. Mireille Rosello, *Declining the Stereotype: Ethnicity and Representation in French Cultures* (London: University Press of New England, 1998), 37.

57. On "technologies of power" and the "politics of respectability," see Evelyn Higginbotham, *Righteous Discontent: The Women's Movement in the Black Baptist Church, 1880–1920* (Cambridge, MA: Harvard University, 1993) 189. Compare Anthony B. Pinn, "Black Theology, Black Bodies, and Pedagogy," *Cross Currents* 50 (2000), 199.

58. Brown-Douglas, *Sexuality and the Black Church* 53 cf. Susan L. Thomas, "Race, Gender, and Welfare Reform: The Antinatalist Response," *Journal of Black Studies* 28 (1998), 419–446, esp. 428–430.

59. Brown-Douglas, *Sexuality and the Black Church* 57. As I shall suggest late, however, one must not buy into a "privileged victim syndrome" which has often been the case when Blacks have portrayed some Black males as victims of a racist criminal justice system even while overlooking the domestic abuse of the same Black males. On this syndrome, see Devon W. Carbado, "Black Male Racial Victimhood," *Callaloo* 21 (1998), 337–361.

60. On this filtering process, see Mary Ann Tolbert, "Defining the Problem: The Bible and Feminist Hermeneutics," *Semeia* 28 (1983), 120.

61. The second category, "reformulation of the bible's function," is taken from Mary Ann Tolbert, "A New Teaching with Authority: A Re-valuation of the Authority of the Bible," in *Teaching the Bible: The Discourses and Politics of Biblical Theology*, ed. Fernando F. Segovia and Mary Ann Tolbert (Maryknoll, NY: 1998), 183.

62. Mattie Udora Richardson, "No More Secrets, No More Lies: African American History and Compulsory Heterosextuality," *Journal of Women's History* 15 (2003), 64.

63. Bryan Strong, "Ideas of the Early Sex Education Movement in America, 1890–1920," *History of Education Quarterly* 12 (1972), 129–161.

64. Richardson, *"No More Secrets,"* 65–66.

65. Randall Bailey, "They're Nothing But Incestuous Bastards: The Polemical Use of Sex and Sexuality in Hebrew Canon Narrative," in *Reading from This Place: Social Location and Biblical Interpretation*, ed. Fernando Segovia and Mary Ann Tolbert (Minneapolis: Fortress, 1994).

66. Ron Liburd, " 'Like . . . a House upon the Sand': African American Biblical Hermeneutics in Perspective," *The Journal of the Interdenominational Theological Center* 22 (1994), 71–91, esp. 79.

67. On this reading, see Christine E. Gudorf, *Body, Sex, and Pleasure: Reconstructing Christian Sexual Ethic* (Cleveland, OH: Pilgrim Press, 1994), 9.

68. Misogyny and sexual repression meet together in 1 Timothy 2:15: "Yet she [a woman] will be saved through childbearing" (NRSV).

69. As William J. Countryman has noted, "Like the rest of Israelite culture, the purity code placed the man at the center and was interested in other beings only as they impinged on him. L. William Countryman, *Dirt, Greed & Sex: Sexual Ethics in the New Testament and Their Implications for Today* (Philadelphia: Fortress, 1988), 34.

70. According to Levirate law, the brother of a deceased man was obligated to marry his brother's widow and thus raise an offspring for the deceased brother. Onan, the brother of Er and son of Judah refused to have a coital relationship with Tamar, Er's widow.

71. Michael L. Satlow, " 'Wasted Seed,' the History of a Rabbinic Idea," *Hebrew Union College Annual* 65 (2001), 137–175, esp. 152–173.

72. Ibid., 163. On self-mastery, see Abraham Smith, " 'Full of Spirit and Wisdom': Luke's Portrait of Stephen (Acts 6:1–8:1a) as a Man of Self-Mastery" in *Asceticism and the New Testament*, Ed. Leif E. Vaage & Vincent L. Wimbush (New York: Routledge, 1999), 99–100.

73. Several scholars have discussed views of the Bible espoused by one or several groups within Afro-America. Thomas Hoyt, Jr., "Interpreting Biblical

Scholarship for the Black Church Tradition," in *Stony The Road We Trod: African American Biblical Interpretation*, Ed. Cain Hope Felder (Minneapolis: Fortress, 1991), 17–39; Peter J. Paris, "The Bible and the Black Churches," in *The Bible and Social Reform*, ed. Ernest R. Sandeed Chico (CA: Scholars, 1982), 133–154; Renita Weems, "Reading Her Way Through the Struggle: African American Women and the Bible," in *Stony The Road We Trod: African American Biblical Interpretation*, ed. Cain Hope Felder (Minneapolis: Fortress, 1991), 57–77; Vincent Wimbush, "The Bible and African Americans: An Outline of an Interpretive History," in *Stony The Road We Trod: African American Biblical Interpretation*, ed. Cain Hope Felder (Minneapolis: Fortress, 1991), 81–97.

74. Mary McClintock Fulkerson, "Church Documents on Human Sexuality and the Authority of Scripture," *Interpretation* 49 (2001), 51.

75. Tolbert, "A New Teaching with Authority," 170.

76. Ibid., 172.

77. All three examples are taken from Tolbert, "A New Teaching with Authority," 172–173.

78. On the text critical autograph problems, see Robin Scroggs, "The Bible as Foundational Document," *Interpretation* 49 (2001), 18.

79. On the harmonization problem, see Fulkerson, 50.

80. Tolbert, "A New Teaching with Authority," 183.

81. On "word churches," see Dyson, *Open Mike*, 312.

82. On public debate, I am here influenced by Cornel West, 30. On bibliolatry, see Dyson, 368.

83. As Michael Dyson has noted, "Reducing black suffering to its lowest common male denominator not only presumes a hierarchy of pain that removes priority from black female struggle, but also trivializes the analysis and actions of black women in the quest for liberation." Michael Dyson, *Making Malcolm: The Myth and Meaning of Malcolm X* (New York: Oxford University Press, 1995), 98. As Monroe notes, moreover, "Since racial oppression is the common reality that all African-American female, male, gay, lesbian, bisexual, and transgendered people confront every day of their lives, we clearly need a model of leadership that articulates simultaneously the multiple oppressions of race, class, gender, and sexual orientation. Because race links us across and between various identities, a racialized understanding of how class, gender, and sexual orientation imbricate patterns of white supremacy would liberate is from the myopic view that only African-American males are endangered members in our communities." Irene Monroe, "Louis Farrakhan's Ministry of Misogyny and Homophobia," in *The Farrakhan Factor: African American Writers on Leadership, Nationhood and Minister Louis Farrakhan*, ed. Amy Alexander (New York: Grove Press, 1998), 296.

5

Vashti

Allen Callahan

Abstract: In a remarkable reading against the grain of the text of the Book of Esther, African American women have seen in the deposed queen Vashti a heroine who refuses to compromise her personal dignity by making her body available to dominating men. The plain sense of the canonical text of Vashti's confrontation with the lords of the Persian court recounts her independence but does not celebrate it. Yet in African American communities even today women are named after the deposed queen. As early as the middle of the nineteenth century African American women were reading Vashti's story as a biblical account of one woman's determination to honor her own body.

Introduction: Vashti

By the middle of the nineteenth century, African American women were reading the story of Vashti, the deposed Persian queen in the opening of the Book of Esther, as a tale of one woman's courageous resistance. Contemporary treatments by African American women continue to celebrate her,[1] and African Americans have given and continue to give the name Vashti to their daughters.[2] In a remarkable reading against the grain of the text of the Book of Esther, African American women have seen Vashti as a queen who loses her throne but holds to her regal bearing.

Remarkable, because the plain sense of the canonical text of her experience in the Persian court recounts her resistance but does not celebrate it.

> On the seventh day, when the king was merry with wine, he commanded . . . the seven chamberlains that served in the palace of

Ahasuerus the king, To bring Vashti the queen before the king with the crown royal, to shew the people and the princes her beauty: for she was fair to look on.

But queen Vashti refused to come at the king's commandment by his chamberlains: therefore was the king very wroth, and his anger burned in him. Then the king said to the wise men ... What shall we do unto the queen Vashti according to law, because she hath not performed the commandment of the king Ahasuerus by the chamberlains?

And Memucan answered before the king and the princes, Vashti the queen hath not done wrong to the king only, but also to all the princes, and to all the people that are in all the provinces of king Ahasuerus.

For this deed of the queen shall come abroad unto all women, so that they shall despise their husbands in their eyes ... Likewise shall the ladies of Persia and Media say this day unto all the king's princes, which have heard of the deed of the queen. Thus shall there arise too much contempt and wrath. If it please the king, let there go a royal commandment from him, and let it be written among the laws of the Persians and the Medes, that it not be altered, That Vashti come no more before king Ahasuerus: and let the king give her royal estate unto another ... And the saying pleased the king and the princes; and the king did according to the word of Memucan ....

After these things, when the wrath of king Ahasuerus was appeased, he remembered Vashti, and what she had done, and what was decreed against her. Then said the king's servants that ministered unto him, Let there be fair young virgins sought for the king ... And let the maiden which pleaseth the king be queen instead of Vashti. And the thing pleased the king; and he did so. (Esther 1:10–2:4)

Where Vashti's name appears in Esther 1:19, 2:1, 4, and 7, it is without her title "queen": by the middle of the first chapter of the book the very silences of the narrative tacitly prepare to dethrone her. After Esther 2:7 we hear nothing more from or about Vashti.[3]

The sense of the Hebrew of 2:1, "After these things, when the wrath of king Ahasuerus was appeased, he remembered Vashti," is that the king remembered his former consort with affection, and suggests in one poignant phrase a pang of regret for his rash actions while "under the influence."[4] In his retelling of the story, the first-century historian Josephus discerns this nuance (*Ant.* XI.195). The targums, "amplified versions" as it were, of Hebrew scriptures translated into the Aramaic lingua franca of Palestine around the beginning of the Common Era, agree that Ahasuerus was visited with remorse.[5] Furthermore, Josephus comments that it was the custom of the Persian men not to allow strangers to look upon the beauty of their wives (*Ant.* IX.191);[6] this raises the ante of Vashti's compliance, suggesting that the queen was in a double bind. On the one hand, she owed obedience to her king and husband. On the other hand, exposing herself to the royal strangers at the banquet would have been a gross violation of Persian custom.

Ahasuerus' command was Vashti's insoluble dilemma. The appreciation for the king's regret and the queen's dilemma in the biblical text is lost to subsequent readers. The translator of the Greek version of the book of Esther missed the nuance of 2:1 in the Hebrew and translates the clause, "And Ahasuerus remembered Vashti no more."[7]

Vashti's complete dismissal in the Greek version becomes outright vilification in rabbinical commentary. Josephus' image of the demure Persian wife is turned on its head. The Talmudic interpretation of Esther 1:11 is that Vashti was commanded to appear before the king and his noble vassals wearing *only* a crown, that is, otherwise completely naked.[8] This is nowhere implied in the text, but from this inference the Talmud then goes on to solve the problem that the inference itself raises: why would the king make such a demand of his own queen. The targum on Esther 1:11 explains, "And the king ordered these seven princes to bring out Vashti the queen naked, on account of her having forced the daughters of Israel to work naked carding wool and flax." The Babylonian Talmud 12b claimed of the phrase "the seventh day," "This teaches that the wicked Vashti would bring the daughters of Israel and strip them naked and make them do work on the Sabbath. For this reason it was decreed upon her that she be slaughtered naked on the Sabbath."[9] The Rabbis understood Vashti's demotion as just recompense for her wickedness. Vashti, as a targum explains, was the evil granddaughter of Nebuchadnezzar, destroyer of the Jerusalem Temple and author of the Babylonian captivity. "And why did this befall her?" asks *Esther Rabba* 5:2 to Esther 2:1, then answers, "Because she would not allow Ahasuerus to give his permission to the building of the Temple, saying: 'What my ancestors have destroyed you wish to build!'"[10] Vashti, granddaughter of the archenemy of Israel, prevents the repatriation of the Jews in Palestine and disdains them in exile. In Jewish midrash, Vashti becomes "wanton," a woman of "sinful intentions."[11]

Compelling Images

Yet as early as the middle of the nineteenth century, African American women found Vashti's story as one more in that repository of tales in which evangelical religion had taught them to find their heroes—the

Bible. As theologian and mystic Howard Thurman put it, "With untutored hands . . . with a sure artistry and genius created out of a vast vitality, a concept of God was wrenched from the Sacred Book, the Bible." The slaves and their descendants were thereby able to "reject annihilation and affirm a terrible right to live."[12] In his classic essay of literary criticism, *The Hero and the Blues*, literary critic Albert Murray writes, "What must be remembered is that people live in terms of images which represent the fundamental conceptions embodied in their rituals and myths. In the absence of adequate images they live in terms of such compelling images (and hence rituals and myths) as are abroad at the time."[13] In the African American collective imagination, the Bible overshadowed the limited influence of the Western classics. The Hebrew Prophets easily eclipsed the Greek Philosophers in the burgeoning, vernacular intellectual tradition of the slaves and their descendents. Moses, not Pericles, would become their model statesman, and the sonnets of Shakespeare would be no match for the Psalms of David. More than any other single literary source, the Bible offered African Americans "such compelling images . . . as are abroad at the time."

Phenomenologist Anthony Pinn's definition of Black religion as a response to the assault on the Black body provides a framework for understanding how African Americans have chosen compelling images from the Bible, and so why African American women have rehabilitated Vashti and made her image—and even her name—their own. It is the "sense of terror or dread" of African American life under slavery and Jim Crow that "gave rise to the historical manifestation of religiosity": "this dread sparks the development of practices, doctrines, and institutional structures earmarked for historical liberation from terror."[14] Pinn has defined black religion as "the quest for complex subjectivity, a desire or feeling for more life meaning. In other words, black religion's basic structure entails a push or desire for fullness."[15] We may understand the "compelling images" fashioned from the Bible as a "push for fullness." Here the push for fullness is not a doctrine, practice, or institutional structure; it is a hermeneutic, a way of making meaning through the interpretation of biblical signs.

The compelling image is a self-representation, a projection comprised of two psychic drives: one, the drive against the terror of Black life; the other, the drive for fullness. These two drives, against terror and for fullness, are balanced differently according to the differing existential and material pressures on the African Americans who coin them. The compelling biblical images of the slaves were heavily freighted against the terror of the slave regime. That terror, with its no-holds-barred assault on the body, was perforce their primary preoccupation. Slaves were the property of their masters—"chattels personal,"[16] over which masters had complete control.[17] The common law that British colonists brought with them had no provision for what Harriett Beecher Stowe would call the "absolute despotism of the most unmitigated form" that American slavery required. Slaves were rendered exempt from that body of common law that afforded rights of personal security and integrity to all persons.[18] The law balanced the rights of "absolute despotism" against those of "absolute property": the violent abuse of slaves would only be construed as criminal insofar as it threatened absolute claims of the master class to enjoy enslaved property. This balance of absolutes was struck, quite literally, on the back of the slave.

Yes, the slaves also formed compelling biblical images that attested to a yearning for fullness, an appreciation for the complexity of their own subjectivity. They insisted that they were moral agents—property with a soul perhaps, as Aristotle once defined the slave, but more important, property with a will. The choice between good and evil was inalienably theirs. That choice, however, was always made a milieu of terror. And so to be compelling to the slave, an image from the Bible had to be an image against terror.

But for free African Americans—"free people of color," as they preferred to call themselves in the antebellum period—the compelling images tended to be freighted toward the push for fullness. Freedom was an existential bulwark against the terror of slavery. That bulwark was fragile, precarious, and subject to breech, but freedom meant nothing if it did not mean a conditional hiatus from the assault on the Black body. Freedom meant that the problem of how the Black body was treated had to be addressed along with the problem of how the Black body was regarded. Free women of color engaged both problems in the image of Vashti.

Terror and Fullness

African American meaning making found in the Bible compelling images to answer the all-out assault on the Black body unleashed by slavery. American slavery not only gave capital complete access to the labor of slaves; it granted capital complete access to their very bodies. One of the first laws of racial differentiation in Virginia colony was that white indentured servants might not be stripped for punishment, as African slaves commonly were.[19] Planters invested a perverse ingenuity into the somatic assault on their slaves. They whipped slaves suspended on tiptoe to increase the pain of torture. They poured salt into wounds opened by their whips. Masters were known to cut open blisters with handsaws, and drip sealing wax or a solution of hot peppers into open wounds. Public castration of slaves had been a common punishment in the early years of slavery, and there is scattered evidence that it continued to be inflicted on rebellious slaves until the fall of the slave regime.[20] Torture was made terror by being perpetrated in plain view of other slaves, who were forced to watch the grisly proceedings.[21] Southern legislatures passed exculpatory laws granting slave masters and other whites legal rights to beat, whip, and under certain circumstances even kill slaves with impunity.[22]

In Virginia, the Carolinas, Georgia, Mississippi, and Alabama, white strangers had the right to perpetrate simple assault and battery against a slave with impunity. South Carolina and Georgia codes stipulated that white strangers who subjected slaves to "cruel punishment" were subject to a fine. "Cruel punishment" of slaves effectively replaced the categories of assault, battery, and mayhem—violent deprivation of another person's use of his limbs resulting in disfigurement or disablement—as crimes of violence against persons recognized by common law. "Cruel punishment" was in effect a crime against the master's property, not a crime against the slave's person.[23] The slave's person did not legally exist. "It is for the benefit of the master, and consoling to his feelings" the General Court of Virginia ruled in 1827, "that a third person [i.e., a stranger] should be restrained under the pains and penalties of felony, from maiming and disabling his slave." The ruling went on to affirm that slaves were covered by the same statutes that prohibited the abuse of pigs and horses.[24]

Slavery in the United States decriminalized violence against Black people. The law, and the property relations that the law was created to protect, developed in the dynamic tension of class interests, inflected—as class interests in America have ever been—by race. Under the slave regime there were élite slave owners, farmers with few slaves, yeoman farmers with none, overseers who directly supervised the work of slaves and thus were a "retainer class" for the élite, and white proletarians—the so-called poor white trash. Because the forces of the state never had the capacity to police the burgeoning populations of slaves that made the political economy possible, whites élites recruited whites from the lower registers to help them forcibly control their slaves around and beyond the boundaries of their estates. To secure collusion between élite and non-élite whites, the planter class instigated laws that established and regulated slave patrols—the hated "patterollers" of African American folksong and folklore. The lower classes were thereby organized into a police force that searched for, and received rewards for the capture of, slaves found away from their plantation without the master's written permission. The 1740 South Carolina slave code tacitly assumed patrollers surveillance: "Any slave who shall be out of the house or plantation where such slave shall live . . . or without some white person in the company with such slave, shall refuse to submit to undergo the examination of any white person, it shall be lawful for any such white person to pursue, apprehend, and moderately correct such slave; and if such slave shall assault and strike such white person, such slave may be lawfully killed."[25] The forerunners of today's American militias, which stockpile extraordinary caches of arms in paranoid preparation for "race war," patrollers were a reserve army retained by the propertied class and paid in arms, money, and skin-color privilege to wage war on Black people.

At the same time, the price of a slave increased robustly from the beginning of the nineteenth century until the outbreak of the Civil War. The United States officially ended the importation of African slaves in 1808, and soon thereafter the invention of the cotton gin made cotton king and slavery indispensable to the American economy. The average price of a prime field hand in Georgia appreciated from $450 in 1800 to $1650 in 1859, reflecting steady increases in slave productivity and profitability.[26] This made the slaves valuable commodities. But slaves were only as valuable as their obedience and submission rendered their bodies available for the master's profit. Because none of that profit redounded to the slave, the slave had no positive incentive to obey and submit. The slave had to be motivated by violence and the real threat of violence—terror. Thus one of several contradictions at the heart of American slavery; slave owners had to continually brutalize their most precious and productive assets. The regime was one unremitting system of ongoing torture, "hell without fire," in the words of one former slave.

And torture is, by definition, a sustained assault on the body. Southern law gave legal warrant to this torture, so necessary to the relation of production and the disciplining of labor under slavery. Jurisprudence in the slave states affirmed the unquestioned right of the masters to abuse slaves as long as the abuse did not result in death. And so the law aided, abetted and all but encouraged the torture of slaves. Seventeenth- and eighteenth-century slave codes explicitly granted masters the right to maim slaves, and laws in South Carolina and Virginia mandated that slaves were to be maimed for certain offenses; between 1723and 1769, the Virginia slave code required that captured runaways were to be dismembered.[27]

The abuse of Black bodies was so inured in the culture of slavery that law limited its otherwise limitless violence. In South Carolina as early as 1712, murder, what common law calls the willful and malicious killing of another human being, was not murder if the victim was a slave. Those found guilty of the crime of killing a slave were fined and required to pay reparations to the slave's master. As for masters, the opinion of North Carolina judge Thomas Ruffin proved to be the guiding principle: "if death unhappily ensue for the master's chastisement of his slave, inflicted apparently with good intent, for reformation or example, and with no purpose to take life, or to put it in jeopardy, the law would doubtless tenderly regard every circumstance which, judging from the conduct generally of masters toward slaves, might reasonably be supposed to have hurried the party into excess."[28]

But even Judge Ruffin could not "tenderly regard" the case of *State v. Hoover,* in which the defendant was convicted of having tortured his female slave to death in the last trimester of her pregnancy. The defendant had beaten the woman "with clubs, iron chains, and other deadly weapons, time after time; burnt her, inflicted stripes over and often, with scourges, which literally excoriated her whole body; forced her out to work in inclement seasons, without being duly clad; provided for her insufficient food; exacted labor beyond her strength and wantonly beat her because she could not comply with his requisitions. These enormities, besides others too disgusting to be particularly designated, the prisoner . . . practiced . . . even up to the last hour of the victim's existence."[29]

Judge Ruffin's 1829 ruling in *State v. Mann,* in which he reversed the conviction of a master found guilty of assault for shooting a female slave who had fled from him as he was beating her, the master has "uncontrolled authority over the body" of his slave. "There may be particular instances of cruelty where, in conscience, the law might properly interfere," wrote Ruffin, ". . . But we cannot look at the matter in that light . . . We cannot allow the right of the master to be brought into discussion in the courts of justice. The slave, to remain a slave, must be made sensible that there is no appeal from his master."[30]

Both men and women suffered the legalized assault on the Black body under the slavery and Jim Crow. Often they suffered the same assaults, albeit with appropriate modifications. One gristly example of this equal-opportunity abuse was the practice of whipping pregnant slaves as they lay face down in a hole in the ground dug to accommodate their protruding bellies. Rape, however, was a pervasive form of assault to which women were especially vulnerable, and no slave who bore witness to the violence of American slavery passed over it in silence. In WPA interviews conducted by black women,[31] 18 percent of ex-slaves described sexual assaults by whites, perpetrated against the interviewees or others on their plantations.[32] Catherine Clinton has called American slavery's reign of sexual terror "penarchy," "a system whereby the males of the elite use sexual terrorism to control women of all classes and races, as well as men within the subordinate classes." It is "a refinement of patriarchy," for whereas "patriarchy defines sexual categories as reflections of biological functions (mother/father) and power relationships are modeled on family roles (father/son, mother/daughter), penarchy emphasizes sexual categories which reflect power relationships and their sexual manifestations."[33] A classic depiction of this peculiar form of sexual terrorism, Harriet Jacobs' autobiographical *Incidents in the Life of a Slave Girl*, shows the master to be a sexual predator who sires "children of every complexion" by the rape of his slaves and "pays no regard to his marriage vows."[34] Jacobs writes of her own master, the lecherous Dr. Flint, "My master met me at every turn, reminding me that I belonged to him, and swearing by heaven and earth that he would compel me to submit to him."[35]

Some slaves, of course, did not submit. The victim of the defendant in *State v. Mann*, after all, had lost her life in flight from her master's cruelty. In the infamous 1855 case of *State of Missouri v. Celia*, Celia, a slave, was convicted of murdering her master. Testimony during the trial established that Celia's master had raped here repeatedly and had made her pregnant. The defenses argued that Celia had slain the rapist in self-defense, and that multiple rape was beyond the pale of the master's property rights. According to Missouri law, the rape of "any woman" was prohibited. The judge ruled that the only rights of standing in the case were those of the master: Celia was his property, and it was his right to do with her as he wished. The anti-rape statute did not include Celia, for as property she was not legally a woman at all. Celia was convicted of murder and sentenced to death. Execution was stayed because Celia was pregnant with her master's child. After giving birth to a baby girl, Celia was hanged.

Proud of her Spotless Name

In 1857, just two years after the case of *State of Missouri v. Celia*, writer, educator, and activist Frances Harper rendered her admiration of the Bible's deposed queen in verse in her poem "Vashti." Frances Harper was born Frances Ellen Watkins to free parents in 1825 in Maryland, then a slave state. Orphaned at three, she lived with her uncle, William Watkins, an activist minister who imparted his religion and his politics to his gifted niece. After receiving a thorough education in her uncle's school, she worked as a domestic—a common occupation for a young African American in antebellum America, regardless of her education—all the while continuing to write and publish poetry. In 1850 she was the first woman to teach at the African Methodist Episcopal Church's newly established Union Seminary near Columbus, Ohio. She subsequently took a teaching post in Little York, Pennsylvania. Her travels brought her into frequent contact with fugitive slaves, further sharpening the radical edge of her politics. She became a fugitive of sorts herself after Maryland outlawed free Blacks and threatened to enslave any free Black persons in the state.

Frances Harper would remain a refugee from her home state until after the Civil War. In 1853 Harper quit teaching, moved to Philadelphia, and became an abolitionist. In the opening stanza of her poem "Bury Me in a Free Land," she writes, "Make me a grave where'er you will, / In a lowly plain or a lofty hill; / Make it among earth's humblest graves, / But not in a land where men are slaves."[36] Written in 1864, one year before the end of the War, Harper declares that she would not want to be caught dead in Maryland.

In "Vashti"[37] the poet once again gives voice to her strident preference for death to disgrace. In response to the lurid king's command, Vashti expresses this preference in her defiance. " 'Go back!' she cried, and waved her hand, / And grief was in her eye; / 'Go, tell the King,' she sadly said, / 'That I would rather die.' " Vashti makes her choice and then pays the price in the story's noble if unhappy denouement.

> Then spake his wily counselors —
> . . . "Then gracious King, sign with thy hand
> This stern but just decree,
> That Vashti lay aside her crown,
> Thy Queen no more to be."

She heard the King's command,
And left her high estate,
Strong in her earnest womanhood,
She calmly met her fate,

And left the palace of the King,
Proud of her spotless name—
A woman who could bend to grief,
But would not bow to shame.

Through the figure of Vashti, Harper gives voice to Black women's quest for dignity that had been and would continue to be marked by both the capacity to bend to grief and the refusal to bow to shame.

"And I am Hard to Force the Petals Wide"

Rape, a staple of terror under slavery, set a perverse precedent for continued sexual violence under Jim Crow. Sexual assault was a pall that continued to hang over African American women long after Emancipation, "the weight and fret of the 'long, dull pain' that the open-eyed but hitherto voiceless Black woman of America."[38] African American educator and activist Anna Julia Cooper had learned of that pain at her mother's knee: she lamented in 1892, "My mother was a slave and the finest woman I have ever known. . . . Presumably my father was her master; if so, I owe him not a sou and she was always too modest and shamefaced ever to mention him."[39] The sexual assault on the Black female body perpetrated under slavery and perpetuated under American apartheid set a precedent for sexual violence that continues to taint our own time: in the United States today an African American woman is six times more likely to be raped than a white woman.[40]

The poem of the reclusive Anne Spencer (1882–1975), "Before the Feast of Shushan" is an exquisitely subtle exploration of sexual violence juxtaposed with a meditation on the virtue of love. While visiting Anne Spencer and her husband Edward on business for the National Association for the Advancement of Colored People (NAACP) James Weldon Johnson discovered Anne Spencer's poetic talent, and convinced her to allow him to publish "Before the Feast of Shushan" in the NAACP's prestigious magazine, *The Crisis*. Johnson later introduced Spencer to the irrepressible H. L. Mencken, editor of the *American Mercury* magazine and one of the most influential American men of letters of his time. Though known and feared for his caustic criticism, he was enthusiastic about Spencer's poetry and offered his support. But though most Harlem Renaissance artists were dependent upon white patrons, Spencer chose to forego Mencken's favor. She resisted Mencken's patronage because he insisted on criticizing her poetry. With quiet, steely resolve Spencer insisted in turn that Mencken was incompetent to do so.

In "Before the Feast of Shushan," Spencer is true to the discursive limits of the biblical account, but ingeniously so. The Bible does not allow Vashti to speak: at least not with words. Spencer speaks with king Ahasuerus' voice, which nevertheless echoes Vashti's sentiments on the eve of her dismissal. Of course, it is not what Vashti says but what she does and refuses to do that bring her character to center stage in the biblical drama and in the African American imagination. The king speaks, but he speaks of what Vashti has said.

> . . .
> Cushioned at the Queen's feet and upon her knee
> Finding glory, for mine head,—still, nearly shamed
> Am I, the King, to bend and kiss with sharp
> Breath the olive-pink of sandaled toes between;
> Or lift me high to the magnet of a gaze, dusky,
> Like the pool when but the moon-ray strikes to its depth;
> Or closer press to crush a grape 'gainst lips redder
> That the grape, a rose in the night of her hair;
> Then—Sharon's Rose in my arms.
>
> And I am hard to force the petals wide;
> And you are fast to suffer and be sad.
> Is any prophet come to teach a new thing
> Now in a more apt time?
> Have him 'maze how you say love is sacrament;
> How says Vashti, love is both bread and wine;
> How to the altar may not come to break and drink,
> Hulky flesh nor fleshly spirit!
> I, thy lord, like not manna for meat as a Judahn;
> I, thy master, drink, and red wine, plenty, and when
> I thirst. Eat meat, and full, when I hunger.
> I, thy King, teach you and leave you, when I list.
> No woman in all Persia sets out strange action
> To confuse Persia's lord—
> Love is but desire and thy purpose fulfillment;
> I, thy King, so say![41]

But as Spencer implies here, the king has his say but does not have his way; the poem is marked by sultry descriptions of the body to which the king will ultimately be denied access. He reclines "Cushioned at the Queen's feet and upon her knee." With indignation, he asks rhetorically if Vashti expects him "to bend and kiss with sharp/ Breath the olive-pink of sandaled toes." Or, lifting his face to her "gaze, dusky/ Like the pool when but the moon-ray strikes to its depth," is he to press a kiss " 'gainst lips redder/ That the grape, a rose in the night of her hair." Vashti is indeed a woman in Persia who "sets out strange action." Though he is "Persia's lord," the king is not a prophet; he teaches and leaves at will, but Vashti has become the prophet "come to teach a new thing." Her oracle: love is not the desire of a man but the sacrament of a woman. The king will prove incompetent to judge Vashti's oracle, and she will ultimately reject his patronage.

Conclusion: The Queen

Vashti is such a compelling image that African American women turned her story on its head and read her text against the grain. Vashti is as they are, "dusky, / Like the pool when but the moon-ray strikes to its depth," with a dark, translucent dignity that even slavery and its ignoble legacy cannot deny. The Bible consigns the deposed queen to oblivion; after Esther 2:7 Vashti disappears. The rabbis would have Vashti "slaughtered naked on the Sabbath." But the Vashti of Frances Harper and Anne Spencer lives on, clothed if not crowned. She so highly regards her body that she will not suffer it to be regarded by others.

Vashti steps down, but she does not bow down. And she does so on her own. Vashti is not a subject merely in relation to other principals— she is not someone's daughter, mother, or property. She is not even, properly speaking, a wife. She is a queen: by definition, authority and agency resident in a female subject. Though we may presume as queen she is married to the king, and though the courtiers claim that her insubordination is a bad example for spousal relations throughout the Persian Empire, the text never refers to Vashti as Ahasuerus' wife. Vashti is defined, in Catherine Clinton's words, neither by "biological sexual categories (mother/father)" or "familial power relationships (father/son, mother/daughter)" of patriarchy, nor by the "sexual categories" reflecting the "power relationships and their sexual manifestations" that mark penarchy. At the same time, Vashti's resistance posits a limit on all these: the authority of the husband, the sovereign, and the state, the reign of custom, and culture. That limit is the dignity of a woman, grounded in her prerogative to make her body unavailable at her own discretion.

African American women's reading of Vashti insists on respect for the female Black body, for the Black woman as woman, as person. Vashti's self-possession and survival were features of a compelling biblical image for free women of color in the United States. They coined from Vashti's story a unique interpretation that they have borne and continue to bear with her name.

Notes

1. See most recently, for example, LaVerne McCain Gill, *Vashti's Victory and Other Biblical Women Resisting Injustice* (Cleveland: Pilgrim Press, 2003).
2. To name only two of the most renown: Bishop Vashti Murphy McKenzie, the first woman elected to the episcopacy of the African Methodist Episcopal Church and national chaplain of the Sigma Delta Theta sorority; Vashti Turley Murphy, one of the founders of Sigma Delta Theta and Bishop McKenzie's paternal grandmother.
3. See *The Expositor's Bible Commentary*, Frank E. Gaebelein, ed. (Grand Rapids: Zondervan, 1979): 4.803.
4. Carey A. Moore, *Esther*, Anchor Bible Commentary, vol. 7B (Garden City, NY: Doubleday, 1971): 17.
5. Moore, *Esther*, 17.
6. Moore, *Esther*, 13.
7. Moore, *Esther*, 17.
8. In Eliezer Segal, *The Babylonian Esther Midrash: A Critical Commentary* (Atlanta: Scholars Press, 1994), 255.
9. Segal, *The Babylonian Esther Midrash*, 255.
10. Segal, *The Babylonian Esther Midrash*, 255.
11. Segal, *The Babylonian Esther Midrash*, 259.
12. *Deep River: An Interpretation of the Negro Spirituals* (Mills College: The Eucalyptus Press, 1945), 127–128.
13. Albert Murray, *The Hero and the Blues* (New York: Vintage, 1995), 13–14.
14. Anthony Pinn, *Terror and Triumph: The Nature of Black Religion*. The 2002 Edward Cadbury Lectures. (Minneapolis: Fortress Press, 2003), 81.
15. Pinn, *Terror and Triumph*, 173.
16. See A. Leon Higginbotham, *In the Matter of Color: Race and the American Legal Process* (New York: Oxford University Press, 1978), 169–170, n. 2.
17. In an important theoretical intervention, Pinn has explained how the American assault on the Black body confounds Michel Foucault's famous and influential analysis of state violence in *Discipline and Punish*, which argues that corporal punishment wanes in the modern period, giving way to kinder, gentler modes of social control. "Whereas the economy of death changes, according to Foucault, there was a time when executions were marked by a prolonging of torture and a ravishing of the body. Torture gives way to the prison system as punishment through loss of wealth or rights. This is a new technique for attacking the body, one less bloody and less visible, but still

somewhat effective. In the context of North America, however, violence against blacks could not transition smoothly because it was not premised upon a recognition of humanity, the type of shared ontological ground held among even Europeans of different classes and backgrounds. True, the desire to remove wealth and rights from blacks existed, but it remained popular thinking that blacks were beasts who deserved such rights as much as horses . . . Blacks never had full exercise of the rights supposedly implicit in their freedom. How, then, could punishment be centered on the restriction of such rights? Punishment had to remain fixated on the body, not on the denial of abstract rights and privileges. Unlike the European prison system, with respect to blacks in the late nineteenth and twentieth centuries, destruction of the physical self was not a by-product of punishment. Rather, it was the purpose of punishment." (Pinn, *Terror and Triumph*, 68.)

Non-European commentators have called attention to the Eurocentric limits of Foucault's analyses. Twenty years ago Edward Said pointed out that Foucault's conception of power allows him "to obliterate the role of classes, the role of economics, the role of insurgency and rebellion." Edward Said, *The Word, the Text, and Critic* (Cambridge: Harvard University Press, 1983), 243. Gayatri Chakravorty Spivak, building on Said's critique, observed that Foucault and other "French intellectuals forget at their peril that this entire overdetermined enterprise was in the interest of a dynamic economic situation requiring that interests, motives (desires), and power (of knowledge) be ruthlessly dislocated." Spivak goes on to suggest, "To invoke that dislocation now as a radical discovery that should make us diagnose the economic (conditions of existence that separate out 'classes' descriptively) as a piece of dated analytic machinery may well be to continue the work of that dislocation." See Gayatri Chakravorty Spivak, "Can the Subaltern Speak?" in *Marxism and the Interpretation of Culture*, ed. Cary Nelson and Lawrence Grossberg (Urbana: University of Illinois Press, 1988), 280.

It is the assault on the Black body both during and after American slavery, however, makes for a final and fatal qualification of Foucault's analysis. Joy James has submitted Foucault's account of modern state violence to a rigorous critique and found it fundamentally flawed. Though "Michel Foucault's *Discipline and Punish* offers a body politics of state punishment and prosecution that is considered by some postmodernists to be a master narrative competent to critique state policing," James shows "this particular work contributes to the erasure of racist violence." James notes that as he writes "about the 'disappearance of torture as a public spectacle'—with no reference to its continuity in European and American colonies where it was inflicted on indigenous peoples in Africa and in the Americas—Foucault weaves a historical perspective that eventually presents the contemporary ('Western') state as a nonpractitioner of torture. His text illustrates how easy it is to erase the specificity of the body and violence while centering discourse on them. Losing sight of the violence practiced by and in the name of the sovereign, who at times was manifested as part of a dominant race, Foucault universalizes the body of the white, propertied male. Much of *Discipline and Punish* depicts the body with no specificity tied to racialized or sexualized punishment." See Joy

James, "Erasing the Spectacle of Racialized State Violence," in *Resisting State Violence: Radicalism, Gender, and Race in U.S. Culture* (Minneapolis: University of Minnesota Press, 1996), 24–25.

18. Andrew Fede, "Legitimized Violent Slave Abuse in the American South, 1619–1865: A Case Study of Law and Social Change in Six Southern States," *American Journal of Legal History* vol. XXIX (1985), 94.

19. Catherine Clinton, " 'With a Whip in His Hand': Rape, Memory, and African American Women," in *History and Memory in African American Culture*, ed. Genevieve Fabre and Robert O'Meally (New York: Oxford, 1994), 208.

20. John Willie Roberts, *From Trickster to Badman: The Black Folk Hero in Slavery and Freedom* (Philadelphia: University of Pennsylvania Press, 1989), 142.

21. Roberts, *From Trickster to Badman*, 141.

22. Fede, "Slave Abuse," 95.

23. See Fede, "Slave Abuse," 127.

24. Fede, "Slave Abuse," 127–129.

25. Cited in Fede, "Slave Abuse," 111.

26. Fede, "Slave Abuse," 108.

27. See Higginbothom, *Color*, 177–178, n. 2.

28. Cited in Fede, "Slave Abuse," 123.

29. Cited in Fede, "Slave Abuse," 123, n. 171.

30. *State v. Mann*, cited in Fede, "Slave Abuse," 138–139.

31. Scholars of American slavery have long been aware of the race and gender of interviewer as a factor influencing the testimony of the ex-slaves interviewed in the Federal Writer's Project's Slave Narrative Collection of the Works Progress Administration. For a classic statement of the problems, see John W. Blassingame, "Using the Testimony of Ex-Slaves: Approaches and Problems," *Journal of Southern History* 41 (1975): 490. A systematic analysis of the Slave Narrative Collection and Fisk interview materials revealed that 72 percent of the ex-slaves interviewed by whites rated the quality of their food as good, while only 46 percent of those interviewed by blacks did. Twenty-six percent of those responding to white interviewers expressed unfavorable attitudes toward their former masters compared to 39 percent of those who responded to Black interviewers. See Paul D. Escott, *Slavery Remembered: A Record of Twentieth Century Slave Narratives* (Chapel Hill: University of North Carolina Press, 1979), 10–11.

32. Clinton, " 'With a Whip in His Hand'," 207.

33. Clinton, " 'With a Whip in His Hand'," 208.

34. Harriet A. Jacobs, *Incidents in the Life of a Slave Girl, Written by Herself*, ed. Jean Fagin Yellin (Cambridge, Mass: Harvard University Press, 1987), 36.

35. Jacobs, *Incidents in the Life of a Slave Girl*, 28.

36. Frances E. W. Harper, "Bury Me in a Free Land," *NA*, 417.

37. Frances E.W. Harper, "Vashti," in Henry Louis Gates and Nellie Y Mckay, eds., *The Norton Anthology of African American Literature* (New York: W. W. Nortan & Company, 1997), 415–417.

38. Mary Helen Washington, "Introduction," in Anna Julia Cooper, *A Voice from the South* (New York: Oxford, 1988), xxxi.

39. Mary Helen Washington, "Introduction," in Anna Julia Cooper, *A Voice from the South* (New York: Oxford, 1988), ii.

40. Clinton, " 'With a Whip in His Hand," 206. This perverse precedent also informs how Black women struggle for and experience the exercise of reproductive rights. "For American white women the concept of property in the self, the ownership of one's body, in relation to reproductive freedom, has more readily focused on the field of events around conception, pregnancy, abortion, and birth," Donna J. Haraway explains, "because the system of white patriarchy turned on the control of legitimate children and the consequent constitution of white females as women. To have or not to have children then becomes literally a subject-defining choice for such women. Black women specifically—and the women subjected to the conquest of the New World in general—faced a broader social field of reproductive unfreedom, in which their children did not inherit the status of human in the founding hegemonic discourses of U.S. society." See Donna J. Haraway, "Ecce Homo, Ain't (Ar'n't) I a Woman, and Inappropriate/d Others: the Human in a Post-Humanist Landscape," in *Feminists Theorize the Political*, ed. Judith Butler and Joan W. Scott, ed. (New York: Routledge, 1992). Reprinted in *The Postmodern Bible Reader*, David Jobling, Tina Pippin, and Ronald Schleifer (Oxford: Blackwell, 2001), 213–214. As Hazel Carby has reminded us, whereas historically in America white women have given birth, often against their will, to the heirs of property, black women, as property under American slavery, gave birth to property. Hazel V. Carby, *Reconstructing Womanhood: The Emergence of the Afro-American Woman Novelist* (New York: Oxford University Press, 1987), 53.

41. *Norton Anthology*, 947–948.

III

Pastoral Studies

6

The Spirit is Willing and the Flesh is Too: Living Whole and Holy Lives Through Integrating Spirituality and Sexuality

Lee Butler

Stay awake and pray that you may not come into the time of trial; the spirit indeed is willing, but the flesh is weak.

—*Matthew 26.41*

When most Christians are asked to think about body issues, notions of purity are frequently central to those considerations. The ideology that resounds throughout the Christian community is that the body is a temple, and we must always put forth great effort to keep the temple pure. These ideas are quite pervasive because of a deep sense that the body and bodily activities are sinful, corrupted, and impure. This understanding has often resulted in an attempt to be disembodied. Having the feeling that the impure activities of the body are unavoidable, Christians have attempted to minimize or escape the body in the name of sanctification.

Through the ages, the formation of a Christian identity has been a traumatizing experience resulting from the difficulties that the Church has had with embodiment. Like Jesus wrestling in the Garden of Gethsemane, we have struggled with the challenge of attachment in life as well as a challenge of being attached to one another. These challenges are most often experienced as a crisis of whether it is better to be embodied or disembodied. The challenge of embodiment sounds odd, but when you consider that most of our physical associations with this world are described in terms of the negative physical pleasures of this life, it should be no surprise that our physical preference is disembodiment in order to make Heaven our home.

Within the United States of America, the challenges associated with the body and embodiment are often guided by a dualistic impulse to make separations and to dissect life. Most of us have been socialized to believe that the best way to understand something is by cutting something open and looking at its internal workings. When we want to try to understand embodiment and the gifts of our creatureliness, however, the impulse to dissect is not for the sake of examination. On matters of the body, our impulse, in actuality, is for the purpose of surgical extraction or amputation. Our preference for disembodiment always perceives our body to be unhealthy and flawed. Due to our understanding of the body as diseased, our dualistic impulse for dissection assumes that there is a dysfunctional component to our being that must be extracted and discarded. This is particularly true when we identify ourselves as sexual beings. Notions of sexual purity tend to always mean adding to life through subtraction from life. As a result, we have dualized spirituality and sexuality as the primary declaration for Christian living, and often extracted and discarded sexuality from our Christian identity.

Finding Harmony

We find it difficult, if not impossible, to conceive opposites coming together to form a harmonious union. Even our characterizations of harmonious union support notions of irreconcilable differences. I know we say things like, "Opposites attract," but our explanation often describes a situation of great struggle in the attraction of opposites. Consider the ways most people talk about marriage. Our most common descriptions of holy matrimony reflect our difficulty to conceive marriage as harmonious union. I regard our basic descriptions of holy matrimony to be expressive of the tragic victimization that is embedded within human existence. Think, for a moment, about the "fuzzy math" we use to describe marriage. We say things like: "I was half and you made me whole;" or we make reference to a spouse being the "better half" ($1/2 + 1/2 = 1$). "I was nothing before you"; or "I am nothing without you" ($1 + 0 = 1$). "Always keep a little something on the side that he doesn't know about" ($1 + 1 = 1$). "I always try on a shoe before I buy it," and because shoes wear out, "a five year marriage is an old couple" ($1 + 1 = 1 + 1$).

When many declare the vital features of a harmonious union using holy matrimony as the prime example, the picture that gets generated is often a function of our dualistic impulse. It is far easier for us to split things and people apart than it is to maintain the integrity of wholeness. This splitting behavior means we are inclined to expressing a misguided understanding of union. Our ideas of union tend to be expressed through the language of subservience resulting from an emphasis on a fallen state of being. As we describe the roles of husbands and wives, the basic descriptions of holy and harmonious union rest upon sex and gender differences that emphasize superior/inferior ideologies instead of stressing equality and mutuality. Through a puritanical "rule of thumb," we promote disembodiment and beat the life out of one another in the name of Christian virtue. Ultimately, we tear our spirits out of our bodies as our way of declaring harmonious union. Rather than promoting a harmony based on communality, there is a tendency to define harmony through a defensiveness based on separation of spirituality and sexuality, which in the end offers a false sense of security regarding holiness.

Continuing to explore the issue of harmonious union, consider the myth of Lilith. According to the myth, Lilith was the first wife of Adam. Although their marital strife seems to be rather specific, the story has been interpreted to say that Adam and Lilith argued about everything. Believing the two of them to be equal, Lilith refused to be dominated in any way. But in the story, here is what actually breaks up the marriage: Lilith refused to be on the bottom during lovemaking. Because of Adam's lack of mutuality, Lilith left Eden. Angels of the Lord visited her, commanding her to return to Adam, and she refused. Her refusal resulted in her becoming the lover of many demons, the seducer of men, and the source of crib death. Among the many things to be concluded from this story, the myth of Lilith suggests that equality is not an option, that equality is not what it means to be spiritual, and that a body without spiritual guidance is destructive. I wonder, can we imagine a harmonious union in the absence of dominance?

Let's consider that question in the context of the gospel of Matthew and the Gethsemane narrative. Jesus is in the garden, separated from his disciples. He throws himself on the ground and begins to pray. He stops praying. He goes back to get some moral support from his disciples, whom he has asked to stay awake. Finding them asleep, he says, "Stay awake and pray that you may not come into the time of trial; the spirit indeed is willing, but the flesh is weak."

Think for a moment of the variety of contexts in which you have heard or said, "The spirit is willing but the flesh is weak." What meaning did you intend or what was the intended meaning when those words were spoken by others? The context for this statement, at the very least, has something to do with Jesus' struggle within life as the necessity of his death drew near. While his statement suggests an awareness of death being imminent, a part of him was hesitant about actually "giving up the ghost." Our typical reading of this text, however, reinforces our notions of spirit power being more potent than physical power. We regularly conclude that spirit is superior to the body. This notion points to an idea that if the spirit simply dominates the body, or if we simply separate ourselves from the body, then the condition of the body is of no consequence. But to emphasize such an idea encourages the escapism that is a natural defense mechanism when we are physically assaulted. In the midst of experiencing the ultimate violent violation of the human soul, we frequently separate ourselves cognitively and emotionally from our bodies in order to escape the horrors of the victimization. In other words, as the victimizer dominates the body, the victim leaves the body. But if this becomes our way of addressing life, that is, separating what we perceive to be our "selves" from our bodies in the midst of struggle, what does it really mean to achieve a harmonious union? Is separating our spirits from our bodies really living?

A Question of Humanity

This for me begs the question that the world has yet to answer to its own satisfaction: "What does it mean to be human?" What is it about this question that throughout the ages we ask, answer, and ask the same question over and over again? Scholars and laypersons of all varieties and disciplines have answered this question ad nauseam, with the latest social hope being the human genome project.

I would like to suggest one reason for our failure to answer this question once and for all. I believe our struggle to answer this question has to do with our division of spirit and body. More directly, our failure to answer this question has to do with our division of spirituality and sexuality. If we considered the two to be parts of the same whole, our understanding of the human experience and condition would be very different. The bifurcation of our being does not simply result in the fracturing of our individual selves, it ultimately results in the destruction of our lives as relational beings. In general, the life of the spirit seeks to bring union, and the body longs to be united to another. We, however, do not tend to see spirit and body as longing for and desirous of the same goal; that is, we do not tend to see spirit and body longing for, desirous of, hoping for the end of an isolated existence. Instead of the positive goal of union being attributed to both spirit and body, we have tended to attribute negative characteristics to the body without realizing that this results in the destructive functioning of the spirit. Attempting to answer the question, "what does it mean to be human," by dividing spirit and body means that a person will always emphasize one part over the other and ultimately declare that emphasized part to be superior to the other part.

The Black Body

Many of my opinions have been formed and informed by African American life. For the remainder of my discussion, much of what I reflect upon has been framed by my views of Black life in America.

Although the dominant ideological split is mind–body, across much of African America, the guiding paradigm for analysis is a spirit–body split. African Americans have an anthropodical (anthropos + theodicy) understanding of the body.[1] That is to say, we have some peculiar ideas about our physical nature as an evil nature. The ideas we have about our own Black bodies make it difficult for us to be "at home in our own skin." Living without a sense of home within means that we are never quite comfortable with another and also suggests that we will be inclined to the colonization of others in order to establish a home.

America's relational systems are regularly described as colorized polar opposites. Whereas we, as a nation, are constituted by a multiplicity of ethnic cultures, America continues to understand its race problems in Black and White and not as a national problem that includes every color of the "rainbow." This interpretative frame is so deep within America that if African Americans were soup, all other ethnic irritations would be described as the "soup de jour." I know today we want to see ourselves as a unified nation committed to fighting against terrorism, but the very terms we use to describe our state characterize us as "the good" fighting against "the evil" in the world. This fight is not seen as being merely temporal. This fight has been described to reflect the eschatological hope of the nation by declaring that God is for us and choosing to not align with us is to stand against God. These contrasting positions, often depicted in Black and White, symbolize life's eternal struggle of evil against good. Furthermore, these contrasting positions have become the defining features of God–human interactions.

In America, White and White bodies have been equated with God and good; and Black and Black bodies have been equated with anti-God and evil. Hence, many of our relational dynamics are expressed as God versus evil. Even today, this is heard in our language of nationalism in the resounding phrases of, "God bless America," "the axis of evil," and "When evil struck America." The male body, which is the temple of God, is considered weak when it is presented with the female body, which is regarded as the evil seductress. Color and body together declare who is acceptable and can belong and who will always be rejected and outcast.

Furthermore, color and body play a part in fantasy life. The human body naturally stimulates erotic senses; but color, among many other features of the body, exaggerates erotic sensations through an identification of the exotic. There is a constructed sense that the exotic is more pleasurable than the "typical." In general, people believe that if they travel to an exotic island, eat exotic foods, and drink exotic drinks, their romantic passions are heightened to superior levels. These fantasies have a similar effect when they are applied to one who is perceived to be exotic. As a result, Black bodies, often thought to be exotic, stimulate extreme ideas of sexual behavior and sexual pleasure. When our puritanical logic is applied to our ideas of the exotic, Black bodies are identified as the embodiment of unbridled passion. This has resulted in spiritual pronouncements being made about Black bodies that have emphasized racialized sexual differences and projected a variety of sexual discomforts and fantasies on to Blackness. Consequently, our Black bodies are frequently seen, and experienced, as the unholy, unclean incarnation of evil in America. We African Americans, therefore, have sought to sacrificially escape our bodies through an over-spiritualization of our lives. We engage in an escapist process to transform that which is thought to be unholy into the holy by separating our sexuality from our spirituality.

Spirituality and Sexuality

African American spirituality, which is rooted in African spirituality, promoted our survival through generations of hard times by an insistence that we maintain our self-understanding as whole and holy human beings. Generally speaking, spirituality is the active integration of our humanity resulting in a singularly directed effort to be in communion with God and others. It is the human spirit moving and being drawn toward God's Spirit. African spirituality has a multilayered, communal understanding of reality. From this perspective, the world is filled with spirits, and God's Spirit is an inescapable presence in the world. Because God is in everything and everyone, the most mundane activity is regarded as a spiritual activity. This is why African spirituality declares there is no separation between the sacred and the secular.

Contrary to the guiding principle of African American spirituality, spirituality and sexuality tend to be seen as separate and unequal. Spirituality is seen as superior and sexuality as inferior. When there is an attempt to describe spiritual poverty, most often the expression is causally related to sexuality. The poor in spirit are thought to be those who are the most worldly and sensual. This, I believe, has led to a denial of our humanity by separating our spiritual lives from our physical lives. If our spirituality instructs that we maintain our holiness by maintaining wholeness, then we must maintain our spirituality and our sexuality as integrated components of our humanity. We cannot say "no separations" and act in ways that establish multiple separations and expect to be whole and healthy human beings.

Whereas spirituality and sexuality should always be considered parts of the same, single whole, they have been described and defined as unrelated parts. An exercise I borrowed from a friend usually helps me to convey this point. The exercise is as follows: On a piece of paper, develop two lists of words. For the first list, describe the feelings that communicate a positive worshipful experience. After giving people an opportunity to develop the first list, for the second list, ask people to describe the feelings of afterglow. What most people discover is they use the same words to describe both experiences. Spirituality and sexuality are not only related, they have the same purpose as the end goal, that is, to integrate human persons with one another and the Divine through the harmony producing activities of communality.

The Damage Done by Splitting

Life is most fulfilling when it is lived out relationally. Spirituality purports to unify all things, yet our Western practices have split our spiritual functioning into the sacred and the profane, the spiritual and the mundane. This action has tended to result in understanding sexuality to be the profane and mundane. The splitting of spirituality and sexuality has meant the splitting of our lives. Rather than spirituality and sexuality being unified to overcome human isolation, we have separated them into independent functions with separate expressions. As a result, our desires to overcome human isolation move us to "pray" or "prey." Because we have been socialized to know that there are appropriate places for "praying" and different places for "preying," and never the twain shall meet, we have come to understand spirituality as the separation from the body, which has promoted the condemnation of sexuality. Within the spiritual world of our making, the body has taken on the description of everything evil, citing that no good can come from the flesh.

This splitting of spirituality and sexuality has had a devastating effect upon African American relationships and our understandings of the body. This American dissection has resulted in African Americans being regarded as being without religion, spirit, or morality, that is, without spirituality. Those who have viewed the African with contempt have thought our nature to be lustful, sensual, and animal, that is, uncontrolled sexuality. Historically, we have been seen as less than human and therefore not spiritual. While only some of us have believed these outsiders' opinions, all of us have been influenced by these opinions whether we believe them or not. Splitting spirituality and sexuality has resulted in our having deviant perceptions about embodiment and how we are to achieve holiness.

For our spirituality and sexuality to be reunited, we must lift high the relational qualities of equality and mutuality. We must return to thinking on the individual, family, and community levels all at once rather than thinking of the individual, family, and community as single, unrelated parts. We are in need of healing to reunite spirituality and sexuality in order to restore our humanity, in order to be resurrected as spirit-filled, embodied beings created in the image and likeness of God from the rich, Black earth of a lush and plush Eden. I see healing as the transformative process necessary for integrating the spirit and body. Healing restores us to life by restoring us to relationship with God and one another.

Mutuality is an essential part of the healing process. It says that our meeting ground, though it may not be common ground, is holy ground. Unfortunately, mutuality is still being avoided by choosing to argue about who is or should be on top. Should the patriarch be on top or should the matriarch? Should a man be over a woman? Should Black be over white? Should the straight be over the gay? We fight to prove that a man cannot be a man if a woman is on equal ground. We are more inclined to promote separation than to encourage mutual relationships. We have separated aspects of life that should always remain together. The Church from the Community, the nuclear family from the extended family, and men from women are all separations upon which we have based our existence. We spend inordinate amounts of time searching to prove how different we are. We energetically seek to validate our ideas of one being superior to the other. These separations, in turn, have divided our humanity. If we are truly going to live in peace with ourselves and others, we must become whole human beings, again. If only we would spend as much time working to establish mutuality as we do in working to maintain a system of dominance!

Encouraging mutuality acknowledges that our spiritual existence effects our physical existence. It also means that our physical existence effects our spiritual existence. Those areas of our lives that have been fractured need to be integrated and made whole. The main fracture that needs to be mended for health is the split that has occurred between our spirituality and our sexuality.

Health and Healing

In order for us to be wholly (holy) human, spirituality and sexuality must be reconciled. We will not be able to restore our full humanity if we maintain this split. The body has frequently been identified as what is bad. If not bad, at the very least, the body tends to be seen as a hindrance to spiritual enlightenment and unity. There is an overwhelming tendency to encourage an absence from the body in order to have a holy experience with God. This condemnation of the body has been conflictive for Africans in America. Historically, we were reduced to being a bodily people only, and as such, seen as less than human and thought to be driven only by primitive desires. Our degraded bodies have been exploited in every way possible: for labor, for sex, and for science. Whereas spirituality has been the strength of our survival, rarely have we been seen as spiritual people.

To our advantage, we also have had another understanding of the relationship between spirituality and sexuality, which points to the possibility for our healing. When we think of health issues, almost everyone is aware of the intimate relationship between spirit and body. In those instances, many of the negative ideas we have about the body are removed. As a result, good health is understood to be when one is "of sound mind and body," that is, good health requires spirituality and sexuality to be together. Consequently, any time we encourage the spirit–body split, we encourage poor health by splitting spirituality and sexuality. When they are kept together, we are fully human and healthier.

Good health is a physical and a spiritual matter. When good health is challenged, healing is required to restore one to health. An unhealthy body is one that has experienced some sort of breakdown in one or more of the body's systems. An unhealthy spirit is one that has experienced some sort of breakdown in the flow of life energy or the lines of communication between the person, God, and others. If the body is unhealthy, it effects the health of the spirit. If the spirit is unhealthy, it effects the health of the body. Healing restores the body and the spirit to a harmonious relationship. Put simply, healing is the process of being restored to a life of relationships. If we are going to obtain and maintain healthy relationships, we must first be healed.

Is the spirit willing and the flesh weak? I do not think that is the lesson we learn from the passion of the Christ child. The message that comes to us from the empty tomb is the spirit is willing and the flesh is too! Without embodiment, why should we have hope in the rapture or dream of walking around Heaven? If the spirit is willing the flesh must also be equally willing. What does it mean to be a "living soul" if not the integration of spirit and body? Maintaining a hierarchical split between spirit and body diminishes our humanity and denies the gospel of the abundant life.

We know what it means to be healthy; but in order to achieve good health, we must be healed. If we continue to conduct "business as usual," the end result will be that the wounds of our relationships will go unhealed. We must mend the fracture that exists between our spirituality and our sexuality. Our healing will restore our humanity. It will restore our community. It will restore our families. Our healing will turn us toward each other and cause us to see one another, perhaps for the first time in a long time. Our healing will turn us into friends and lovers. It will turn the hearts of children toward parents and parents toward children. Our healing will make us whole and holy, spiritual and sexual, human beings.

Note

1. See, Lee H. Butler, Jr., *A Loving Home: Caring for African American Marriage and Families* (Cleveland: Pilgrim Press, 2000).

7

When and Where I Enter, Then the Whole Race Enters with Me: Que(e)rying Exodus

Irene Monroe

African American males from various Christian denominations and the Nation of Islam have interpreted Exodus from the "endangered Black male" perspective. Irene Monroe challenges that reading since it excludes African American women and translesbigays, thus legitimizing misogyny and phobias of sexual minorities. She propose a more inclusive and liberative reading of Exodus from an embodied and sexual praxis.

Of the many liberation motifs used in the African American biblical canon, none is so central as the Exodus narrative. In analyzing the Exodus narrative in light of the struggle for Black freedom, the trials and tribulations of the Israelites under Egyptian domination parallel those of African Americans under the reign of white supremacy in the United States. From the hermeneutical perspective that God's liberating actions for the oppressed take place in history and as history, African Americans' appropriation of the Exodus motif functions as a historical account of God's omnipresence in Black life. As permanent outsiders to American mainstream society, the Exodus narrative affords African Americans the social location of privileged insiders in the scriptural drama for liberation.

However, as a liberating paradigm for African Americans, the Exodus narrative has never been fully exegeted in the context of Black physical bondage. Just as it was for the Israelites during Egyptian slavocracy, American slavocracy was the working and controlling of racialized subjugated bodies and sexualities. Forced into compulsory heterosexuality for the economic purpose of replenishing an enslaved labor force, both Black men and women were subjected to the vagaries of a racialized system of gender and sexual domination. The Exodus narrative has always been a coming-out story for all African Americans. It is a story about coming out from the fetters not only of racial captivity but also of physical and sexual captivity. Because both Black heterosexual male Christians as well as Muslims construct the Exodus narrative around a narrow racially gendered discourse on the "endangered black male," the narrative remains in both gender and sexual captivity. As an African American lesbian feminist my struggle in fully coming out and being accepted in the Black community, as the Exodus narrative calls for, is inextricably tied to the liberation of all my people, because when and where I enter the struggle for Black liberation both within my community and within the dominant culture is where the whole race enters with me.

Although this appropriation of the Exodus motif is touted as being liberating and inclusive to all Black people, from the social locations of women and lesbian, gay, bisexual, and transgender people in the Black community, this reading has been nothing but a ball and chain around our necks. By unhinging the Exodus motif from its patriarchal theme of the "endangered black male," as this essay attempts to do, the traditional Africentric male narrative becomes inclusive and emancipatory for all people in the African American community to freely come out of the closet of gender and sexual slavery.

The Exodus narrative is the first of stories in the African American biblical canon that sets the stage for African Americans to come out of Black physical bondage. Every since 1619, when the first cargo of enslaved Africans was brought to America, liberation from racial oppression was and continues to be a central theme and necessary preoccupation for the livelihood and survival of Black people. With over two hundred years of slavery followed by a provisional emancipation in 1865 due to both hegemonic ideologies and legislative edicts of Jim Crowism, segregation, and now reverse discrimination, liberation for African Americans in this country has at its best been nominal and has at its worst been blatantly denied. Given America's tenuous commitment to Black freedom, African Americans sought out an authority that would give them both an unwavering spiritual succor and an unshakable earthly foundation: the Exodus narrative.

As the formation and framer of a Black world order, the Exodus narrative has iconic status and authority in African American culture. With constitutional rights not guaranteed to African American citizenry in this country, the Decalogue handed to Moses on Mount Sinai and the civil and religious laws called the Covenant Code (Exod. 20–23) functioned as our very own Declaration of Independence and our Bill of Rights through the labyrinth maze of American's unyielding racism. Intended by slavers to make Africans, not better Christians, but instead better slaves, the Bible was the legitimate biblical sanction for American slavery. However, my ancestors, enslaved Africans, turned this authoritative text, which was meant to aid them in acclimating to their life of servitude, by their reading of Exodus into an incendiary text that fomented not only slave revolts and abolitionist movements but also this nation's civil rights movement. As a road map for liberation, the Exodus narrative told African Americans how to do what must be done. And in so doing, Nat Turner revolted against slavery, and Harriet Tubman conducted a railroad out of it.

The clarion call for all Israelites to come out of physical bondage, and by extension for all enslaved Africans, is heard in Exodus 5:1, when both Moses and Aaron went to the pharaoh to relay God's message, which said, "Let me people go." So commonly heard in sermons, protest speeches and spirituals by African Americans, and in the refrain of the best known of all the spirituals "Go Down, Moses," "Let my people go" was one of the first calls for Black revolt. So stirring and electrifying were the words that singing the spiritual was prohibited on many plantations, especially since it was believed the song was composed to honor insurrectionist Nat Turner, whose slave revolt in Virginia in 1831, the bloodiest of the 250 slave revolts, first introduced America to the meaning of Black rage and tore asunder its myth of the docile slave.

"Let my people go" is a command from God to come out of physical bondage. The command calls for all enslaved Black people to come into their bodyselves. In the African American folktale of High John de Conquer, he espouses a command to come out of physical bondage and into our bodyselves when he ordered the slaves, "Just leave your worktired bodies around for him [the master] to look at, and he'll never realize youse way off somewhere, going about your business"[1] By claiming our bodyselves African Americans can then reclaim their bodyrights and sexualities. Since our bodies and sexualities have been demonized by white culture, the reclaiming of Black Bodyrights and sexualities has to begin with self-love, which in the African American community has been in short supply. Baby Suggs in *Beloved* invites a self-love of black bodies and sexualities when she said:

> Here . . . in this place, we flesh: flesh that weeps, laughs; flesh that dances on bare feet in grass. Love it, Love it hard. Yonder they do not love your flesh. They despise it. . . . And O my people they do not love

your hands. Those they only use, tie, bind, chop off and leave empty.
Love your hands! Love them. Raise them up and kiss them. Touch others with them, pat them together, stroke them on your face 'cause they
don't love that either. You got to love it, you! . . . And all your inside
parts that they'd just as soon slop for hogs, you got to love them.[2]

Unfortunately, Black bodies and sexualities are just as repugnant to
many African Americans as they are to white Americans. To be
trapped in undesirable bodies creates a hatred for all sexualities
because, as Christine E. Gudorf states, "Sexuality is who we are as
bodyselves—selves who experience the ambiguity of both having and
being bodies."[3]

Whereas the Black community executed God's injunction of "Let
my people go!" against the dominant culture, it has not been obedient
in executing the injunction within its community. By incorporating the
Judeo-Christian mind/body dualism coupled with a history of both
physical and sexual abuse due to slavery, African Americans are cut
off not only from their bodies but also their sexualities. With a strong
embrace of fundamentalist Christianity that has embedded in its tenets
as asexual theology, African Americans' bodies and sexualities, which
were once systematically usurped by white slave masters, are not ritu-
alistically harnessed by the Black church.

God's words "Let my people go!" is a command to come out of
physical bondage to not only reclaim our bodies but also to rebuild a
broken Black humanity that includes lesbians, gays, bisexuals, and
transgender people. By creating an interpretation of Exodus that is
imbued with either the tenets of racial essentialism or of Black nationalism, we see that the metal chains from physical bondage left Black
bodies after slavery but the mental chains remained intact. Racial
essentialism purports that there is a monolithic "black experience,"
and therefore, it views women, queers, and their sexualities as inauthentic representations of the race. Black Nationalism puts "the race"
or "the nation" above individual gender and sexual identities; therefore, it views feminists, lesbians, gays, bisexuals, and transgender
people as counterrevolutionary to the cause of Black liberation for all
people.

Since both racial essentialism and Black nationalism are dismissive
of the lives of people who experience multiple forms of oppression—
that is, women, lesbians, gays, bisexuals, and transgender people—
they promote a Black male heterosexuality as the icon of racial
suffering and for Black liberation. Combining the icon of racial suffering and racial liberation into the sole image of the Black heterosexual

male creates a gendered and sexual construction of Black racial victimhood that has come to be known as "the endangered black male". Kristal Zook states, "the Endangered Black man narrative speaks to the very real assaults on the material well-being of black men. But it is part of a larger myth of racial authenticity that is cultivated in ghettocentric culture, a myth that renders invisible the specific contours of living in female, working class, gay and lesbian black bodies."[4]

An important antecedent that gives rise to the belief that the African American heterosexual male is an endangered member in his community who must be saved in order to liberate his entire people is the gender and sexual biases in African American Muslim and Christian appropriation of the Exodus motif. As a central paradigm for liberation and leadership, the Exodus narrative has shaped African American Christian and Muslim theologies and has called both groups to social protest and action.

Just as the curse of Ham in Genesis 9:25–27 was used as the legitimate biblical sanction for slavery, in the African American Christian and Muslim communities Exodus 1:22 is the legitimate biblical sanction for heterosexism, expressed in terms of the "endangered black male." The early biblical roots about an oppressed male's life being endangered drive from this text. The narrative opens with Moses' life precariously floating on water because of the pharaoh's edict in Exodus 1:22, which is to "take every newborn Hebrew boy and throw him into the Nile, but let all the girls live." The subversive acts of the midwives, pharaoh's daughter, and Moses's mother and sister, all working in concert, saved Moses' life and defied the pharaoh's infanticidal decree on Hebrew males. Unarguably, Israel's liberation from Egyptian bondage had its beginning with these women. However, the female-centered story abruptly moves to and remains fixed as a male-centered narrative, consequently focusing solely on the oppression of the Israelites and the election of Moses as their divine leader. The uncritical use of the same interpretation and images over and over again keeps the narrative in patriarchal captivity. Therefore, what we miss in the Exodus narrative is the fact that women make possible the survival and growth of Moses, that they refuse to cooperate with the Egyptian pharaoh's decree because their obedience to God takes precedence, and that there is strength in females bonding against patriarchal oppression. However, what we derive from the fixed interpretation of the narrative is imbalanced gender relations between men and women: women who act independently against male authority are ignored, and women are excluded from leadership positions. Nevertheless, when interpreted within the patriarchal constraints of the African American experience the Exodus narrative tells African American women that only their men's lives are endangered. As women we are to nurture, save, and protect our men for the survival of the race. As men they have the ordained right to lead our liberation movements, and we are to organize and follow them. As Michael Dyson states, "Reducing black suffering to its lowest common male denominator not only presumes a hierarchy of pain that removes priority from black female struggle, but also trivialized the analysis and actions of black women in the quest for liberation."[5]

Although the African American appropriation of the Exodus narrative is no different from that of most white Christian churches nationwide, our enactment of it has spearheaded social and political movements such as the abolitionist movement, the Garvey movement, the civil rights movement, and the Black theology movement. These movements have all showcased male leadership. Our Moses figures in history have been male, from Nat Turner to Martin Luther King, with the exception of one: Harriet Tubman, conductor of the Underground Railroad.

Although Tubman was an exception to the rule, she neither negates nor disrupts the andocentric thought and base of African American leadership from slavery to the present day. Many African American men have argued that it doesn't matter than Tubman was female because they are "gender blind" when it comes to her leadership role in the emancipation of African American people during slavery. Others have argued that they see her as female but ostensibly in a male role. Her husband, a free Black man during slavery, saw her as a disobedient wife. He attempted to dissuade her from fleeing for her freedom, but Harriet Tubman, nonetheless, went north. When she returned home months later to get him, she discovered that her husband had taken up with another woman. As one who had transgressed the prescribed gender role for African American leadership, Tubman paid a heavy price: her marriage.

The Exodus narrative assumes a heterosexual orientation not only because Moses is the icon of the Black endangered male but also because the narrative is one of the pillars that upholds and institutionalizes male leaders in the Black church. If the Moses narrative did not exist, the Black church would have had to invent it.

In the Nation of Islam, the Exodus narrative is one of the central motifs in its theology and its social protest and action. It is buttressed by both a selective interpretation of scripture and an Africentric creation myth of the Original Man. In the Original Man story, African men were the original inhabitants of the earth. As descendants from the tribes of Shabazz, these thirteen tribes constituted an African Nation united by Black skin color, the Islamic religion, and reverence for Allah, a supreme Black man among Black men. The creation of the white race was an experiment in human hybridization by a brilliant but demonic African scientist named Dr. Yakub. Derived from the Original Man sprang forth a race of "blue-eyed devils," known as the Caucasian race, who were genetically programmed to promulgate evil in the world. The Original Man story is basic to the Nation of Islam's fundamental premise of reclaiming for all men of African descent their central place in the creation and leadership of the universe. Former minister of the Nation of Islam, the Honorable Elijah Muhammad stated, "When the world knows who the Original Man is and only then wars will cease. For everything depends on knowing who is the rightful owner of the earth."[6]

The creator of the Original Man story was Wallace D. Fard, a mysterious but charismatic door to door salesman in an African American neighborhood in Detroit, who told his followers in the 1930s that "I come from the Holy City of Mecca. More about myself I will not tell you yet, for the time has not yet come. I am your brother. You have not yet seen me in my royal robes."[7] Fard's purpose as the self-proclaimed Supreme Ruler of the universe and the incarnation of Allah was "to bring freedom, justice and equality to the black men in the wilderness of North America" and "to reconnect with his lostfound nation [to] raise from among them a messenger."[8] Thus began the Islamization of the "endangered black man" theme through appropriation of the Exodus story.

To explain the upcoming demise of white world supremacy, the Nation of Islam's theology of the Original Man inscribes the Exodus motif into the New Testament apocalyptic narrative, the book of Revelation. Fard argues that because white domination throughout the world "became too morbid and bestial . . . Allah himself was touched by the suffering and decided to send a mulatto prophet Moses in 2000 B.C.E. to assist in reforming the white race and free it from the clutches of barbarism."[9] Reascendancy of the Original Man will begin with a global conflagration of the Caucasian race and the death of Christianity and Judaism in the year 2000. Keeping consistent with the theme of the "endangered black man," the end of the Black man's plight begins with the second advent of Fard. Before being forced out of town because of police harassment, Fard promised to return in order to deliver his "lostfound" African brothers in the wilderness of North America from the yoke of white oppression. His parting words to his crying followers outside the Temple of Islam, which he founded, were, "I am with you; I will be back to you in the near future to lead you out of this hell."[10]

Whereas Fard was the creator of the Original Man myth, the Honorable Elijah Muhammad, who headed the Nation of Islam from 1934 until his death in 1975, was its messenger. Louis Farrakhan, on the other hand, is now the sustainer of the Original Man theme. Mattias Gardell states that "Moses is Elijah Muhammad, who prepared to go and meet with God [Fard] and assigned Farrakhan to be his Aaron, leaving the Nation and his legacy in his charge."[11]

The Million Man March was a rearticulation of Farrakhan's theme of the "endangered black man" by a ritualized production of African American–male uplift. The belief that an emasculated African American–male image is to be salvaged by reinstitutionalizing Black patriarchy with Black puritan mores only affirms heterosexual male domination and control over women, children, lesbians, gays, bisexuals, and transgender people. It creates a gender and sexual hierarchy that keeps women, children, and queers subordinate to heterosexual men and subject to patriarchal violence should they step out of their prescribed gender and sexual roles.

Many out-of-the-closet gay men attended the Million Man March to make their presence visible and to stand in defiance against Farrakhan's homophobic pronouncements. The march's theme of articulating the racial problems of African American men impelled many African American gay men to go and to stand in gender solidarity with their heterosexual brothers, hoping the issues of sexual orientation and AIDS would be addressed. However, homophobia prevailed because last-minute decision changes due to "time constraints" and "priority factors" canceled the only openly gay speaker. Nonetheless the clarion call for African American men to save and to liberate the African American community echoed across sexual orientations because it also spoke to some gay men's belief that they too are to lead in correcting the entire African American community's problem. Keith Boykin, former executive director of the National Black Gay and Lesbian Leadership Forum, stated, "And who is better suited to lead the long overdue revolution against patriarchy and violence against women than black gay men."[12] Of course, replacing heterosexual patriarchy with homosexual patriarchy replicates the same male power dynamics that Farrakhan espouses. Boykin's statement shows how the foundation of African American leadership is rooted in an Africentric messianic male tradition.

In carving out a racial essentialist or Black nationalist identity with the Exodus narrative, African Americans have done it at the expense of leaving their bodies and sexualities behind. The theme of the "endangered black male" within the Exodus narrative has turned a liberation motif into a policing one because it keeps all African Americans—heterosexuals and queers, males, and females—in both gender and sexual captivity. The African American interpretation of Exodus, from its inception to present day, has been merely the ritualization of Black heterosexist patriarchy, which is modeled after and in competition with white male supremacy. The liberation of Black bodies and sexualities using the Exodus motif is as impossible as the liberation of Black bodies under the domination of white male supremacy. Both racial essentialism and Black nationalism vie for the social ordering and policing of Black bodies and sexualities. African Americans have always been in the closet about sexuality, especially as it relates to sexual abuse, and both maintain the two salient features that shape Black sexuality: sexual exploitation and sexual violence because of its scapegoating of woman and queer sexualities. Also both maintain the cultural hysteria and iconography of Black sexuality as "other."

When unhinged from the patriarchal theme of the "endangered black male," the Exodus narrative is a liberation story about the renewal of Black life and the healing of Black relationships to the world and to each other. Having been bombarded with a history of stereotypes, violence, and abuse, neither whites nor African Americans know what Black sexuality is. African Americans' silence speaks volumes of that history. Our fractured relationships between and across genders and sexualities in the Black community are testimony to the pain and confusion. Policing women, lesbians, gays, bisexuals, and transgender people gives Black heterosexual men what they could not have during slavery and what they only have nominally today: power.

As a coming-out story, Exodus is about the celebration of being freed from Black physical bondage. It is the discovery of our body-selves and bodyrights that allows for the affirmation of Black bodies and the validation of Black sexualities within our community and in the world. In talking about human freedom, African American philosopher Cornel West states, "We must be strong enough to resist the prevailing forms of bondage yet honest enough to acknowledge our weaknesses . . . This honesty about our weaknesses is itself a supreme form of strength that precludes paralysis and impotence."[13]

When the African American community owns up to weaknesses by dismantling its dominant belief that racism is the only and ultimate oppression African American people face in the country, then the community can begin to address the sexism and homophobia within its fold. In order for African American leadership to be both effective and inclusive, we must implement a new emancipatory reading of Exodus that encompasses a comprehensive analysis of race. Since racial oppression is the common reality that all African American females, males, gays, lesbians, bisexuals, and transgender people confront every day of their lives, we clearly need a model of leadership that articulates simultaneously the multiple oppression of race, class, gender, and sexual orientation. Because race links us across and between various identities, a racialized understanding of how class, gender, and sexual orientation are linked to the pernicious and intricate patterns of white male supremacy would liberate us from the myopic view that only African American males are the endangered members in our communities.

Until we dismantle this hierarch of oppressions, which makes people fight among themselves and believe that one oppression—their oppression—is greater than any other oppression, the Black liberation movement in this country will not cease to function in a Sisyphean pattern. The struggle against racism is only legitimate if we are also fighting anti-Semitism, sexism, classism, and the like. All of these isms are merely tools of oppression, which will continue to keep us fractured instead of united toward the common goal of a multicultural democracy. Bernhard W. Anderson stated that "those who followed Moses in flight from Egypt, as we have seen, were a variegated company, a 'mixed multitude' as we are told specifically (Exodus 12:38), who were held together primarily by their common desire to be free from slavery."[14] As an African American, my liberation is tied to the freedom of my people, but my liberation is also tied to the struggle of women and queers everywhere the integrity of their bodies and sexualities is compromised.

The Exodus narrative calls us all to come out of whatever bondage enslaves us. For African Americans, our bodies and sexualities are in as much need for freedom as our skin color is. The controlling of racialized bodies and sexualities in this country requires an embodied reading and praxis of Exodus in our future social protest and speeches about liberation. As an African American lesbian, when and where I enter both my body and sexuality into the struggle for Black liberation is where the whole race enters with me.[15]

Notes

1. Garth Baker-Fletcher, *Xodus: An African-American Male Journey* (Minneapolis: Fortress Press, 1996), 61.
2. Toni Morrison, *Beloved* (New York: Alfred A. Knopf, 1987), 88.
3. Christine E. Gudorf, *Body, Sex, and Pleasure: Reconstructing Christian Sexual Ethics* (Cleveland: Pilgrim Press, 1994), 171.
4. Devon W. Carbado, ed., *Black Men on Race, Gender, and Sexuality: A Critical Reader* (New York: New York University Press, 1999), 4.
5. Michael Dyson, *Making Malcolm: The Myth and Meaning of Malcolm X* (New York: Oxford University Press, 1995), 98.
6. C. Eric Lincoln, *The Black Muslims in America*, 3d ed. (Trenton: Africa World Press, 1994), 71.
7. Ibid., 12.
8. Mattias Gardell, *In the Name of Elijah Muhammad: Louis Farrakhan and the Nation of Islam* (Durham: Duke University Press, 1996), 59.
9. Claude Andrew Clegg III, *An Original Man: The Life and Times of Elijah Muhammad* (New York: St. Martin's Press, 1997), 53.
10. Gardell, *In the Name of Elijah Muhammad*, 127.
11. Ibid.
12. Keith Boykin, "Gays and the Million Man March," in *Atonement: The Million Man March*, ed. Kim Martin Sadler (Cleveland: Pilgrim Press, 1996), 17.
13. Cornel West, foreword to *Go Down Moses: Celebrating the African-American Spiritual*, by Richard Newman (New York: Clarkson Potter, 1998), 9.
14. Bernhard W. Anderson, *Understanding the Old Testament*, 4th ed. (Englewood Cliffs, NJ: Prentice-Hall, 1986), 84.
15. E. Franklin Frazier, *Black Bourgeoisie* (New York: Macmillan Publishing Co., 1957), 71.

8

Toward a True Black Liberation Theology: Affirming Homoeroticism, Black Gay Christians, and Their Love Relationships

Horace Griffin

Black Sexual Bondage

The internalization of dark skin as ugly and in need of lightening; coarse hair texture as bad and in need of straightening; writhing Black bodies as nasty and in need of saving; sexual attitudes as dirty and in need of purifying; Black sexual longings as uncontrollable evil and in need of taming; and sex talk as inappropriate and in need of silencing, have made it difficult for Black people to love their bodies and contributed to an understanding of their own sexual expression as nasty. When Black film director Spike Lee popularized a common Black cultural understanding of sex as "doing the nasty," few African Americans may have grasped the negative implications of shame and filth that come with such a reference, even when the reference is made in a humorous manner. Negative associations about Black sexuality are familiar to both Anglo and African Americans. Since the Atlantic slave trade and the post-Enlightenment's racial classification of humans, Europeans have identified the sexuality of African peoples as debased, immoral, perverse, and generally grotesque. European Americans wielded their power to brand Black sexuality as everything having to do with badness: African peoples were understood to be oversexed, to have animalistic large genitals and to be characterized by predatory sexual behavior. For the past century, in the post-slavery Americas and postcolonial Africa, African and African American scholars, like W. E. B. Dubois, along with political and religious leaders, have been engaged in a perpetual reaction to this past by adopting dualistic notions of sexuality and promoting conservative sexual mores in order to gain respectability from the mainstream white ruling class.[1] On Black college campuses and in Black elite social clubs, Victorian sexual mores reigned supreme. Such reactions left African Americans with unresolved perspectives related to sexual thought and practice.

While most African Americans could hardly be considered sexually repressed to the degree of that the educated Black bourgeoisie class has been (the display of sex in Black hip-hop music and music videos and a disproportionate number of teenage pregnancies would disprove such a claim), historical circumstances that demonized Black sexuality are largely responsible for African Americans' current prudishness or public silence about sexuality. Although African Americans engage their sexual desires with the same sense of wonderment, intensity, and angst as the rest of humanity, they also experience some particular struggles around sexuality directly related to their difficult past. Being considered the "despised sexual other," which often caused Black people hardship and loss of life, Black people learned all too well to remain publicly silent about sex. The outrage that most Black people felt toward Anita Hill and their refusal to show outrage after President Bill Clinton fired Black U.S. Surgeon General Jocelyn Elders (for her statement, in response to a citizen's question, that masturbation was a healthy sexual expression) stemmed from Hill's and Elders's uncovering of a painful history that appeared to validate whites' assertions about Black sexual obsessions and proclivities.

Like heterosexuals who highlight and exaggerate the sexual misdeeds of the despised gay while ignoring heterosexual sexual transgressions (often more common and gruesome), whites historically projected onto all Blacks the notion of being highly sexed and Black men as preying on and being sexually obsessed with white women while refusing to account for their own sexual obsession and sexual violence heaped on Black men and women.[2] This common reality reminds us that those in power have the privilege of using sex to demonize and punish the despised group while the powerful escapes ridicule and repercussion.

Since history largely determines the present, it is understandable that African Americans, in an effort to overcome sexual demonization, would be especially disturbed about and averse to any association with contemporary understandings of sexual perversion, including homosexuality. The power of sex to control, to silence, to instill discomfort, emerges, in all too familiar, yet unfortunate ways, especially for Black lesbians and gay men. It is unfortunate because a negative understanding of homosexuality causes Black people to internalize another negative understanding about themselves, about their sexual longings, their lovemaking and their capacity to appreciate sexual intimacy and orgasm. Thus, heterosexual supremacy, like white supremacy, male supremacy and so forth, further imposes bondage upon Black people, a spiritual estrangement that prevents them from loving their Black bodies.

In this chapter, as a middle class gay African American Christian pastoral theologian and seminary professor, I challenge the present assumptions that Black love is uniquely heterosexual and that heterosexuals are the only ones with the capacity to love their bodies. I explore the theological perspectives that shape the present "homosexuality as immoral" view, contributing to Black Christians' mode of resistance to a different Christian understanding. I also offer a position located in the Black erotic, that *loving* sexual desire, in whatever form, enables the union of body and spirit, and becomes a religious undertaking, a Christian act, that allows one to feel the joy, life, wholeness, and liberation that come from God. I call for pastoral persons not only to teach Black heterosexual Christians to love their bodies as they share with each other but to provide the care and empathy for Black gay Christians that will ultimately lead them to love their bodies and those with whom they share their bodies. In such a community, heterosexuals will experience spiritual transformation on homosexuality and gays will find health from a loving community.

Understanding and appreciating homosexuality as a legitimate sexual expression continues to be a challenge for all people, especially African Americans. Even amid the significant number of gays, lesbians, and bisexuals in Black families and communities; the ever-growing number of openly gay and lesbian African Americans, like the Black icon, Angela Davis; and the awareness of prominent and revered Black gay and lesbian Christians from the past such as George Washington Carver, James Cleveland, Barbara Jordan, Blacks continue to display a stubborn resistance to viewing homosexuality as anything but a negative, a white aberration, often dismissing its relevance to Black people.[3]

It is difficult to determine exactly when Africans and African Americans integrated negative views about homosexual expression into their theology and espoused anti-homosexual pronouncements in Black religious and social communities. One of the first recorded accounts of a Black minister leading an organized protest against homosexuality and Black gays can be traced to the early twentieth century. In 1929, during the Harlem Renaissance that gave birth to a number of gay African American artists, including Richard Bruce Nugent, Claude McKay, Countee Cullen, Alain Locke, and Wallace Thurmond, the African American pastor, Adam Clayton Powell Sr., of the famous Abyssinian Baptist Church in Harlem, New York "initiated a vigorous crusade against homosexuality."[4] Powell's "crusade" reflects a rather common response made by African American ministers regarding homosexuality and gay people.

As Black gays gain more visibility in the latter twentieth century and early twenty-first century, African American ministers continue to play an active role in condemning the love relationships of Black gays in their sermons, conversations, and political activism.[5] African American ministers were some of the first voices to decry AIDS as "God's punishment to homosexuals" and actively participate in supporting discrimination against Black gay citizens at the federal, state and local levels.[6]

While generally Black Church leaders and their denominational positions are not monolithic, on the issue of homosexuality, there is little variance. All of the Black denominations define homosexuality as sin. For most Black Christians, viewing homosexuality as anything other than immoral, sinful, and a sexual expression contrary to God's will, would be considered unchristian. Many fear that believing homosexuality not to be sin is straying away from God's intention for humankind and that they will suffer God's punishment for their change of belief and practice. They, like most Christians, quickly state that the Bible commands them to respond in such a manner, even when they fail to adhere to other passages alongside the few opposing homosexual activity. This Christian position that identifies gay Black people as sinful because of their sexual difference and consequently deserving of the discrimination and oppression imposed on them by a heterosexual majority flies in the face of the claim that defines the Black church and more generally Black people, according to Black theologian Dwight Hopkins, as in the "spirit of liberation."[7] What causes such an unbending and negative response to homosexual expression and ultimately to Black gay people? The answer lies in history. The apostle Paul is often blamed for the gender and sexual restrictions practiced in some form or another in every Christian denomination. While it is true that Paul's invoking a host of teachings about "sexual sin" contributes to the present difficulty in seeing other moral sexual responses, Paul's ambivalence is also present in scripture; he asserts that in Christ there is no male or female as he calls for women's subordination in church and family structures, for example. Whatever ambivalence can be attributed to Paul, "the Church Fathers in the first five centuries . . . were far less ambivalent about the sexual body . . . By and large, they were simply negative."[8]

The stricter sexual positions of Paul and the mind–body dualisms of the Gnostics became standard within Christian teachings. In her important work, *Body, Sex and Pleasure*, Christine Gudorf identifies why so many Christians approach sex and the body with an enormous amount of discomfort.

> St. Augustine is often used to exemplify an understanding of sexual pleasure that was predominant in the early church. He saw sexual pleasure as dangerous because it is virtually irresistible. St. Jerome agreed, and one of his strongest arguments for virginity was that only those who have never experienced sexual pleasure can be freed of its dangerous tentacles. Pleasure which is irresistible causes a loss of control over our activity, makes us irresponsible and, therefore, causes us to neglect our moral duties . . . Aquinas . . . maintained that sexual pleasure is something that humans have in common with animals. It is part of our lower animal nature, and not part of the higher rational nature which links us to the Almighty and which is characteristically good . . . [sex] is not a truly human good.[9]

Likewise, the enormous amount of disdain that church leaders expressed over the course of history regarding homosexuality, significantly contributes to the ongoing unease and outright disdain of many heterosexual Christians today. Augustine states that homosexual practices are transgressions of the command to love God and one's neighbors and declares that those shameful acts against nature, such as were committed in Sodom ought to be detested and punished, for example.[10] While Aquinas did not celebrate sex between men and women, he, nonetheless argues, "it is not evil, for it is part of our God-given nature";[11] he does not feel the same way about homosexual expression. In Aquinas' opinion, homosexuality is not only evil, but it is the "unnatural vice," the "gravest of all" vices, the worst abomination that a human can commit with another human being.[12] In Europe and the Americas, Catholic and later Protestant missionaries and ministers followed suit, preaching sex negative views as they converted Africans into the Christian body. Puritans were no less committed to a theology of sexual sin than the church fathers, and they identified homosexuality as "wicked," "disgusting," "vile," and "horrible."[13] Whatever their earlier beliefs might have been, Africans exposed to missionary teaching learned that homosexuality was to be feared. They discovered that European Americans would enact the ultimate punishment of death for homosexual practice. As early as 1646, an African in America, Jan Creoli, "was sentenced to be 'choked to death and then burned to ashes' for a second sodomy offense."[14] Although African American Christians usually rejected the white racist uses of the Bible, which commanded them to be obedient slaves, there is no evidence, especially regarding sexual theology about the body, that these Christians rejected other white Christian teachings.[15] Thus, African American Christians generally take on a sexually restrictive and negative position, in large part due to sex negative teachings from the Catholic and Protestant missionaries and ministers who converted them during slavery.

Throughout history, Christians differed on a number of issues while maintaining their claim of being Christian. Christians, for example, supported and opposed slavery using the same Bible. By the same token, being Christian, white, Black, or other, does not necessitate opposition to homoeroticism. To be sure, the dominant Christian position, from its origins, has identified sex generally as negative, dangerous, and sinful, but there have also been Christian sects resisting these restrictive and oppressive responses to sexuality.

During the nineteenth century, Christian groups like the Quakers and the Oneida community both stressed female and male equality with the latter opposing the dominant Christian repressive sexual attitudes and practices. Even in nineteenth century Mormonism, "in almost every instance Mormon leaders who served . . . were more tolerant of homoerotic behaviors than they were of every other nonmarital sexual activity."[16] The increased anti-homosexual sentiments of today's Mormon leaders, like those of African American church leaders and Black college administrators (demonstrated in their resistance to address homosexuality in progressive ways, if at all), perhaps is related to the long-held desire to be viewed as morally fit by the dominant religious culture. Following slavery, many of the African American leaders received their education about the body from "Puritan" New England missionaries (founders of the first Black colleges); later Black educators instilled in young Black minds negative messages about the sexual expression of Black bodies by stressing that "it was only 'common' Negroes who engaged in premarital and unconventional sex relations . . ."[17] As famed Black sociologist, E. Franklin Frazier notes in *Black Bourgeoisie*, Black educators on

Black college campuses put forth this image of the "chaste" Black body as "proof of respectability in the eyes of the white man, who had constantly argued that the Negro's 'savage instincts' prevented him from conforming to puritanical standards of sex behavior."[18]

Black feminist Paula Giddings correctly asserts that The Clarence Thomas/Anita Hill hearing was a reminder to African Americans that there is a price to be paid for being perceived by society as sexually deviant, perverse, and wanton. Thomas cleverly imposed the word "lynching," helping everyone in the nation make the connection with a shameful racist history of sexually demonizing Blacks that "got black men lynched and black women raped."[19] Most African Americans watched the Thomas/Hill hearing with Emmett Till's story seared in their memory, knowing that any sexual misstep, regardless of how small, could rain down sexual shame and even death on Black people.

The internalizing of these experiences have had a major negative effect on Black people and can be seen in the ongoing devaluing of Black bodies as Black people impose violence and death upon Black women and men everyday. Womanist theologian Kelly Brown Douglas argues in her groundbreaking work, *Sexuality and the Black* Church, that this internalized negativity related to Black bodies can still be observed in behavior expressed by Black church members such as the women covering their legs when sitting in the pew.[20] While the Till case raised perhaps the greatest offense to white society (white heterosexual men): a Black man with a white woman, this cultural hostility toward Black men with white women is quite similar to its hostility toward love between two men or two women. In *Queering the Color Line*, Siobhan Somerville writes about the nineteenth century race and sex categories that pathologized Blackness and homosexuality: "whereas previously two bodies, the mulatto and the invert, had been linked together in a visual economy, now two tabooed types of desire—interracial and homosexual—became linked in sexological and psychological discourse through the model of abnormal sexual object choice."[21]

Thus, in addition to being carriers of the strong anti-homosexual Christian teachings, African Americans are also invested in an effort to establish themselves within the society's definition of sexually moral beings, in the face of a culture that historically cast them as sexually perverse and predatory in the same manner as it presently attributes to gay men. Toward this end, African Americans strongly oppose homosexuality and lesbian and gay equality within churches and often dismiss the relevance of homosexuality and gay issues within Black settings by identifying same-sex lovemaking as having been imposed on them by Europeans.[22] This perspective prevents not only gays and bisexuals from expressing their erotic feelings toward the same sex but inhibits heterosexual men in particular from being close or affectionate with other males or simply saying that another man is nice looking.

In their brilliant work, *Boy Wives and Female Husbands: Studies of African Homosexualities*, anthropologists Stephen Murray and Will Roscoe simply refute the latter claim by stating that "although contact between Africans and non-Africans has sometimes influenced both groups sexual patterns, there is no evidence that one group ever 'introduced' homosexuality to another."[23] Considering the prevalence of homosexual practice or homosexualities throughout time and space in nature and the world (see Arlene Swidler's *Homosexuality and World Religions*), and since homosexuality is a part of human sexuality and nature, identified in various forms on all continents by anthropologists and sociologists, it is arguably a racist claim to state that Africans do not express themselves with same sex love or sexual activity like the rest of God's creation. Despite Zimbabwean leader Robert Mugawbe's, and Temple University Africentric professor Molefi Asante's position that the present anti-homosexual attitude of many Africans and African Americans is in keeping with their African tradition, there is no record that Africans castigated and killed African homosexuals, like their European counterparts, prior to the slave trade. In spite of their denial that homosexuality is authentically Black, history supports the notion that Africans, like other cultures throughout the world, engaged in homosexual expression.

The corresponding implication that homosexuality was widely accepted in Europe prior to the Atlantic slave trade is also inaccurate; most of Europe held rather negative views about homosexuality in any form. Ironically, Africans who, like some Native Americans, expressed themselves sexually with the same sex, frequently in transgenderal homosexuality, actually experienced condemnation rather than a condoning or encouraging of their homosexual expression by European Christian missionaries.[24] Early documents containing "African men's own testimony also shows that they generally expected and often feared the stern disapproval of whites and sought, for that reason, to keep their homosexual practices secret."[25]

As African Americans become more informed about historical homosexualities in African cultures, one wonders why so many Africans and African Americans still resist the suggestion that there has been a homosexual presence in Africa. But in a world that continues to view Africans and African descendants as less developed, less moral and perhaps less human, and given the stigma of homosexuality as a sexual taboo, an immoral expression, the myth that homosexuality did not exist in Africa satisfies a Black cultural need for validation. Hence, the view that homosexuality is an outside aberration imposed on sacred African people. The lack of social power held by Blacks does not prevent them from also demonizing white sexuality. Like whites who cast their own insatiable sexual desires and practices onto despised Blacks, this assertion, that homosexuality is a perverse sexual practice of Europeans imposed on Africans, is another example of the human tendency to attribute one's stigmatized sexual behavior onto the "sexually despised other."

Ultimately, it is irrelevant as to how Africans view or respond to homosexuality. Even if Africans uniformly opposed homosexuality (and it is clear that Africans are not monolithic in their views on this or any issue), African Americans do not adopt African cultural practices just because they are practiced by many Africans. African Americans tend not to become Islamic or a part of traditional African religions, do not practice polygyny and rightfully oppose the more common African practice of clitorectomy. Many African Americans are using "Africa," in the same way that they use the Bible: worthy of citing as a justification for their resistance to homosexuality and unjust treatment of Black gays, but something that they can ignore when it goes against their other views.

Recently, a number of non gay African American Christian scholars and ministers such as Kelly Brown Douglas, Michael Dyson, Jeremiah Wright, and Dwight Hopkins are responding to African Americans using the Bible as justification for Black church homophobia and heterosexual supremacy. Hopkins agrees, "the Bible is brought into conversation as a justification to oppress lesbians and gays . . . as condemning homosexuals to hell without salvation unless they become heterosexuals."[26] He further asserts that these Christians call for this theological response to gays while at the same time stating that "the [Biblical] stories are wrong when they call on slaves to obey your masters, and Black heterosexual women argue that the passages proclaiming women should obey men are sinful."[27] Although this point is not new, African Americans express much resistance to the slavery parallel. Hopkins, and other heterosexual Christian allies recognize this paradox and argue that if Black Liberation Theology, and more importantly Black Christians, expect to maintain credibility when asserting that God sides with oppressed people and is opposed to unjust attitudes and practices enacted on any people, then there must be opposition to a Christianity that embraces the sin and evil of homophobia and heterosexual supremacy.[28]

Why do so many Black Christians use the Bible frequently as an injunction against Black gays, Christian and otherwise, while entertaining a variety of Christian responses on other issues? Since African American Christians (like other Christians) demonstrate the ability to choose selectively parts of the Bible as authoritative while not adhering to other parts, it is becoming more and more difficult for Black ministers, seminarians, and scholars who advocate Black liberation theology for Black people to resist liberation in Black churches and communities for *all* Black people, including lesbians and gays.

Toward a True Liberation Theology: Affirming the Homoerotic and Lesbian and Gay Christians

More than fifty-five years after Adam Clayton Powell Sr. led his crusade against Black gays in New York City, at another famous New York City church, the Riverside Church, Dr. Channing Phillips, an African American heterosexual supremacist, had these demeaning words to say to gays and their love relationships on May 5, 1985 in his sermon, taken from the Gen. 1:27 passage:

> Male and female God created them . . . it is difficult to avoid the conclusion that heterosexuality . . . is being lifted up as the model of human sexuality. . . . Those are hard words . . . that imply that deviation from the parable of heterosexual relationship ordained by marriage is contrary to God's will—is sin. . . . And no theological or exegetical sleight of hand can erase that word of the Lord.[29]

Reminiscent of the time a century and a half earlier when Christians stood divided on whether to honor Biblical passages that validated slavery, many at the Riverside congregation, led by a heterosexual man, stood that Sunday in opposition to this use of the Bible to justify oppressive treatment of God's people and their relationships. According to the progenitor of Black Liberation Theology, James Cone, Black Liberation Theology "must take seriously the reality of Black people—their life of suffering and humiliation . . . When Black people affirm their freedom in God, they know that they cannot obey laws of oppression. [And in light of] the Biblical emphasis on the freedom of [humans], one cannot allow another to define his [or her] existence."[30] If liberation is at the heart of the historical Black church as Cone and others claim and if it is to be consistent with Jesus' gospel mandate "to liberate the oppressed" (see Luke 4: 18, 19), then: Black heterosexual Christians must ultimately work to end the immorality of laws that allow police in a number of states to arrest gays anytime they make love in the privacy of their homes; legal discrimination against and firing of gays in employment as well as in other sectors of the society; legal discrimination that permits the government to remove children against their will from the homes of their gay parents; and church teachings and practices that are demeaning to Black gays and contribute to their suffering and death.

Only a relatively few African American Christians presently concur with Hopkins and accept the ethic of Black Christian liberation and equality for gays and their relationships. Instead most African Americans are like Channing Phillips, selectively choosing parts of the Bible to support an anti-homosexual position and identifying gay lovemaking as nasty, filthy, disgusting, and an immoral expression outside of God's will. African Americans like Alveda King, gospel music artists Debbie and Angie Wynans, and ministers Reggie White, Calvin Butts, and James Sykes go farther than their local congregations in making this point, gaining national attention for their repudiation of any social or religious effort to recognize gay oppression or validate gay sexual relationships as moral equivalents to heterosexual ones. They use the Bible as a tool for imposing oppression on gays, superimposing irrelevant hostile texts onto those with loving same sex sexual desires, expressions and relationships.

This is why no prominent African American heterosexual condemned the comments of Rick Santorum, on April 7, 2003. Responding to the Supreme Court case that will abolish or uphold the criminalizing of gay lovemaking at the state level (to be decided in June 2003), Santorum asserted,

> If the Supreme Court says that you have the right to consensual sex within your home, then you have the right to bigamy, you have the right to polygamy, you have the right to incest, you have the right to adultery. You have the right to anything.[31]

Since African Americans have encountered similar discrimination based on religious or moral reasoning, one might question why they did not condemn Santorum's comments. The reason why there was no African Americans speaking out reflects a sad reality: most African American heterosexuals agree with Santorum.

While it is true that slightly more Black heterosexuals than white heterosexuals support the civil rights of gays, that support should not be overstated.[32] Based on a recent study conducted by Dr. Robert Franklin, the majority of Black heterosexual Christians perceive homosexuality to be immoral.[33] White heterosexual Christians are more varied, with more white Christians than Black viewing homosexuality as moral. This different moral understanding and response can be observed by the implementing of nondiscrimination policy changes, theological statements, open and affirming congregations, gay–lesbian support groups, and anti-homophobia workshops, teaching and training in many white educational institutions, places of employment, theological seminaries, and some denominations throughout the country. The lack of similar progress in Black settings seriously challenges the claim put forth by some Blacks that Black heterosexuals may be more accepting of gays than their white counterparts.

Even when Black heterosexuals in theory should support civil rights for gay citizens, their understanding of homosexuality as immoral precludes such support and complicates their stand against oppression. Although most white heterosexuals, like Black heterosexuals, are homophobic and supremacist in their attitudes and practices, it is especially disturbing to find African American heterosexuals using arguments of morality similar to those used against them to oppress gays. There is no evidence that African American heterosexuals would accept discrimination against themselves and their sexual relationships. Such practices send forth a message, rightly or wrongly, that concern for oppression is only a concern when the oppression is against Black heterosexuals. It is indeed ironic that when it comes to issues of sexual justice and equality within the church, many of the proponents are white and many of the opponents are Black, with few Black heterosexuals advocating for gay equality in Black churches.

More than occasionally, I am struck by the fact that heterosexual Christians in general feel that when they are asked to change their understanding of homosexuality as immoral, they are being asked to do something that Christians in the past never had to do: admit that a "Christian" view was wrong and change it. Christians today express difficulty in understanding that Christians in the past were just as convinced that slavery was a moral practice as they presently feel that homosexuality is an immoral practice. For the most part, it was not until whites experienced African Americans in a way that challenged and disproved long held racist views and theories that white pastoral persons were compelled to reconsider traditional understandings of scripture related to slavery and to the people they thought to be subhuman, African Americans. If slavery, which after all can be supported biblically, nevertheless can also be opposed on the grounds that its oppressive nature is out of the will of a just and liberating God, then it is impossible to justify another set of scriptures that imposes oppressive treatment onto a group, whether it be women or gays.

Nineteenth-century African American Christian leaders such as Daniel Payne, David Walker, Nathaniel Paul, and Sojourner Truth, declared that they were also Christian, while at the same time, as African American New Testament scholar Vincent Wimbush notes, "interpreted the Bible differently from those who introduced them to it."[34] This point informs us that it is too simplistic to say that African Americans are Bible Christians. African American Christians have always resisted certain Bible passages and, as a result, already do what I suggest they should do in relation to passages related to homosexual activity: engage in a prayerful and critical reflection on those passages, resisting the oppressive nature of scripture that runs counter to the just and liberating God also testified to in scripture. The rejection of these scriptures that defined God as accepting slavery by Howard Thurman's grandmother, Nancy Ambrose, is just one example dispelling the myth that African Americans are bound to all scripture as authoritative.[35] While there are still references by some heterosexual Christians to the non-procreative sex of gay and lesbian couples, the fact that they do not apply the scripture "to be fruitful and multiply" to non procreative heterosexual couples (through their choice or infertility) informs us that they can recognize that certain scriptures are limited and inapplicable. Black women church leaders as ministers in the Methodist and Pentecostal traditions and the contemporary reality for African American women cutting their hair without wearing head coverings are other examples of ways in which African Americans are unencumbered by some portions of scripture.

In *Heterosexism: An Ethical Challenge*, Patricia Jung and Ralph Smith argue that Paul's writing in Romans 1, often cited to justify a common Christian condemnation of homosexuality, must be placed in context. It is important to note that "Paul presupposed that all same-sex desires and behaviors among the Gentiles resulted from their insatiable lust for sexual variety, rooted intimately in their idolatry."[36] Given that there is no scriptural reference that addresses loving same sex sexual relationships characterized by long-term care and commitment, many argue with good reason that it is inappropriate to use the Bible when responding to the very different reality of lesbians and gays within the twenty-first century world. In fact, in the first century world that Paul lived in, there was no understanding that someone's sexual attraction toward persons of the same sex might be deeply ingrained, in the way that we imply today when we use the phrase "sexual orientation".[37] Jung and Smith argue,

> Paul might well conclude that the Fall results in both the sexual disordering of desires and behaviors and the sexual disorienting of some of us. However, were he a part of our world, it is also possible, and we think theologically consistent, for Paul to conclude that although sin has disordered everyone's sexuality, it has disoriented no one's.[38]

This approach to Paul's writings does not mean, however, that Black gay and heterosexual Christians disregard scripture altogether or refrain from judging right and wrong behaviors. Like other Christians, I understand sin as those behaviors that violate, destroy, and abuse our fellow human beings and our relationships with them. Homosexuality, in and of itself, does not belong in the category of sin anymore than heterosexuality, in and of itself. Abusive and destructive sexual relationships between two men or two women are just as wrong, but no more wrong, as abusive and destructive sexual relationships between a man and woman. Loving heterosexual relationships that mutually value the body should be honored alongside loving mutual homosexual relationships that mutually value the body. The affirmation of gay relationships is in no way intended to disregard or diminish heterosexual relationships but rather broaden the concept of family in Black faith and social communities.

If Black heterosexual church leaders and Christians continue to resist changing their treatment of scripture and understanding of gays, however, they will continue fostering dishonesty among their gay relatives and fellow congregants. As a pastoral counselor, I encounter many Black gay men in particular who marry heterosexual women simply to avoid the harsh condemnation they would experience as gay, or as a result of the coercion they receive to marry the opposite sex. Many of the heterosexuals condemn these gays for "living a lie" when it was heterosexuals' homophobic attitudes that led these gays to marry in the first place. The Black Church must become a place that upholds sexual integrity, valuing its lesbian and gay members; otherwise it will fail its members, creating more situations like the following tragedy.

Ten years ago, a young pastor, Kevin (pseudonym) shared with me the psychic pain, the constant shame and guilt that remained with him for marrying a woman simply because of family and church pressures.

Much of this internal conflict had to do with the decision he felt that he had to make: marry a woman rather than the man he loved and preferred. He had met this man in an African country almost ten years prior to our discussion. The African man, Ajen, had much affection for Kevin and shared a deep love for him. Their relationship evolved in such a manner over time that they realized that they could not endure a separation by the Atlantic Ocean. Ajen decided to leave his country and move to the United States to be with Kevin.

Kevin told me that they shared a passion with other, often spending hours together talking, laughing, holding each other, and giving thanks to God for blessing them with each other. At the same time, Kevin's family objected to him spending so much time with Ajen instead of a woman. They began questioning why he did not have a girlfriend, telling him that people had begun talking about the absence of a woman with him. Kevin described that such harassment caused a lot of stress in his life, leaving him depressed and confused about what he should do. He admitted that he began to break under the pressure. At the end of what seemed like many months of torture, Kevin concluded that if he were going to pastor a church in his Baptist denomination, he would have to get married. Reluctantly, Kevin began to put distance between Ajen and himself and as a result of family and community coercion, began a relationship and married Sheila. Ajen expressed to Kevin that he was extremely hurt. Ajen said to Kevin that he loved him so much that he left his country for him and that it was difficult to think about Kevin leaving him for Sheila because of others' intolerance. Kevin told me that he lived with much sadness and that if the church and society were different, he would have shared the rest of his life with Ajen. He said that there will always be a void in his life.

This poignant story reflects the story of so many gays who fear retaliation and rejection from an unaccepting heterosexual majority. While many still carry the Black church teachings that their lives are immoral, they also struggle with the feelings that their love is unnatural and that they are unworthy of love. For African Americans, the life of the Black church and family are integral parts of our being, and so Black gay Christians often sacrifice their feelings, health, and a great deal of life's happiness that could be found in relationships, to remain in the church. They feel that the alternative, a rejection of Black church homophobia, which may also mean a severing of church and family ties, would be unbearable.

The life of Kevin is one of many examples of how the Black church is failing its lesbian and gay sisters and brothers. The present silence about or condemnation of homosexuality further promotes unhealthy mixed sexual orientation relationships that not only create low self-esteem, low self-worth and depression for gays but an undue burden on heterosexuals, especially heterosexual women, who find themselves unfulfilled and longing for adequate sexual companionship. Ultimately, institutions that force people to deny their sexual desires and needs either through celibacy or by marrying the persons to whom they are not sexually attracted inflict indelible harm on God's people. Teachings against homosexuality, and in essence against gays, are problematic and are destroying Black families, leaving family members in tears, miserable with the feeling that their loved ones are sick, sinful individuals to be pitied. They often fear embarrassment should their lesbian and gay family members ever be known.[39]

It is rare to find a Black church that affirms Black gays and their love relationships. The progress that has been made on gay equality in some predominantly white environments, including some Christian denominations, for example, the United Church of Christ and the Episcopal Church, leads many Black gays to such places. If Black heterosexuals are "less homophobic than whites," as some suggest, it is indeed curious as to why a significantly lower percentage of Black gays come out in Black settings and churches than their white counterparts.

While only "29 percent of Blacks surveyed said that homosexuals should remain in the closet, while 65 percent disagreed" many Blacks continue to argue that they "do not object to homosexuality [but] object to *open* [emphasis mine] expressions of it."[40] Such a position is necessarily contradictory. To say that a gay person is accepted as long as she/he does not demonstrate the very thing that makes her/him gay is no acceptance at all. This attitude is strikingly similar to that of white racists who feigned acceptance of Blacks as long as Blacks stayed in their place or exhibited behaviors that did not reflect Black cultural thoughts or practices. The expectation for gays to be invisible, even when there is a simultaneous claim for them to be out of the closet, reflects the shame and embarrassment that African Americans harbor about bodily expressions between the same sex. Given that no heterosexual is saying that heterosexuals should not be open about their heterosexuality, this reaction is more than cultural modesty of sexual relationships. Rather, this kind of silencing is a means of control over gays and, like all silencing, works toward the death of a people.

Historically, the Black Church has been a place attentive to the spiritual, political, social, and emotional needs of Black people. It has sought to provide holistic ministry, affirming people and offering liberation from society's definition of them as immoral and inferior. As Womanist scholars have already pointed out, just as Black theology consistently identifies whites oppressive actions against Black people, it "must also unmask oppression or domination within its own tradition as well."[41] Church leaders should continue to embrace scriptures that offer life, love, and liberation. Jesus' command that we treat others as we want to be treated is a scripture that should be maintained in that it reminds us to be just and loving people of God. When we do this, we honor the gospel and the Black tradition of liberation.

There is no need to impose a theological view that unfairly and significantly harms gay Christians. As African Americans eventually spoke out and resisted the injustice, pain and suffering that racist whites in the church as well as society inflicted on them, Black gays and lesbians must also oppose oppression directed toward them by "coming out" and telling their stories of pain that heterosexuals constantly inflict on gays through heterosexuals' "theological constructions of the imago Dei, that pervasively insist that lesbian and gay people are inferior and evil."[42] Gay Christians must do this for their own survival and health. I agree with gay therapist Richard Isay that "any gay man or lesbian who does not oppose the prejudice and discrimination of organizations [and I would add churches] to which he or she may belong remains enslaved by the self-hatred such institutions engender."[43]

The "coming out" and sharing of Black gay Christian narratives— stories that reflect a Christian witness and faith comparable to that of God's people within scripture—will do two things: (1) demonstrate that "all human beings are capable of reflecting the imago Dei—when their concrete and everyday lives and relationships are truthful, loving, creative, just and diverse"; and consequently (2) assist in transforming the understanding of many Black heterosexuals so that they will come to recognize that Black gays and their loving sexual relationships are also moral. As Pastoral Theologian Larry Kent Graham notes, when this occurs, the imago Dei becomes "embodied communally within a web of just diverse and creative [Black] relationship characterized by honest and loving communion."[44]

In light of Black Christian liberation and Black Christian resistance to oppressive scripture, there is no reason why Black heterosexual church leaders cannot move toward a true Black liberation theology that affirms all loving sexual relationships and commitments as reflecting God's purpose in creation. Black pastoral persons can offer healing to lives that are broken by homophobia and reconcile those lives with family members, gay and heterosexual alike. The visibility of gays and of their relationships in Black church settings sheds more light into our capacity to see God's love and presence in community in a variety of ways. Black pastoral care must move toward celebrating all loving sexual relationships within church communities, for it is in such relationships that we find intimacy, health, and wholeness. This embrace allows us not only to appreciate our sexuality, whether we express those sexual yearnings in a mutual way with persons of the same or opposite sex, but also to experience God's goodness within that sexual expression. In that this connection makes us whole beings, we can become better stewards, providing care in our communities and opposing the violence and injustice that seek to abuse and destroy us.

As we begin the twenty-first century, we have an opportunity to love our bodies more than ever. As other writings in this volume suggest, we must bring the spirit and flesh together in healthy ways as opposed to seeing them in dualistic ways and a never-ending tension. History allows us to learn better ways of being and relating in the world. I agree with Douglas that as Black people, much of our present negative attitudes toward our bodies and many times, sex itself, stem from this country's Puritan past and Victorian influence and "the way Black sexuality has been impugned by white culture."[45] However, I hasten to add, along with Douglas, that

> there is an individual and communal responsibility for violating the humanity of another and precluding her or him from fully experiencing what it means to be created in the image of God . . . . A Black sexual discourse of resistance is also constrained to make clear that homophobia and concomitant heterosexist structures and systems (those structures and systems that privilege heterosexuals while discriminating against non heterosexuals) are sin . . . [Black and Womanist theologies] should reveal the basic contradiction between homophobia and the church's belief in a God of justice.[46]

My challenge to African Americans is to engage seriously and critically the relationship between Christianity and homosexuality in the same faithful way that we have typically offered a critical engagement of Christianity and race.

As African American Christians, we now have an opportunity to reject the unfortunate sex negative messages, shedding the past about our sexuality as nasty and loving our bodies as God's gift to us. Our acceptance and celebration of lesbians and gays and their relationships, as we celebrate heterosexuals and their relationships, will welcome and affirm our sisters and brothers who, in their faithful commitment to their sexual gifts, allow us to appreciate the beauty of God's diverse creation. In doing this, in affirming the erotic in all of us, we will proclaim a true Black liberation theology, and in so doing, we will honor God.

Notes

1. Thomas Wirth, *Gay Rebel of the Harlem Renaissance* (Durham and London: Duke University Press) 2002, 46–47; and E. Franklin Frazier, *Black Bourgeoisie* (London and New York: Macmillan Publishing Co.), 71.
2. Calvin Hernton, *Sex and Racism in America* (New York: Grove Press, Inc., 1965), 66.
3. James Sears, *Growing Up Gay in the South* (New York and London: Harrington Park Press, 1991), 5; Jessie Carney Smith, ed. *Notable Black American Men* (Farmington Hills, MI: Gale Publications, 1999), 211–212. and J. Jennings Moss, "Barbara Jordan: The Other Life," *The Advocate* (Los Angeles, CA: Liberation Publications, Inc.), issue 702, March 5, 1996, 38–45.
4. Thomas Wirth, *Gay Rebel of the Harlem Renaissance*. (Durham and London: Duke University Press, 2002), 22. Jervis Anderson's *Troubles I've Seen*, notes that Congressman Adam Clayton Powell Jr. (also a minister) would follow in his father's footsteps of anti-gay sentiment by attacking long-time gay African American Civil Rights activist, King advisor and architect of the 1963 March on Washington, Bayard Rustin, which eventually led to Rustin's resignation from SCLC. Rustin's resignation from SCLC was prompted amid threats from a Powell source that if he did not resign "Powell would announce publicly that King and Rustin were involved in a sexual relationship." 229–230.
5. Although homophobic actions impose pain and suffering on all gays and lesbians, for the purposes of this writing, this essay will address how such behaviors by Black heterosexuals affect Black gays and lesbians more acutely and directly. Considering the culture's focus and general understanding that anything related to homosexuality has to do with white gays and lesbians, typically ignoring a Black gay reality, this discussion underscores the fact that homophobia and heterosexual supremacy also harms and destroys Black people. Also, Black bisexuals should be considered in discussions that include same or opposite sex sexual expressions and relationships. The terms African American and Black will be used interchangeably. Gay will be used to include lesbians and, in terms of same sex relationships, bisexuals.
6. Keith Boykin, *One More River to Cross*. (New York: Doubleday, 1996), 124 and Cathy Cohen, *AIDS and the Breakdown of Black Politics* (Chicago: The University of Chicago Press, 1999), 256.
7. Dwight Hopkins, *Introducing Black Theology of Liberation* (Maryknoll, New York: Orbis Press, 1999), 3.

8. James Nelson, *Embodiment* (Minneapolis: Augsburg Fortress Press, 1978), 52.

9. Christine Gudorf, *Body, Sex and Pleasure: Reconstructing Christian Sexual Ethics* (Cleveland, Ohio: The Pilgrim Press, 1994), 82–83.

10. D. Bailey, *Homosexuality and the Western Tradition* (New York: Longmans Green, 1955), 82.

11. Christine Gudorf, *Body, Sex and Pleasure: Reconstructuring Christian Sexual Ethics* (Cleveland, Ohio: The Pilgrim Press, 1994), 82.

12. Thomas Aquinas (translated by fathers of the Dominican) *The 'Summa Theologica' of St. Thomas Aquinas* (London: Burns, Oates and Washbourne, Ltd., 1932), 11: 11 q.154 art. 12.

13. Jonathan Katz, *Gay and Lesbian Almanac: A New Documentary* (New York: Carroll and Graf Publishers, Inc., 1983), 245.

14. Ibid., 61.

15. Kelly Brown-Douglas, *Sexuality and the Black Church* (Maryknoll, New York: Orbis Press, 1999), 83.

16. D. Michael Quinn, *Same Sex dynamics among Nineteenth Century Americans* (Urbana, Illinois: University of Illinois Press, 1996), 265.

17. E. Franklin Frazier, *Black Bourgeoisie* (New York: Macmillan Publishing Co., 1957), 71.

18. Ibid.

19. Kelly Brown Douglas, *Sexuality and the Black Church* 48 and Paula Giddings interview with Ofra Bikel, 1992 Frontline Documentary, "Public Hearing, Private Pain: The Anita Hill/Clarence Thomas Hearings."

20. Kelly Brown-Douglas, *Sexuality and the Black Church*, 31, 83.

21. Siobhan Somerville, *Queering the Color Line* (Durham and London: Duke University Press, 2000), 34.

22. Keith Boykin, *One More River to Cross*, 189, 196–197.

23. Stephen Murray and Will Roscoe, *Boy Wives and Female Husbands* (New York: St. Martin's Press, 1998), 267.

24. Ibid., 174 and Walter Williams *The Spirit and the Flesh* (Boston: Beacon Press, 1986), 133.

25. Stephen Murray and Will Roscoe, *Boy Wives and Female Husbands*, 218.

26. Dwight Hopkins, *Heart and Head: Black Theology Past, Present and Future* (New York: Palgrave, 2002), 187.

27. Ibid.

28. Ibid., 188.

29. James Nelson, *Body Theology* (Louisville, KY: Westminster John Knox Press, 1992), 55.

30. James Cone, *Black Theology and Black Power* (New York: The Seabury Press, 1969), 117, 137–138.

31. Lisa Neff, "Santorum: Not Sorry" in *Chicago Free Press*, April 30, 2003, vol. 4 #37, 1.

32. Keith Boykin, *One More River to Cross*, 187–189.

33. Robert Franklin, *Another Day's Journey: Black Churches Confronting the American Crisis* (Minneapolis: Fortress Press, 1997), 79–80.

34. Vincent Wimbush, ed. *African Americans and the Bible: Sacred Texts and Social Textures* (New York: Continuum Press, 2001), 17.

35. Howard Thurman, *Jesus and the Disinherited* (Nashville, T N: Abingdon-Cokesbury Press, 1945), 30–31.
36. Patricia Jung and Ralph Smith, *Heterosexism: An Ethical Challenge* (Albany, N Y: State University of New York Press, 1993), 80.
37. Ibid.
38. Ibid., 82
39. Karen McClintock, *Sexual Shame: An Urgent Call to Healing* (Minneapolis: Augsburg Fortress, 2001), 80.
40. Kevin Boykin, *One More River to Cross*, 188.
41. Dale Andrews, *Practical Theology for Black Churches* (Louisville: Westminster John Knox Press, 2002), 109.
42. Larry Kent Graham, *Discovering Images of God: Narratives of Care Among Lesbians and Gays* (Louisville, KY: Westminster John Knox Press, 1997), 169.
43. Richard Isay, *Becoming Gay: The Journey to Self-Acceptance* (New York: Henry Holt and Company, 1996), 159.
44. Larry Kent Graham, *Discovering Images of God: Narratives of Care Among Lesbians and Gays* (Louisville, KY: Westminster John Knox Press, 1997), 172.
45. Kelly Brown Douglas, *Sexuality and the Black Church*, 7.
46. Ibid., 126–127.

IV

Theology

9

Embracing Nimrod's Legacy: The Erotic, the Irreverence of Fantasy, and the Redemption of Black Theology

Anthony B. Pinn

Black theology has traditionally understood itself as a tool for troubling non-liberative discourse in part through a theological repositioning of Black bodies in public spaces. One must understand this process as a positive religious move in that it problematizes and moves beyond the traditional attempt to escape the body as a prerequisite for maintenance of our ultimate orientation related to our ultimate concern. While talk of the incarnation should have rendered the Cartesian duality unreasonable, illogical, it only entailed a contradiction Christians have been willing to accept as an act of faith.[1] Black theology undoubtedly has wrestled against this duality, but with limited success. One of the reasons for this limited success: Black theology has not responded to erotic realities and relationships that make up the religious quest as I have defined it elsewhere.[2]

I am interested in exploring a potential corrective to this problem on the level of theological theory and method. Such a corrective first entails a moment of de-construction, a recognition of the manner in which both Black Christianity and Black theology have failed to give adequate attention to eros as a vital dimension of bodies in relationship. My objective here is not to advocate for the legitimacy of certain erotic actualities over against others. I am concerned with the development of an alternate hermeneutic, one that is capable of uncovering and articulating the erotic dimensions of human meaning and interaction without flinching; one that moves theological discourse beyond the unnatural confinements of existing sex(ual) norms.[3] Yet the development of a sex(ual) moral code is not my intent. Although an important discussion, one started by scholars such as Kelly Brown Douglas, what constitutes proper sex(ual) expression and the proper impetus—and dynamics of consent—for sex(ual) activity is beyond the scope of this essay.

My goal is to disrupt what had been a comfortable discourse which, while heated, has been sex(ually) non-threatening and unable to approach the deep structures and attitudes that promote other-ing, dis-ease and the dread of being "different." This, a comfortable discourse, has been the theological route taken in Black theology to this point, and it is far from adequate. My concern is with highlighting a way by which theology can take seriously Black bodies as erotic realities and note this acknowledgment as an undeniably important dimension of religiosity and theological discourse. To fall into the trap of simply providing alternative norms with respect to discrete sex(ual) activities and attitudes would be as problematic as to continue embracing exist-ing norms. I am interested in the ways erotic realities might alter the very doing of theology and the meaning of Black religion. Both Black theology and Black religion have pushed for the equality of bodies, but what are the theological and religious consequences of "eroticiz[ing] their equality?"[4]

Many in Black religious studies and more progressive Black minis-ters associate sex(uality) with relationship, but can the modalities of "loving relationship" be narrowly defined, as they currently are, with-out actually denying the activities of parts of God's human creation, or denying that "loving" is a matter of eros—erotic desire and activity? Sex(ual) assumptions lurking in Black theological discourse and reli-gious practices must be exposed and challenged, thereby allowing for the development of complex and pleasurable modalities of identity and relationship, without apology. In a bizarre twist it seems Black Christianity's push toward liberation has in fact rendered certain bodies (gays and lesbians for example) invisible and thereby undeserving of pleasure. It is as if liberation efforts within the context of the Christian faith's theology and practice expressed in Black communities wonders out loud the line Tina Turner made famous: "What's love got to do with it?" That is, when love is eros.

Black Theology on Agape and Philia

It is eros that makes Black Christianity and Black theology uncomfort-able. Agape and philia are easily identified elements of theological discourse and components of practice. Attendance of any Black church service will point to both, as members speak of their love for God and their love for "neighbors." Black theology's emphasis on liberation also entails an embrace of both as required ways of being in the world, one feeding the other. In fact, critiques of classism, racism, and sexism imply this commitment to love in that proper relationship with God means a certain relationship with humanity as the reflection of God. By extension, both modalities of relationship are deformed by the dehumanizing effects of oppression in its various forms. Furthermore, the basic claim of liberation theologies, that God sides with the oppressed, is given its logic through appeal to the love of God because, as James Evans remarks, "the partisanship of God is the political and historical manifestation of God's love." According to James Cone, this love, agape, is inseparable from God's being and consequently, "when religionists [deviate] from the *agape* motif, the result [is] always a distortion of the authentic Christian conception of God."[5] The love of God provides the epistemological groundwork for the recognition of others as fully human and of deep and lasting importance, as well as the historical manifestation of this recognition through justice. In fact, turning again to Evans, "self-sacrificial love is the modality of *agape*, but the purpose of *agape* is justice."[6]

In keeping with the theological ancestors of the Black community such as Howard Thurman, Cone, with a bit more passion, emphasized in emerging Black theology a recognition of love (agape and philia) as a radical and aggressive call for historically based transformation. This involves relationship with God through acceptance of the Christ event and the framing of this connection to the divine through a new image of self and others. First noted in terms of an ontological, epistemological, and existential significance to "blackness," Cone expresses this dynamic of love as an acceptance of blackness, loving "it as a gift of the Creator," doing so with the recognition that acceptance of the Black self is a prerequisite without which it is impossible to love God and others with justice and righteousness.[7] This synergy of sorts or mutuality between agape and philia facilitates a way of being in the world. The mantra "black is beautiful" gains theological weight as love becomes a hermeneutical principle and also a mode of conduct. Agape, from a transcendent yet immanent being toward humans, makes necessary as part of its demand, to use Sharon Welch's phrasing, a "love for life enabling the transcendence of social structures that destroy life"[8] manifest in proper relationship with God's creation. This sense of divine love means "it is blasphemy to say that God loves white oppressors unless that love is interpreted as God's wrathful activity against them and everything that whiteness stands for in American society."[9] To the point, "the wrath of God is the love of God in regard to the forces opposed to liberation of the oppressed."[10]

An assertion of the theological importance of divine love/justice and the demands it places on human relationships remains strong within Black theology, although it is nuanced and refined. What I am referring to here is the emergence of womanist theology. Framed by a theory of theological discourse from the work of Alice Walker, womanists as of the mid-1980s, first in the pioneering work of Katie Cannon and Delores Williams, spoke in terms of a fierce commitment to the experiential and epistemological holdings of Black women. What is of particular importance for this discussion is the manner in which womanist thought, if true to Walker's definition of "woman-ish," promotes concern with complex relationships of love because a womanist is:

> Also: A woman who loves other women, sexually and/or nonsexually. Appreciates and prefers women's culture, women's emotional flexibility (values tears as natural counterbalance of laughter), and women's strength. Sometimes loves individual men, sexually and/or nonsexually. Committed to revival and wholeness of entire people, male and female.[11]

While womanist scholarship is not without some disagreement on the "acceptability" of an embrace of same-sex relationships, most have recognized the importance of love as a dimension of Christian life properly conceived.[12] As Walker's definition notes, wholeness requires the ability to love. Theologian Karen Baker-Fletcher echoes, within the theistic orientation prevalent in Black community's, Walker's sensibility when saying, "we cannot love God if we refuse to love what God loves, and God loves us. . . . Something within black culture recognizes the wholistic nature of God, which identifies with humanity in its fullness as male and female."[13] As was demonstrated with regard to Black theology, womanist thought also expresses recognition of love and justice as being linked. Turning again to Baker-Fletcher, who appeals to Alice Walker's character Celie from the *Color Purple*, one finds these words: "Like the awakened Celie, who learned that God loves freedom, everything and everybody, we are called to arise from whatever oppressive, repressive, depressive slumber seduces us to inaction and to act with God, who is on the side of justice."[14]

With all this said, the appeal to love as central to the meaning and purpose of life, I am left wondering: What about sex(uality)? Walker's definition, embraced by womanist scholars, involves explicit reference to sexual pleasure. When, theologically speaking, is love "sexy"—a matter of pleasuring and being bodily pleasured? When is it not philia nor agape, but something much more comfortable with or at home in the "fleshy" nature of the body?

Black Theology and Erotic Discomfort

Emilie Townes and others call for an understanding of the importance of the erotic as a dimension of embodied theology, yet this call receives little attention and most theological discussions (in and outside the academy) on the erotic are awkward and superficial, while also limited to a certain range of acceptable modalities of eroticism. What is the erotic in Black theological reflection and/or religious practice? Are there Black theological discussions of masturbation? Of homoerotica? Of sadomasochism? Are there ways in which this discourse addresses what Renée Leslie Hill refers to as "intersections, in-between places, and borderlands of identities"?[15] No, at best Black theological discourse addresses issues that are in essence matters of manhood and womanhood either embraced or critiqued.

Without attention to erotic sex(uality) as a dimension of meaning, liberation as discussed by theologians becomes a festish. If Black theology urges the bringing of one's experiences to scripture, to religion, in what way is the excluding of the erotic dimensions of life right, particularly when the erotic (as sex[ualized] pleasure) has been used against Blacks as scholars such as Kelly Brown Douglas note?[16] Shouldn't liberation mean an embrace of the full capabilities and meaning of our bodies? There is a fluidity between private and public that religion seeks to regulate using theology as the language of control—coitus interruptus. Hill and others have pointed out the problem, the slippage in Black theological discourse, but how might one address this dilemma? Greater attention to the diversity of sex(uality) within Black communities is a basic need. But how might one go about bringing in substantial ways the erotic into theological discourse and religious aesthetics that is not limited to discussions of inadequate health care, dis/ease, sex(ual) positions, and positions on sex?

Limited engagement of the erotic in part results from a failure to recognize the deep connections between eros and cultural creativity, the developments that serve as a major source for theological reflection and the substance of religious practice and aesthetics. That is to say, sex(uality) has been discussed within Black theological discourse or Black religious studies in more general terms in ways that separate it from the erotic. Sex(uality) is discussed as a political matter in the same way that race, class, and gender have been discussed with regard to political space, individual, and collective social identity. This seems the case, for example, in Hill's call for new theological work:

> We need to be prepared for the fact that what might not seem lethal to us in our particularity might become lethal if we remain ignorant of our own complexities, or if we lose track of our need to form networks of solidarity with other marginalized people. The homophobia that we ignore because it is "not our issue" might well turn out to affect a dearly loved family member. The sexism that is "not at the top of our agenda" might be followed up by racism that is used to deny us our livelihoods or even our lives. One aspect of human identity that holds potential resources for new forms of black power, black affirmation, and healing is sexuality.[17]

Hill at times calls for attention to sex(uality) as physical intimacy, but how might this happen within theological discourse? Black theology as a form of liberation theology proclaims the mutual dependency between spirit and flesh, spiritual and social, and attention to eros (which includes but is not limited to libido desire and fulfillment) might foster a deeper sense of this. Such is the case because, "theological reflection that does not separate prayer times from meal times cannot separate prayer times from those of intimacy; from times of going to bed with someone. That is the point for a theology without underwear, made by people whose sexual misfortune, personal or political, need to be reflected upon as part of our theological praxis."[18] Hill and others push for the erotic, but in what I would consider a rather limited sense, in terms of sex(ual) pleasure.

The Erotic Reconsidered

Paul Tillich, although, like most of us, failing to completely work out these issues in his personal life, offers an alternative grounded in an understanding of eros in cultural creativity. This reframing of the erotic makes eros an indispensable component of the meaning of human existence.[19] Eros is a force that gives shape to human ingenuity and expression on a variety of fronts and in a variety of forms. It is libidinal and as a result concerned with physical pleasure, but it is more than this because it is also concerned with the "beautiful" in far-reaching terms and the desire to create relationships saturated with this beauty.[20]

To attempt a reduction of eros to individualized pleasure—what others give—is to rob it of its drive beyond the self to mutuality and relationship. Eros and the erotic involve the body, but in spaces of relationship that are not confined to sex(ual) release or sexual repression.[21] Eros reality is not synonymous with sex(ual) release; nor is it strictly a matter of sex(ual) politics or the politics of sex(uality).[22]

Such an understanding of eros is important in that it can serve to move Black theology away from a preoccupation with agape devoid of "libidinal impulses and erotic feelings."[23] The binding together that is in one aspect religion involves the connections and pleasures of eros defined relationships. Put another way, "the erotic drives us 'towards union with the forms of nature and culture and with the divine sources of both.' "[24] Eros ties together the various relationships of meaning and pleasure that mark appreciation of self, contact with others and, for those who are theist, the divine. And, it does so in ways that recognize the integrity of those encountered. In this sense eros properly conceived seeks to bring together and unite with agape and philia as a uniting of love, power, and justice.[25] The erotic is the mark of embodiment fully, but critically, embraced and celebrated as a way of holding in tantalizing tension the "inside" and "outside" of history. Without recognition of the erotic, the body loses its relational elasticity, so to speak. This situation of rigidity has ontological implications in that what it means to "be" and be in connection to others, is minimized.

There is no opposition, then, between agape and eros. They are in fact connected because the former is always "erotically charged."[26] Black theology and religious communities such as the Black Church have focused on agape as the ground of all meaningful interaction.[27] And while agape is certainly important, its emphasis has come through philia at the expense of meaningful attention to the erotic. Exclusion of eros in Black theology stems from a warped moralism based on questionable social norms and misleading interpretations of scripture. Resulting from this is an odd arrangement—a discourse that is somewhat politically and economically progressive while sex(ually) "descent," to borrow from Marcella Althaus-Reid, and acceptable to the very social system it seeks to dismantle.[28] Strange bedfellows indeed!

Neglecting the erotic fractures the logic of Black theology in that maintaining a profound appreciation for embodiment as the essence of religious engagement within the world is attempted by cutting us off from a celebration of a fundamentally important impetus for relationship between various bodies. Work of transformation presented by black theology and religious activism, therefore, is missing passion and deep enjoyment. But, in contrast, as Alexander Irwin remarks, "eros as Tillich describes it is an energy of connection-making. This is the common demonstration that underlies the many different areas in which the erotic finds expression. Eros opens us, draws us out, moves us beyond ourselves into sustaining relationship with things, ideas, and beings."[29]

There are ways in which a call for attention to the erotic as a necessary dimension of theological discourse is irreverent. But this is a good thing, not because of its shock value, a forcing of a particular theological agenda through the manipulation of religious grammar. Rather such irreverence or "indecency" is vital in that it brings into question theological norms and religious boundaries in creative ways, and in so doing breaks down the parameters of what are considered proper relationships in terms of "sexual and political praxis."[30] Such a process of de-construction does important damage to the meta-narrative of relationship guiding human interaction such as troubling depictions of gay and lesbian interaction as "unnatural" or at least unspeakable. Theology that takes seriously the irreverent power of eros gains a vulnerability that opens it to seeing the beauty in relationships and interactions that were once despised. The erotic, put another way, entails "the sharing of joy with another and in the bodily act of creativity, when released in our lives it prevents us from simply accepting oppression and the numbness that necessarily comes with it. The erotic propels us out of a sense of powerlessness, but it also prevents the use and abuse of others."[31]

Embodied Theology and the Imagination Paradigm

The proposition housed in the above quotation involves a different relationship to the body. Again, Black theology and Black religion acknowledge the body through the language of embodiment. However, this language entails what James Nelson refers to as "one-directional" discourse—beginning with the transcendental nature of religion and moving toward the body. I suggest giving erotic realities centrality entails beginning with the body, the "fleshly experience of life—with our hungers and our passions, our bodily aliveness. . . ." Such a change of position involves an appreciation for the body and the spaces it occupies, while bracketing the natural theological tendency to establish normative patterns for the movement and use of the body.[32]

Some might refer to this as "body theology," the formation of a theological discourse through attention to the body in ways that acknowledge both bodily sensations and the workings of the mind.[33] An emphasis on bodily experience as presented in body theology highlights connections between truth and experience. Put differently, body theology involves "celebration of embodiment beyond all definitions, enjoying a body for its own sake. It is an attempt to allow people to be framed by their bodies and not by culture or doctrine."[34] There seem ways in which those advocating body theology suggest sex(uality) has intrinsic value, but it also points beyond itself to more fundamental notions of relationship and connection.

In spite of potential dangers, consideration of such a theological approach to the body is worthwhile within Black theological discourse given its rhetoric of embodiment. It holds great potential regarding a proper recognition of the erotic as an important paradigm shift. How does one open theologically to this recognition of the erotic within a social context and religious environment opposed to it? How does one affect such a paradigm shift? But first, on a more fundamental level, what is the paradigm currently in place within Black theological discourse?

Black theological discourse has been premised on the workings of imagination. By this I mean it is based on a type of wishful thinking supported by activism within the confines of the existing social order. It is the thinking up of new life options, but within the general confines of the "establishment." It involves the same process as the dream of winning the lottery within the confines of the capitalist system: what would you do with one hundred million dollars, regulated by the established late capitalism rules of the game? Imagining so conceived entails the abstract exercise of re-envisioning a world of healthy life options, but done without a radical break with the fundamental elements of order.

Nonetheless, imagination within the context of Black theology is a mode of protest in that it seeks to increase the subjectivity of despised bodies. Yet it is a limited and rather weak form of protest in that it leaves too many of the existing restraints on human potentiality in place. The imaginary proclaimed by Black theology critiques the "real" promoted by existing social systems but it is only able to step but so far outside the established matrix of the status quo. I am not implying that imagination is a limiting form of protest because it does not achieve it ends. No, I suggest it is a limited because it is able to posit only a rather safe range of new possibilities because, for the purposes of this essay, it cannot perceive the movement of erotic realities.

Although Charles Long does not make use of the same language, it strikes me that his critique of theology—"an explicitly theological apologetic tradition"—as a method for studying Black religion high-lights a concern similar to my lament of Black theology's limited vision. I suggest that Black theological discourse up to this point has involved a paradigm of imagination, which does not allow for creative movements that challenge on a fundamental level-social entrapments of Black bodies. The apologetic tradition Long identifies in Black theo-logical discourse leads "to a narrowness of understanding and the fail-ure to perceive certain creative possibilities," due to a rather static notion of human experience and interaction. The "normative frame-work of Christian theology" that marks Black theological discourse is indebted to certain religious and social sensibilities that are not neces-sarily amenable to the re-framing of Black bodies in relationship.[35] Furthermore, this apologetic preoccupation is incapable of appreciat-ing (or even recognizing) the full range of Black experiences, and this oversight is particularly telling with respect to the erotic as modality of relationship in the Tillichian sense. What Long labels the apologetic tradition paradigm I would call, for the purpose of this project, the paradigm of imagination.

To imagine is to work one's passive will within a context which maintains something of the survival impulse. It is to be shadowed by the meta-narrative of the dominant social structure. Imagination, all things considered, is a rather polite mode of re-envisioning in that it does not call into question the elemental nature of the grammar of dis-course. It is a rumbling within the social matrix that fails to challenge its basic design and intent because such disturbances do not radically compromise intent of the social matrix. These disturbances simply cre-ate acceptable alternatives within the framework of the social order. Put yet another way, imagination as the agent of liberation does not call into fundamental question the essential "realness" of the reality promoted by the dominant social system. It may rebel against certain aspects of it (e.g., racism, sexism, classism), but it fails to cause the type of damage to the social system that does more than necessitate a change in its symbol system. Imagination is important, but it is not the stuff by which relationships are examined and reconceived in ways that pose long lasting damage to things as they have been.

The Fantasy Paradigm as Corrective

Where imagination falls short, fantasy provides new possibilities for appreciating a fuller notion of relationship, one that can easily incor-porate the erotic realities of life. But fantasy is despised.

I would like to offer an example of the manner in which theological discourse and religious practice despise the fantastic and also the ways in which an embrace of the fantastic, in spite of this negative response, might be a way of "saving" theological discourse from itself. I also see this example as an opportunity to demonstrate the manner in which the paradigm of fantasy—with its hermeneutic and mode of practice—can uncover the importance of the indecent and utilize the irreverent to forge more life affirming modalities of erotic realities.

I seek to put the paradigm of fantasy to speculative use by providing a positive reconstruction of a particular scriptural legend in light of it. Mindful of social restrictions on relationship and interaction that mark the contemporary and ancient worlds, scripture cannot be taken as is.[36] Feminist and Womanist scholars have already demonstrated problematic dimensions of the biblical text and the ancient world.[37] Hence, we know scripture must be reassessed in opposition to codes of conduct and constructions of meaning that seek to stifle self-image and self in relationship. The theological and religious import of scripture must be re-thought, and I suggest this be done in light of fantasy, and its bearing on the erotic. As the criterion for this reevaluation of scripture, and this is important, I make use of erotic realities, as defined above, as the normative ground of complex and rich relationships and interactions as fundamental to human life in freedom. By using this criterion, within the context of a heuristic exercise, I seek to note the importance of the liberation emphasis of traditional Black theology, but use the erotic to also extend this norm of liberation beyond its present relational boundaries.

The legend I have in mind involves the briefly mentioned but strongly despised figure in Genesis—Nimrod (Genesis 10:8–15; 11:1–9).[38]

After the great flood that destroyed all but a remnant of humanity, and after the presentation of the table of nations, comes the awkward mention of Nimrod and the "cultural legend"[39] of the tower of Babel. This legend does not provide a great deal of substantive information concerning Nimrod and, as is the case with legends, it has been handled and mishandled by countless interpreters but without losing its negative impact.[40] Readers know that he is the descendent of Ham, with all the commonly imposed "dark" connotations of such a connection to the person who faced Noah's wrath: "Nimrod was black: his grandfather Ham was the first Negro; his father Cush was the ancestor of Ethiopians; he personifies human nature's darker side."[41] As Stephen Haynes notes, Nimrod—"savage rebellion personified"[42]—was often linked with Ham in pro-slavery theological discourse in order to maintain the dehumanization of African Americans. For instance, according to Josiah Priest, an antebellum pro-slavery thinker, Nimrod's kingdom and proposed tower were meant to stifle the divinely ordained servitude of Blacks to whites.[43] Beyond the period of slavery, Nimrod served as a consistent scriptural/theological reminder that segregation (i.e., dispersing of groups) is God's way and rebellion by African Americans (the children of Nimrod) must be controlled as a part of social order and religious commitment.[44]

The depiction of Nimrod as outside the will of God (and we can assume the accepted social order) is enhanced by his alleged possession of the clothing worn by Adam and Eve upon their expulsion from the Garden. While these items gave Nimrod, the legend goes, unusual abilities, they are also articles of clothing connoting shame and disregard, the great sin of the original two.[45] Although possession of these garments does not constitute Nimrod's crime, they serve as a symbol of his dangerous ambitions and desires. And so, for religious traditions that make use of this scripture, he is consistently portrayed as "the greatest sinner since the Flood," although a more positive assessment is possible based on sources that present Nimrod as opposed to the tower.[46] An example of this positive assessment comes from a pamphlet by African American minister Harvey Johnson (Union Baptist Church, Baltimore). In 1889, Johnson argued that Nimrod's success with respect to political development as the first great king, combined with his achievement in the area of architecture, point to the merits and capabilities of those of African descent, the children of Nimrod. It is in the location of his kingdom, "in the valleys, and along the river banks, such as the Tigris, Euphrates and Nile; and the great Shinar valley, where the first kingdom was formed, and the first king, Nimrod, the grandson of Ham, reigned. Yes, it was here that man began to distinguish himself in the arts and sciences of government and architecture, by the building of the city and tower of Babel; this is admitted by all."[47] Johnson provides a favorable assessment of Nimrod, but within the confines of the established social structure—its rules and regulations. For example, he does not bring into question the rules of the social system; he simply seeks to make room for African Americans through a glowing commentary on Nimrod. Even so, the positive assessment is not the dominant reading.

It is stated in Genesis 10:8–10 that Nimrod is a great hunter. Some scholars say of wild game, others, including several of the church patriarchs, claim him to be a hunter against God who despises God and seeks to destroy humanity through the Tower of Babel.[48] This information, his political and social talents (Genesis 9–14), is important and serves to frame the larger legend. In fact, "the great success that attended all of Nimrod's undertakings produced a sinister effect. Men no longer trusted in God, but rather in their own prowess and ability, an attitude to which Nimrod tried to convert the whole world."[49] From Rabbinic commentary, through various generations of Christian commentary, Nimrod's infamy intensified. He went from being "a paragon of unrighteousness" to the personification of satanic will and influence, one who seeks to destroy the religion and people of God through excessive attention to sensual realities and human pleasure.[50] His assumed rebellion would become a marker for all forms of social destruction.

Whether the story is a referent to Babylon and whether Nimrod is a composite of cultural hero or a deity is of little importance here in that such considerations have not effected the meaning of the story for Christian communities.[51] As biblical scholar Hermann Gunkel notes, "the name of the city, which was to have brought humanity fame and honor, became its disgrace and shame. Whenever one hears the name 'Babel' one simultaneously hears of the insolence and shame of ancient humanity."[52] Legends speak to community values and concerns, and this one in particular sought to answer questions concerning the "origins of current differences in language and dwelling places" for humanity. The lesson readers are to gather from this story and the commentary surrounding it has remained significant and in the foreground of biblical teachings on humility and regard for what Karl Barth called the infinite and qualitative distinction between God and humanity.

> Then they said, 'Come, let us build ourselves a city, and a tower with its top in the heavens, and let us make a name for ourselves. . . . [53]

Humanity, through the construction of a tower reaching into heaven, sought to secure a "name" or "fame," much to God's displeasure, because God "the Eternal One, alone wants to have an eternal name." God's name "will be remembered from generation to generation," but humanity must fade away with death.[54]

The legend teaches a negative lesson that does not in actuality promote healthly life options: Human ingenuity, creativity, and ambition result in destruction. Common interpretations of Nimrod and the tower of Babel promote at best human imagination in that gains made and advances sought must remain within imposed limits—whether one considers these imposed by God as this ancient legend does, or imposed by the invisible hands of the social system.

This legend and its morality lesson rejects fantasy as irreverent, as an indecent challenge to the established order, and imposes—through the story of dispersal—a limited sense of relationship. Nonetheless, I propose another interpretation based on the significance of fantasy for theological discourse on the nature and meaning of relationship.

The confusing of languages by which God ends communal construction seeks to void fantasy by placing restrictions on articulation of reality, reducing the ability to shape life and celebrate meaning. God's response to human desire for relationship and meaning is to impose social structures that prohibit growth and unity. In juxtaposition to Nimrod, readers encounter a God who is involved in the affairs of humans, but "almost afraid of the growing might of humanity."[55] God's response is to frustrate human activity and thereby tame human self-importance:

> And the Lord said, "Look, they are one people, and they have all one language; and this is only the beginning of what they will do; nothing that they propose to do will now be impossible for them. Come, let us go down, and confuse their language there, so that they will not understand one another's speech." So the Lord scattered them abroad from there over the face of all the earth, and they left of building the city.[56]

It is precisely this challenge to the established order that is of value because it extends the capacity of humanity to make meaning through an expansion of what it means to be in relationship. Community, a beneficial arrangement, from the perspective of the social structure (in scripture established by God) is despised to some degree. The oppressive manner of this restriction is more keenly felt when one is mindful of pro-slavery theological discourses utilization of Nimrod's punishment for seeking to keep people unified—together—as grounds for enslavement of Africans and their social segregation.

Through a movement from the restrictive paradigm of imagination to the irreverence of fantasy new possibilities for living emerge. It becomes clear that existing social structures (including certain notions of divinity and divine will) seek to artificially limit human creativity and connectedness through a denial of relationships that threaten the system. Social arrangements—not Nimrod's actions—are problematic. This is certainly one way to read the following statement concerning the impetus for the tower's construction:

> With the spread of mankind corruption increased. While Noah was still alive, the descendants of Shem, Ham, and Japheth appointed princes over each of the three groups—Nimrod for the descendants of

Ham. . . . Ten years before Noah's death, the number of those subject to the three princes amounted to millions. When this great concourse of men came to Babylonia upon their journeyings, they said to one another: 'Behold, the time is coming when, at the end of days, neighbor will be separated from neighbor, and brother from brother, and one will carry on war against the other. Go to, let us build us a city, and a tower. . . . [57]

Imagination involves certain arrangements of relationships, a recognition of which modalities of interaction are worthy and which are damaging. Fantasy involves a rupturing of existing standards as they relate to relationship and in this way it opens toward opportunity to embrace what was once despised. Fantasy within this context means the push against relationships and interactions—against normative structures of being and meaning—in the form of an impulse toward the subversive. That is to say, fantasy entails "trac[ing] the unsaid and the unseen of culture: that which has been silenced, made invisible, covered over and made 'absent'" by which an attempt is made to "realize desire, to make visible the invisible and to discover absence."[58]

This process is not limited to the political aggressiveness that marks much of Black theological discourse. Fantasy includes this concern with political developments, but it is not defined by this interest. Its target is "dominant hierarchical systems" more broadly conceived.[59] Fantasy involves a concern with an opening of new possibilities of meaning through an embrace of modalities of relationship (only some of which involve sex[ual] gratification) over against socially normative claims against them. In a sense, it can be said to point "to the edges of the 'real'," if the real is understood as the socially sanctioned modalities of relationship as meaning. So conceived, fantasy bears important ontological and epistemological weight because it refocuses and reshapes what it means to be.[60] Fantasy entails a lifting of "life" layers to expose modalities of being (in relationship) that the normative social narrative seeks to hide.[61]

Distinguishing the Truly Fantastic

I am not the first to recognize fantasy as a worthy subject of theological inquiry. Theologian Harvey Cox, for example, gave attention to both feast and fantasy in his text *The Feast of Fools: A Theological Essay on Festivity and Fantasy*.[62] We, however, operate based on differing notions of the fantastic. Cox laments the manner in which, as of the late 1960s, the fantastic has actually become "predictable and politically impotent" and thereby incapable of inspiring "genuine social transformation."[63] Mindful of this, I label what Cox refers to as imagination and not fantasy. First, the fantastic as I understand it is concerned with more fundamental social structures that include the sociopolitical but are not limited to it. On the other hand, imagination involves the limitations he laments in that it is restricted to the modalities of relationship presented by the social system and can therefore only act as reaction within the context of these restrictions. Furthermore, Cox understands fantasy as being "advanced imagining" whereas I see it as a radically different process.[64]

Even when Cox acknowledges a rebirth, so to speak, of the fantastic, the manner in which he seeks to provide "radically alternative life situations" does not have the scope I understand the fantastic to entail.[65] In a word, Cox's version of the fantastic is not as indecent as mine.

I agree with Cox that fantasy involves "the riches sources of human creativity," but I disagree on the range of that creativity and the manner in which it is in essence irreverent.[66] He sees fantasy constituting a new take on history, the constructing of new selves with new realities within the context of history. I see fantasy as bringing history into fundamental question, destroying history by toppling the social structures and relational possibilities that frame it. By way of illustration, the manner in which Pop Art, for example, raised questions concerning the fundamental nature and meaning of art, fantasy raises a challenge to the nature and scope of relationship.[67]

Cox sees Christian liturgy as being capable of housing the fantastic whereas I do not see this as the case.[68] Fantasy cannot be fully borne out in existing rituals because these rituals are confined to existing social arrangements and sensibilities. Social structures by their very nature do not "facilitate freedom."[69] In fact, the fantastic calls into question many of the basic assumptions of the Christian faith's sense of relationship. Unlike Cox, I see no connection between fantasy and mediation, for example. From the perspective of Christian faith and its liturgy as currently presented, the fantastic is indecent. Fantasy does not involve work to occupy the terrain taken from fallen social lies. It does not seek to merely impose new boundaries; rather, it confronts "a culture with that which it cannot stand, possibilities of alternate universes. . . . Thereby it explores the limits of civilization, decomposes humanist and religious sanctions, concerning what is 'proper', 'decent', and 'acceptable. It invites the individual to trespass. . . . ' "[70]

In more general terms, it "reveals that which must be concealed so that one's internal and external experience may be comfortably known, so that one may get along day-to-day in the communal world. . . . The fantastic confronts civilization with the many faces it must repress in order for it to remain whole, functioning, and successful."[71] Hence, the fantastic is not important because it fits the faith, but rather because it poses fundamental challenges to the notions of relationship and meaning that the faith embraces to the determent of its followers.

Cox sees fantasy as beneficial in that it can result in the restructuring of life options, with positive political consequences. Theologian Sallie McFague has the opposite view: Fantasy is detrimental to transformation of attitudes and circumstances. She argues that the development of a proper relationship with nature entails in part the development of a "loving eye" whereby we pay "attention to another person or thing" in healthy ways. Such a stance, however, requires the ability to "pay attention to individuals in all their particularity: we look at a sunset, a building, even another person simply to appreciate them in their difference and detail" made possible through "aesthetic distance."[72] According to McFague what often prevents us from forming an "aesthetic distance" is fantasy, which involves concern with our "own wishes." In this respect, fantasy is unable to do the heavy work involved in reconstructing relationship with nature in that it is preoccupied with the wishes and interests of the individual. It does not transform situations in that it allows for an unusual distance from others, a safe space in which to simply project our own desires.

It strikes me in both the case of Cox and of McFague that the difference in their perspectives on fantasy and mine revolves around their closeness to Samual Taylor Coleridge's perspective on what he labels fancy and my interest in a more existentialist notion of fantasy as rebellious—particularly when coupled with the existentialists concern with subjectivity as the essential concern prior to the emergence of social structures and regulations.[73] I agree with Coleridge that imagination and fantasy are different faculties. Imagination (composed of primary and secondary imagination) is connected to perception and as a result has great importance. Fancy, on the other hand, lacks the creative element implicit in perception—"as a repetition in the finite mind of the eternal act of creation"—in that it involves only non-contextual memory.[74]

For Coleridge imagination is vital, but fancy is not. Both operate within human life, but only the former is a "higher intellectual power." The content of fancy is made available through what the imagination has accomplished, yet fancy is incapable of remaking these memories.[75] Such an understanding of fancy easily lends itself for constructive and liberation theologians to a perspective on fantasy as having limited transformative muscle. McFague seems to hold such an opinion and moves on to replace fantasy with perception. But what McFague disregards is neither imagination nor fantasy but at best an inactive hopefulness and at worse it is what must liberation theologians condemn—a pernicious modality of voyeurism by which the predicament of others is "experienced" from a safe distance through which the relationship between the two—the observed and the observer—remains essentially the same. It, fantasy, demands a subjectivity that can be denied by imagination.

Finally, through the process of fantasy as a corrective to Black theological discourse it becomes possible to appreciate a more complex web of relationships in that fantasy gives high regard to what has been traditionally despised, including erotic realities. Not only will this new paradigm serve as a corrective for warped notions of relationship that render sexism, homophobia, and heterosexism normative stances, it, more importantly, pushes toward a more fundamental appreciation for relationships as an act of profound love, an act that ties together in beautifully indecent ways a variety of possibilities for interaction. It is in this way, and only in this way, that Black theological discourse can speak a word of transformation and provide a vision for the meaning of life that is not bound by the dangerously restrictive codes of relationship this discourse actually seeks to dismantle. In this sense it is "good" to be "bad."

Notes

1. Lisa Isherwood and Elizabeth Stuart, *Introducing Body Theology* (Sheffield, England: Sheffield Academic Press, 1998), 15.
2. This brief definition of religion relates to and extends with respect to the dread/terror of warped sex(uality) the notion of religion I provide in *Terror and Triumph: The Nature of Black Religion* (Minneapolis: Fortress Press, 2003). I continue to hold to religion as the quest for complex subjectivity over against efforts to dehumanize, and in this essay I argue that warped sex(uality), a denial of erotic realities is a component of the dehumanization religion at its best seeks to undo.
3. I use sex(ual) and sex(uality) as a way of highlighting a duality of meaning and interconnectedness between sex and sexuality, the latter defined as extending "beyond our physicality to encompass all of the ways in which the physical is rendered meaningful." See "Introduction," in *Religion and Sexuality in*

Cross-cultural Perspective, ed. Stephen Ellingson and M. Christian Green (New York: Routledge, 2002), 2.

4. This phrase is drawn from Lisa Isherwood and Elizabeth Stuart, *Introducing Body Theology* (Sheffield, England: Sheffield Academic Press, 1998), 32.

5. James H. Evans, Jr., *We Have Been Believers: An African American Systematic Theology* (Minneapolis: Fortress Press, 1992), 70; James H. Cone, *A Black Theology of Liberation*, second edition (Maryknoll, NY: Orbis Books, 1986), 66. This love, however, does not mean acceptance of humanity without attention to the demands of justice; theological order requires a creative tension between love and justice. As Martin Luther King, Jr., rightly noted, without justice, love is weak and without love, justice is harsh and without mercy. It is this fellowship with God that allows humans, in turn, to initiate and sustain proper relationship with self and with other the created order.

6. James Evans, Jr., *We Have Been Believers*, 70.

7. James H. Cone, *Black Theology & Black Power*, 20th Anniversary Edition (New York: Harper & Row, Publishers, 1989), 53.

8. Sharon D. Welch, *A Feminist Ethic of Risk* (Minneapolis: Fortress Press, 2000), 180.

9. Cone, *A Black Theology of Liberation*, 70.

10. Cone, *A Black Theology of Liberation*, 71.

11. Alice Walker, *In Search of Our Mothers' Gardens* (San Diego: Harcourt Brace Jovanovich, 1983).

12. For a debate on this point see Cheryl Sanders, "Christian Ethics and Theology in Womanist Perspective," *Journal of Feminist Studies in Religion* 5, no. 2 (Fall 1989).

13. Karen Baker-Fletcher, *Sisters of Dust, Sisters of Spirit: Womanist Wordings on God and Creation* (Minneapolis: Fortress Press, 1998), 113.

14. Karen Baker-Fletcher, *Sisters of Dust, Sisters of Spirit*, 121–122.

15. Renée Leslie Hill, "Disrupted/Disruptive Movements: Black Theology and Black Power 1969/1999" in *Black Faith and Public Talk: Critical Essays on James H. Cone's Black Theology & Black Power*, ed. Dwight N. Hopkins (Maryknoll, NY: Orbis Books, 1999), 138.

16. See Kelly Brown Douglas, *Sexuality and the Black Church: A Womanist Perspective* (Maryknoll, NY: Orbis Books, 2002).

17. Hill, "Disrupted/Disruptive Movements: Black Theology and Black Power 1969/1999" in *Black Faith and Public Talk: Critical Essays on James H. Cone's Black Theology & Black Power*, ed. Hopkins, 144–145.

18. Marcella Althasu-Reid, *Indecent Theology: Theological Perversions in Sex, Gender and Politics* (New York: Routledge, 2000), 28.

19. Althasu-Reid, *Indecent Theology*, 88; See Alexander C. Irwin, *E.R.O.S Toward the World: Paul Tillich and the Theology of the Erotic* (Minneapolis: Fortress Press, 1991).

20. Alexander C. Irwin, *E.R.O.S Toward the World: Paul Tillich and the Theology of the Erotic* (Minneapolis: Fortress Press, 1991), 1, 5, 6.

21. Feminist scholars have provided a great deal of important work that unpacks the manner in which sex(uality) has served as a tool for the maintenance of patriarchy and other modalities of oppression; nonetheless, sex(uality) can be

taken back, celebrated. Black theological reflection must take seriously this work and incorporate its insights and challenges into its work. See for example Carole S. Vance, *Pleasure and Danger: Exploring Female Sexuality* (Boston: Routledge & Kegan Paul, 1984).

22. In not wanting to limit the erotic to sexual pleasure, I am in agreement with much of the work done by feminist scholars. However, I am also unwilling to limit the erotic to its political and economic dimensions as well.

23. Alexander C. Irwin, *E.R.O.S Toward the World: Paul Tillich and the Theology of the Erotic* (Minneapolis: Fortress Press, 1991), 12.

24. Paul Tillich, *Love, Power, Justice,* 22, 30 in *E.R.O.S Toward the World: Paul Tillich and the Theology of the Erotic,* ed. Irwin, 12.

25. Paul Tillich, *Love, Power, and Justice: Ontological Analyses and Ethical Applications* (New York: Oxford Unviersity Press, 1954), 116–117.

26. Irwin, *E.R.O.S Toward the World,* 28.

27. Alexander Irwin argues that feminist and womanist theologians have embraced the importance of eros. However, his text does not actually support this claim with respect to womanist theology. Rather he makes a rather convincing argument for thinking of African American literature by figures such as Alice Walker as committed to a healthy notion of the erotic.

28. Althasu-Reid, *Indecent Theology,* 22. I am indebted to Althasu-Reid for her insights into the political/theological nature of terms such as decency, indeceny, and irreverence.

29. Alexander C. Irwin, *E.R.O.S Toward the World: Paul Tillich and the Theology of the Erotic* (Minneapolis: Fortress Press, 1991), 89.

30. Marcella Althaus-Reid, *Indecent Theology: Theological Perversions in Sex, Gender and Politics* (New York: Routledge, 2000), 4.

31. Isherwood and Stuart, *Introducing Body Theology,* 99.

32. James B. Nelson, *Body Theology* (Louisville, KY: Westminster/John Knox Press, 1992), 41, 42–43.

33. One must be careful, however, to avoid slipping back into dualism premised on the body and the non-body. It is also vital to recognize that the body does not serve as a "pure" source of information because the body, as Mary Douglas notes, must also be understood as a construct, a creation that mirrors the social system. The body does provide knowledge, information on the worlds we hold dear; yet, this knowledge must still be approached critically. Religion denies this knowledge, although it should house the information regarding the body's struggle against dehumanization including the warping of sex(uality).

34. Isherwood and Stuart, *Introducing Body Theology,* 28.

35. Charles H. Long, *Significations: Signs, Symbols, and Images in the Interpretation of Religion* (Philadelphia: Fortress Press, 1986), 173–174.

36. What I present here is just a preliminary sketch, and more work is certainly need. In future projects related to the theme discussed in this section of the essay, the work of scholars such as Elisabeth Schüssler Fiorenza and Rosemary Radford Ruether will be useful resources.

37. See for example Elisabeth Schüssler Fiorenza, *In Memory of Her: A Feminist Theological Reconstruction of Christian Origins* (New York: Crossroad,

1987); *Bread Not Stone: The Challenge of Feminist Biblical Interpretation* (Boston: Beacon Press, 1984); Delores Williams, *Sisters in the Wilderness: The Challenge of Womanist God-Talk* (Maryknoll, NY: Orbis Books, 1993).

38. If the story of Ham required the work of a new hermeneutic of suspicion, the story of Nimrod requires re-theologizing based on erotic realities and the process of fantasy as ground for healthy relationship and interaction.

The story of Nimrod is a rich narrative, one I have also used to frame the nature of African American humanism. See *Africian American Humanist Principles: Living and Thinking Like the Children of Nimrod* (New York: Palgrave Macmillan, forthcoming). I am grateful to three colleagues, Calvin Roetzel, Allen Callahan, and Matthias Henze for their assistance with my thinking on Nimrod.

39. Hermann Gunkel, *Genesis, translated and interpreted by Hermann Gunkel* (Macon, GA: Mercer University Press, 1997), xiv.

40. Gunkel, *Genesis, translated and interpreted by Hermann Gunkel*, xxvi–xxvii.

41. Stephen R. Haynes, *Noah's Curse: The Biblical Justification of American Slavery* (NY: Oxford University Press, 2002), 61.

42. Haynes, *Noah's Curse*, 10.

43. Haynes, *Noah's Curse*, 107.

44. Such a move also requires critique of the misguided analysis offered by African Americans such as James W. C. Pennington, who also saw Nimrod as marked by rebellion and rejection of proper religion (and one can assume social sensibilities and structures), and attempted through critique of Nimrod to better position African Americans within the existing social system. Social Gospeler Reverdy C. Ransom gives a sermon in which uncritical attention is given to the Tower of Babel and the confusion of language as metaphor. See "Thanksgiving Sermon: The American Tower of Babel; or, The Confusion of Tongues," in *Making the Gospel Plain: The Writings of Bishop Reverdy C. Ransom*, ed. Anthony B. Pinn (Harrisburg, PA: Trinity Press International, 1999), 102–111.

45. Louis Ginzberg, *The Legends of the Jews, I: Bible Times and Characters from the Creation to Jacob*, translated from the German manuscript by Henrietta Szold (Philadelphia: The Jewish Publication Society of America, 1909), 177.

46. *The Anchor Bible*, Genesis: A New Translation with introduction and commentary by E. A. Speiser (New York: Doubleday, 1962), 1117.

47. Harvey Johnson, The Hamite (Baltimore: J. F. Weishampel, 1889), 66. Found at: <http:lcweb2.loc.gov/cgi-bin/query/r?ammem/murray:@field(FLD001+ 91898142+):@@@&REF$

48. Haynes, *Noah's Curse*, 46.

49. Ginzberg, *The Legends of the Jews, I*, 178.

50. Haynes, *Noah's Curse*, 45–61.

51. For useful information on such topics see E. A. Spesier, *Oriental and Biblical Studies: Collected Writings of E. A. Speiser*, edited with an introduction by J. J. Finkelstein and Moshe Greenberg (Philadelphia: University of Pennsylvania Press, 1967), 41–61.

52. Gunkel, *Genesis, translated and interpreted by Hermann Gunkel*, 97.

53. Genesis 11:4 (Revised Standard Version).

54. Gunkel, *Genesis, translated and interpreted by Hermann Gunkel*, 96.
55. *Genesis, translated and interpreted by Hermann Gunkel*, xii.
56. Genesis 11:6–8 (Revised Standard Version).
57. Ginzberg, *The Legends of the Jews*, I, 175.
58. Rosemary Jackson, *Fantasy: The Literature of Subversion* (New York: Methuen, 1981), 4.
59. Jackson, *Fantasy: The Literature of Subversion*, 4.
60. Jackson, *Fantasy: The Literature of Subversion*, 23.
61. For information on my understanding of archaeology see *Varieties of African American Religious Experience* (Minneapolis: Fortress Press), chapter five.
62. Harvey Cox, *The Feast of Fools: A Theological Essay on Festivity and Fantasy* (Cambridge: Harvard University Press, 1969).
63. Cox, *The Feast of Fools*, 4.
64. Cox, *The Feast of Fools*, 62.
65. Cox, *The Feast of Fools*, 7.
66. Cox, *The Feast of Fools*, 59.
67. There are ways in which Pop Art transforms art into philosophy through the forcing of this question: What is art? It also brings an end to history in a certain sense. I am indebted to Arthur Danto's philosophy of art for this take on Pop Art, particularly: Arthur C. Danto, *Philosophizing Art: Selected Essays* (Berkeley: University of California Press, 1999); *After the End of Art: Contemporary Art and the Pale of History* (Princeton: Princeton University Press, 1997). Readers interested in more information concerning my use of Danto's philosophy of art should see *Terror and Triumph: The Nature of Black Religion* (Minneapolis: Fortress Press, 2003), chapters 7–8.
68. Cox, *The Feast of Fools*, 68–79.
69. Cox, *The Feast of Fools*, 78.
70. Lance Olsen, *Ellipse of Uncertainty: An Introduction to Postmodern Fantasy* (Westport, CT: Greenwood Press, 1987), 22.
71. Olsen, *Ellipse of Uncertainty*, 22.
72. Sallie McFague, *Super Natural Christians: How We Should Love Nature* (Minneapolis: Fortress Press, 1997), 112–114.
73. Jean-Paul Sartre, *Existentialism and Human Emotions* (New York: The Wisdom Library, 1957), 17.
74. Samuel Taylor Coleridge, *The Collected Works of Samual Taylor Coleridge, Biographia Literaria or Biographical Sketches of My Literary Life and Opinions*, I, edited by James Engell and W. Jackson Bate (Princeton: Princeton University Press, 1983), 304, 305.
75. I. A. Richards, *Coleridge on Imagination* (London: Kegan Paul, Trench, Trubner & Co. LTD., 1934), 75.

10

The Construction of the Black Male Body: Eroticism and Religion

Dwight N. Hopkins

Like the pounding blows of a steam hammer, devastating images of the African American male body repeatedly hit the U. S. public's psychic during the end of the 1990s. Recurring themes of sexual lust akin to religious fervor acted as foundational planks in this construction of what it means to be a Black man in America. Yet the stereotypical blueprinting of the African American male identity actually began to intensify at the close of the 1980s, specifically in the 1988 presidential campaign. Indeed, we will see that the American Black male body, individual and corporate, is defined by eroticism and religion.[1]

Triangle of Desire

The 1988 presidential elections pitted the Republican George Bush against the Democrat Michael Dukakis. Hoping to ensure a victory in the Fall elections, Bush drew on a tried and true formula from the U. S. cultural matrix and psychological reflex. In a vicious attack media advertisement, which proved quite successful, Bush drew heavily on then Massachusetts Governor Dukakis' apparent record of being soft on crime. The state of Massachusetts, under the governor's leadership, had released African American Willie Horton, who, during his furlough, was convicted of raping a white woman. With this lurid case, Bush launched a national crusade to discredit Dukakis as a wimp regarding law and order. The image of Bush, the white patriarch, defending the sanctity and purity of the innocent, American white female citizen from the rapacious copulating appetite of the out-of-control,

Black brute criminal saturated the air waves. If not the decisive nail in the proverbial coffin of Dukakis' failed bid for the White House, this compelling story line of sex, sanctity, and race at least added to Bush's victory in November.[2]

The following year, a pregnant white Bostonian female, Carol Stuart, died from a gunshot blast. Her baby expired also after a Caesarean section. White male Charles Stuart, the husband, claimed that this double homicide as well as his gunshot wound had been inflicted by an overpowering Black man. The state authorities apprehended at least three African American men in the process of discovering which Black male in Massachusetts had committed such a heinous crime—the violation of innocent, white female motherhood in America.

> Somewhere along the line the narrative failed and Charles Stuart committed suicide. Shortly thereafter, it became clear that he had concocted the ploy in order to kill his wife. Charles had rehearsed the events with his brother, who met the car shortly after the shooting to take away Carol's pocketbook, which also contained Charles's gun. At the end is the corpse of the white family as social construction, the feared result of violation from the "nigger rapist."[3]

These two sensationalized strategies of Bush and Stuart symbolized an ongoing U. S. legacy of the primal archetype drama: white male and Black male protagonists moving through scenes of violence of the Black sexual body, religious-like obligation to defend white female body, and intervention of the white male body, all foregrounded by the erotic. "A common structure, a triangle of desire, unites these cases on a paradigmatic level with the death of Emmet Till. Although each is a variation, the triangle positions Black men and white men as adversaries in a contest over the body of women."[4]

Threshold of the Twenty-First Century

The 1990s exemplified the triangular dynamic with even more force, often clouded over with intimations of erotic pleasure at the expense of Black bodies. For instance, after falsely arresting him, New York City police raped Abner Louima, a Black man, by driving the handle of a toilet plunger up his anus. And what could be considered an ecstatic climax of orgiastic violence, New York City police executed Amodou Diallo, a Black man, with nineteen shots because they feared that this dark male body threatened their safety. (Diallo was actually reaching for his wallet.) The Federal Bureau of Investigation captured on tape District of Columbia Mayor Marion Barry in a hotel room with nonprescription drugs and a woman who was not his wife. The surveillance video suggested that the mayor planned to move in sexually on the woman after consuming the illegal substance. Michael Jackson endured strip-searching and examination of his pubic hair by state authorities who implied that he had sexually molested a child. A group of white male, citizens of Texas lynched James Byrd, Jr., a Black man, by dragging his body from the back of a moving vehicle through the street. Byrd lost his penis in the ordeal. The U. S. Senate's confirmation hearings of Clarence Thomas to the U. S. Supreme Court exhibited white men judging the fate of a Black man in the midst of sexual predator accusations and high-tech lynching charges. (And who will ever forget the television framing of direct shots of Judge Thomas with a white wife on one side and a white male patron senator on the other.)[5] Rap star Tupack Shakur was accused of participating in a gang rape of a female.[6] A jury acquitted O. J. Simpson of murdering blond, blue-eyed Nicole Simpson while doubts persisted about his guilt and prior sexual and emotional domestic violence complaints.[7] Los Angeles police officers repeatedly dealt near-lethal blows on Rodney King's Black body because they sensed he might over power them with brute (erotic?) strength. (King had two prior arrests for domestic abuse.)[8] In fact, one of the terrorist-like officers referred to King as "Gorillas in the Midst." And the judicial courts convicted boxing heavy weight champion, Mike Tyson of date rape and two counts of "deviant sexual conduct."[9]

Despite disparate instances and differing scenarios in the above narratives, what we want to argue is that the "triangle of desire" serves as the overarching backdrop for Black men's American identity in U. S. culture and mentality. Moreover, the *ménage a trois* signifies the intertwining of eroticism and religion in the construction of the Black male body. The United States' obsession with eroticism of the Black corporeal identity is akin to if not actually a religion, revealed in Christianity and the wider U. S. culture.[10]

A Sexualized Beast Body

Conceptually, the Black male body has been constituted from several sources. The Frenchman, Rene Descartes' theoretical reflections on the mind and body separation helped lay the seeds for and, thereby, influenced greatly the eighteenth century European Enlightenment's understanding of a material and immaterial split in what it means to be a human being. In a word, the mind, symbolized by whites in Europe, strove for loftier goals in the human situation, while the body, embodied in Blacks and other darker peoples of the globe, longed for expressions of the carnal. The body's traits mean "passion, biology, the inside, otherness, inertness, unchanging, statis, matter—a more primitive way of being. To the mind is attributed reason, the self, the same, action, movement and intelligence, a more developed way of being or *not* being."[11] In Descartes' *Discourse on Method* (1637, and furthered elaborated on in his *Meditations* 1641), the mind is pure thought, the body mere materiality. The mind can affect the body. The body can only be acted upon by the mind. In this sense, the body becomes an object and a mechanical instrument—a machine.[12] Particularly for Black folk, in this anthropological model, Black body results from external factors and lacks power to think, decide, impact history, or forge a spirituality on its own. The Black body is deficient by nature and creation. The white mind is pure intellect, decision making, or a proactive anthropology. The Black body succumbs to fate; the white mind indulges in freedom.[13] The white mind exhibits rational, calm deliberation. The Black male body, in particular, thrives on raw, animal eroticism.

Descartes' structures of thought have dangerous implications for African American Christians. Despite the sensuousness of play found in Black church worship, most Black Christians attempt, at all costs, to drive the funkiness of the Black body out of its domain. Rarely is the erotic mentioned and, in instances of sex-talk, it becomes prohibition: don't have sex before marriage, don't cheat on one's wife, don't have homosexual sex, don't let sex be your driving force in life, don't look at women's bodies, God sees what you're doing in the bedroom, and so forth.

> We continue to live in Cartesian captivity: the mind–body split thought up by philosopher Descartes flourishes in Black theologies of sexuality. Except it is translated as the split between body and soul. Black Christians have taken sexual refuge in the sort of rigid segregation they sought to escape in the social realm—the body and soul in worship are kept one place, the body and soul in heat are kept somewhere else.[14]

The irony is African American Christians have opposed white Christian racists on grounds that they continue to pit a gospel of spiritual liberation against a gospel of material freedom for Black folk. For example, African American believers oppose white supremacists for telling Blacks to have faith in a theology of "you can have the world, just give me Jesus" while, in the really real world, when Blacks turn toward heaven, whites control earth. Yet, Black Christians then unite with the same theological structures of thought regarding the body–soul bifurcation. Conceptually, the split between body and soul or body and mind fervently preached in too many Black churches implies double trouble for Black believers. First, the church fails to craft a positive theology of eroticism for the Black body (especially the male identity), which helps to drive many Black men away from Christian institutions. Second, the notion of the split perpetuates further the dangerous myth that a theology separating mind and body reinforces religious claims that Black people are "body" people. They embody carnal tastes, nasty sex, and lustful libido. So, Blacks who advocate this split are actually affirming theories about their own bestiality and lasciviousness.

An additional conceptual piece in how religion and eroticism contribute to the making of the Black male body is a prudish theology. Such a religious way of thinking springs from two reactionary ways of believing—self-denial Puritanism and conservative Victorianism. To be pure entails restricting the mind from thinking about body eroticism and, above all, a guilt whipping to prevent engaging in such activities. A Victorian, in this instance, upholds high culture and advanced civilization, both of which contrast radically with the sexual consumption of the peasant masses.

> In sharp contrast to the heat of most Black worship experiences, there emerged almost immediately in Black churches a conservative theology of sexuality. In part, this theology reflected the traditional teachings of white Christianity. Out of moral necessity, however, Black Christians exaggerated white Christianity's version of "p.c."—Puritan Correctness. Later, many Black Christians adopted white Christianity's Victorian repression to rebut the myth of Black sexuality being out of control.[15]

A theology of antagonistic dualism and a theology of prudishism, in the realms of eroticism and religion, undergird the construction of the Black male body. The material and immaterial separation arises from Descartes' narrow, personal experiences. The Victorian accent overcompensates for white Christians' negative depiction of Blacks. The Puritan thrust derives from a European legacy and the biblical Paul.[16]

Finally the idea of the male Black as Beast haunts the triangular interplay of African American male body on (white) female body defended by white male (authority) body. This prominent notion seeks to seduce us in various disguises. But, perhaps in the popular imagination, an old television commercial of National Basketball Association star Patrick Ewing propagandizes a most sensational pornographic portrayal. In this television advertisement, Ewing, then with the New York Knicks, is seen scaling the New York City Empire State Building, itself thrust into the heavens as an emblematic phallus. A blaring echo of King Kong movies is hammered into the viewer's conscious and subconscious mind. With dark skin, flaring nostrils, close-cropped hair, and broad lips, the prostituting portrayal of Ewing strikes a similar pose of the sexual bestiality of the Kong freak. In the King Kong movies, one has an overpowering gorilla from the wilds of Africa brought into civilized New York City; and of the eight to ten million inhabitants, he stalks a blond, blue eyed white female to hold in the palm of his gigantic hand. Could a Black male thing so big actually physically love a white woman without crushing and splitting her open? And, following the predominant American cultural script, it is powerful white men who perceive their sacred crusade to destroy this ugly, Black man-monkey.[17]

Moreover, this religious-like fervor against the erotic Black beast forces the most egregious acts of all American males onto the Black man's body. It is "an established fact that our culture links manhood to terror and power, and that Black men are frequently imaged as the ultimate in hypermasculinity. . . . The cops who beat Rodney King and the jury who acquitted King's assailants openly admitted that the size, shape, and color of his body automatically made him a threat to the officer's safety."[18] Somehow Black men have become a primary cathartic scapegoat for the evils committed by maleness at large.

Benefits of Scapegoating

Scapegoating inevitably entails a sustained and systematic elaboration of an ultimate lie—ultimate in the sense of life and death meaning in particular. To maintain singular focus on African American males as the ultimate center of all American male perversion, one has to comprehensively dress up falsehood with the air of scientific objectivity. But, such scientism or common sense beliefs evade the true notion of erotic insecurity of the dominant male community in the U. S. For, it "is still true, alas, that to be an American Negro male is also to be a kind of walking phallic symbol: which means that one pays, in one's personality, for the sexual insecurities of others."[19] The dominating culture prosecutes and perpetrates insecurities on Black others because of the white tradition's simultaneous fear and fascination, dislike and desire. Yet the push–pull of apparent polar opposites masks a fundamental cornerstone of erotic phobia about the Black other's potential prowess in contrast to a white legacy of self-perceived impotency. There is "probably no greater (no more misleading) body of sexual myths in the world today than those which have proliferated around the figure of the American Negro. This means that he is penalized for the guilty imagination of the white people who invest him with their hates and longings, and is the principal target of their sexual paranoia."[20]

Imaginative scapegoating, therefore, draws together a comprehensive Blackening of the other in order to paint a narrative portrait of common sense metaphor and scientific image. Colorful metaphor conjures up a collation of complex caricatures—sexually aggressive, violent, animalistic. And vibrant image offers visual frames and memorable pictures—primal brute, kinetic sensuality, superhuman genitalia. Is this eroticism (that is, the addiction of focusing on Black male, perverse body) and religiosity (that is, an ultimate life and death fixation) in mainstream construction of the Black body simply about penis size envy and, hence, the notorious need to protect white womanhood?[21]

Perhaps. But the triangle of desire (i.e., Black male body–woman body–white male body) is, as indicated previously, what too many white men fathom and deploy for definite self-serving goals. "With respect to rape, for example, and as the white feminist Andrea Dworkin has observed, white men often employ and invoke the image of the Black male rapist to obscure, deny, or excuse their own participation in this crime."[22] As a result, part of the Black man's burden is to carry a disproportionate load of the legacy of white men's evil sexual acts against white and Black women. To be a male rapist in America translates into being an African American man.

However metaphor and image must have sanction from a more powerful institution in order to convince the broad populace and have transcendent longevity. Enter the state apparatus—which even today is still controlled by a minority of U. S. citizens: powerful white men in executive, judicial, and legislative branches. The U. S. state apparatus originates the concept of Black men raping white women. This idea is not spontaneous. "It does not come from the people, who knew better, who thought nothing of intermarriage until they were penalized for it: this idea comes from the architects of the American state." Similarly the state fosters and manipulates the notion of Black bodies as labor commodities for capitalism. "The idea of Black persons as property, for example, does not come from the mob. It is not a spontaneous idea."[23]

And the (white) state functions in collusion with, if not at the behest of, the small minority of white families who monopolize the majority of the wealth in the U. S.[24] To provide free (under slavery) and cheap (until today) Black labor for white profit and further accumulation of wealth, the state works with the wealthy to evangelize the American public that Black citizens are sensuous commodities. Toward this end, the white republic treated Black folk as less than human and then justified the treatment by grooming the public's mind that Blacks were, in fact, less than human.

For instance: the thirteen colonies' and the U. S. government's support of slavery; the 3/5ths clause in the U. S. Constitution; the government's providing land for white citizens in the Western "frontier"; the federal administration's backing of segregation well into the 1960s; federal, state, and local officials providing pro-wealthy financial policies with a negative impact on the poor comprised disproportionately of African Americans; the state's removal of Black people from their land or housing to make way for wealthy developers, and the state's collaboration with the wealthy elite to divide and conquer Blacks and other minority citizens[25]—all indicate that the humanity of Black folk (and brown, red and yellow peoples) represents a low priority in America . The subordination of African Americans "was not an act of God, it was not done by well-meaning people muddling into something which they didn't understand. It was a deliberate policy hammered into place in order to make money from Black flesh."[26] Furthermore, one could argue persuasively today that the inordinate amount of virile Black men in prison in the twenty-first century results from a deliberate collaboration between monopoly capitalist-related prison industries and local, state, and federal governments. Someone is making billions of dollars from the incarcerated labor of Black male bodies.

Echoes of the Past

The religious concept of sexualized Black beast body (cemented in a theology of antagonistic dualism and a theology of prudishism) did not fall from the sky. A historical legacy has birthed it with white, European Christianity as a prime architect. "The church officially reinforced this entanglement of aesthetics, carnality, and negativity of Blackness at the fifth-century Council of Toledo."[27] White religious men decided that Satan was a monster with a huge penis. Three centuries later, one finds a naked black Devil painted in Europe. Given this genealogy of their Christian European ancestors, it is not totally surprising that when European ethnic groups came to the U. S. and changed their identity into "white" people (against Blacks),[28] white Christianity and the broader U. S. civic religion (that is, white monopolization as a god-complex) enslaved Africans and African Americans.[29] Indeed, white "anxiety about alleged erotic allure of Blacks exploded in America as early as 1662, when the British colony of Virginia passed a law that forbade sexual relations between Black male slaves and white women." The white male rulers of the Virginia colony cited biblical warrant as justification.[30]

During the British colonial (1607–1776) and U. S. slavery (1619–1865) periods, white Christians instituted the castration of the Black male body for at least two reasons. One rationale asserted the necessity of subduing "spirited" Black men accused of raping white women. Another suggested a form of freaky voyeurism among segments of the dominant white population. Castration, here, was "linked to carnal curiosity about the Black male's phallus," a perversion going back to ancient Greek and Roman civilizations.[31]

The Reconstruction era (1865–1877) saw the relative success of former enslaved Blacks stretching into government, civic, and business areas, domains of exclusive monopoly of privileged white men. As a result, lynching of Black men became the order of the day. White Christian terrorists orchestrated beatings and hangings in the Black community. "The closer the black man got to the ballot box, one observer noted, the more he looked like a rapist."[32] Lynching during post-Reconstruction, Jim Crow America became as common as "mom's apple pie." On one Sunday afternoon (the day of Jesus Christ), April 23, 1899, over two thousand white folk congregated and frolicked to witness the lynching of the Black male, Sam Hose. Like the overwhelming amount of cases, no evidence was produced. After chaining Mr. Hose to a tree, "they cut off his ears, fingers, and genitals, and skinned his face. While some in the crowd plunged knives into the victim's flesh . . ." Jubilant participants removed his liver and heart while others broke up his bones. The festive crowd of Christians fought over these precious souvenirs. Crucified on resurrection Sunday, Hose's dying body deteriorated near an adjacent sign declaring "We Must Protect Our Southern Women."[33]

Throughout the South and Midwest, lynching persisted well into the twentieth century. It became a religious ritual signified by both its Sunday occurrences but also by a sense of (white) ethical duty to engage in an American pasttime. White terrorists often held prayer services prior to hangings. Christian fathers and mothers brought their girls and boys along with picnic baskets. Some chartered trains to attend the affair of entertainment. Newspaper reporters flooded the scene and ordinary citizens flashed their kodak cameras. Industrious white men made instant postcards on the spot with white citizens taking pictures beside Black men's castrated bodies, and then having these scenes developed into postcards to send to friends and relatives. White bankers, lawyers, merchants, and landed gentry occupied prime seats.

Yet the accused African American man rarely had had sex with a white woman. As a true motivation, wealthy white men, backed by those who followed them, sought accumulation of more wealth under capitalism. A leading (1916) South Carolina newspaper wrote: Black property "ownership always makes the Negro more assertive, more independent, and the cracker can't stand it."[34]

Black Creativity in Eroticism and Religion

Despite lethal blows in the construction of the Black male body, African American men built creatively the scaffolding for their own self identity. Theirs was a comprehensive crafting of healthy eroticism and positive religiosity in the manufacturing of individual and collective body. In contrast, the larger architecture of American civil religion equated carnality and bestiality with Black manhood. Black men, on the other hand, even with all their own shortcomings, laid the foundations of transcendent meaning within immanent manifestations. In a word, religion took on an ebony body. And this body displayed, acted out, and embraced eroticism. For our purposes of asserting the proactive posture of Black male body construction, the expressions of eroticism and religion follow.

> "Eroticism": The powerful life force within us from which spring desire and creativity and our deepest knowledge of the universe. The life force that flows like an inscrutable tide through all things, linking man to woman, man to man, woman to woman, bird to flower, and flesh to spirit. Our ancestors taught us this in their songs of love, their myths of creation, their celebrations of birth, and their rituals of initiation. Desire. Pleasure. Wholeness.[35]

Eroticism speaks to Black men's identity flooded with a life force in their very bodies. Here, eroticism distances itself from the dominating culture's and oppressive religion's planks in the building of the Black male body. Yes, eroticism includes sex; yet it surpasses sex by situating it within a fluid and broader framework. Eroticism works itself from the inside out. The inside consists of a transcendent life force, an integrated spirituality clinging sensuously to flesh. The flow of the force of life is communal and interactive among human, animal, and plant life, as well as the natural elements. It recognizes its cornerstone as the holy legacy of Black ancestors. Consequently, eroticism is history, knowledge, desire, pleasure, wholeness, and creativity.

And religion means orientation— "orientation in the ultimate sense, that is, how one comes to terms with the ultimate significance of one's place in the world. The Christian faith provided a language for the meaning of religion, but not all the religious meanings of the Black communities were encompassed by the Christian forms of religion." How does the Black male body construct itself to come to terms with the ultimate (that is, the holy, the sacred) in its being, its consciousness, its feelings, and its doing? How does it come from within and overflow itself in experience, rhythms, behaviors, styles, motivations, and intentions?[36] That which is ultimate (in terms of life and death—meaning the sacred) resides in embodiment. It is life force. Religion, therefore, is erotic.

For example, Jesus Christ, in Black Christianity, is body revelation of sacred life force. "Jesus Christ clearly signifies that God loves us not in spite of or apart from our bodies, but that God loves us in our bodies as uniquely embodied creatures."[37] Simultaneously, the blues moan and groan out another revelation of sacred life force. In the blues, physicality and spirituality exist as a dynamic quilting of the life force among Black folk. The folk perceive a powerful "spiritual function of the human body." The sacred and the secular, the divine and human coalesce. "For black people the body is sacred, and they know how to use it in the expression of love."[38]

And so, Black men redesigned the definitions of eroticism and religion to create their own plumbline in Black male body construction. Specifically, a set of building blocks in the positive self forging of the Black male body can be seen in an African American man's reworking of Alice Walker's notion of "womanism."[39] Learning from how Black women have renamed themselves, African American men are renaming a new mode of masculinity.

> "1. From *High John the Conqueror*: A mode of masculinity for Black men who are committed to the liberation and survival whole of Black people. Inspired by a trickster figure in African American folklore also known as Jack who is the human analogue of Brer Rabbit. As a slave, John is a redemptive, transgressive, and resourceful figure who achieves advantages over 'Old Massa' through motherwit, laughter, and song. He lives in the slaves' quarters of plantations and in the conjure root that bears his name.

2. *Also*: A man of courage who routinely 'beats the unbeatable.' A man who laughs at himself and also understands the many uses of laughter. As the hope-bringer, a man who's been 'down so long that down don't bother' him. Unflappable. Responsible, as in: 'Takes care of business' or 'On the case.' Traditionally capable, as in: 'able to make a way out of no way and can hit a straight lick with a crooked stick.' A man of strength possessing confidence and a durable constitution, as in: 'Ain't no hammer in dis lan strikes like mine.' Admirable and honorable, as in: 'You de man.' (Opposite of trifling, jive, half-stepping, irresponsible, player, not serious.)

3. In his youth: mannish. From the Black folk expression of elders to male children: 'You acting mannish,' i.e., like a man. Often referring to bodacious, defiant, willful, and risky behavior, as in: 'He's smelling himself' or 'You trying to be grown.' Evincing a premature interest in adult activities and privileges.

4. Loves the Spirit. Loves men (sexually and/or nonsexually) and the society of men. Loves women (sexually and/or nonsexually) and the society of women. Loves children. Loves his ancestors. Loves difference. Loves creativity, song, and dance. Loves the beautiful/ugly. Loved by others: as in, 'My main man' or 'Show me some love.' Loves movement: as in, 'Gotta highball thru some country.' Loves himself. *Irregardless.*

5. Free, as in 'I ain't worried about that.' Spunky. Crazy but got good sense. Regular. Committed to coalitions, but capable of independent action. Nonviolent, but capable of self-defense. Persevering and enduring, as in 'Keep a-inchin' along lak a po' inch worm.' A man who flourishes in the 'Be class,' as in: '*Be* here when the ruthless man comes and *be* here when he is gone.' Cool.

6. 'A bottom fish,' as in values knowledge, truth, and wisdom. Values process and improvisation. Values collective work and solitude. Values dialogue, listening, and harmony. Values tenderness. Values the strength in feelings and tears. Values freedom and its responsibilities. Values justice. Values peace.

7. A mode of masculinity for Black men who are committed to the abolition of emasculating forms of masculinity; a mode of masculinity for Black men who are committed to the abolition of racism, sexism, homophobia, and other ideological traps."[40]

I would argue that this new mode of Black masculinity is constituted by at least healthy eroticism and empowering religion. We remember that eroticism is pleasurable life force internal to the body; this force draws on history, knowledge, desire, pleasure, wholeness, and creativity. And religion is orientation toward the ultimate in one's life and death. Thus, erotic religion or religious erotic of the Black male body concerns the ultimate living in the body and a spirituality clinging to every dimension of the flesh.

Part 1 of the above definition lifts up the Black male identity as pro-liberation and survival whole of all Black people. The Black male body transcends itself, first of all, by being dedicated to the entire community. This allegiance equals a religious commitment or ultimate faith in the sense of one's life and death calling to be there for the entire extended family and not mainly focus on the individualism of the self. Commitment, faith, and ultimate suggest that part of being an African American male is to put one's Black body on the line for others. The internal life force inspiring this liberation-survival commitment consists of definite attributes; that is, redemption, transgression, and resourcefulness. Moreover, a flesh life force of being present for other bodies enables the new mode of Black masculinity to practice both survival (i.e., to make do within negative structures) and liberation (i.e., to transform radically entire systems and establish new ones).

To follow the life force within toward liberation and survival, furthermore, necessitates courage, part 2 of the definition. Any Black male in America called to put his body on the line against nonintentional (i.e., liberal) and intentional (i.e., conservative) white supremacy is either insane or courageous. By being there, in crisis and out of crisis, the visibly present Black male body helps to engender hope, responsibility, strength, confidence, admiration, and honor.[41]

Part 3 honors the younger generation of Black males. "Mannish" is a term bantered about between father figures and male youth. By seemingly criticizing precocious manhood, the elder male is actually teaching the young about what he is up against when the youth thinks, acts, and has faith like a man. In other words, the older figure is training the younger how to come to terms with the calling of the life force within his Black male body, the spirituality clinging to the throbbing of his flesh. The boy needs to properly comprehend the implications of the sacred legacy of a man's erotic body, especially when "he's smelling himself."[42]

One of the most challenging aspects of the life force–flesh dynamic, for the grooming of young Black males, is confusion about, volatility of, and ambiguity about love. For the flesh to endure the pleasures of a healthy eroticism, it must first embrace the Spirit. This is the ultimate life force already present in the erotic Black body. Love of the Spirit in oneself provides the condition for self body-love and male–male, male–female body love (sexually and non-sexually). It enhances love of the ancestors (i.e., the living dead), the unborn (i.e., those spirits preparing to enter the realm of body flesh), and the children (i.e., the embodiment of ancestral inheritance). The ultimate Spirit love, put differently, fosters a universal love of all humans, plants, animals, and the natural elements. As a foundational plank, Black men must love religiously their own erotic body, "irregardless."[43]

A spirit filled body produces an outward love that sees and treats one's lover as a full independent human being. Referring to Black men in hetero-erotic relations, we perceive deep and broad love in the following.

> The strength of a man isn't in the deep tone of his voice. It's in the gentle words he whispers. The strength of a man isn't in the weight he can lift. It's in the burdens he can carry. The strength of a man isn't in how hard he hits. It's in how tender he touches. The strength of a man isn't in how many women he's loved. It's in how true he can be to one woman.[44]

Building a sacred erotic Black male body with this perspective facilitates an understanding that love precedes sex. Sex, here, is the culmination of an ongoing sensuous body interchange of talking, reliability, and the unsolicited surprise. In a monogamous commitment, foreplay starts with the hug and kiss good-bye as one leaves the home in the morning. "Which was followed up by taking out the trash and dropping her clothes off at the cleaners. The foreplay was continued by the phone call in the middle of the day to see how her day was going, to removing the dinner plates from the kitchen table, and helping the children with their homework." A love of commitment to one's partner and allegiance to the Spirit will naturally lead to Black bodies in spiritualized eroticism of the flesh.[45] This is what it really means for the Black male body to hit the right spot.

Parts 5 and 6 help us to understand that freedom comes from the inside out. In this manner, the Black male body is never a slave. He might be *enslaved*, but still remain free within. Consequently, external chains of slavery don't determine the inner life force of the eroticized body. So he can "be here when the ruthless man comes and be here when he is gone." With this sense of what's in his body, a Black man is free to leave options open from nonviolence to self-defense, from joint work to independent action. And the practice of the "bottom fish" prompts the ethics of dialectical values. That is to say, freedom on the inside allows for a both-and embracing of seemingly polar opposites in the man's thought, talk, and walk.

Finally part 7 instructs us about the abolition of emasculating structures of Black masculinity. To build a Black male body, one has to also repair fundamental fault lines in Black masculine identity. The struggle against white supremacy cannot succeed if Black men (here we mean heterosexual male) construct walls of hierarchy against and exclusion of others who endure similar barriers of oppression in their body lives. The fight against the power of racism and for healthy individual and collective masculine healing will succeed when the humanity of one individual depends on aiding the humanity of others.

"Reading men in the context of race is thus a dialectical intervention: an attempt to understand men at the (construction) site of specific power relations, each relation mediating the reproduction and transformation of another."[46] The new Black male identity helps in the empowerment and health of working-class people, African American women, and Black lesbians and gays. While all African American men endure the sinister, subtle, and shocking cases of white supremacy, Black middle and upper income, heterosexual male bodies occupy a status of privilege vis-a-vis the working class, the poor, women, and lesbians and gays.[47]

And so the Spirit grounded in flesh is a location of different power dynamics. A foundational question is whether the new mode of Black masculinity fosters an equalization of resources and rights among African Americans as well as between the whole of Black people and the dominating society. If we answer "yes," we enlarge our own definitions of who we are and, consequently, destroy emasculating structures. Therefore to struggle for the other as well as the self opens the door to a new type of theology—that is, critical self-reflection on how Spirit dwells in flesh. In other words, the construction of the Black male body with a positive religion and healthy eroticism requires surveying the implications of a theology of eroticism. "We must recover the erotic use of our bodies from the distortions of white racism and the traps of Black exploitation. We must liberate ourselves to embrace the Christian bliss of our Black bodies." And we can quickly add that so-called secular Black spirituality (seen in the creative genius of Marvin Gaye, Prince, Howlin' Wolf, and Lightnin' Hopkins) has already succumbed to the seductive possibilities of the Black male body in music and song.[48] Actually the Saturday night Black love of "oh, yes, baby, I'm yours, baby . . ." is not too far from the Sunday morning church irruptions of "oh, yes, Jesus, I'm yours, Jesus . . . " As long as the body focuses on the sacred life force within, both nighttime and daytime forms of erotic release point to a proactive self-love and self-empowerment.

Notes

1. For an insightful thesis on the global Black body, refer to Radhika Mohanram, *Black Body: women, colonialism, and space* (Minneapolis MN University of Minnesota Press, 1999), chapters 1–2.
2. See Robert Hood's *Begrimed and Black: Christian Traditions on Blacks and Blackness* (Minneapolis, MN: Fortress Press, 1997), xi.
3. George P. Cunningham, "Body Politics: Race, Gender, and the Captive Body," in *Representing Black Men*, ed. Marcellus Blount and George P. Cunningham (New York: Routledge, 1996), 148.
4. Ibid., 134–135. Emmet Till, a 14-year-old Black boy from Chicago visiting relatives in the Delta of Mississippi, was lynched in 1955 by two local white men because they explicitly stated they needed to protect southern white womanhood from Black male sexual predators. Examine Stephen J. Whitfield, *A Death in the Delta: The Story of Emmet Till* (New York: Free Press, 1988), and "Eyes On the Prize: America's Civil Rights Years 1954–1965. 'Awakenings (1954–56)' Series 1 Volume 1."
5. See an excellent analysis of the implications of the Thomas–Hill hearings in Marcia Y. Riggs's *Plenty Good Room: Women Versus Male Power in the Black Church* (Cleveland, OH: Pilgrim Press, 2003), 54–55.
6. Devon W. Carbado, "The Construction of O. J. Simpson as a Racial Victim," in *Black Men on Race, Gender, and Sexuality*, ed. Devon W. Carbado (New York: New York University Press, 1999), 159.
7. Ibid., 172. Toni Morrison deepens this conversation in her edited work, *Racing Justice, En-gendering Power: Essays on Anita Hill, Clarence, and the Construction of Social Reality* (New York: Pantheon Books, 1992).
8. Carbado, op. cit., 159.
9. Examine Michael Awkward's " 'You're Turning Me On': The Boxer, the Beauty Queen, and the Rituals of Gender," in Carbado, op. cit., 129.
10. On the notion of American civic or civil religion, Leroy S. Rouner offers a compelling analysis. For my purposes, I would add race-wealth-gender to his discussion. Compare Leroy S. Rouner, "What Is an American?" in *The Key Reporter/The American Scholar* (www.pbk.org/pubs/keyreporter/spring99/rounder.htm).
11. Mohanram, op. cit., 199.
12. Observe Dalia Judovitz's *The Culture of the Body: genealogies of modernity* (Ann Arbor, MI: The University of Press, 2001), 68–69.
13. See Lewis R. Gordon, *Bad Faith and AntiBlack Racism* (Amherst, NY: Humanity Books, 1999), 101.
14. Michael Eric Dyson, "When You Divide Body and Soul, Problems Multiply: The Black Church and Sex," in *TRAPS: African American Men on Gender and Sexuality*, ed. Rudolph P. Byrd and Beverly Guy-Sheftall (Bloomington, IN: Indiana University Press, 2001), 316–317.

15. Ibid., 313.
16. Though Paul was not among Jesus' twelve disciples and never met Jesus on earth, Paul occupies much more of the Christian Scriptures than Jesus' words. Hence Paul's theology carries a great deal of weight for Black Christians. Furthermore, he believed that Jesus' return to earth was rather imminent and the main thing was to prepare one's soul for the second coming of the Redeemer. So Paul is not known for embracing a positive theology of the body.
17. For other constructions of the Black male body in the U. S. popular culture, refer to Phillip Brian Harper, *Are We Not Men? Masculine Anxiety and the Problem of African–American Identity* (New York: Oxford University Press, 1996).
18. Robin D. G. Kelley, "Confessions of a Nice Negro, or Why I Shaved My Head," in *Speak My Name: Black men on masculinity and the american dream,* ed. Don Belton (Boston, MA: Beacon Press, 1995), 15.
19. James Baldwin, *Price of the Ticket: collected non-fiction 1948–1985* (New York: St. Martin's Press, 1985), 290.
20. Ibid., 273.
21. In his *Constructing the Black Masculine: identity and ideality in African American men's literature and culture* (Durham, NC: Duke University Press, 2002), 32, Maurice O. Wallace argues that "Black men come to embody the inverse picture necessary for the positive self-portrait of white identity." This picture is what he calls an "ideograph for the American propensity to see Black men half-blindly as a blank/Black page onto which the identity theme of American whiteness, with its distinguishing terrors and longings, imprints itself as onto a photographic negative."
22. Ishmael Reed, "Buck Passing: The Media, Black Men, O. J., and the Million Man March," in Carbado, op. cit., 46.
23. Baldwin, op. cit., xix.
24. Regarding the white wealthy minority that control the U. S. and their impact on Black America, refer to Robert L. Allen, *Black Awakening in Capitalist America: An Analytic History* (Garden City, NY: Doubleday & Company, 1969); Manning Marable, *How Capitalism Underdeveloped Black America* (Boston, MA: South End Press, 1983); David Rockefeller, *Memoirs* (New York: Random House, 2002); Nelson W. Aldrich, Jr., *Old Money* (New York: Vintage Books, 1989); Michael Parenti, *Democracy for the Few* (New York: St. Martin's Press, 1977); G. William Domhoff, *Who Rules America Now?* (Englewood Cliffs, NJ: Prentice-Hall, Inc., 1983); Richard C. Edwards, Michael Reich, and Thomas E. Weisskopf, eds. *The Capitalist System* (Englewood Cliffs, NJ: Prentice-Hall, Inc., 1972); David N. Smith, *Who Rules the Universities?* (New York: Monthly Review Press, 1974); Frances Fox Piven & Richard A. Cloward, *The New Class War* (New York: Pantheon Books, 1982); and Felix Greene, *The Enemy: What Every American Should Know About Imperialism* (New York: Vintage Books, 1971).
25. Review Derrick Bell, "The Sexual Diversion: The Black Man/Black Woman Debate in Context," in Carbado, ed., op. cit., 239.
26. Ibid., 328–329.
27. Robert E. Hood, *Begrimed and Black: christian traditions of Blacks and Blackness* (Minneapolis, MN: Fortress Press, 1994), 89.

28. There exists a beginning but vibrant intellectual tradition on the study of how European ethnic and tribal groups became "white" once they left their ancestors' continent and came to the land of the Native Americans (e.g., now the United States). For instance, see Thomas K. Nakayama and Judith N. Martin, eds. *Whiteness: The Communication of Social Identity* (Thousand Oaks, CA: Sage Publications, 1999); Joel Kovel, *White* Racism: A Psychohistory (New York: Columbia University Press, 1984); Birgit Brander Rasmussen, Eric Klineberg, Irene J. Nexica, and Matt Wray, eds. *The Making and Unmaking of Whiteness* (Durham, NC: Duke University Press, 2001); Richard Delgado and Jean Stefanici, eds. *Critical White Studies: Looking Behind the Mirror* (Philadelphia, PA: Temple University Press, 1997); Mike Hill, ed. *Whiteness: A Critical Reader* (New York: New York University Press, 1997); Matthew Frye Jacobson, *Whiteness of a Different Color: European Immigrants and the Alchemy of Race* (Cambridge, MA: Harvard University Press, 1998); and Theodore W. Allen, *The Invention of the White Race: Racial Oppression and Social Control, volume one* (New York: Verso, 1994).

29. See Dwight N. Hopkins, *Down, Up & Over: slave religion and Black theology* (Minneapolis, MN: Fortress Press, 1999).

30. Hood, op. cit., x.

31. Ibid., 150–151.

32. Leon F. Witwack, "Hellhounds," in *Without Sanctuary: Lynching Photographs in America* (no editor cited) (Santa Fe, NM: Twin Palms Publishers, 2000), 30.

33. Ibid., 9–10.

34. Ibid., 28. Also examine Don Belton, "Introduction," in *Speak My Name: Black men on masculinity and the american dream*, ed. Don Belton (Boston, MA: Beacon Press, 1995), 2.

35. Miriam DeCosta-Willis, "Introduction," in *Erotique Norie: Black Erotica*, ed. Miriam DeCosta-Willis, Reginald Martin, and Roseann P. Bell (New York: Anchor Books, 1992), xxix.

36. Charles H. Long, *Significations* (Philadelphia, PA: Fortress Press, 1986), 7.

37. Kelly Brown Douglas, *Sexuality and the Black Church: A Womanist Perspective* (Maryknoll, NY: Orbis Books, 1999), 123.

38. James H. Cone, *The Spirituals and the Blues* (New York: The Seabury Press, 1972), 128.

39. Alice Walker, *In Search of Our Mothers' Gardens: Womanist Prose* (New York: Harcourt Brace Jovanovich, 1983), xi–xii.

40. Rudolph P. Byrd, "Prologue. The Tradition of John: A Mode of Black Masculinity," in *TRAPS*, 1–2.

41. On the notions of staying, being there, and setting examples, see James Baldwin, *The Evidence of Things Not Seen* (New York: Henry Holt and Co., 1995), 20–21; Arthur Flowers, "Rickydoc: The Black Man as Hero," in Belton, ed., op. cit., 263; and Randall Kenan, "Mr. Brown and the Sweet Science," in Belton, ed., 66.

42. Compare Dennis A. Williams, "A Mighty Good Man," in *Speak My Name* where he describes the reflections of a younger man on the older and young Black male interchange: "I can only now begin to appreciate how much effort

and genius that requires—to guide without commands, to correct without rebuke, to set limits without saying no," 84–85.

43. This type of love, I believe, would encourage more Black men to stay in church and relish the company of their wives and, in the process, reaffirm their wives' authority. See Dennis A. Williams, "A Mighty Good Man," in Speak My Name, 24–25.

44. Sadie B. Gandy, "Blessed Boys!," in *What Keeps Me Standing: letters from Black grandmothers on peace, hope, and inspiration*, ed. Denis Kimbro (New York: Doubleday, 2003), 181.

45. Elder Sharon T. Jones, "The Love We've Lost" in ibid., 205.

46. Michael Uebel, "Men in Color," in *Race and the Subject of Masculinities*, ed. Harry Stecopoulos and Michael Uebel (Durham, NC: Duke University Press, 1997), 2.

47. Examine Marlon T. Riggs, "Black Macho Revisited: Reflections of a SNAP! Queen," in Carbado, 308; and Devon W. Carbado, "Introduction," in Carbado, 4–9.

48. Michael Eric Dyson, "When You Divide My Body and Soul, Problems Multiply: The Black Church and Sex," in *TRAPS*, 313, 316–317.

11

The Erotic in Contemporary Black Women's Writings

Karen Baker-Fletcher

This essay considers Black women's understandings of the erotic as it has been represented in the literature of Black women novelists, poets, writer/activists and theo-ethicists. It focuses on the questions and agenda of Black women. I employ the poet/writer Audre Lorde's understanding of the erotic. It examines wisdom regarding *eros*.

This essay considers wisdom regarding *eros* found in the writings of Black women. The objective of the essay is first, to recommend literary resources healing of Black women, second, to dialogue with black men, and third, in a circular fashion, to contribute to possibilities for healing and wholeness within Black communities. I write with a sense of the "hush harbor," the sacred space where Black women discover self in relation to God and community. In several places I intentionally employ the pronoun "our" to emphasize that this essay is written from one subject to other subjects. The essay rejects white feminist, post-modern arguments that "this is essentialist" as a nonagenda item for Black women who find healing in acknowledging a common history in relation to the transatlantic slave trade.

While white feminists are busy deconstructing self, Black women are still claiming the selves that a racist, sexist, classist society relentlessly essays to render invisible. The same is true of the cultures representative of Black communities. While we are diverse, there is a common "we" and "our" that we can point to in our shared social-historical and cultural experiences. But, this essay is not written for white feminists. While they are welcome to listen and learn from those who are different, the present agenda is independent of their unique concerns.

In the West African cultural tradition that has been transmitted to the descendants of Africans in North America for several centuries, there is an understanding that "I am, because we are." It is similar to the understanding that is also found in Korean understandings of self and community. In the Korean language, there is no word for "I." The word *ouri* means "I and we." The English language is insufficient for understanding traditional African and African American non-individualistic understandings of self/and community. My purpose in employing "we" and "our" at certain points in the essay is to subvert the objectifying tone of much of academic genre as defined by traditional Western patriarchal norms, while also contributing scholarly observations. The section on the "hush harbor," in particular, is subjective, metaphorical, and creative in style.

I have four aims regarding the content of the essay. First I define *eros* and *erotic*, because many Black women are not aware of the precise, historical, and actual meaning of these terms. Many women associate *eros* and *erotic* with the "adult" films that reduce women to sexual objects or with mere physical, sexual desire. Many churchwomen treat the very words *eros* and *erotic* as profane. They are not aware that the love of Christ for the Church, the love of a bridegroom for his bride and the bride's love for the groom is *eros*. *Eros* is simply unifying power, the love of mystical union with the divine as we shall discuss below. The world of pornography, Hollywood, music videos, and a host of media controlled by patriarchal forces have done women a great disservice by reducing the meaning of the terms *eros* and *erotic* to objectifying sexual pleasure.

Second, I consider distinctions between the sacred space from which Black women's sexual-spiritual wisdom emerges and the closet of internalized homophobia and oppression in which wisdom is silenced. I call the sacred space of wisdom the "hush harbor" from which Black women's sexual-spiritual wisdom emerges. Positively, this "hush harbor" approach is characterized by quiet grace, invisible dignity and unshouted courage approach by which many Black women have lived their sexual-spiritual lives. Negatively, one may confuse it with "the closet."

Third, I introduce some of the womanists who have already contributed publications on Black women's sexuality. These womanists include but are not limited to Delores Williams, Katie Cannon, Kelly Brown Douglas, Cheryl Kirk Duggan, and Emilie Townes. Third, I consider Black women's literature as a resource for some of the wisdom regarding sexuality-spirituality that has emerged from Black women's real-lived experience. I begin with Walker, because she writes with particular honesty about the range of situations in which Black women historically have found themselves and about the range of possibilities in which Black women find their sexual identities. I also consider the insights of Black women's spiritual-sexual wisdom in literature by other Black women writers. It is not sufficient to limit the discussion to one authorial voice. Therefore, I will make references to the types of wisdom depicted by authors like Audre Lorde, Tina McElroy Ansa, Julie Dash, Toni Morrison, and J. California Cooper to broaden the discussion. Some of these authors are very explicit in their sexual content, so this essay is for the mature reader.

Eros and the *Erotic*

Lorde's definition of the erotic applies to women of all sexual orientations. In Greek there are four forms of love: *agape*, *filia*, *epythymia*, and *eros*. *Agape* is the form of love that Martin Luther King, Jr. taught Americans to embody in relation to one another. *Agape* is the unconditional love that God has for creation and is the form of love that New Testament authors most frequently ascribe to God and followers of Christ. In the African American Christian tradition it is often understood in relation to other understandings of God's impartial treatment of human beings across ethnic and cultural differences. For example, Paul describes God as "no respecter of persons" (Romans 2:11). The author of Acts 10:34 writes that Peter, after receiving a vision of God's removal of dietary restrictions regarding clean and unclean animals, goes to the Gentile Cornelius to preach with the understanding that "of a truth I perceive that God is no respecter of persons, but in every nation the ones that fear God and work righteousness are accepted with God." Black communities of faith tend to focus on *agape*. *Filia* is the love that friends have for one another. *Epythymia* is sexual love and the love of procreation, a drive for union. The Greeks understood *eros* as "a unifying force."[1] It is more than the sexual love of *epythemia*. *Eros* includes passion and desire for the beloved. Plato, in the *Symposium*, presents Socrates discussing *eros*. Socrates teaches that sexual desire "can be developed into the pursuit of understanding the Form of beauty."[2] Neo-Platonists understood *eros* as mystical union with Being. For Christians, the desire for union with God is *erotic*—a desire for that which is supremely beautiful, good, and true.

Black women, in all that we do—from cooking greens, to braiding hair to making love—are often suspicious of *eros*, associating it with popular understandings of the *"erotic"* in pornography or with "doing the nasty," as if authentic lovemaking could ever be "nasty"—impure or unclean. But this is a false understanding of *eros* and the *erotic* learned from patriarchal structures that denigrate women's power to love in a way that unites body with spirit. Pornography and Hollywood falsely appropriate the term *erotic*. We need to remove these oppressive images and meanings from our mind in order to free our imaginations to reclaim the power of *eros*. Very few of the films produced by Hollywood and none of the pornography marketed in red-light districts and "Adult" stores, are *erotic*. They are at best *epythymic*.

Properly understood, *eros* is the desire for union with the sacred. The sacred may be found in those whom we love passionately, in the work that we love, in the creation that loves us back with sunshine or rain, and in all that is beautiful. The sacred may be found in all that God has created, because the sacred is the depth, breath, integrity, and energy of all God has created. *Epythemia* is superficial and functional, but *eros* seeks spiritual depth. Pornography is not *erotic*. Pornography is *epythymic*. *Epythymia* satisfies temporary biological wants and instincts. It leaves Black women feeling used and dispensable. Pornography is the most superficial form of *epythymia*. *It does not seek spiritual union with the other.*

Eros is the desire for union with the other. *Eros* satisfies body and *soul*. It has the power to heal the spirit as well as the body.[3] While Black church folk traditionally have not employed the word *eros* to describe our understanding and experience of sexuality, we have experienced what scholars mean by *eros* in our own, unique cultural styles. A love of good music, food, roundness, and good lovemaking that satisfies the soul as well as the body go together in traditional Black folk culture like smoked meat in greens. It forms a rich cultural code that works toward abundant life. It is possible for those who are not part of the culture to eat the greens, enjoy the music, see the artistry of it all, even learn to "walk black" or "talk black" from a preponderance of videos and never understand it. The combination of this code and others like it in Black folk culture, form family recipes that lose something in translation. Not all of the people in our community have caught the code. There are strands of contemporary rap and hip-hop music videos that speak soley to *epythemia* in its crudest, most unloving forms. Comedians like Steve Harvey challenge such artists to learn from their elders about the ways Black artists, like Marvin Gaye, used to sing about love. It is not the rap or hip-hop rhythm that needs to be challenged, but the content of the lyrics. Healthy Black sexuality, like God, is a mystery found in the interstices of laughter and tears. The blues singers, the jazz artists, the rhythm and blues singers, the hip-hop and rap artists dance around it sometimes richly and sometimes crassly, to present an echo of the best and worst of Black sexuality. Its full meaning is in the dance of the Spirit that surrounds the coded tone of all our words. The code is not meant to be broken or understood by the curious onlooker or the voyeuristic other.

The erotic satisfies more than physical hunger and tastes. The power of it heals the soul and the bones. It is fitting that down-home African American cooking is called "*soul* food." Those who partake of collard greens with smoked meat, candied yams, cornbread dressing with sage, and sweet potato pie feel connected to the joy and sweetness of the God who created collards, sweet potatoes, cinnamon, and every kind of spice from their tongues all the way down into their hearts. In Tina McElroy Ansa's novel, *The Hand I Fan With*, Lena's love relationship with Herman makes her very insides hum sweet melodies in perfect pitch. While Christian authors might find a disconnect between the spirituality of the novel, which transcends Christian faith and their own, the lovemaking that emerges from Lena's and Herman's connection with God, the ancestors and the universe is sweet enough for Christians and Black readers from other faith traditions alike to learn from. When Lena thinks of Herman, she remembers how he "played her like a Stradivarius. She felt that way in his hands, like a masterpiece, a one-of-a-kind treasure that was being cherished."[4]

Lena noticed that if she simply thought about Herman, "her vagina sang." "What's that lovely song you're humming?" people asked her when she was out shopping or on an elevator?[5] This makes Lena blush the first few times that she becomes aware that the very thought of Herman makes her body hum lovely music. She has to leave the grocery store with her shopping half done. She learns to get the music under control so that only she and Herman can hear it while they are alone. Herman does not only teach Lena's body to hum, but also teaches her to laugh, to pick berries, to enjoy fresh dark honey from the honeycomb, and enjoy cooking delectable food in the kitchen together. He teaches her to love others more deeply, so that she becomes a mother to runaway children who find shelter in a family home she owns on Four fifty-five Forest Avenue. Through the children and her renovation of the house, this home takes on life it never had when her parents were living. Herman does not simply merge with Lena's body during lovemaking but with her soul. This is *eros*.

Returning readers to the Greek understanding of *eros* as a unifying force, Audre Lorde describes *eros* as one of many types of power. She associates it with women's power, although the Greeks did not limit it to women. For Lorde, only by being in touch with this power within ourselves can women work effectively against oppression. "The erotic," Lorde writes, "is a resource within each of us that lies in a deeply female and spiritual plane, firmly rooted in the power of our unexpressed or unrecognized feeling."[6] Eros, "creative power and harmony," when asserted is "the erotic . . . the life-force of women . . . that creative energy empowered" and reclaimed in "our language, our history, our dancing, our loving, our work, our lives."[7] It is not limited to sexual intercourse but is the response of life to life in all that we do. It is that form of love that unites life with life. Lorde observes that oppression perpetuates itself by corrupting or distorting various sources of power. "For women," she continues, "this has meant a suppression of the erotic as a considered source of power and information within our lives."[8] Women have come to distrust this power, which has often been used against us by men. This distrust results in internalized oppression of women's creative power. Moreover, it is important to add that women participate in perpetuating this oppression. Therefore, this essay considers not only the womanist wisdom that is passed on from mother to daughter, but the problem of what Alice Walker calls the women's folly that is also passed on from mother to daughter.

The Hush Harbor

Many Black women were taught by our mothers or other-mothers "Don't speak everything you think," "Don't believe everything you read," and "Be careful what you write." Moreover, the injunction to young girls to "Keep your mouth shut and your legs closed" around menfolk associates speech with sexual looseness. Keeping one's mouth shut on the subject of sexuality functions as a sign that one is not loose, immoral, available, open to all and any who desire to enter or maim. However, Black women must take care not to turn our hush harbors of sacred wisdom and mystery into closets of shame and internalized oppression.

Historically, Black women have felt safe pouring our hearts out to God in the hush harbor. In the hush harbor there is not silence, as much as conscious separation from unwelcome, outside ears and tongues that oppress Black women's inherent right to claim ownership of our bodies, hearts, and minds. Specifically, white men, white women, and some Black men historically have claimed the right to define Black women's sexuality for them. Therefore, in Black women's real-lived experience, these groups have not been privy to certain kinds of conversation between Black women and God or Black women and one another. Black women often have engaged in separatism in this area of our lives for reasons of health.[9]

The hush harbor is where the slaves would go late at night, a place away from white people, yet a place where one might pray into a pot to make sure the slave master would not hear. This was the only place and way they felt relatively safe to speak their hearts. For Black women today, our hush harbors are different. We are not always limited to meeting at night. Our hush harbors include the kitchen table, a reading group, women's retreats, a room filled with sister-friends or other types of women's space. Black people, male and female, maintain a variety of metaphorical "hush harbor" spaces for healing and wholeness. "Hush harbor" space is sacred space. It is a space that draws boundaries between peace and violence, life and death, healing and sickness, freedom and captivity, love and hate, faith and fear. It defies the prison of shame and hate, that oppressive forces produce to contain, control, break, and destroy the sexual-spiritual lives of the subjugated. We need this space to retrieve, hear, and remember our own wisdom. When one emerges from the hush harbor, one is empowered, like Sojourner Truth, to speak the truth.

I use the term "hush harbor" metaphorically to describe safe, separatist space for finding spiritual freedom to name God and self in relation to community and the wider world. A "hush harbor" is different from a "closet." In the hush harbor, there is unity between the human spirit with the Spirit that reveals itself in creation. The hush harbor is not a tiny, enclosed room, but a prayer space outdoors. You have to "enter the creation" to go into that sacred space. The challenge to us all is to know the difference between the "hush harbor," which provides empowerment for liberation and "the closet," which perpetuates oppression. The "closet" is the place where heterosexual, bisexual, transgendered, gay, and lesbian persons alike accept the power of lies over the power of truth. In the closet, we may find heterosexual, lesbian, bisexual, or transgendered persons who deny their sexual-spiritual freedom to be self-defining in relation to the larger community and wider world. Some of us are seeking answers in the hush harbor while others of us are stuck in the closet. There are many of us who are not "out," straight *and* gay, who pretend to like what we do not like or be what we are not in order to please others, who live a half life to "fit in," instead of a whole life to be free.

Sometimes we are "closeting" ourselves when we fail to engage in explicit discussions of sexuality. Other times, we are simply claiming separate space in which to hear our own voices clearly without interference from the racist, sexist, and heterosexist agendas of historically oppressive others. One of the tasks for womanist scholars is to carefully discern the difference between the "hush harbor" and "the closet" in a community with a diversity of black women across economic classes. While the hush harbor is a sacred space for black women to clearly hear their own voices and God's response, the closet is an oppressive space of shame in which black women's voices are silenced. "Hush" is an invitation to listen carefully to those who are speaking, praying, and passing on wisdom. "The closet" stamps out the freedom to speak. I write here, emerging from the sacred space of the hush harbor to share some of the wisdom learned there from ancestors, elders, and black women writers about human sexuality.

The "hush harbor" is a place where black women name sexual-spiritual freedom in relation to one another. The "closet" is a place where sexual-spiritual freedom is never named; it is a place of shame. I make these distinctions, because Black women's struggle for sacred space on the one hand, is as difficult a struggle as Black women's struggle for freedom on the other hand. The task of womanists in our struggle for freedom, survival, and abundant life is to share the social-historical wisdom of Black women's understandings of sexuality while at the same time resisting the evil of oppressive voyeuristic others. A healthy womanist discussion of sexuality celebrates Black women's sexuality, in all its orientations, while also resisting the evil of oppression.

Note that Alice Walker, whose name means "Truth Walker" or "Walker of Truth," writes freely about a range of sexual responses to others in *The Color Purple, Possessing the Secret of Joy, In the Light of My Father's Smile*, and in her numerous collections of essays while also maintaining quiet grace, invisible dignity, and unshouted courage. In recent years, she has explicitly stated that she is "bi-sexual," although she finds this term limiting in relation to all that she can love—the creation. Yet, she maintains the space of the hush harbor by writing literature that resists the consumerist desire for the merely sensational. I will say more about this below. In reality, Black people as a whole maintain a variety of metaphorical "hush harbor" spaces for healing and wholeness. "Hush harbor" space is sacred space. It is a space that draws boundaries between peace and violence, life and death, healing and sickness, freedom and captivity, love and hate, faith and fear. It defies the prison of shame and hate that oppressive forces produce to contain, control, break, and destroy the sexual-spiritual lives of the subjugated.

Womanist Theo-Ethical Discourse on Black Women's Sexuality

In her book, *Black Womanist Ethics*, the first book published by a womanist scholar of religion (1998), Katie Geneva Cannon writes that womanist ethics is characterized by quiet grace, invisible dignity, and unshouted courage.[10] Cannon explores the life and writings of Zora Neale Hurston with reference to Black women's social-historical "real-lived" experience to support her claims. While Cannon does not devote her text entirely and explicitly to Black women's sexuality, a careful examination of her work reveals that it is certainly included. For Cannon, Hurston was fully human and sexual. Her sexuality is part of the whole of her response to life. It includes the way she writes about Black women's bodies, particularly Janie's in *Their Eyes Were Watching God*. Janie's response to her own body as she develops a sense of moral agency from the time she is six years old and sees her face in a mirror for the first time, to the time she is sixteen amidst flowering trees and budding passions, to the times she marries men who control her body, to the time she frees herself, reveals Hurston's understanding of a woman's sexual *and* moral freedom. While Cannon may not say this in her analysis in so many words or in quite this way, the connection between sexual and moral freedom is apparent in *Black Womanist Ethics*. Moreover, in her collection of essays *Katie's Canon: Womanism and the Soul of the Black Community*, she writes not only of Hurston's life and literature as a resource for a womanist constructive ethic, but she also writes incisively about Black women's sexuality. She affirms, for example, Alice Walker's criticism of Judy Chicago's feminist artistic statement "The Dinner Party." Cannon shares Walker's astonishment that in this artistic depiction of plates that are imagined as vaginas, with one that looks like lettuce, another like butterflies, and other natural images, Chicago's imagination fails to imagine black women with vaginas. Walker puts it this way:

> All the other plates are creatively imagined vaginas (even the one that looks like a piano and the one that bears a striking resemblance to a head of lettuce: and of course the museum guide futters about talking

of "butterflies"!) The Sojourner Truth plate is the only one in the collection that shows—instead of a vagina—a face. In fact, *three* faces. One, weeping . . . another screaming, and a third in gimcracky "African" design, smiling . . . It occurred to me . . . that white women cannot imagine black women have vaginas.[11]

It is not surprising that a Black woman did not write "The Vagina Monologues," not we whose foremother the Sarah Bartman, suffered the humiliation of white men displaying her genitals at the Museum of Paris and whose remains were not properly buried in her homeland until the turn of the twenty-first century. Historically our bodies have been forcefully displayed and spread for curiosity, amusement, observation, and consumption. To be private about sexuality is a freedom for which Black women are still fighting at great cost.

Yet, one finds no lack of imagination regarding Black women's sexuality in Black women's literature. Our stories are not all negative. There is positive experience and wisdom available in our history and present lives. It is important to recognize this positive experience and wisdom, to learn from it, and to pass the positive stories on. Tina McElroy Ansa's *The Hand I Fan With* with its characters Lena and Herman (see above) is an example of Black women's literature that imagines Black women as fully embodied spirits who know and enjoy their inner and outer beauty apart from white feminist or even misinformed Black communal understandings of Black women's bodies. Moreover, the turn to Hurston that Walker and Cannon share is a turn to Black women's experience and understanding of sexuality and the body. The turn to Black women's literature brings readers to a more authentic understanding of Black women's love of the body—self and other—than other resources that claim to represent Black women.

Cannon's discussion of Hurston's life does not separate Hurston's moral agency from her understanding of her sexuality. I lift up Cannon to observe that while the complaint is often made that womanists "have not written enough about sexuality," I would say that we write about sexuality more often than readers have taken note. Sexuality can not be separated from spirituality, from understandings of moral agency, from appreciation of the aesthetic in creation and human art, or from understandings of God. Sexuality is about more than "sex," as in genital sexual intercourse. Sexuality involves the understanding of one's entire person and one's response not only to intimate partners but to the whole of life. Once individuals and communities understand this, it is possible to discern what Alice Walker calls "women's folly" and move into the "womanist" wisdom that she celebrates. For Walker, womanist wisdom leads to freedom. Women's folly leads to bondage. Women's folly includes platititudes like the following in relation to child bearing: "*That* little pain. . . . That pain is over before you know it," or "The thing about that kind of pain is that it does a funny thing to a woman . . . the more it hurts . . . the more you love the child . . . Sometimes the pain . . . isn't even real."[12] In contrast to the women's folly that she has heard from her mother, the essay's in *In Search of Our Mothers' Gardens* are commited to the wisdom she and other Black women have learned from her mother and other mothers. She celebrates, for example, the wisdom of her mother's creativity and is committed to the liberating activity of Harriet Tubman. From her own experience of giving birth, Walker learns that birth is miraculous, in part, because a woman has two wombs:

> The point was, I was changed forever. From a woman whose "womb" had been, in a sense, her head—that is to say, certain small seeds had gone in, and rather different if not larger or better "creations" had come out to—to a woman who . . . had two wombs! No. To a woman who had written books, conceived in her head, and who had also engendered at least one human being in her body.[13]

Walker honors two wombs—her mind and her reproductive organs—for their generative, generating power. Each gives life. Each is associated with sexuality and the power of life. Most of her children, she observes, have emerged from her mind. These children are books, poems, and essays. She has borne one child from her literal womb and vagina. But the activity of giving birth to ideas that are produced in concrete form is as powerful and as important as giving birth to children.

Alice Malsenior Walker was born in Eatonton, Georgia in 1944. She describes herself as a Black, pagan, bi-sexual woman. She finds the term "bi-sexual" limiting, because she has always believed that she could love anyone or anything that she loved. That Walker's writings form the core material for discussion requires us to note not only spirituality or theology, but the matter of religion. The religions that many womanist theologians and ethicists belong to are relatively conservative on the matter of sexuality. Whether one claims Christianity, Islam, or traditional African religions like Yoruba as one's tradition, such belief systems tend to emphasize compulsory heterosexuality. Religion has a silencing effect of a different nature. The non-pagan spirituality of most womanist theologians and ethicists contributes to the habit of the Closet. Christianity is particularly problematic when addressing the scope of sexuality that Walker freely affirms. In spite of Walker's liberating, spiritual, sexual definition of what it means to be a womanist, a black feminist or feminist of color, few of us are as free as Walker. Many of us are bound to religious institutions whose administrative leadership is repressive. It is no wonder that Walker is a pagan.

Alice Walker turns to Native American and African indigenous spirituality. Her ideal of womanhood is a womanist writer's pagan remembrance of ancestors her Native American great-grandmothers and the most ancient and nearly forgotten African women of the rainforest. As her characters in *Possessing the Secret of Joy* reveal, Walker longs for a womanist spirituality that has been lost even in African traditional religions, a type of womanhood that most Africans deny has ever existed. In contrast, those of us who are not pagan, wrestle with heterosexist scriptural texts and oral traditions.

Walker's work is not simply about Black women's sexuality, but about human sexuality. She demonstrates that Black women fall within the range of sexual orientation and expression that is possible for all women. Moreover, she demonstrates that Black men fall within the same range of sexual possibilities as all men. Walker's understanding of sexuality neither begins with *The Color Purple*, nor stops there. Moreover, *The Color Purple* is about the blues, food, roundness, God and creation as much as it is about the relationship between Shug and Celie, Celie and Mister, and Shug and Albert. In *Possessing the Secret of Joy*, Walker includes a character who is "pansexual." *Possessing the Secret of Joy* is a controversial book that criticizes traditional practices of female circumcision. Activists against the practice, including Walker, call this practice female genital mutilation (FGM) and anthropologists call female genital cutting. Within the narrative there is a discovery of ancient dolls with their genitals intact in postures of self-pleasure and pleasure with others. Moreover, Walker describes the sexuality of a minor "pansexual" character who was once the lover of the bi-sexual character Pierre who is an anthropologist. The character Adam offers the following narrative regarding Pierre's only woman lover:

The only girl he ever loved, for instance. A Berkeley student with whom he often went horseback riding. She rode bareback, always, he tells me ... She experienced orgasm while riding the horse ... She'd been brought up by pagan parents, earth worshippers ... She could experience orgasm doing almost anything. She sais that at home there were favorite trees she loved that she rubbed against. She could orgasm against warm, smooth boulders, like this one we're sitting on; she could come against the earth itself if it rose a bit to meet her. However, says Pierre, she'd never been with a man. Her parents had taught her early on that it wasn't absolutely necessary, unless she wanted to have children.[14]

The name of Pierre's lover is Queen Anne, after Queen Anne's lace, a wildflower with a delicate, doily-like appearance that is strong and sturdy. While Walker's depiction of coming to orgasm while riding horseback is not terribly original, she makes an important point, especially as the narrative continues. Queen Anne has an intimate awareness of her body in relation to creation, whether a waterfall or the earth itself. She describes a union between Queen Anne and creation that is merely suggested in *The Color Purple*. Queen Anne is not simply masturbating, the character Pierre explains, because "she was making love."[15]

Sexuality, for Walker, is connected to the Spirit and to beauty. The Spirit is in the beauty of creation. A womanist, in Walker's definition loves the Spirit. The Spirit loves. Moreover, as a writer-activist, Walker emphasizes that "anything we love can be saved," in a book by the same title.[16]

Delores Williams, in her article "Womanist Theology," offers the earliest, full description of Walker's understanding of womanist identity. She includes the section of Walker's four-part definition that describes a womanist as not only loving women's tears and laughter, but as loving women sexually and non-sexually as well as loving men sexually and non-sexually. *Williams*'s discussion demonstrates that Alice Walker's understanding of sexuality can not be separated from her understanding of spirituality. To the extent that womanist theologians and ethicists teach the poetry, fiction, film and essays of Black women artists like Audre Lorde, Zora Neale Hurston, Ntozake Shange, Nikki Giovanni, Tina McElroy Ansa, Julie Dash, Bernice Johnson Reagon, Sweet Honey in the Rock, Toni Morrison, and Alice Walker there is a movement to address not only the pain of existence but the lushness of life. Here we find the food Black women cook and how it tastes, the love Black women make in a celebrative way, and the words of music that the world misunderstands.

Literature, music, poetry, film, and artwork are comfortable places for womanists to introduce material that portrays the richness of Black women's experience, body and soul, in the classroom. Black women artists offer holistic presentations, refusing to compartmentalize Black women's sexuality as somehow different from Black women's textured, spiritual, daily living. I imagine that if more womanist theologians and ethicists were novelists, painters, composers, and poets that we would present our understanding of Black women's sexuality in these genres. Consider the difference between womanist presentations during the annual meeting of the American Academy of Religion, and womanist presentations at the Womanist Consultation which is exclusive to womanists. We offer original, artistic presentations on separate occasions—in our figurative hush harbors. Alice Walker writes that a womanist is a separatist only on occasion for reasons of health. Womanists are still healing.

The academy, predominated by white men and some white women, is not a place where Black women enter into such discussion easily or lightly. Quite frequently, once womanist theologians and ethicists have defined the term "womanist" in our writings the matter of sexuality recedes to the background or loses visibility altogether. The reasons for this are varied. For womanists who do love other women sexually, the socio-economic repercussions of heterosexist responses to public, explicit discussion of sexuality are ever-present demons that one does not easily choose to disturb. For heterosexual womanists who love women's tears, laughter, minds, spirits, and bodies "non-sexually," some level of homophobia and heterosexism enter in. These are the obvious reasons. But audience also plays a large role as one considers who is in the classroom or who will be reading what one writes. There are long, historical reasons that evoke hesitance, reluctance, and what Katie Cannon calls quiet grace, unshouted courage, and invisible dignity[17] from Black women around the subject of sexuality.

Not only during slavery, but through the Reconstruction period and throughout the period of segregation, Black women were vulnerable to rape by white men. During slavery and after as domestic workers or day laborers, Black women were raped by white men. Today, like other women, Black women still are vulnerable to sexual assault and abuse from within the ranks of men of all races. We are often raised to talk about sexuality in code, if at all. One gets the sense that if we speak about it only with one another, in the absence of men and white folk, then we can protect our womanhood. In public, if we speak of our sexuality in code, or not at all, then the historical demons of rape and abuse may not afflict us. To speak of it in mixed company may awaken the old accusations that the Black Women's Club Movement fought so roundly—that Black women are loose, sexually available, and immoral.

Notes

1. Robert Audi, ed., *The Cambridge Dictionary of Philosophy* (New York: Cambridge University Press, 1995), 240.
2. Ibid.
3. For the purpose of this essay, I am using "body" and "soul" synonymously as they are often used in black folk culture.
4. Tina McElroy Ansa, *The Hand I Fan With* (New York: Doubleday, 1996), 218–219.
5. Ansa, 219.
6. Audre Lorde, *Sister Outsider: Essays and Speeches by Audre Lorde* (New York: The Crossing Press, 1984), 53.
7. Lorde, 55.
8. Ibid., 53.
9. See Alice Walker, "Womanist," in *In Search of Our Mothers' Gardens*, (New York: HBJ, 1983), for her definition of "womanist." A womanist is most succinctly a Black feminist or feminist of color. She is concerned about the survival and wholeness of entire communities, male and female. She is not a separatist, except on occasion for reasons of health.
10. Katie Cannon, *Black Womanist Ethics* (Atlanta: Scholars Press, 1988).
11. Alice Walker, "One Child of One's Own," *In Search of Our Mothers' Gardens*, (New York: Harcourt Brace Jovanovich, 1983), 372–373.
12. Ibid., 367.
13. Ibid., 368.
14. Alice Walker, *Possessing the Secret of Joy* (New York, San Diego, and London: Harcourt Brace Jovanovich, 1992), 175–176.
15. Ibid., 177.
16. Alice Walker, *Anything We Love Can Be Saved* (New York: Random House, 1997).
17. Katie Cannon, *Black Womanist Ethics* and Katie Cannon, *Katie's Canon* (New York: Continuum, 1997).

V

Musical Studies

Salome's Veiled Dance and David's Full Monty: A Womanist Reading on the Black Erotic in Blues, Rap, R&B, and Gospel Blues

Cheryl A. Kirk-Duggan

In most of the colonial states of the Western Hemisphere, slaves taught or caught reading or writing could lose a limb or a life as a lawful penalty: reflecting a fear of the body and by default sexuality; indicative in Puritan sensibilities, notably Hawthorne's *The Scarlet Letter.* Consequently, antebellum law specifically prohibited slave education with severe penalties enforced against both the teacher and the taught. When these poor chattels owned a book, especially within the Christian tradition, it was probably the King James Bible, wherein dates of births, marriages, and deaths were recorded. These "souls of Black folk" lived close to the earth and were sensual, sexual folk. Slave owners used Black women as brood mares and Black men as studs, especially when the importation of newly captured slaves from Africa was halted by international treaty in the early 1800s. Intrigued and intimidated by blackness and the mystery of their African origins, coupled with a need to categorize slaves as non-human "property" for both legal and cultural needs, base, ignorant stereotypes about blackness and Black folk arose among Blacks and whites alike. In response, Black folk redacted scripture to support their humanity and liberation.

Fittingly, this essay uses the metaphors expressed by Salome's veiled dance (Matthew 14:6) and David's full Monty (2 Samuel 6:14), to explore the erotic in African American songs: blues, rap, R&B, and gospel-blues. After providing an overview of a Womanist biblical theological method, I exegete the two biblical texts in defining my metaphorical rubric of the Black erotic. My analysis continues with an overview of these four musical genres with a brief biography of four musicians and their work: blues, Alberta Hunter; R & B, Marvin Gaye; rap, Tupac Shakur, and gospel blues, Shirley Caesar. I conclude with an extrapolation and synthesis of the erotic in these genres.

Womanist Biblical Theological Method

Womanist theory, an interdisciplinary, spiritual field of study and thought, takes the oppressive experience of race/sex/class/age/ability seriously. *Womanist*, derived by Alice Walker[1] from the term "woman-ish," refers to women of African descent who are audacious, outrageous, in charge, and responsible. *Womanist* theology,[2] the study or discipline of God-talk that emerges out of the experience of Black women, analyzes human behavior with the Divine, witnessing the misuse of power and the politics of language. Womanist theology exposes and desires to transform all categories of oppression that seek to make invisible, ameliorate, or destroy those deemed other, frequently depicted in the lives of poor Black women. Womanist thought includes, but is not limited to issues in theology (identity, spirituality dialogue, sacrality, and power); Bible and/or other sacred texts (authority, characters, language, rituals, history); ethics (value, visibility, integrity, behavior, and praxis); and context (autobiography, culture, aesthetics, ecology, and community). My Womanist biblical theology needs a hermeneutics ranging from tempered cynicism to the comedic.

Tempered cynicism or suspicion questions texts deeply amid hopeful embedded faith and a complexity of ideas and method. Creativity lets us explore texts in new ways. Courage helps one do credible analysis despite sameness or mystery. Commitment to the hearing and just appropriation of texts undergird the route of relevant discovery. Candor exposes oppression within the written and living texts of secular and sacred communities. Curiosity presses a quest of the sacred toward inclusivity, mercy, justice, and love. The comedic supports balance and healing in gratitude of difference. Womanist biblical scholarship, located in the academy and the church, signifies the fire and passion of Womanist scholars who teach, write, interpret, preach, and minister, seeing education as transformative power. Womanist biblical scholars do textual analysis to expose pathological oppression and the misuse of power toward change, balance, immediacy, and inclusivity. Though some biblical texts are problematic, I seek and propose a rhythm and blues of sacred words, toward healing and liberation.

A Veiled Dance, A Full Monty: Metaphors of Dress and Undress

The *Erotic* involves interdisciplinary analysis of the beauty of human sensuality and sexuality, the fluidity of sexual boundaries, deep intimacy, sexual love and desire, emotional expression, and the related power. Erotic, from Eros, the Greek god of erotic love, symbolizes the aggregate of life-preserving instincts manifested as stimulus or catalysts to gratify basic needs. Plato speaks of Eros as sublimated impulses, impulses to protect and preserve the body and mind; love as a pivotal creative impulse containing a sensual element. Audre Lorde incarnates her notion of the erotic.

For Lorde, the erotic is a provocative, replenishing, deeply rooted power, a resource of a human inner, feeling, sensual self. A labyrinth of self-awareness and strong passion, the erotic is an emotional, psychic vitality; women's life force. Such empowered creative energy involves an epistemic reclaiming of story, work, love, and culture; embracing spirituality—the emotional and psychic—the political and the intellectual, toward a great capacity for joy. Deep within, the erotic is fluid and aesthetic, as it bolsters one's entire being. This deep desire, to be embraced not feared, involves sharing with integrity, respect, recognition, and participation.[3] The erotic involves the lyrical sounds and sights that express the abundance and the aesthetics of sex.[4] These feelings resound in the sensuality often skimmed over in the stories of Salome and David.

Matthew 14:3-11—Salome's Story

People will chastise, if not kill over matters of power and authority, symbolized by Salome's[5] dance. In Matthew 14, John the Baptist gives unsolicited public testimony: it is incest for Herod to engage in sexual intercourse with his sister-in-law, Herodias, his brother Philip's divorced wife. With his authority challenged, Herod has John arrested and imprisoned. Herod decided to wait to execute John, until public outrage over his arrest of this prophet diminished. On Herod's birthday, Herodias' daughter Salome performs a dance for Herod and his court at Herod's drunken birthday celebration. Herod's response to his post-pubescent niece/step-daughter's dance was likely his own erotic arousal. So aroused with sexual desire for Salome, Herod vows before his guests, to reward Salome anything she desires. On the advice of her mother, who is Herod's incestuous partner, Herodias,

Salome asks for the head of John the Baptist on a platter. [A reasonable speculation is that Herodias' vehemence and rage against John is that of a woman scorned, since John may have spurned Herodias' offer to share her favors with him.] Herod does not yet wish to kill John, but having made a solemn promise before his guests, he has no choice. The guards behead John and bring his head to Salome, who carries it to her mother. Thus the question, for this essay, is: What does Salome's dance intimate?

Herod seems to have been sexually aroused by his stepdaughter's erotic dancing, although the Biblical text is less than explicit. Why would a drunken Herod make that promise? Was he a proud step-parent or a lascivious male or both? Was the dance sensuous, erotic or pornographic? (That is, in modern terms did she do a break dance, a pole dance or a lap dance?) Was this a young woman coming of age? Could it or did it arouse Herod? Lois Miriam Wilson[6] claims that the causes of John the Baptist's beheading are beyond any dance Salome would have done. When a group of twentieth century teen-age girls were invited to act out her story, their dancing was neither provocative nor seductive, albeit Wilson's debutantes did not perform for a group of dirty old men. Wilson also questions the historicity of the account and its portrayal of women. She concedes that John gets into trouble because he attacks Herod's marriage to Herodias, one of incest and divorce.[7] Salome's reputation seems to come from Richard Strauss' opera *Salome*, and her "Dance of the Seven Veils." Yet, Josephus does not mention a dance or a banquet. Some argue that Salome's social status would have prohibited her from dancing before such a besotted audience.[8]

Strauss' opera, is a one act drama with erotic, sensuous music based on the libretto from Oscar Wilde's play of the same name. After Salome performs the dance and demands the head of John the Baptist, the soldiers bring the head on a platter. She addresses it and kisses the dead lips. Herod orders her crushed beneath the soldiers' shields.[9] Wilde's play uses the biblical text to create a story of lust, revenge, unbridled desire, and wickedness. Salome shows indifference to Herod's lust and obsesses over John the Baptist. Such blasphemy with the erotic sensationalizes Salome's dance and the Baptists' death. Salome seizes the shield with John's head on it and wants John to look at her as she hungers for his body. After she kisses the prophet's mouth, Herod orders the soldiers to kill her.[10]

Wilde's version of Salome's dance, as metaphor for the erotic, shows desire and sensual movement that celebrates the mind, spirit, body connection, and it sensationalizes and connects sex and beauty with violence. Too often, many spiritual descendents of Augustine view the erotic, nudity, and sensuality as base; flesh as weak and evil. Dance indicates an embodiment often missing in abused and addicted persons. Dance as ritual is a vehicle of praise, protest, and passion.

"Salome's Dance" serves here as a metaphor for a political, spiritual aesthetic of embodied, sensual, intimate desire. And what of David's full monty?

2 Samuel 6:1-16—David's Full Monty

The context for David's full monty is the disposition of the ark of the covenant. David was afraid of the Lord and of having the ark with him. Instead of bringing it to the city of David, he left it in the house of Obed-Edom the Gittite, whom the Lord blessed. Having learned about the blessing, David went down and brought up the ark of God to the city of David, and sacrificed a bull and a fattened calf. Then wearing only a linen ephod,[11] David danced before the Lord with all his might, while he and the entire house of Israel brought up the ark of the Lord with shouts and the sound of trumpets. As they entered the city of David, Michal, Saul's daughter, saw King David leaping and dancing before the lord and she despised him in her heart.

Was Michal upset because David danced, of the way David danced, or regarding David's attire, or lack thereof, or a combination? Does Michal resemble people today who would rather the body be less sensuous, less vital, and more disconnected from the total person? The text does not reveal Michal's cognitive process. The emphasis indicates that David only wore an ephod—a linen apron, with a back and front panel, and shoulder straps. While many biblical scholars focus on David's dance as a ritual commemorating the installation of the ark at Jerusalem, with great focus on worship, pageantry, and holiness, wearing such a garment and dancing "with all his might," suggests his dance could have been a "full monty," which might reveal David's manhood in full bouncing arousal—this prince of a man so revered throughout scripture, despite a complicated life, rife with violence, multiple wives and concubines. "The Full Monty," a British dramatic comedy film released in 1997 popularized the term, which means "the whole thing; everything."[12] In the film, unemployed British steelworkers with no prospects of work gathered their friends and produced their version of the Chippendales show—full frontal male nudity, sans thong—they took everything off and left nothing to the viewer's imagination. The origins of the term "full monty" are unknown. (The term is not confined to taking off all one's clothes, rather it means "going all the way.") Interestingly, there are no sexually provocative moments in the film and the full frontal male nudity is discretely handled. There is a great deal of spontaneity in *The Full Monty* that makes the movie's climactic scenes more believable and enjoyable.[13] Thus, the *Full Monty* in this film connects economics, sexuality, and sensuality, with class, nobility, and good taste. One can appreciate nudity from the realm of the erotic, without it being eroticized, cheapened, and denied. Here and in David's dance, sexuality is embodied in the dance form itself.

David's *Full Monty*, as metaphor for the erotic, expresses divine witness and human testimony to the beauty of the sensual, sexual body in praise of God and in honor of life, connecting politics, power, and pageantry.

Taken together, Salome's Dance and David's *Full Monty*, make available a lens with which to focus onto and wrestle with the multiple dimensions of the erotic: a political, spiritual physical, powerful aesthetic of embodied, sensual, intimate desire.

"Salome's dance," as a metaphor for the erotic, shows desire and sensual movement that celebrates the mind, spirit, body connection, as it sensationalizes and connects sex and beauty with violence. "David's Full Monty," as metaphor for the erotic, expresses divine witness and human testimony to the beauty of the sensual, sexual body in praise of God and in honor of life, connecting politics, power, and pageantry. These metaphors can serve as vehicles for wrestling with the erotic in African American music, beginning with the Blues.

Lady Sings the Blues: Alberta Hunter

The Blues, as a song form developed at the turn of the twentieth century, ethnographically arise out of the concept "Blue Devils," an eighteenth century Anglo-American term for depression or despondency, an absence of serenity, a coldness. These responsorial, empathetic, cosmological Psalms that chronicle the Black experience beyond, yet often in concert with the Black church, evolved from the spirituals, cries, work songs, hollers, and ballads, from their improvisational, unaccompanied musical speech beginnings to a codified form of twelve-bar Blues vocal melody, based on a five-tone scale with three stanzas and instrumental accompaniment.[14]

   Alberta Hunter (1895–1984), "Prima Donna of Blues singers," was a phenomenal Blues/cabaret/jazz singer, recording artist, songwriter, Broadway star, entertainer, chanteuse, humanitarian, and nurse. Known as the "dusty songstress," "Lady Hunter," "Apostle of Gaiety," and "Hospital Mommy,"[15] she moved from a life of poverty to being a renowned proclaimer of the Blues. Hunter did not let sexism or racism obstruct her determination to become a singer. Born in Memphis and moving later to Chicago, she went from washing dishes to performing in elite clubs, there, in New York, and Europe. She retired from singing in 1956, and then Hunter volunteered at the Joint Diseases Hospital in Harlem. She was rediscovered upon her mandatory retirement from nursing in 1977, and continued to sing until her death. For Hunter, the Blues were a language of love; one could sing the Blues because one has experienced hurt.[16]

   Hunter's music[17] depicts the erotic as sensual, sexual, lived expression of an embodied really, real self. In her earliest music, there is a sophisticated elegance in music that has the ethos of easy listening, classical ballroom, swing-style music backed by swing bands, with a warm, embodied sensual sound. Her later vocal timbre is gutsy, earthy, energetic. Her eroticism emerges as she is sensual and signifies seduction in the double entendre in her lyrics and the strong empathy in her accompanying band, small combos, or solo piano. Those doubles may concern relationships, where "Daddy" is not her father figure, but her lover; it may concern touching various body parts, as in her song "My Handy Man Ain't Handy No More," when he can shake her ashes, grease her griddle, churn her butter, or stroke her fiddle. With vocal coloring, rhythms, and word inflections, one is clear that the churned butter has nothing to do with oleomargarine to spread on toast. Hunter sings about the complexity of love and the dynamics of relationships. Theologically, one of her constants is the notion of "you reap what you sow." In the process, she does not bifurcate her sacred and secular reality, as she sings about the need to change and put aside bad behavior, so that one can experience salvific glorious feelings, which are free for everyone. Her songs celebrate desired touch, and right relationships, with an import for the individual and the individual connecting with others. Love is a powerful force, as it is embodied through touch, sight, and smell. Love, like her faith is old-fashioned, which signals romance, constancy, and her appreciation for time. Many songs deal with life and death through time. Hunter names the reality of life's hard times, injustice, and celebrating life as a free spirit. Through "Salome's dance," Hunter's singing celebrates the total self as sexual, sensual beauty personified amid an elegance that heightens the intensity of simple lovemaking. Her eroticism is real and accessible, amid a "reap what you sow" ethic that condemns injustice, violence, or wrongdoing, as one has to pay the price for misbehaving. Via "David's Full Monty," Hunter brings together an intimacy between the sacred and secular in her life. A very private person, Hunter offers commentary on the beauty and gift of life in the real, lived world. Decades later another person who understood the intimacy between sacred and secular proclaimed his message through R&B.

Priest of Sexual Healing: Marvin Gaye

Rhythm & Blues (R&B)[18] emerged in the 1940s from the Spirituals, Blues, Gospels, and Jazz, when *boogie woogie* was already popular and bebop was on the rise. Not a culturally derived term, the name *Rhythm & Blues*[19] was a marketing concept to replace the politically incorrect term *Race Music*. R&B included Chicago Blues people, especially ensembles with vocals, rhythm, and supplemental sections, but not the categories like Blues, Jazz, and other folk genres earlier subsumed by *Race Music*. *R&B* peaked and evolved into rock 'n' roll in the 1950s. Within the 1960s, Soul Music[20] became the term the music industry used to classify Black popular music with *R&B* influence.

Reared by a doctrinaire Pentecostal minister father, Marvin Gaye (1939–1984), the Prince of Motown, rebelled against an abusive home life by moving to secular music. Gaye's sensual and charismatic persona[21] embraced songs about love, sexuality, ecology, inner city life, drugs, peace, and war, cruelty, and human divisiveness and needs. Gaye remained tormented from his relationship with his father, and just before his forty-fifth birthday, Marvin's father murdered Gaye.[22] This father, a crossdresser, abused and confused Gaye. Into this insane mix, Gaye found solace and harmony for the angelic and the demonic in his music. Gaye had an *agape*, Christocentric ethic with a spiritual faith, amidst the warring duality within.[23] Thus, a recurring theme in his songs is that of love: the salvific, with romantic-erotic-sexual notions, religious issues about God: his notion of sexual healing.[24] Gaye, a "brooding genius,"[25] composed and performed most of his own music with a prophetic witness.

Gaye's music[26] celebrates, signifies the erotic and makes seduction sacred. His symphonic-type music underscores sensuality, sexuality, eros, and deep passionate concern for individuals and community. His tremendous empathy causes him to name injustice, criticize war, and ask about the health and sensibilities of his community. The music alone is sensual and suggestive, supporting the message of the lyrics. He wants anyone who cares to try to save the world from itself, with a particular sensitivity to children. Gaye connects mind, body, spirit in a most religious, notably Christian language. Heartfelt, luxurious accompaniments parallel the rich, dynamic words about love, change, and relationality. Gaye is a masterful architect as he notes sounds, smells, colors, textures, and cultural dynamics. He has a keen political awareness and an ethics of love and peace. For Gaye, all of reality connects with the salvific, as he presses to focus on the wholeness of reality in its holiness. Seeing holiness casts full lighting on the depths of poverty and the scandal of war. In his album of ballads, Gaye celebrates dignity, intimacy, passion, and deep caring, as he examines the notion of choosing to be lovers, and the related needs and wants. Such musical expression unfolds in Gaye's changing moods: "exultation, sadness, reflection, remorse, hope, despair. He achieves this through overdubbing his own distinctive three voices: piercing falsetto, smooth midrange, and impassioned growl."[27] In much of his music, Gaye explores a large range of emotion. His quintessential erotic song is "Sexual Healing," where he explores harmonious embrace of the complex web of romantic-erotic-sexual desires, social-economic-political-ecological experiences, and theological-religious-salvific needs.[28] This holy, poetic song evokes sensual, sexual, spiritual healing, bringing together a sense of joy, goodness, and blessed intimacy. Viewed through "Salome's Dance," Gaye's music boldly celebrates desire, sensuality, sexuality, and love as salvific, honoring the entire persona, as framework for criticizing violence especially in war, against children, and the environment. As "David's Full Monty," Gaye's music is an aesthetics of the sensual, sexual body in praise of God, honoring life as testimony, lived in the real world of power and politics. Almost two decades later, another songster celebrates the body as aesthetic tapestry, yet sensationalizes violence, and like Gaye, dies a violent death.

Dead Man Rappin': Tupac Shakur

Rap Music, a genre stemming from the mid-1970s among Black and Hispanic performers in New York City, was linked with breakdancing. From a 1960s slang term for dialog or conversation, *rap* involves chanted, often improvised street poetry set to a mixture of popular recordings, usually disco or funk music. Some criticize rap music for glorifying violence and misogyny. Others admire it as an imaginative handling of cultural idioms in critical sociopolitical commentary. *Rap* is rhythmically spoken, accented words with an underlying rhythm section; hip-hop is the background music which accompanies the rapper.[29] Michael Dyson calls Tupac Amaru Shakur (1971–1996) a Renaissance man. Shakur read vociferously, was a keen observer of life, listened to music, from rap to classical repertoire, and critiqued the expendability of poor Black children and political policy.[30] His emotional roller coaster in part derived from his mother, Afeni Shakur, a former Black Panther, who was militaristic, political, and an addict. His experiences with her resulted in low self-esteem, insecurity, root-lessness, and perpetual chaos.[31] In sum, Tupac's life mirrored the con-flicted symbolism of the hopes and failures of the Black Panther revolution. As cultural icon, secular guru, and ghetto saint, Shakur was a workaholic, a gifted poet and musician, who embodied his thug image: hyper-Black masculinity, misogyny, an intense intellect; and a forthright, prophetic, charismatic entrepreneur.[32] Shakur's scripted, tattoo-adorned body signified ambitions and tensions experienced by young Black males: objections to pop conformity, bewilderment, and confusion about racial politics and the entertainment industry.[33] After prison, Shakur took on the alias Makaveli[34]—as his alter ego. Using hip-hop as a language system to describe Black life,[35] he developed this persona to be larger than life.

Questions of the erotic are closely linked with death, violence, and inner city or ghetto life in Shakur's music.[36] Such destructive elements penetrate the very resonance, tapestries, and inflammatory language of lyrics and rhythmic melody—which often include gunshots or simu-lated bomb detonations. Shakur's music embodies the erotic as he brings together the secular, visceral, earthy day-to-day life with talk of God and Jesus. His music is visual imagery in motion. Theologically, he engages God, critiques the church, and explores theodicy, which he often answers with compassion. The human body becomes the target of assault and decimation. At the same time, one's senses are keen to observe the drama unfolding around, including the objectification of sex; there is no beauty or empowerment related to sex. Often Shakur uses sexualized language to indicate disrespect of himself or others. Sometimes when he talks about having sex, it is for gratification, with "hoes," nameless women from the street that by definition relinquish any need for respect, though he counts "getting pussy" as the "sweetest joy" second only to revenge.[37] Yet, Shakur chides those in power for disrespecting inner-city folk. There is a driven intensity in this skewed eroticism that reflects the desperation and futility of the street, the ever-present shadow of death and the hard lessons of life. With all of the misogyny and violence, religious language frequents his texts. Thus in signifying about God and the begotten son, Shakur venerates Mary and talks about the Eucharist as the eating of Christ's flesh. Several prayers evoke an awareness that highlights feelings, hearing and being heard, and having a pure heart. His laments include invocations to those in power, with the lament proper that proclaims suffering, along with petitions, motivation, and a certainty of hearing. Throughout his music, he uses numerous metaphors from everyday life to signal a particular message that ultimately connects with the senses, the body, life in community, and power in search of love and peace. As "Salome's Dance," more than the other musicians, Shakur's eroticism sensationalizes sex and connects it with violence and death, with a strong objectification of the body due to all of the disrespect, drugs, and poverty he sees around him. Through "David's Full Monty," Shakur gives testimony to the beauty of the body through the adornment of his own body and he makes deep lament over all of the pain around him. His music honors God and offers commentary on all of the problems he sees, skewing a healthy notion of the erotic. A songster from the realm of Gospel looks to Jesus in her proclamation of an aesthetic.

Songs from the Heart: Shirley Caesar

Gospel music focuses on the Christian church and Jesus' teaching and ministry, especially the doctrine of salvation by grace. The name Gospel for these songs developed because many of the lyrics are from the first four books of the New Testament. When the Spirituals that arose in a rural setting were unable to help many African Americans cope in their new urban settings where they had migrated, Gospel music came into its own in the Northern states. Poor people had a strong resonance with poor people. Though initially Gospel was unwelcomed in many churches, it has evolved from a music that blended Blues tunes and sacred texts for church, to include secular Gospel performed in nightclubs and concert halls. The combined, diverse melodic, rhythmic, and harmonic configurations express personal experience in solo or choral Gospel blue[38] using various types of accompaniment from solo piano to full orchestra, with lyrics that proclaim blessings, the Trinitarian God with major emphasis on Jesus, joy, praise, sorrows, and overcoming. These songs involve a theology of experience and imagination, for God is ever present and one can remain hopeful. Gospel songs include a theology of grace where one can be intimate with God and know liberation, and a theology of survival where God assists one daily, despite monumental oppression.

Shirley Caesar (1938–), a contemporary gospel singer from North Carolina, signifies as she blazes forth, an educated saved soul singer, filled with the spirit, a marionette for Jesus.[39] A civic leader and a minister, Caesar skillfully and energetically dances, shouts, moves. She is one of twelve children. At the age of twelve Caesar's father died and she was left with an invalid mother. Having sung with other small groups, Caesar joined the *Caravans* in 1958. By 1961, she had taken the famed Apollo Theatre by storm with her singing, in a folk-preacher song-sermonette style, becoming an evangelist along the way. Her style grew with using blue notes, slurs, and achieving rhythmic effects by repeating consonants, using intense nasality, and high or very low "yeahs" with the heavy breathing of an old country preacher.[40] She cut her first solo LP in 1966, "I'll Go." Known as the Queen of Gospel and the First Lady, with six Dove awards and five Grammys Caesar continues to do ministry, record, and work on behalf of youth.[41]

Caesar's[42] music depicts the erotic as a Jesus-focused, cosmological testimony of love and transformation. The music for her Gospel songs involve sensual embodiment: one engages in participatory listening, toe tapping, hand clapping, and swaying from side to side. When she performs, as with many Gospel singers, her back -up singers have choreographed movement, some rehearsed, others improvised. The erotic in Caesar's music is framed as intimacy. One has to have a close, devoted relationship with Jesus, which allows one to feel deeply as they wait on the Lord. The ability to feel emerges from embodied faith and a deep awareness about the realities of others: that babies cry, one can touch a leaf, the importance of being honest, the sadness that comes when one is forgotten. Caesar's aesthetic testimony knows the cycles of life, the impossibility of God to fail, and the need for us to reach out and touch each other. This testimony is kinesthetic, for human contact through touch and sound are quintessential for the lost to be found, to feel better. Only through the deep intimacy with Jesus does one discern their deep needs, even as they grasp the gift of the pleasures of life. Moving from being lost to found is part of the salvific process. Much of the Jesus-focused erotic is the gift that Jesus gives to others, helping the blind to see, the lame to walk, by being a lifeline. Jesus is the one who fixes life within the framework of the

Christ-event: birth, death, and resurrection. Caesar also contrasts the kinds of feelings felt by Jesus during his journey that most of us will not feel: being spat upon, being ridiculed, being wounded, or carrying a cross upon our back. Yet she realizes that life is not a bed of roses, as one remains open to living a life that is merciful, dutiful, true, kind, and faithful. In her song, "No Charge," she contrasts the desires of the son for payment for household chores over against no charge for the full cost of her love that carried him and took care of him, which then is paralleled with the gift of the redemptive acts of Jesus Christ. As "Salome's dance," Caesar's songs and music embody the erotic as sensual, kinesthetic movement when singing, and as transformative, redemptive movement in life through a personal relationship with Jesus Christ. As "David's Full Monty," Caesar's music is a dialogical testimony of what Jesus has done and will do, and the witness of the lives of those who have been changed, as she connects with the politics of existence in the lives of people in all walks of life.

The Erotic Revisited

To go forward, first invites reflection on where we have been. In review, the erotic involves the awareness and beauty of human sensuality and sexuality, the fluidity of sexual boundaries, deep intimacy, sexual love and desire, emotional expression, and the related power, as provocative, replenishing, energizing source for human integrated living of mind, body, spirit. "Salome's dance," as metaphor for the erotic, depicts a deep yearning and sensuality in motion that honors the mind, spirit, body relationality, as it heightens the intensity of and connects beauty and sex with violence. "David's Full Monty," as metaphor for the erotic, communicates divine observance and human acknowledgment to the aesthetics of the sensual, sexual body in worship of God and in tribute of life, connecting politics, pomp, and power. Each singer reflects a distinctive sense of the erotic in their work, reflected through the lens of Salome's Dance and David's Full Monty.

Through "Salome's dance," Hunter's singing celebrates the erotic in the total human self and proclaims "you reap what you sow" as she decries wrong. Via "David's Full Monty," Hunter takes a holistic approach to celebrate beauty and gift of life in the real, lived world. Viewed through "Salome's Dance," Gaye's music fully integrates the erotic as salvific, and from that context offers sociopolitical and religious commentary against anything that violates creation. As "David's Full Monty," Gaye's music offers testimony as aesthetic, lived praise.

As "Salome's Dance," the sensationalized violence in Shakur's music overshadows erotic beauty as he lives the thug life and comments on all the pain within and around him. Through "David's Full Monty," Shakur music is like the psalms of lament without the final thanksgiving. As "Salome's dance," Caesar's songs and music embody the erotic as sensual, kinesthetic movement through performance and a personal relationship with Jesus Christ. As "David's Full Monty," Caesar's music is a Christocentric witness and a promise of hope and transformation.

Imagery and themes of the erotic exist in the music of African Americans, particularly those of blues, Rhythm & Blues, rap, and Gospel, a statement which flies in the face of convention for many, particularly Gospel. Yet, the texts and performances speak for themselves. The music comes alive when performed through the human voice and body, in the artist and the listening, often participating audience. People do not sit still, but clap hands, sway, jump, tap feet, or dance. People make love to some of the music, and pray and meditate to others. Recognizing the deep passion, power, and provocative energies within this music is a place to begin to allow ourselves to embrace our own experience of the erotic more fully. How great and marvelously made is the human body, mind, and spirit. What a shame that some of us allow fear, false guilt, and shame to rob us of ecstasy.

Dancing, ooh, so fine
Elegant sway of hips,
Seductive flip of wrist:
Swaying along, with the Divine
Who made me
And I glory in it.
Releasing any shame
You might have tried to put on me
'Cause I love me
I love my body
I ain't ashamed
To be really, real in it!

Notes

1. Alice Walker, *In Search of our Mother's Gardens: Womanist Prose* (New York: Harcourt Brace Jovanovich, 1983), xi.
2. Diana L. Hayes, "And When We Speak: To Be Black, Catholic, and Womanist," in Diana L. Hayes, and Cyprian Davis, *Taking Down Our Harps* (Maryknoll, NY: Orbis Press, 1998), 102–119.

3. Audre Lorde, "Uses of the Erotic: The Erotic as Power," in *Erotique Noire: Black Erotica*, ed. Miriam DeCosta-Willis, Reginald Martin, Roseann P. Bell (London: Doubleday, 1992), 78–83.

4. Charles L. Blockson, "African-American Erotica and Others Curiosities: "The Blacker the Berry, the Sweeter the Juice . . ." in *Erotique Noire: Black Erotica*, ed. DeCosta-Willis et al., 87.

5. Most ancient manuscripts identity the dancer only as Herodias' daughter. Neither Matthew nor Mark identity her by name, though tradition names the dancer, Salome. See Carol Myers, ed., *Women in Scripture: A Dictionary of Named and Unnamed Women in the Hebrew Bible, the Apocryphal/ Deuterocanonical Books, and the New Testament* (Grand Rapids, MI: William B. Eerdmans, 2001,) 411.

6. Lois Miriam Wilson, *Stories Seldom Told: Biblical Stories Retold for Children & Adults* (n.p., Canada: Northstone), 1997.

7. Herodias' first marriage was an incestuous one, where she married her Uncle Philip. She later divorced Phillip and married his richer and more powerful brother, Herod Antipas. Some cultures reject marriages between uncles and nieces, and others do not. Jews at Herod's Court would take offense at accusations of incest and unlawful divorce, particularly if they did not regard Herodias' sex with both her uncles as scandalous. With all the drama unfolding about her, how interesting that Herodias has no speaking voice and really has no say in the party activities.

8. Wilson, 122–123.

9. David Ewen, *Encyclopedia of Opera* (New York: A. A. Wyn, 1955), 451. Strauss used the German translation by Hedwig Lachmann. The opera premiered December, 1905, and at the New York Metropolitan Opera House, January 1907.

10. http://www.sparknotes.com/drama/salome/summary.html, July 26, 2003.

11. An ephod is an embroidered vestment believed to resemble an apron with shoulder straps, worn by priests in ancient Israel; it was made of fine linen, and consisted of two pieces, which hung from the neck, and covered both the back and front, above the tunic and outer garment, a Biblical jock strap or male miniskirt. http://www.wordreference.com/english/definition.asp?en=ephod, July 26, 2003; http://bibletools.org/index.cfm/fuseaction/Def.show/RTD/Easton/Topic/Ephod, July 26, 2003.

12. http://www.worldwidewords.org/articles/monty.htm, July 5, 2003.

13. http://movie-reviews.colossus.net/movies/f/full_monty.html, July 5, 2003.

14. Leroy Jones (Amiri Baraka), *Blues People: The Negro Experience in White America and the Music That Developed from It* (New York: Morrow, 1953), x, 3, 5, 50–51; Sandra R. Lieb, *Mother of the blues: A Study of Ma Rainey* (Amherst: University of Massachusetts Press, 1981), 4.

15. See Frank C. Taylor with Gerald C. Cook, *Alberta Hunter: A Celebration in Blues* (New York: McGraw Hill, 1987), 44, 61, 153, 205, 252.

16. Ibid., 198–203; 232.

17. See the following: *Alberta Hunter with Lovie Austin's Blues Serenaders*, Riverside Records, 1984, CD OBCCD-0510-2; *Alberta Hunter: Amtrak Blues*, Columbia Records, 1980, CD CK 36430; *Young Alberta Hunter, The*

20s & 30s, Jass Records, 1988, CD J-CD-6; *The Legendary Alberta Hunter, The London Sessions*—1934, DRG Records, 1981, CD CDSL 5195.

18. Samuel A. Floyd, Jr., *The Power of Black Music: Interpreting Its History from Africa to the United States* (New York: Oxford University Press, 1995), 161–206. 175–176, 136, 143.

19. Ibid., 161.

20. A term used by Black musicians in the mid-1950s.

21. Paul Friedlander, *Rock and Roll: A Social History* (Boulder, CO: Westview Press, 1996), 184.

22. Ibid., 184–185.

23. David Ritz, Program Notes, Marvin Gaye, *Midnight Love & The Sexual Healing Sessions,* Columbia/Sony Music Entertainment, 1982, 1998 CD C2K-65546, 16.

24. Orea Jones, "The Theology of Sexual Healing" *The Theology of American Popular Music: A Special Issue of Black Sacred Music: A Journal of Theomusicology* 3 (1989), 69–70.

25. Ibid., 21.

26. See the following: Marvin Gaye, *Super Hits,* Motown Records, 1970, CD 374353012; Marvin Gaye, *What's Going On,* Motown Records, 1998, CD 314530853; Marvin Gaye, *Let's Get It On,* Motown Records, 1998, 1973, CD 31430885-2; Marvin Gaye, *Midnight Love & The Sexual Healing Sessions,* Columbia/Legacy, 1998, 1982, CD C2K 65546.

27. See Marvin Gaye, *Vulnerable,* "Liner Notes," by David Ritz. Motown, 1997. CD 314530786-2.

28. David Ritz, *Divided Soul: The Life Of Marvin Gaye* (New York: Da Capo Press, 1985, 1991), x.

29. http://www.lclark.edu/~ria/MAINRA~1.HTM, Ben Trieger, "Rap and Hip Hop"; Also see *The Columbia Encyclopedia* viewed August 31, 2003.

30. Michael Dyson, *Holler If You hear Me: Searching for Tupac Shakur* (New York: Basic Civitas Books, 2001), 70–83, 94–100.

31. Ibid., 21–25, 31–43.

32. Ibid., 11, 13–16, 21.

33. Armond White, *Rebel for the Hell of It: The Life of Tupac Shakur* (New York: Thunder's Mouth Press, 1997), 84–90.

34. Machiavelli, the sixteenth century Florentine philosopher, celebrated power as amoral and exercised "an any means necessary" notion of gaining power.

35. Armond White, *Rebel for the Hell of It,* 164–172.

36. See the Following: Tupac Shakur, *Makaveli,* "Hail Mary," Beverly Hills, CA: Death Row Records, 1996, 2001, CD 2870630122; 2 PAC, *All Eyez on Me,* Death Row Records, 1995, CD DRR 63008-2; 2 PAC, *2Pacalypse Now,* Interscope Records, 1991, CD 01241-41633-2; 2 PAC, *Strictly 4 My Niggaz,* Interscope Records, 1993, CD 01241-41634-2; 2 PAC + Outlawz, *Still I Rise,* Interscope Records, 1999, CD 0694904132.

37. Tupac Shakur, *Makaveli,* "Hail Mary," Beverly Hills, CA: Death Row Records, 1996, 2001, CD 2870630122.

38. Eileen Southern, *The Music of Black Americans: A History* (New York: Norton, 1971), 401–2; Horace Clarence Boyer, "Contemporary Gospel Music," *Black Perspective in Music* 7 (1979): 5–6, 10; Michael Harris, *The*

Rise of Gospel Blues: The Music of Thomas Andrew Dorsey in the Urban Church (New York: Oxford University Press, 1992), xvii, 100, 209.

39. Tony Heilbut, *The Gospel Sound: Good News and Bad Times* (New York: Anchor Books/Doubleday, 1975), 238; Horace Clarence Boyer, "Shirley Caesar," in *Black Women in America: A Historical Encyclopedia*, ed. Darlene Hine, Elsa Brown, and Rosalyn Terbory-Penn (Indianapolis: Indiana University Press, 1993), 214; "Shirley Caesar: Putting the Gospel Truth into Politics," *Ebony* (December 1988), 66–67, 70.

40. Heilbut, Gospel Sound, 240–241; Boyer, "Shirley Caesar," 215.

41. Promotional materials, Shirley Caesar Outreach Ministries, Durham, NC, Summer, 1995.

42. See the following: Shirley Caesar, *Shirley Caesar's Treasures*, HOB Records, 1992, CD HBD-3501; Shirley Caesar, *Why Me Lord*, HOB Records, 1992, CD HBD 3510; Shirley Caesar, *First Lady*, HOB Records, 1992, HBD 3515; Shirley Caesar, *Sailin'*, Word/Epic, CD EK 48800; Shirley Caesar, *Throw Out the Lifeline*, HOB Records, 1993, HBD 2802.

13

Black Spirituals, Physical Sensuality, and Sexuality: Notes on a Neglected Field of Inquiry

Arthur C. Jones

A curious aspect of the vast scholarly literature on the spirituals—the sacred songs created and first sung by enslaved Africans in North America in the seventeenth, eighteenth, and nineteenth centuries—is the relative absence of substantive analyses that center on themes in the songs that relate to sexuality. This dearth of commentary on erotic matters is especially curious given the longstanding perception of the spirituals as reflecting a comprehensive, wide-ranging oral repository of Black life and culture during the experience of North American slavery. For example, the poet James Weldon Johnson, in his now-classic 1926 essay on the spirituals, wrote:

> In the Spirituals the Negro did express his religious hopes and fears, his faith and his doubts. In them he also expressed his theological and ethical views, and sounded his exhortations and warnings. . . . But in a large proportion of the songs the Negro passed over the strict limits of religion and covered the whole range of group experiences—*the notable omission being sex.* . . . Indeed, the Spirituals taken as a whole contain a record and a revelation of the deeper thoughts and experiences of the Negro in this country for a period beginning three hundred years ago and covering two and a half centuries. (emphasis added)[1]

If indeed the spirituals "contain a record and a revelation" of African Americans over a nearly three hundred year period, why is sex a "notable omission"? Unfortunately, Johnson does not elaborate, and there is little help to be found in the writings of other well-known scholars and researchers.

Twentieth-Century Definitions of "Negro Spiritual": Cultural and Societal Dynamics

One line of investigation that has received surprisingly little attention is the influence of overarching cultural and societal forces in the very definition of what is considered a "spiritual." From this perspective, one possible reason for the seeming omission of issues of eroticism in discussions of spirituals is the somewhat arbitrary classification of songs as secular or spiritual during the Harlem Renaissance of the 1920s and 1930s, when scholarly, literary, and musical treatments of the spirituals reached a peak. During this period there was a significant push within segments of the Black intellectual elite to showcase African American cultural products as significantly worthy of esteem and praise from the dominant artistic community. The thinking that guided this dynamic was the idea that promoting the superior moral and intellectual capabilities of prominent Black artists and writers would serve as a source of cultural uplift for the entire Black race. For example, according to the Harlem Renaissance folklorist Zora Neale Hurston, many of the songs that were labeled as "spirituals" during the Harlem Renaissance were actually the product of conscious efforts by African American composers, trained in the European classical music tradition, to present musical arrangements of spirituals that could stand side by side with the great choral works of Europe. (This is a tradition that was pre-figured by the famous tours of the Fisk Jubilee Singers in the 1870s.[2]) Hurston calls these works neo-spirituals, distinguishing them from the folk spirituals that were created by enslaved Africans. While she allows for the importance of this neo-spirituals tradition for African Americans and others, she believes it is important to distinguish it from the folk spirituals tradition:

> There never has been a presentation of genuine Negro spirituals to any audience anywhere. What is being sung by the concert artists and glee clubs are the works of Negro composers or adaptors based on spirituals. Under this head come the works of Harry T. Burleigh, Rosamond Johnson, Lawrence Brown, Nathaniel Dett, Hall Johnson and Work. All good work and beautiful, but not the spirituals. These neo-spirituals are the outgrowth of glee clubs. Fisk University boasts perhaps the oldest and certainly the most famous of these. They have spread their interpretation over America and Europe . . . But with the glee clubs and soloists, there has not been one genuine spiritual presented.[3]

For Hurston, and for others of similar persuasion, our collective impression of what is actually included in the category of "the spirituals" has been shaped largely by this neo-spirituals tradition, which was originally driven by social forces that few scholars have acknowledged. Not only did these new musical forms emulate European art; according to Hurston they also presented a sanitized picture of Black life, devoid of earthy concerns or preoccupations. It can be argued that this way of thinking about spirituals—as songs echoing lofty religious values devoid of the realities of ordinary earthly life, has persisted in the culture throughout the last several decades.[4]

Following this line of argument, the question of what constitutes genuine spirituals becomes relevant, particularly with respect to the issue of whether such songs, in their original form, did in fact provide commentary on experiential aspects of Black sexuality and, more broadly, physical sensuality. Hurston's stance on this issue is crystal clear. In her view, there was little artificial compartmentalization in traditional African American folk expression. Such compartmentalization existed only within the realm of the refined "neo-spiritual" that was the product of a circumscribed community of Negroes seeking acceptance in the larger American cultural arena. In contrast, traditional African American cultural forms gave full voice to issues ranging from religious conversion to sex. This was true whether the form of expression was story, song, or dance. The variety of life domains covered, according to Hurston, was unlimited:

> Its great variety shows the adaptability of the black man: nothing is too old or too new, domestic or foreign, high or low, for his use. God and the Devil are paired, and are treated no more reverently than Rockefeller or Ford.[5]

Moreover, in the specific realm of sexuality, Hurston is even bolder in her assertions:

> Likewise love-making is a biological necessity the world over and an art among Negroes. So that a man or woman who is proficient sees no reason why the fact should not be moot. He swaggers. She struts happily about. Songs are built on the power to charm beneath the bed-clothes.[6]

Clearly, for Hurston, traditional Black songs cannot be confined into artificial categories or classifications. Their domain is the entire range of Black life experience.

The Spirituals versus the Blues: Chicken, Egg, or Bedfellows?

Cultural critic Angela Davis echoes Hurston in her view that the dominant social mores of the 1920s and 30s operated to exclude the natural tendency within Black cultural communities to give direct voice to experiences of physical sensuality and love-making. In fact, argues Davis, female blues artists such as Gertrude "Ma" Rainey, Bessie Smith, and Billie Holliday offered their art, at least in part, as a counter to the prevailing norms of the larger culture, emulated by the Black intellectual elite of the 1920s and 30s, that would portray the ideal life (particularly for women) as one in which sexual urges and desires are minimized:

> ... African-American blues lyrics talk about love.... By contrast, the popular song formulas of the period demanded saccharine and idealized nonsexual depictions of heterosexual love relationships. Those aspects of lived love relationships that were not compatible with the dominant, etherealized ideology of love—such as extramarital relationships, domestic violence, and the ephemerality of many sexual partnerships— were largely banished from the established popular musical culture. Yet these very themes pervade the blues.[7]

It is customary, of course, to think of the blues as an entirely separate genre from the spirituals. In the prevailing view, blues songs are secular music, while the spirituals are sacred music. Within Davis's framework, we might conceptualize the work of blues artists like "Ma" Rainey as essentially reverting to traditional forms of African American artistic expression, in which all realms of life are available for comment. This would counter the evolving values embraced by the composers and performing artists nurtured within the culture of the Harlem Renaissance, in which the songs presented as "spirituals" (and classified by Hurston as "neo-spirituals") were stripped of all erotic themes.

Standard discussions of African American music history present the blues as a twentieth-century musical genre associated with the new-found freedom of a people who were no longer slaves.[8] According to this conceptualization, such issues as sexuality and travel—issues presumably of secondary concern to people confined in physical bondage— could now be explored fully in the new music—the blues—that was arising.[9] Africanist Delridge Hunter, in a recent work, challenges this bedrock assumption of African American music history inquiry. Hunter argues,

> Blues are as old as anyone can remember. As many of the slave songs reveal, blues were a sound, a moan, a grunt, a sigh, a lyrical poem about the oppressive nature of slavery. As the songs evolved, they became social commentary, meditative prayer, of wanting to be loved and held by the one you loved.[10]

The evidence compiled by Hunter to support his view of the blues as pre-dating the spirituals includes oral history transcripts from conversations with African and African American storytellers and folklorists, who consistently report the early existence of blues-like songs among both the indigenous African communities from which North American slaves were captured, and among enslaved Africans in North America in the seventeenth and eighteenth centuries. According to these accounts, songs addressing broad issues of life, as well as the specific exigencies of sexual and romantic relationships, were pervasive, pre-dating the sacred songs that were later called "spirituals." Within this framework, the subsequent development of religious songs influenced by Christian conversions among slaves would be regarded as almost secondary to the primary impulse to create music that addresses comprehensively all the daily experiences of life, particularly when times were hard, as was almost always the case in the slave quarters. Hunter's argument would also lead logically to the idea that within the slave community, the classification of songs into the categories sacred versus secular would be inconsistent with the African-derived cultural roots of the slaves, in which all aspects of daily life, including physical eroticism and sensuality, would be incorporated naturally into the songs and other cultural products of the community.

The Spirituals and Religious Prohibitions Within the Slave Community

Despite the persuasive argument constructed by Hunter concerning the comfortable incorporation of themes of eroticism and sensuality in early slave songs, there is also considerable evidence that there were factors within the increasingly Christianized culture of the slave community that conspired to separate body movement and physical sensuality from the realm of religious life, including the act of singing sacred songs.[11]

The title of ethnomusicologist Dena Epstein's book, Sinful Tunes and Spirituals, is particularly revealing in this regard. Epstein's choice of this title for her work reflects her well-documented research into the evolution and cultural functions of various slave songs, revealing that the slaves themselves frequently categorized their songs as recreational or secular versus sacred. This is not simply a fictionalized categorization. At some levels, it was experientially real for the slaves themselves, and increasingly stronger as time progressed.[12]

One example of the self-imposed separation of secular and sacred in slave culture is the evolution of the ring shout, which is the ceremonial dance ritual in which early spirituals were created and performed. Several scholars have documented the African roots of this counter-clockwise circle dance ritual.[13] However, the ring shout as it developed in North America seems to have been employed as the container for songs with a narrowly defined religious orientation, to the exclusion of other aspects of Black life, particularly within the erotic domain. For example, it was in the North American context that the practice seems to have evolved wherein participants in the ring shout were prohibited from crossing their legs when performing the ritual. This prohibition appears to have emerged in response to the clear message from Christian missionaries that dancing was an un-Godly activity.[14] However, this prohibition conflicted with longstanding African traditions, in which not only body movement, but physical sex as well, were incorporated fully within the realm of sacred life, as noted by John Mbiti:

> In African societies sex is not used for biological purposes alone. It also has religious and social uses . . . . There are African peoples among whom rituals are solemnly opened and concluded with actual or symbolic sexual intercourse between husband and wife or other officiating persons. This is like a solemn seal or signature, in which sex is used in and as a sacred action, as a "sacrament" signifying inward spiritual values.[15]

It was likely very difficult to eradicate such longstanding and deeply rooted African cultural sensibilities and practices. Newly converted slaves, therefore, must have found themselves in a bind. They were being asked, in essence, to eradicate all aspects of body movement and eroticism in worship settings. In order to embrace their new religion, they were being asked to abandon psychologically significant cultural practices and sensibilities.

To resolve this conflict, slave participants appeared to have struck a brilliantly creative compromise: They made a decision to retain the essential African impulse to engage in body movement, while reconceptualizing the ring shout as an exclusively religious activity outside the realm of dancing. Within this reframed conceptualization, to cross one's legs was to dance. In contrast, to move one's body in a steady shuffle, in the absence of leg crossing, was to engage in solemn worship. Seemingly, there was no middle ground; one was either dancing or not dancing. However, this reframing appeared to provide a subtly creative way for enslaved Africans to retain old traditions of sacredly sanctioned body movement and sensuality without violating tenets of their newly acquired religious beliefs, in which such activity was considered sacrilegious. Folklorist Harold Courlander puts it this way:

> Among West Africans, dancing in combination with other elements is regarded as a form of appeal to supernatural forces, and this tradition remains alive in New World African cults. . . . In the Euro-Christian tradition, however, dancing in church is generally considered a profane act. The ring shout in the United States provides a scheme, which reconciles both principles. The circular movement, shuffling steps, and stamping conform to African traditions of supplication, while by definition this activity is not recognized as a "dance."[16]

It also appears that enslaved Africans participating in ring shout ceremonies sometimes stretched the limits as far as they could go. For example, it is fascinating to note some of the erotic-tinged language used by members of early African American communities in the lyrics of their shout songs. Take, for example, the lyrics of an early shout song known as "Move, Daniel":

> Move, Daniel, move, Daniel . . .
> Rock, Daniel, rock, Daniel . . .
> Shout, Daniel, shout, Daniel . . .
> Move, Daniel, move, Daniel . . .
> Shout, Daniel, shout, Daniel . . .
> Rock, Daniel, rock, Daniel..
> Go the other way, Daniel . . .
> Sinner in my way, Daniel . . .
> Do the eagle wing, Daniel . . .
> Shout, Daniel, shout, Daniel . . .
> Rock, Daniel, rock, Daniel.[17]

Traditionally, as shouters performed this song, they engaged in a "sensual, rocking motion of the hips" whenever the line "Rock, Daniel, rock, Daniel" was sung.[18] Moreover, despite the seeming reference in the song to the Old Testament figure Daniel, present-day shouters from coastal Georgia describe the apparent origins of the song as actually coming out of a specific practical situation in the experience of a slave community:

> Daniel is "not the Daniel in the Bible," bur rather a slave who, having stolen some meat, is fleeing the master's whip. The shout becomes a dramatic symbolic expression of solidarity between Daniel and his fellow slaves, as they instruct him to move, turn the other way, and in a beautiful gesture of arms extended birdlike from the shoulders, "do the eagle wing" as he evades the master.[19]

We therefore see that, despite the proscriptions against dancing in the newly adopted Christian doctrine, there was a whole other layer of dynamics operating, including the creative incorporation of sensual body movements against the backdrop of cleverly disguised, open defiance of the slave master. This is consistent with what is known about the complex system of coded and clandestine messages and cultural functions of the spirituals as they were sung during slavery.[20] However, it is also evident that the layering of meanings was even more intricate and multidimensional than has been reported previously.

The picture that begins to emerge from this kind of analysis is a tension between the dictates of the new Christianity among slaves (in which slave worshippers are encouraged to view body awareness, movement and sensuality as sinful), and longstanding African sensibilities, in which body awareness, physical movement and sensuality, along with the confident assertion of the rights of self and community, were prevalent. To resolve this tension, slaves appeared to be able to institute intricate cultural practices that allowed allegiance to both extremes of a complex bi-cultural matrix.

With respect to coded messages within the spirituals, the most frequent context that has been the subject of study has been the use of spirituals for secret communication of plans for escape, rebellion, and worship.[21] However, it appears that the same process of layered meanings may have been employed in many other realms, including individual experiences of romantic attachment and physical attraction. One example where this dynamic is expressed is a song entitled "Poor Rosy," transcribed in the first published collection of spirituals, Slave Songs of the United States, which first appeared in print in 1867:

Poor Rosy, poor gal,
Poor Rosy, poor gal.
Rosy break my heart;
Heav'n shall-a be my home.
I cannot stay in hell one day,
Heav'n shall-a be my home.
I'll sing and pray my soul away,
Heav'n shall-a be my home.[22]

The collectors indicate, in a footnote, that the chorus may be varied, substituting "Poor Caesar, poor boy" in place of "Poor Rosy, poor gal." It is obvious that this song, employing surface references to Heaven and a presumed preoccupation with life after death, also provides direct commentary on the loss of an important relationship, and most likely a romantic one. Whether it is a woman grieving the loss of "Caesar" or a man grieving the loss of "Rosy," there is a clear hint that the source of the singer's distress is the loss of a loved one, and that the cause of the loss may have been separation on the auction block, since the singer is not only distressed, but also concerned for the fate of the lost partner, "poor" Rosy (or Caesar). Much has been written about the physical abuses of slavery, but separation of families on the auction block, including the cutting off of loyal romantic liaisons, was likely an equal, if not greater source of emotional distress.[23]

While the above discussion demonstrates that themes of sensuality and sexuality were not as absent in slave spirituals as may have been previously assumed, there are good reasons why scholars have viewed the spirituals in a category separate from secular songs and devoid of commentary concerning the realms of sex and the erotic. The lyrics of the vast majority of songs in the Allen collection, for example, focus almost exclusively on religious themes. "Poor Rosy" stands out as an exception rather than as a representative song from the collection. The influence of narrowly proscribed Christian practice in the slave community is a reality that cannot be denied. Nevertheless, it is also clear that the ongoing influence of African derived conceptions of spirituality as inclusive rather than exclusive of sexuality and sensuality is worthy of further study. The issues are far more complex than have previously been assumed. For example, in the ongoing struggle to reconcile the tension between religious belief and the exigencies of physical and romantic attraction, it is not surprising that the resolution was not always comfortable or unaccompanied by feelings of guilt. An example of the uneasy tensions is illustrated in the lyrics of one other spiritual documented in the Allen collection:

> I saw the beam in my sister's (brudder's) eye,
> Can't see the beam in mine.
> You better lef' your sister door,
> Go keep your own door clean.
> And I had a mighty battle like-a Jacob and de angel,
> Jacob time of old.
> I didn't tend to lef' 'em go,
> Till Jesus bless my soul.
> And blessed me, and blessed my,
> And blessed all my soul.
> I didn't tend to lef' 'em go,
> Till Jesus bless my soul.[24]

This song may simply have reflected the traditional idea that one must account for one's own sins before judging the sins of others.

However, the "sister" may also be viewed as a sexually attractive member of the community, and the ensuing feelings of sexual desire (symbolized by the issue of whether the singer should leave the sister's "door") may be both overwhelming, and accompanied by guilt. The singer identifies the conflict as akin to the epic struggle of Jacob and his wrestling with the angel, who turns out to be God Himself. In the biblical story, the struggle does not end until God blesses Jacob.[25] The slave singer attempts to deny the "beam" in his or her own eye (i.e., to deny that he or she actually shares in the sexual attraction being perceived as coming from the other person), but cannot succeed in overcoming his or her own physical urges. Ultimately it takes the intervention of Jesus to resolve the struggle, to "bless my soul," similar to the blessing administered by God in the biblical story. Even so, this appears to be an uneasy resolution!

A New Field of Inquiry

Heretofore there has been very little investigation of the intricacies of sexuality and physical sensuality in Black spirituals. While the work of Zora Neale Hurston and other scholars points in some interesting directions, any comprehensive understanding of underlying themes of sensuality and sexuality in the spirituals will require going against the grain of decades of research. For example, even Angela Davis, in her attempt to resurrect a clear understanding of the role of sexuality in the artistic creations of African Americans, especially African American women, writes as if she has embraced core parts of the conventional wisdom concerning the relatively minor role of themes of sexuality in the spirituals and other slave songs:

> Themes of individual sexual love rarely appear in the musical forms produced during slavery. . . . The spirituals and the work songs confirm the individual concerns of Black people expressed through music during slavery centered on a collective desire for an end to the system that enslaved them. This does not mean that there was an absence of sexual meanings in the music produced by African-American slaves. It means that slave music—both religious and secular—was quintessentially collective music. It was collectively performed and it gave expression to the community's yearning for freedom.[26]

The view that slave songs reflected strong collective aspirations for freedom is undeniable.[27] However, there is clearly much more to the story. It is fascinating, in many respects, that there seems to have been a relatively unspoken assumption among scholars that expressing collective aspirations for freedom would somehow be incompatible with expressing individual physical longings and desires. Even the most oppressed of human beings are still human, and sexuality and physical sensuality are significant parts of their humanity. Among the community of enslaved Africans in North America in the seventeenth, eighteenth, and nineteenth centuries, the story of how they managed to retain their full humanity has not yet been explored fully. It will be interesting to see what future lines of investigation uncover in the attempt to elucidate the ways in which experiences of sensuality and sexuality were played out in the creation of the spirituals, as well as in the creation of other forms of artistic expression in the slave community.

Notes

1. James Weldon Johnson and J. Rosamond Johnson, *The Books of American Negro Spirituals*, preface to Book 2 (New York: Da Capo Press, 1973, originally published 1926), 12–13.
2. The best treatment of the story of the Jubilee Singers is provided by Andrew Ward, *Dark Midnight When I Rise: The Story of the Jubilee Singers Who Introduced the World to the Music of Black America* (New York: Farrar, Straus and Giroux, 2000).
3. Zora Neale Hurston, *The Sanctified Church* (Berkeley, CA: Turtle Island, 1981), 80.
4. See, for example, Hazel V. Carby, *Race Men* (Cambridge, MA: Harvard University Press, 1998).
5. Hurston, *The Sanctified Church*, 56.
6. Hurston, *The Sanctified Church*, 61.
7. Angela Y. Davis, *Blues Legacies and Black Feminism* (New York: Vintage Books, 1998).
8. See, for example, Eileen Southern, *The Music of Black Americans (3rd edition)* (New York: Norton, 1997), 332–340; and Tilford Brooks, *America's Black Musical Heritage* (Englewood Cliffs, NJ: 1984), 51–60.
9. See Peter R. Aschoff, "The Poetry of the Blues," in *The Triumph of the Soul: Cultural and Psychological Aspects of African-American Music*, ed. Ferdinand Jones and Arthur C. Jones (Westport, CT: Praeger Publishers, 2001), 35–68.
10. Delridge L. Hunter, *The Lyric Poet: A Blues Continuum* (Brooklyn, NY: Caribbean Diaspora Press, 2001), 17.
11. The story of Christian conversion among slaves is a complicated one, with both slave masters and slaves resisting the idea of conversion for different but equally compelling reasons. Eventually, after the "Great Awakening" of the 1740s, slaves began to convert to Christianity in significant numbers. By the early nineteenth century, an Africanized form of Christianity was firmly established among most slaves. See Lawrence Levine, *Black Culture and Black*

Consciousness (New York: Oxford Press, 1977), 3–81; Albert Raboteau, *Slave Religion* (New York: Oxford Press, 1978); and Arthur C. Jones, *Wade in the Water: The Wisdom of the Spirituals* (Maryknoll, NY: Orbis Books, 1993), 64–101.

12. Dena Epstein, *Sinful Tunes and Spirituals* (Urbana, IL: University of Illinois Press, 1977).

13. See Sterling Stuckey, *Slave Culture* (New York: Oxford Press, 1987), 12–16; Lydia Parrish, *Slave Songs of the Georgia Sea Islands* (Athens, G A: University of Georgia Press, 1992), xxxii; Samuel A. Floyd, Jr., *The Power of Black Music* (New York: Oxford Press, 1995), 37–40; Art Rosenbaum, *Shout Because You're Free: The African American Ring Shout Tradition in Coastal Georgia* (Athens, GA: University of Georgia Press, 1998), 4–5, 17–20.

14. Rosenbaum, *Shout Because You're Free*, 21.

15. John S. Mbiti, *African Religions and Philosophy (2nd edition)* (London: Heineman, 1989), 142–144.

16. Harold Courlander, *Negro Folk Music, U.S.A.* (New York: Columbia University Press, 1963), 195.

17. Rosenbaum, *Shout Because You're Free*, 123–124.

18. Rosenbaum, *Shout Because You're Free*, 121.

19. Rosenbaum, *Shout Because You're Free*, 121.

20. See Jones, *Wade in the Water*.

21. Jones, *Wade in the Water*, 39–100.

22. William Francis Allen, Charles Pickard Ware, & Lucy McKim Garrison, *Slave Songs of the United States*, reprint of 1867 publication (Bedford, MA: Applewood Books), 7.

23. On the psychological consequences of separation of parents from children, see Jones, *Wade in the Water*, 18–21. The separation of marital and sexual partners was likely equally devastating in its emotional consequences. See Henry Wiencek, An Imperfect *God: Washington, His Slaves, and the Creation of America* (New York: Farrar, Straus and Giroux, 2003), for an extensive treatment of the central issue of separation of marital and romantic partners as a source of psychological trauma for slaves.

24. Allen et al., *Slave Songs of the United States*, 17–18.

25. Genesis 32: 22–31.

26. Davis, *Blues Legacies and Black Feminism*, 4

27. See especially Jones, *Wade in the Water*; and John Lovell, Jr., *Black Song, the Forge and the Flame* (New York: Paragon House Publishers, 1986).

VI

Hermeneutics and Cultural Criticism

14

Loving Our Black Bodies As God's Luminously Dark Temples: The Quest for Black Restoration

Riggins R. Earl, Jr.

Prejudice against color is nothing short of hating God's image because he has dyed it a darker hue

. . . .

If God hates one sin, more than all others, it is the hating of his image in his afflicted colored brethren in the United States-Samuel Cornish .[1]

I excitedly accepted this assignment from the editors of the project based on my ceaseless scholarly interest in the study of the phenomenon of the Black body in American thought. The idea of Blacks loving their bodies as God's luminously dark temples[2] must be critically probed in light of the following: (1) White Christianity's creation of the white soul/black body salvation dilemma type that required that Blacks hate their bodies; and (2) The redemptive God-consciousness type of Blacks' love/hate dilemma for their dark bodies. These constructs illuminate Blacks' theological and moral challenges of loving their bodies as God's luminously dark temples. They are challenges that have their origin in slavers' interpretations of sin and Blackness as being synonymous. This interpretation of salvation, in the name of Jesus' blood, for the African's soul created in him/her a white soul/black body anthropological salvation dilemma.

White Soul/Black Body: The Anthropological Salvation Dilemma[3]

At the heart of American law, politics, economics, religion, and morality has been the question, implicitly or explicitly, of Blacks' bodily color and worth. It is for this reason that the idea of Blacks loving their bodies as God's luminously dark temples cannot start with traditional classical Christian theologians' and ethicists'[4] presuppositions of self-love. It must, instead, start with Blacks' response to the Christian challenge to love themselves in an antiblack society as creations of God. It must struggle with blacks' need to see themselves as having been created in God's image as well as re-creators of themselves. Blacks' perennial struggle to love their Black bodies as sacred creations must be seen as an act of defiance against slave Christianity's construal of blackness as sin and Black persons as sinful. How have Blacks' valued their bodily selves in a society that literally divested their bodies of all sacred worth? This is the question that surfaces when the issue of "blacks loving their black bodies as God's luminously dark temples is engaged. My first major scholarly engagement of the idea of the slave's body took place in the publication *Dark Symbols, Obscure Signs*.[5] In this text, I sought to show how the issue of Christian conversion as total (body/soul) self-awareness manifested itself in slaves' conversion language. This phenomenon was a counter response to the slave master's construal of conversion language for the salvation of the slave's soul. Such language fostered a false dichotomy of the slave's soul and body. The challenge of Blacks' loving their Black bodies as God's dark temples[6] has its genesis, as we presently know it, in western slave culture. This challenge must be seen as Blacks' response to whites' categorical claim of the sinfulness of the African's blackness of body and soul. Slave culture created in the consciousness of Blacks and whites a complex love/hate dilemma for the latter's definition of sin as blackness and blackness as sin. Blacks' dilemma of both loving and hating their Black bodies as sinful creations has just as much shaped the racist history of America as it has been shaped by that history. This fact is heard in white America's constant bemoaning of Blacks' seemingly obsession with race and color. Whites are heard to say to Blacks, "Why can't you people talk about an issue without bringing up race and color?" Blacks' counter question is, "How can white people pretend that American justice is color blind when the nation's foundational document (i.e., the Constitution) reflects its founders' antiblack philosophy? Whites fail to realize that Blacks must always bring their Black presence to the forefront of this debate.

The Value Contradiction

The issues of color and race are deeply rooted in the very fabric of American culture. They originated religiously and morally out of whites' racist redemption requirement of *Africans'* souls. Whites required slaves to have their souls washed in Jesus' blood, making it possible for slaves to have white souls in irredeemable Black bodies. Blacks' bodies were declared to be beyond divine redemption. Whites' racist antiblack belief was polar to the notion in the book of Genesis that what God created was *good*. Whites denounced Blacks as being representative of evil. This notion of the evil of blackness placed Black people in a difficult position of trying to explain why God created blackness. Slaves who were washed in Jesus' blood were seen by pious white Christians as having white souls in Black bodies (i.e., Christian oreos). This invariably led to the love/hate dilemma of the body/soul in Black consciousness. The soul is loved for its whiteness and the body is hated because of its blackness. This love/hate dilemma uniquely emerged in the consciousness of Blacks as a result of the Euro-American slave experiment. It created a false value dichotomy between the sacred worth of the slave's soul and the mere utility value of his/her body. It denied any existence of a sacred value correlation between the converted slave's sacredness of a white soul in Jesus' blood and the slave's Black body as property of the slave owner. Here we have the making of a racist redemption requirement dilemma regarding *blackness* as sin and *sin* as blackness. In spite of their belief that Jesus' blood could wash Blacks' souls white, whites were unwilling to concede that anything could be done for the slave's Black body's lack of intrinsic worth. Whites' foregone conclusion was that the slave's bodily worth did not exceed that of property status. The idea was that a divine curse upon Blacks' blackness of body had deprived them of any possibility of sacredness. Whites' saw all counter arguments as being contradictory to the politics of slavery.

This racist redemption requirement created a paradoxical anthropological model for stereotypically valuing and devaluing Blacks. It declared Christian converted Blacks as being simultaneously good white souls and evil black bodies, saved and heathen. Its advocates' idea was that the pre-Christian African's primitive condition of benighted blackness presented no anthropological contradiction of self. Teachers of redemption presumed that the unredeemed African's self symbolized evil interiorly and exteriorly. The Black African was deemed totally evil. Ironically, the Black African redeemed in Jesus' blood could only be declared *semi-evil* and half good (i.e., possessing a good white soul in an evil Black body). This was pious white Christians' contradictory response to what they considered to be the divine *curse* of *blackness*. Their belief was that Black persons could only be partially (e.g., spiritually) saved. No social or political salvation was conceivable for Blacks' bodily selves in the white man's society.[7]

In the stereotypical eyes of whites, the Black slave could only experience the salvation of the soul. Radical Blacks saw that the white man's Jesus' white soul requirement actually compromised the sacredness of the African's self. On the contrary, whites believed that their white Jesus' soul whitening power lifted the African from zero value status as a heathen to a tolerated subhuman level. Blacks' faith in whites' Jesus would place them in an oppressive anthropological contradiction of self-consciousness unique to whites' enslavement of them. This oppressive anthropological paradox fostered in Blacks' consciousness a self-valuation dilemma of extreme value deficits and surpluses. On the one end of the valuation continuum, it has required that Blacks put too much emphasis on their souls' heavenly rewards at the expense of their earthly needs. On the other end of the valuation continuum , it has required that Blacks' assign superfluous value to their bodies' utility worth at the expense of their spiritual needs. It created a dilemma of how to love the self holistically.

The Love Question

Racists' redemption requirement that slaves attain a white soul, by being washed in the blood of Jesus, is the root pathological cause for Blacks' bodily self-hatred of their blackness. It fostered a false sense of racial inferiority in Blacks and one of racial superiority in whites. This has amounted, too often, to Blacks hating themselves for being Black and for whites hating Blacks for being Black. While racist whites have used Christianity to justify their dehumanizing treatment of Blacks, Blacks have used Christianity as shield and buckler against whites' hatred of them. Whites' salvation requirement of Blacks drove them to a narcissistic love for their own *whiteness*. It often drove Blacks to a self-contradictory disposition about their holistic self-worth. Realistically whites' notion of Christianity was intended to save the slave's soul. It was not intended to teach slaves to love themselves holistically. In short, whites used Christianity to make the slave a more effective tool of labor. The question of Blacks loving their own Black bodies assumes a connection or disconnection between their fallen condition of creation and redemption.

Redeeming Fallen Creation

Blacks loving their Black bodies as God's dark temples begs the question of their understanding of slave Christianity's interpretation of their blackness in relationship to the biblical stories of *creation, the fall* and *redemption*. Only a word can be said here about the concepts of *creation*, the *fall* and *redemption* as it relates to Blacks' challenge to love their Black bodies as God's luminously dark selves.

Debates pursued among whites, during slavery and afterward, over the question of where Blacks stood in the biblical doctrine of creation and the fall. I am of the persuasion that whites' racist redemption requirement of Blacks' souls is the starting place for trying to understand them religiously and morally. It is in the face of the white soul/black body stereotypical dilemma that Blacks must work out their agency. It is in response to the black body/white soul salvation formulary that Blacks must work out their understanding of agency. Here Blacks come to see themselves in relationship to the biblical myths of creation and the fall. Redemption possibilities of the African's soul in Jesus is where the Christian slave master and the slave make contact with each other religiously and ethically. Whites' question of the Africans' redemption possibilities provokes critical questions about creation and the fall. This redemption question harks back to what historian Charles Long calls the "creation myth." Long has mythically alluded to the American slave experience as Black Americans' second creation that they must dialectically deal with in relationship to their first creation. Recounting a "creation myth" pertaining to the arrival of enslaved Africans to the Americas, Long concludes.

> The oppressed must deal with both the fictive truth of their status as expressed by the oppressors, that is their second creation, and the discovery of their own autonomy and truth-their first creation. The locus for this structure is the mythic consciousness which dehistoricizes the relationship for the sake of creating a new form of humanity-master slave dialectic.[8]

Long's assumption of the first and second creation myth begs the question of how Blacks have understood original sin and the fall. Mythically, if Blacks are twice-created, are they twice-fallen? The subsequent redemption question is, what are the salvation requirements of twice-fallen Blacks? Are the salvation requirements of twice-fallen Blacks different from those of once-fallen whites? If the African's Black body is furthered devalued via the white man's white soul/black body stereotypical redemption requirement of Blacks, how do Blacks love their bodies as God's luminous dark temples?

The major difference seemingly between the once-fallen white Adam and Eve and the twice-fallen Black Adam and Eve is that of whites' single debtorship versus Blacks' double debtorship. Once-fallen whites would be single debtors to God only for the sins of the soul via the fall of Adam. Whites stereotyped twice-fallen Blacks as being double debtors to God and themselves: (1) To God for saving their Black souls in Jesus' blood; and (2) to the white slave owners for bringing Blacks from benighted Africa into slavery so that they could be introduced to Jesus.

Slaves such as Phyllis Wheatley internalized and expressed gratitude poetically for what she believed was God's mercy displayed through colonizers, slavers, and missionaries. This resonates in Wheatley's heralded poem "On Being Brought from Africa to America." In the lyrics she pictured Africa as a sanctuary of paganism and from which Christianity had liberated blacks. Ironically, she insists that Blacks, even in their "diabolic" color, are within God's redemption plan:

> 'Twas mercy brought me from my Pagan land,
> Taught my benighted soul to understand
> That there's a God, that there's a Savior too;
> Once I redemption neither sought nor knew,
> Some view our race with scornful eye
> "There color is a diabolic die."
> Remember Christians, Negroes, Black as Cain,
> May be refined and join th' angelic train.[9]

The *Christian oreo (black body/white soul)* revels in the faith knowledge that Jesus has whitened his/her soul for eternity. This Christian oreo primarily delights in knowing that a white soul has eschatological value despite the white man's devaluing his body. This plants in Blacks' consciousness the idea of what will be spoken of later as an *in spite of doctrine* of Black redemption. The following quote from whites' memorialization of a slave, named Caesar, in the last quarter of the eighteenth century is a case in point:

> In Memory of Caesar
> Herein lies the
> best of slaves
> Now turning into dust:
> Caesar the Ethiopian craves
> A place among the just.
> His fled soul has fled
> To realms of heavenly light
> And by the blood of Jesus shed

Is changed from black to White
Jan. 15, he quitted the state
In the 77th year of his age
1780.[10]

Slave Christianity presupposed theologically that the blackness of slave's body was the results of the Hamitic curse that Noah invoked upon his son Ham following the flood. The underlying presupposition was that God could save the slave's Adamitically cursed Black soul *in spite of* its entrapment in a Hamitically cursed body of blackness. The Hamitically cursed blackness of the African's body placed the slave in a double-jeopardy-sin-cursed category. George Kelsey has categorized it as the condition of the twice-fallen which he believes resulted from the racist skewed interpretation of the biblical myths of Adam's sin and the Hamitic curse invoked by Noah upon his son Ham. The Adamic myth claims that God cursed Adam for his disobedience; the Hamitic myth declares that the father, Noah, cursed his son, Ham, for the latter looking upon his drunken father's nakedness. In The Adamic story, it is a paternalistic case of God cursing man. While in the Noah story it is the case of man cursing man. The historical fact in the American experience is that of white identity with Adam in the first story and with Noah in the second story. For whites theological consciousness of being the once-fallen before God gave them a sense of superiority over Blacks in every way. It gave them the theological rationale for justifying slavery.

White slavers used the doctrine of the Hamitic curse to reinforce the myth of Blacks' natural inferiority of body and soul. Physical blackness of the soul was thought to be the proof of this curse. Dianne Stewart notes that the physical blackness of Blacks has been alluded to as the cause for what George Kelsey has referenced as the second fall.[11] Stewart's critical read of Kelsey's thesis is profoundly insightful:

> The history of black religious experience in the United States bears out Kelsey's thesis. The double fall, especially the second "racial fall," has impacted the African American Christian tradition so negatively precisely because of its inability to distinguish "blackness" as a human identity from evil, shame, sin, guilt, and other self-abnegating experiences known by many practicing Christians.[12]

The second racial fall myth shaped the way that white slave masters valued blacks' bodies. Slave masters' compromising view of slaves' bodily worth generated the following stereotypical images of Blacks (1) the bodyless soul and the soulless body stereotypes; and (2) the mindless body and the bodyless mind stereotypes. This stereotypical dichotomization of the Black self, which originated in slavery, continues to impact the way Blacks see themselves in relationship to whites and vice versa.

In this discussion, a brief word about the soulless body and the mindless body stereotypes is sufficient.

The Soulless Body

Whites' soulless body stereotypes of Blacks as tools of servile labor and objects for public torture is graphically delineated in American history from slavery to the present. Numerous contemporary Black scholars tend to reference this fact.

As Tools of Servile Labor

From slavery to the end of the industrial revolution Black bodies were seen as tools of servile labor, as capitalistic investments. During slavery, the big nigger buck, or mandingo type was viewed by slave masters as model tools for servile labor and breeding. Black females were used as tools of reproduction and labor as well. Slavers bred this type with selected females so as to increase the strength of slave laborers as well as the market value of slaves' offspring. During the beginning of the American industrial revolution, the legend of a Black worker by the name of John Henry took on mythic proportion. Legend has it that John Henry was such a consummate steel driver that his boss had him compete with a steel driving machine. This myth dramatizes the extent to which the industrialized society reduced Blacks—males and females,[13] to tools of labor. The post-industrial society values Blacks bodies as incarcerated commodities. The balladeer of the John Henry ballad notes that his wife replaces him in the steel driving competition during her husbands mandatory sick leave. A line in the ballad says: "John Henry took sick and had to go to bed and Pollyann drove steel like a man. Lord! Lord! Pollyann drove steel like a man!" Contemporary high technology has redefined physical labor itself and its lack of need for Blacks' bodily strength. America's prisons have become the new slave ships for the society's useless black bodies. Black bodies are valuable to a prison culture that is driven by a need for economic profit. Blacks as tools of labor have been no less objects of public torture.

As Objects of Public Torture

Rituals of public torture have been white America's way of reducing the Black person to a soulless body stereotype. Common during and after slavery, rituals of public torture such as whippings, lynchings, and maiming typified whites' techniques for controlling Blacks through fear. Anthony Pinn's recent book on slavery and religion insightfully exams the way that Black bodies were made objects of torture.[14] Pinn seems to ignore the sacred/non-sacred dilemma in his informative discourse about the Black body as an object of whites' terrorization.

I think that Pinn could have made an even stronger case for the issue of the Black body's value and its devaluation had he given more attention to what I call in *Dark Symbols, Obscure Signs* the slave owners' soulless body and bodyless soul stereotypes. No period was more inclined to behave brutally towards Blacks as stereotypical soulless bodies than that of Jim Crow. It was this era in which whites denied Blacks all personal (e.g., slave owner) or legal protection. During this era a moderate white preacher's expressed trepidation for the harmful consequences of lynching to the souls of white lynchers with total disregard for the sacredness of the Black lynched victim "is instructive": "The great peril at this hour where outbreak and lawlessness are at the surface is not that the negro will lose his skin but that the Anglo-Saxon will lose his soul."[15]

Blacks as soulless body stereotypes dominated the consciousness of America as the public rituals of lynching Blacks make clear. The following description of whites lynching of a Black male on Sunday April 23, 1890 in Newnan, Georgia is an example of this fact. The event attracted participant observers from Atlanta. The guilt of the victim had not been proven in a court of law. Photographed pictures of the event show that no attempt is made on the part of the lynchers to conceal their identity. Many of them are upstanding citizens. Historian Litwack's summation of the white mob's behavior at Sam Hose's lynching in Georgia indicates their stereotypical devaluation of him as a soulless body:

> After stripping Hose of his clothes and chaining him to a tree, the self-appointed executioners stacked korsene-soaked wood high around him. Before saturating Hose with oil and applying the torch, they cut off his ears, fingers, and genitals, and skinned his face. While some in the crowd plunged knives into the victim's flesh, others watched "with unfeigning satisfaction" (as one reporter noted) the contortions of Sam Hose's body as the flames rose, distorting his features, causing his eyes

to bulge out of their sockets, and rupturing his veins. The only sound that came from the victim's lips, even as his blood sizzled in the fire, were, "Oh, my God! Oh Jesus." Before Hose's body had even cooled, his heart and liver were removed and cut into several pieces and his bones were crushed into small particles. The crowd fought over these souvenirs. Shortly after the lynching, one of the participants reportedly left for the state capitol, hoping to deliver a slice of Sam's heart to the governor of Georgia, who would call Sam Hose's deed "the most diabolical in the annals of crime."[16]

The media reported, "The next morning, smoldering ashes and a blackened stake were all that remained." On the trunk of a tree near the scene, a placard read, "*We must protect our Southern Women*," and One Georgia woman, Rebecca Felton gave voice to that sentiment: "*The Premeditated outrage on Mrs. Crawdford was infinitely more intolerable than the murder of her husband.*"[17] As for Hose, Felton claimed any "true-hearted husband" or "*father*" would have happily dispatched the "*beast*" with no more concern than if he were shooting down a mad dog: indeed, "*The dog is more worthy of sympathy*".[18]

The Mindless Body

"The drum and its influence need to be mentioned in proper perspective. Misapprehension resulted in the Negro's being associated with an orgiastic drum beat."[19] Defending intellectual integrity has been a constant struggle for Blacks. Portraying Blacks as mentally inferiors or as mindless bodies has been a propaganda tactic of whites for control of them. Euro-American arguments for the mindless body stereotype of Blacks often bordered on the ludicrous as the following quote suggests:

> You can dress a champanzee, house break him and teach him to use a knife and a fork, but it will take countless generations of evolutionary development, if ever, before you can convince him that a caterpillar or cockroach is not a delicacy. Likewise, the social, political, economic and religious preference of the Negro remains close to the caterpillar and the cockroach.[20]

Lemuel Johnson notes that the Negro was seen (1) as a literary toy, and (2) a most important economic discovery. Johnson proceeds to note that:

> The Negro, in so far as he was black and physically different, became an incarnation of the incongruous and the anti-thetical. He was seen as an apt metaphor for ethic and ethical caricature. Insofar as he was black,

he was a metaphor for darkness and for the unholy. So he became the Devil, "being hels [sic] perfect character." To the extent that his features and behavior were crucially different he became a Buffoon. But these same features, black skin and blubber-lipped, flat-nosed, could also be perceived as uncomfortably close caricatures. Seen in this light he became as negatively decorative and slightly obscene as a Gargoyle.[21]

As Objects of Public Ridicule and Shame

White America made the stereotyped Black body the object of public ridicule and shame. Minstrel shows and films were the means for perpetuating the image of the Black as a mindless body stereotype. Toms, coons, mulattoes, mammies, and bucks were popular degrading metaphors that whites used to publically ridicule Blacks. Donald Bogle rightly notes about these degrading metaphors: "All were character types used for the same effect: to entertain by stressing Negro inferiority. Fun was poked at the American Negro by presenting him as either a nitwit or a childlike lackey."[22] The film industry merely reproduced the stereotypes of Blacks that arose out of the slave culture.

Numerous movies arose, starting at the beginning of the nineteenth century, for the purpose of portraying Blacks as mindless Black bodies who were best suited for entertaining whites. Movies such as Mr. Bojangles and Stepin Fetchit taught Blacks to make fun of their own buffoonery; despising themselves as mindless bodies. Blacks' loving their bodies as God's luminously dark temples has been shaped by a mosaic history of redemptive God-consciousness that has its genesis in slavery.

Redemptive God-Consciousness Types of Blacks' Love for Their Bodies

In a religion such as Christianity, the image of God in the minds of many Christians is that of a kindly, benevolent, bewhiskered white man, seated on a white throne, surrounded by blond and brunette angels who stand ready to serve Him in praises or as messengers. The Devil, on the one hand, is the Prince of Darkness while the imps of the devil are black. Hence the phrase "black as imp." Now this is strong medicine even for the pure of heart. What a vote of confidence it must have been to a white person to feel that the Creator of the Universe was made in his image. Of course, there is nothing universal about the notion that God is imaged in accordance with the ideal of the beholder. The advantage is obvious.[23]

We have shown above that redemptive God-consciousness has shaped the way that Blacks have loved their bodies as God's luminously dark temples in an antiblack society. It continues to shape Blacks' love/hatred for their bodies. To be a Black American is to be undeniably influenced by the reality of America's history of redemptive God-consciousness, that is, whites' definition of what constituted Christian redemption of the soul for those in black bodies. Blacks have inevitably internalized the different types of redemptive God-consciousness as they have struggled with the question of loving their Black bodies. At least four evolutionary types of redemptive God consciousness are discernable in Black America's struggle to love their Black bodies as God's sacred temples: (1) the redemptive white racist God-consciousness type; (2) the color-blind God-consciousness type; (3) the Black power God-consciousness type; and (4) the Black restorationist God-consciousness type.

The Redemptive White Racist God-Consciousness Type

This is the chief cornerstone of all the redemptive God-consciousness types. Architects and managers of slavery were theologically informed by this type. All subsequent types derive from the redemptive white racist God-consciousness one. The God of this type, on the one hand, sees and devalues blackness as *being-evil in-itself* and *being-evil to-God*; on the other hand, the God of this type sees and values whiteness as *being-good-in-itself* and *being-good-to-God*. Advocates of this type of God-consciousness are antiblack body and pro-white body. Physical blackness is irredeemable in the salvation project of the God of this type of consciousness. For this type being washed in Jesus' blood can do nothing to mitigate the evil of the blackness of the body. This type's God's antiblack body philosophy manifests itself in the racist redemption requirement of Blacks having the white soul/black body as a result of being washed in Jesus' blood. As we noted above, this left the redeemed Black subject in a salvation dilemma of being an interiorly good white soul self in an exteriorly evil Black bodily self . This soul-in-body entrapment created an existentially *oh wretched man* that I am crisis. It left Blacks saying "When I would be satisfied with my soul having been washed white in Jesus' blood, the black stain of my body is always present." Who or what can deliver me from my body of blackness?" becomes the existential cry of the Black of this type.[24]

The redemptive white racist God-consciousness type posits the implied theological presupposition that God loves people's souls *in spite of* the blackness of their bodies. This *in spite of* theological presupposition reeks with the Christian colonizers' false notion of racial superiority. On the one hand, God saves white people because they are white and favored. On the other hand, God saves Blacks' souls *in spite of* the irredeemable blackness of their bodies. It must be concluded from the *in spite of* theological presupposition that God of this type does not love Black people holistically. Moreover, the God of this type makes it problematic for Blacks to love themselves holistically in themselves or in God. Black people, under this typology, are given only partial status with God because of the irredeemable blackness of their skin. In this case, they cannot say, "God loves the sinner but hates his sin." Instead, the Black person must say that "God loves my soul washed white in Jesus' but hates my body because it is black."

This white racist redemptive God-consciousness type has dominated western religious discourse for hundreds of years primarily because it has translated blackness into an evil hegemonic ideology. Eulalio P. Blatazar's statement of a process theology of blackness delineates the complex historical evolution of the variant interpretations of the darkness/light dilemma in human consciousness.[25] He notes that white, western theology has given roots to racism not only by supporting a color symbolism that separates white from Black as good from evil, but by its insistence on light, clarity, rationalism, and conceptualization. The God of this type presupposes that Black people are accountable for the evil of their own physical blackness. This spurious presupposition provokes such questions as: What sin did Blacks commit against God to warrant God making them black? How did blackness become evil? The racist hegemonic nature of this type has presented God as an enemy of Black people's blackness. It made sin and blackness synonymous. Blacks of this type are given no space to challenge whites' definitions of sin, guilt, redemption and restoration. The question in this type of whether black people love God and themselves is rather easy. The more difficult question is: Does God really love Black people?

This type of God-consciousness inevitably has shaped the way that Blacks have sought to love themselves as God's luminously dark bodies. It has fostered in blacks a pathological hatred for the blackness of their bodies that has its antecedents in what we noted above as slave ideology's false creation of them. Bold black religious leaders, from Henry McNeal Turner to Malcolm X,[26] have vigorously attacked the demonic theological presuppositions of this type. Defiantly they have demanded that Blacks love their blackness, as the third type will show, as God's sacred creation. Nowhere did these leaders teach Blacks to love their blackness as God's image. Much of this probably had to do with the fact that Black leaders have only attempted to address this question of blackness in response to whites' public denigration of them. This is why the redemptive color-blind God-consciousness type has had a critical place in the consciousness of Blacks.

The Redemptive Color-Blind God-Consciousness Type

The color-blind idea is that the God of this type does not see blackness or whiteness. For the color-blind God whiteness and blackness do not exist at all when it comes to persons. Both Black and white practitioners of religion have espoused the color-blind theory of God. Blacks have been inclined to use the color-blind theory as a buffer against their internal feelings of rage at the idea that God really does favor whites over Blacks. In short, both Blacks and whites who invoked the color-blind God, in response to racism, often did so to escape the painful reality of the negative politics of race and color that the idea of a white God elicits. Oppressed people probably have a greater need than their oppressors for a God who does not get involved directly in the politics of race and color. Neither a color-blind God nor such a God's followers are encouraged to bring the issue of color to public discourse. Black masses for generations have had a utopic longing for a color-blind God who sees people for their human worth only. That hankering is expressed in Martin King, Jr's celebrated 1963 march on Washington "I have A Dream Speech."[27] King said he dreamed of a day coming in America "When my four little children will not be judged by the color of their skin but by the content of their character." Because they have believed that God is color-blind, Blacks have longed for a color-blind society. It, perhaps, has kept them from at least venting their rage against God and their oppressors. It has mitigated their hostility against what seemed to have been God's impotence to liberate the darker peoples of the world. It possibly countered the raging question of the blues songster who, employing the collective I, asked for all Black people: "What did I do to be so black and blue?" The God is color-blind antidote cooled blacks' internal anger, born out of physical and psychological abuse, that caused them to wonder aloud and silently, "Is God a white racist?" Black scholars' struggle with the white racist question of God's color and possible favoritism of whites goes back to W. E. B. DuBois' query of God following the 1903

Atlanta race riot. In his litaneutical probing, DuBois wondered aloud as to whether God was white.[28] He expressed undoubtedly the fear of untold numbers of Blacks for generations.

For Blacks the idea of God being color-blind has undoubtedly served as an antidote against the venom of white racism borne by the redemptive white racist God-consciousness type. It had antidotal value for previous generations who uttered such popular phrases as: "God does not see color." Or, "God treats all of his children alike regardless of their color. Color means nothing in the eyes of God." Ironically, most Blacks do not practice such idealism about God and color toward each other. Patricia J. Williams has probably captured the truth of the color-blind aspiration theory when she writes: " . . . I embrace color blindness as a legitimate hope for the future, I worry that we tend to enshrine the notion with a kind of utopianism whose naivete will ensure its elusiveness."[29] The issue of color-blindness provokes the question of God's trustworthiness for Blacks. It elicits the question of whether God is merely some cosmic being who is unable to distinguish certain colors. If this is the case, does this constitute an optical defect in God's being? If Black people are made to suffer because of their color, should not people of color have a God who can distinguish between the color of the oppressed and that of the oppressor? The color-blind type is very problematic theologically because it assumes that God is unable to totally identify the peculiar ethnic differences in God's creation.

Despite this faith claim about God, blacks know that the issue of color runs deep in the consciousness of the American society. The kind of value preference that Blacks make of the difference in the different colors of skin among themselves borders on being pathological. Although, they might have longed for a color-blind God, blacks have never, even among themselves, been able to approximate color-blindness in relating to each other.

The Redemptive Black Power God-Consciousness Type

The God of this type is the polar opposite of both the white racist redemptive God-consciousness type and the color-blind redemptive God-consciousness type. Many advocates, academics and practitioners, of the Black power redemptive God-consciousness type think of God as being Black. For this reason the God of this type has no problem loving Black people's body as well as their souls. Early Black

Christian leaders, even before the founding of the country have been unequivocally committed theologically and ethically to Black people loving their own Black bodies as God's luminously dark temples. Richard Allen was committed to this principle when he led a group of Blacks in a kneel-in protest against racial exclusion at the altar of the Saint George's Methodist Church of Philadelphia. In response to whites' rejection of Blacks, Allen led the Blacks from the church and founded the historic Mother Bethel African Methodist Episcopal Church in Philadelphia. Moral leaders such as Richard Allen, Henry M. Turner, Alexander Crummell, David Walker, Sojourner Truth, Ida B. Wells, and Marcus Garvey all represent certain variations of the Black power redemptive God-consciousness type. Very few of these leaders would have advocated the idea of God being Black. We might safely say that these leaders were more concerned about God's power and love of Black people than God's color. Most leaders, except Marcus Garvey, believed that God would favor and empower Black people because of their blackness.

Blacks of this type have been expected to love their bodies as God's luminously dark temples either because God is Black or because God is colorless. The belief of this type is that the colorless God favors Black people because they have suffered unduly for being Black. God's relationship with Black people grows out of a *because of* theological motive. Two reasons undergird this *because of* theological motive of God's love for Black people and Black people's love for God and their own Black bodies: (1) Black people love their Black bodies because God is metaphysically and physically (i.e., Jesus of history) Black. (2) God, although colorless, loves Black people because God is empathetic toward the less fortunate (i.e., Blacks and browns) of the earth. The academic side of liberation theology is grounded in the idea of God being metaphysically Black. James Cone has been the principal proponent of this position about God . A few prominent practitioners of religion have espoused this view of God such as Albert Cleage and Elijah Muhammed. These leaders have been unquestionably the exception to the rule. By and large, Black religious practitioners, especially of the Christian church, have been very timid about embracing the notion of God being Black. A few Christian pastors have gone along with the idea of the blackness of the historical Jesus. Black Christian pastors have been more inclined to embrace the notion of a colorless God than that of God being Black. For them, of course, this colorless God sees and loves God's created children in spite of their different colors. They would say that God loves those victimized of

God's creation in a special way because of their unmerited suffering. Ironically, the colorless God of this type affirms Black people's quest for Black power and the need to love their blackness.

A great ethical tension has existed between the notion of a colorless God in their struggle for Black power and Blacks' love of themselves and those who want a Black God. Advocates of the colorless God notion wants a God who will affirm their quest for Black power and Black love without offending white people. On the contrary, advocates of a Black God or messiah want a deity who affirms Black people's quest for Black power and love of their own Black bodies by offending white people by whatever means necessary. The contrasting leadership styles of Martin L. King, Jr. and Malcolm X symbolize these ethical polarizations in Black consciousness.

The God of this type offers holistic redemption for the Black body and soul from an antiblack world. On the one hand, God of the redemptive Black power type devalues whiteness as *being-evil-in-itself* and *being-evil-to-God*. On the other hand, God of this type values blackness as *being-good-in-itself* and *being-good-to-God*. This devaluation/valuation polarity provokes the question of God being totally for black people. Radicals of the Black power redemption God-consciousness type have been reluctant to see God as redeemer of both races. They present God with the challenge of either being for oppressed people or against them.

All of the above typologies of God-consciousness certainly illuminate the complex theological and ethical challenges that Blacks have faced in their attempt to love their blackness as a *created good*[30] of God. The need is for a restorationist God-consciousness type that restores blackness and whiteness to their primal status of created goodness.

The Black Restorationist God-Consciousness Type

I have deliberately chosen to call this the restorationist God-consciousness type because the latter term gets at the idea of rebuilding what has been torn down. Black theologians have generally used the term reconciliation when speaking of race and liberation. Deotis Roberts[31] saw reconciliation as one of the main foci of Black liberation theology. Crafting his theological discourse against the back drop of the civil rights movement, Roberts was concerned to accent the reconciliation motif of Black liberation theology. He accented the need for America to revisit the biblical notion of God's atonement in Christ for understanding reconciliation. Roberts understood this to be the vertical dimension of reconciliation. He noted that the horizontal dimension had to do with the restoration of good relationships between Blacks and whites. Roberts clearly noted that horizontally reconciliation, as taught in the scriptures, presupposed an event between equals. I make the case here that the concept of redemption fails oppressed people's attempt to understand their blackness in relationship to God and sin. It presupposes that Blacks need redemption from the blackness of their bodies. This would mean that Blacks owe some primal debt to their Creator for being Black.

Blacks need a savior to save them from this dilemma of the sinfulness of blackness. The notion of restoration seems more persuading in that it presupposes one who makes restitution for something taken away or lost. In this case, white Christians' enslavement of Blacks amounted to them robbing Blacks' blackness of its created goodness. It taught blacks to hate that natural part of themselves that God had called *good*.[32] It is this issue of God's *created goodness* that causes me to veer from Olin Moyd's[33] call to make redemption the premier theological category for Black theological reflection. Moyd thinks that redemption is a broader category than that of liberation. I part with Olin Moyd's call for redemption as a critical category for Black theology because his argument does not help us to see how blackness as a symbol is redeemable in a Christian world view that is antiblack.

The God of this type affirms the fact that the being of both blackness and whiteness have been robbed of their created (primal) goodness through slavery and institutionalized racism. It presupposes that blackness both was-good-in-itself and was-good-to-God. It, also, presupposed that whiteness was-good-in-itself and was-good-to-God at the genesis of creation. The need of this restorationist type is for a God who will help Blacks restore whiteness and blackness to their originary status of created goodness. Given that blackness was created good, the need is for the restoration of blackness. The idea of the restoration of blackness to its original goodness presupposes that blackness will have to become a metaphor of theological and moral goodness. Does this mean that God of this type will have to be Black? Only when blackness becomes a theological and moral metaphor for goodness will the discourse of Black theology be taken to another level. When blackness becomes a metaphor for goodness, as opposed to being only a metaphor for evil, even whites will find it indispensable to their redemption. This means that blackness will be-good-in-itself; it will be good-to-God and it will be-good-for-non-blacks.

Blacks of the restorationist God-consciousness type have the moral duty to lead whites in restoring whiteness to its primal state of goodness. Given the fact that it has been given preeminence in our value system, whites often find it problematic in seeing how they have corrupted the symbol of whiteness. Blacks are probably more capable of helping others to see how whites, in the name of whiteness, have robbed the symbol of its originary goodness. Blacks partnering with whites might be the best solution for helping all to see the need for smashing and restoring the symbol of whiteness. If symbol rebuilding will require partnership between oppressed and oppressor with God, is the goodness of the restored symbol reflected in the act of mutual cooperation between all parties? Or, is goodness God's gift to the restorationists?

Conclusion

It has been shown above that the challenge of Blacks' loving their bodies as God's luminously dark temples is ensconced in a redemption history of the evolutionary struggle of God-consciousness types. No one God-consciousness type adequately mirrors how Blacks have loved their Black bodies. All the named typologies are necessary for understanding that for Blacks, loving themselves is rooted in the pathological history of American religion and racism.

Notes

1. Samuel Cornish Roger in the *Colored American*, October 7, 1837, December 22, 1838. Samuel Cornish and John Russwurm were cofounders of Freedom's Journal in New York, the first Black U.S. newspaper.
2. Dark temple is a paraphrasing of the Apostle Paul's analogization of the body as the temple of God. In I Corinthians 6:19 Paul asks the Corinthians whether they knew that their body is the temple of the Holy Spirit. When I speak of the Black body as God's luminously dark temple, I am making reference to its sacred nature.
3. Black theological discussion has been rather silent on the question of a Black anthropology. Maybe it is a bit early for addressing such an issue. It is difficult to talk about agency without struggling with the complex issues of conceptualizing a Black anthropology out of the Black experience. Dianne Stewart has written one of the best essays on the subject of which I am aware. See Stewart's article: "Christian Doctrines of Humanity and the African Experience of Evil and Suffering: Toward a Black Theological Anthropology" in *The Ties that Bind African American and Hispanic* (New York: Continuum, 2001), 169–183.
4. For a comprehensive interpretation of the classical theological arguments about the body see Benedict M. Ashley's O. P. *Theologies of the Body: Humanist and Christian* (The Pope John Center: Braintree, Massachusetts, 1985).

5. I sought to address this issue formally in *Dark Symbols, Obscure Signs: God, Self, and Community in the Slave Mind* (Orbis Books: Maryknoll, New York, 1993. Reprinted at Knoxville, Tennessee: University of Tennessee Press, 2003).

6. "Do you not know that your body is the temple of the Holy Spirit?" is a constant theme of conservative Black preaching. Preachers, male and female, use it to generally chide the congregation about it sexual impropriety.

7. Numerous studies in the last thirty years have drawn heavily upon the primary sources of slavery to reveal the complexities of the minds of slave holders and slaves. One of the most comprehensive studies was Eugene Genovese's *Roll, Jordan, Roll: The World the Slave Made* (New York: Vintage Books, 1967).

8. Charles H. Long, "The Oppressive Elements in Religion and the Religions of the Oppressed," in *Significations: Signs, and Images in Interpretations of Religions* (Philadelphia: Fortress Press, 1986, reissued in 1999 by The Davis Group), 170.

9. Phillis Wheatley, *The Poems*, 10. London: Printed for A. Bell, Bookseller, Aldgate; and sold by Messrs. Cox and Berry, King Street, Boston ADCCL XXIII

10. Quoted in Joseph Washington's *Antiblackness in English Religion* (New York: Mellen Press, 1984), 351–353.

11. See George D. Kelsey, *Racism and a Christian Understanding of Man* (New York: Charles Scribner's Sons, 1965), 25–26.

12. Op. cit., Dianne Stewart, 176.

13. Joan Martin, *More Than Chains and Tools: A Christian Work Ethic of Enslaved Women* (Louisville, Kentucky: Westminister John Knox Press, 2000).

14. Anthony Pinn, *Terror and Triumph: The Nature of Black Religion* (Minneapolis: Minnesota, 2003).

15. Quoted by Leon Litwack's in his article "Hellhounds" in *Without Sanctuary: Lynching Photography in America*, eds. James Allen, Hilton Als, Congressman John Lewis, and Leon F. Litwack (Santa Fe, New Mexico: Twin Palms Publishers, 2000), 22.

16. Ibid., 8.

17. Ibid.

18. Ibid., 8–9.

19. Lamuel Johnson *The Devil, The Gargoyle, and the Buffoon: The Negro as Metaphor in Western Literature* (Port Washington, New York: National University Publications, 1969), 19.

20. Quoted by Carl T. Rowan, "How Racists Use Science to Degrade Black People," in *Ebony*, vol. XXV, no. 7, May 1970), 31–40.

21. Op. cit., Lemuel Johnson, 19.

22. Donald Bogle, *Toms, Coons, Mulattoes, Mammies, and Bucks: An Interpretative History of Blacks in American Films* (New York: Continuum International Publishing Group, Inc. 2001, originally published in 1973).

23. Howard Thurman, *Luminous Darkness* (New York: Harper & Row, 1965), 59–60.

24. The inspiration came from the Apostle Paul's autobiographical account of his struggle with sin from Romans chapter 7. In contrast to Paul, I am using blackness as a metaphor for sin.

25. Eulalio R. Baltazar, *The Dark Center: A Process Theology of Blackness* (New York: Paulist Press, 1973). Baltazar's treatment of the whole color symbolism phenomenon as regards the issue of evil is the most valuable source yet on the subject. Also see Robert E. Hood's *Begrimed and Black: Christian Traditions on Blackness* (Minneapolis, Minnesota: Fortress Press, 1994). For an excellent collection of essays on blackness see *Existence in Black: An Anthology of Black Existential Philosophy*, ed. Lewis R. Gordon (New York: Routledge, 1997). Also, see Franz Fanon, *Black Skin, White Masks*, trans. C. L. Markmann (New York: Grove, 1967).

26. See Edwin S. Redkey, ed., *Respect Black: The Writings and Speeches of Henry McNeal Turner* (New York: Arno Press, 1971); Alex Haley *The Autobiography of Malcolm X* (New York: Ballantine Books 1965, reprinted 1987).

27. Coretta Scott King ed., *The Words of Martin L. King , Jr.* (New York: Newmarket, 1983, 1987), 95–96.

28. W. E. B. DuBois "The Atlanta Litany" in *Dark Waters* in *The Seventh Son: The Thought and Writings of W.E.B. DuBois* vol. I Edited and with Introduction by Julius Lester (New York: Vintage Book, 1971), 422–427. DuBois wondered about God: "Surely Thou too, art not white, O Lord, a pale, bloodless, heartless thing!" Ibid., 425.

29. Patricia J. Williams, *Seeing A Color-Blind Future: The Paradox of Race* (New York: The Noonday Press, 1997), 4.

30. The notion of blackness as created goodness has been given practically no scholarly attention. Victor Anderson's work is most valuable in summarizing the strengths and weaknesses of Black theologians' treatment of the subject. Anderson's work, however, is too quick to dismiss the myth of blackness as God's created goodness. As fascinating as it seems to be, Anderson's religious and cultural criticism does not get us beyond the reality of the challenge of ontological blackness.

31. J. Deotis, *Liberation and Reconciliation: A Black Theology* (Philadelphia: Westminister Press, revised edition 1971; Maryknoll, NY: Orbis Books, reprinted 1994).

32. See James Cone *Black Theology and Black Power* (New York: Seabury Press, 1969; San Francisco: HarperCollins, 1989). One of Cone's greatest contribution in his first publication was to challenge Blacks to deconstruct the racist contamination of the primal symbols of whiteness and blackness. While he alludes to the problem rhetorically, Cone does not develop the idea. The challenge facing Black theology and ethics is to develop an argument of blackness for goodness and vice versa.

33. Olin P. Moyd, *Redemption in Black Theology* (Valley Forge, PA: Judson Press 1979).

15

Desiring Booty and Killing the Body: Toward "Negative" Erotics[1]

Edward Phillip Antonio

I

As a prelude to a consideration of the Black erotic, I first argue that celebrations of the Black body and of Black sexuality in modernity ought to be tempered by the memory of Black suffering since, for Blacks, it is precisely in their bodies that that memory of pain and suffering is etched.[2] Yet there is a paradox which recognition of this creates. For is not the body also the site where the erotic, at least in its sexual form, is experienced? If so, it would appear then that there is a fundamental sense in which pain and pleasure are determinative forms of the structure of Black desire. But this means that at the center of representations of the body that I address here (and the sexuality they entail) lie contradictions and ambiguities—whose substance is essentially racial and political—that can only be understood, though not necessarily resolved, in terms of the excesses of the operations of desire as it manifests itself in and through the erotic.

I first proceed by way of proposing an approach that I call "negative erotics." The idea of the "negation" or the "negative" is of course not new in philosophy. It is, for example, central to Hegel's philosophy of identity and difference and to Adorno's work. Its application to the domain of sexuality can be found in the works of Freud and Lacan where it more or less means refusal, denial, and even repression. My use of it here is, however, more in the Hegel/Adorno tradition than it is in the tradition of Freud and Lacan. I am especially interested in Adorno's rendition of "negative dialectics." For him, rather than promoting any synthesis between things as they are (or as they appear) and as they ought to be or between the identity of identity and non-identity, thought and political practice ought to be negative in the sense of being socially and politically (i.e. critically) attuned to the totalizing forces of oppression. Its tasks include that of constantly undoing any such synthesis by refusing everything that claims the status of the self-constituting given.[3] Hence Hegel's argument that being for the other is negation of being in itself.[4]

Negative erotics as I define it does not seek to cancel or deny the erotic without any further ado; it is not negation of desire as such; rather it is a style of thinking that refuses to invoke the erotic in black experience without at the same time recalling that historically the black body has been a veritable site of horrendous pain repeatedly inflicted on it in the name of biological (racial) identity. As I suggest toward the end of this essay, this pain is unforgettable, which of course, is to say that as well as being etched in our bodies it is also etched in our memory. As a style of thinking, negative erotics proceeds on two planes. On the first— as a necessary act of historical solidarity with the Black victims of modernity—it involves a recollection of all the negative instances of the pain inflicted on the Black body in history. Ultimately, the point of such a recollection is to relativize and undercut any impulse toward facile "celebrations" of Black sexuality such as we see in rap music, pornography and other venues of cultural expression.

But such a recollection is also required because any enjoyment or celebration (facile or otherwise) of desire, love, and the erotic is always confronted by its historical other—that is, the pain emblazoned on the body. Corporeal pain is recalled precisely because it actively constitutes one (though not the only one) of the fundamental modes of black self-understanding. It was inflicted by whites in order to define Blacks as nonhuman, to take away their human identities. Administering bodily pain on the Black subject was the negative articulation of the denial of Black being; as such its ends were never gratuitous but always political. The result of this was the creation in Black being of a matrix of loss characterized by want, absence and lack. But if, as Plato's Symposium, Hegelian dialectics and Lacanian psychoanalysis have all suggested in their different ways, desire is lack, want, and absence then clearly there is a sense in which desire is the central arena within which the possibility of Black identity is fleshed out at the intersection of pain and pleasure.

The second plane on which negative erotics proceeds is its determinate refusal to reduce Black corporeality to the exclusive object of either pain or pleasure or, indeed, to any unambiguous conceptualization of the relationship of corporeality to desire. Furthermore, this refusal seeks to rethink the Black body beyond its representations in modernity.

To take seriously the contradictions and ambiguities of desire, black sexuality, and the erotic as suggested above is, in a certain sense, a task that pertains to what Foucault in the second volume of his *History of Sexuality* calls the "moral problematization of sexual conduct." Foucault is discussing the goal and purposes of moral reflection among the Greeks, the questions that define and regulate desire: how and under what conditions does one enjoy sexual pleasure? With what principles is such enjoyment to be explained and justified?[5] Given the contradictions and ambiguities regarding the history of the Black body hinted at above these questions are obviously not irrelevant to the present discussion. For surely, to attend to the historical mapping of pain and pleasure on the Black body is to ask about the "conditions and modalities" of their manifestation and their ethical implications. However, for the purposes of this essay I want to redefine the task of the moral problematization of sexual conduct somewhat so as to focus not on sexual conduct per se but rather on the representation of the Black body as the material condition for the emergence of a certain kind of discourse about Black sexuality.

So, then, my goal in this essay is to consider the sexual, "scientific" racial and aesthetic ambiguities of representing the Black body both a as the site of pain, desire, and erotic experience as well the production of racialized knowledge about sexuality. In it I summon and interrogate the term "booty" as a historical trope by means of which the body, especially the Black female body and, through this, desire and the erotic, are reified into the fetish. What I wish to do is to explore how the term "booty" represents one way in which Black female sexuality has been constructed by men by reductively organizing it around certain parts of the female anatomy, especially the buttocks. I shall argue that these constructions span a wide range of discursive practices marked at the one end of the spectrum by the pseudo-sciences of the eighteenth and nineteenth centuries, which were deeply preoccupied with the measurement of human bodies including, as we shall see, the female buttocks, and at the other, by portrayals of the female behind as a site of the "erotic" in modern pornography so that, in the end, there is little difference between both.

In between these two extremes reside all the jokes, euphemisms, slips of the tongue, and other forms of misogynistic parapraxes that have come to define the signifiers in terms of which the meaning of "booty" is popularly elaborated. One of the most interesting parts of the argument that I wish to develop here is that historically the discourse on "booty" straddles conflicting, though overlapping, racial, sexual, "scientific" and "aesthetic" practices. It is a discourse in which at different levels and in different ways, both Black and white males are implicated.

Of course, the term booty in its sexualized sense is a modern word and, as reported by Peter Jennings and Todd Brewster of ABC news, has only recently (as of 2002) been given official status by being included in a dictionary where it means buttocks.[6] As will become evident later on my argument here is that this term is fundamentally an extension of its "scientific" counterpart—steatopygia, defined, according to the *Merriam-Webster's Collegiate Dictionary* as "an excessive development of fat on the buttocks that occurs especially among women of the Hottentots and some black peoples." Explaining the process through which words are given dictionary status, Jennings and Brewster quote Tom Pitoniak, one of the lexicographers at Merriam Webster: "It's not enough for a word to be used once to be included in the dictionary . . . *There've got to be clear signs that it is gaining widespread acceptance.*" And the report by Jennings and Brewster adds that every year the *Merriam-Webster's Collegiate Dictionary* defines words in "mainstream use."[7] As we shall see, over and above its current lexical popularity, the term historically links up with the violence of war, slavery, and piracy and thus with the logic of power, ownership and control. But of immediate concern to this essay is how words enter into our everyday consciousness and experience; how they come to function as metaphorical signifiers both of our conceptions of and the way we identify others. Robert B. Baker has called these signifiers "metaphorical identifications." One example of this are the historical uses of the pronouns "boy" or "girl" in white paternalism to refer to adult African Americans. In such uses the attributes associated with boys and girls such as immaturity, irresponsibility, infantile behaviour and the like are automatically projected onto adult Blacks in precisely the same way that the slang terms we use for women—piece of ass, cunt, fox, babe, bitch, and so on, transfer to women the characteristics of the objects to which those terms refer.[8]

Although some of the terms that Baker analysizes in his essay have more or less fallen out of use, I want to argue here that others have replaced them. As indicated earlier, I am particularly interested in the disturbing history of men's fixation with Black female buttocks and how that fixation has now been translated, under the neologism booty, into everyday ways of thinking about women and their sexuality in such a way—and this even more disturbing—that some Black women have, in fact, come to accept the conception and identification of their identities entailed by use of that neologism. I want to use the story of Saartjie Baartman both to give historical context to men's preoccupation with Black female buttocks as well as to set the stage for my argument that the practices that history discloses are ongoing.

II

There can be no doubt that the distressing story of Saartjie Baartman, the so-called Hottentot Venus, traces in *nuce* the deeply problematic history of the staged representations of the Black female body and its sexualized semiotics in modernity. I recount the story in some detail. My reasons for doing so are given later.

Baartman was a Khoisan woman born in colonial South Africa in 1789 near the Great Fish River in the Eastern Cape. Before she left South Africa for Europe in 1810 she worked either as slave or as a servant of Dutch farmers. Baartman's ethnic identity and social status as either servant or slave are not minor details of the history of what happened to her body. Her ethnic identity is important because the Khoisan were regarded by many Europeans throughout the eighteenth and nineteenth centuries as the most primitive and barbaric race. Her social status is important because it circumscribes the power dynamics that led to her plight. Baartman had large buttocks and a "reputed" *sinus pudoris* (the so-called Hottentot apron or extended flap of skin dangling from the vagina which gave the latter an elongated form). These features of her genitalia attracted the attention of western sexual voyeurism. Hendrick Cezar, the brother of Baartman's employer and Alexander Dunlop, a surgeon on a British Naval ship offered to take Baartman to Europe to display her body to the European public for money and promised to share the profits with her thereby making her wealthy. This, of course, amounted to asking Baartman to go and sell her body as a viewable commodity. As I argue later on, this is of the same generic scope as the manipulation of Black female bodies in pornography today.

When Baartman arrived in London she was taken to Piccadilly where she was put on display right away. Her buttocks and rumors of the size of her vagina aroused intense fascination and attracted large crowds of people from all social classes. This was the beginning of the story of the ignominious display of her body in bars, exhibitions, circuses, universities and medical laboratories and eventually, after her death, in the Musée de l'Homme in Paris.

In these shows Baartman was sometimes caged and presented on a platform raised a few feet off the ground in order to give those who came to see her genitalia a better view. She became a subject of jokes and caricature.

It is interesting that Baartman did not leave South Africa without official colonial "intervention." Indeed, the governor of the Cape gave his permission for her to be taken overseas. It is, therefore, also interesting that it was The African Association for Promoting the Discovery of the Interior of Africa established in 1788 that took up the cause of Baartman with the courts in London. The story of Baartman was framed by the pragmatics of colonial history. Appearing before the court of the King's Bench one of the representatives of the association described the way in which Baartman was displayed to the public:

> "On being ordered by her keeper, she came out . . . The Hottentot was produced like a wild beast, and ordered to move backwards and forwards and come out and go into her cage, more like a bear in chain than a human being."[9]

The court case which, as Rosemary Wiss has shown was essentially about "the colonization and enslavement" of Baartman's body focused on two main issues: whether she had consented to be displayed to the public and whether the manner of her display was indecent. Although the court raised, as its central concern, the question of pain that might be caused to Baartman by being exhibited, it sidelined its own question by concentrating, instead, on the "problem" of public sensibility and moral "delicacy." Throughout the proceedings Baartman was not given the opportunity to speak for herself, although she could speak Dutch, English, and later on, some French.[10] Her silence was no doubt the function of her colonial subjection.

The colonial dynamics that undergirded both this court case as well as the cruel and inhumane treatment of Baartman must be understood against the background of the overall history of the oppression of her country and her people. As I have already pointed out, not only were the Khoi and the San regarded in Europe as paradigmatic examples of the most backward race, thus giving rise to the suspicion that they might not be human, their country was seized, their land expropriated, and their identity effectively denied by the Dutch and the British colonizers. They could not speak for themselves and they had no rights. It goes without saying that it was these historical circumstances that made possible the fate of Baartman. But once removed from her land, dispossessed of her freedom, and treated as subhuman, Baartman's body came to stand for the history of her country. In the face of these colonial dynamics, it was rather disingenuous of the court of the King's Bench to try to ascertain whether Baartman had consented to be put on display. Both her lack of voice and the fact that she did not possess rights or freedom in her country were facts with which the court was perfectly familiar.

It is little wonder that the court case did not change Baartman's condition and she continued to be put on display in London as well as in other parts of England. In 1814 she was removed to Paris where Henry Taylor exhibited her before passing her on to various owners including an animal trainer. Depressed and in despair she became an alcoholic and a prostitute. She died poor and lonely on January 1, 1816.

After her death, the renowned comparative anatomist Georges Cuvier performed the autopsy. He cast her in plaster and then dissected her body. It is said that the first parts of her body that he examined were her vagina, the vulva, and the anus. He then went on to remove the brain. All the body parts were placed in formaldehyde jars and were kept on display at the Musée de l'Homme in Paris until 1976. Baartman's body remains were only recently returned to South Africa after a prolonged diplomatic wrangle between the South African and French governments, the end result of which was the passing of special legislation by the French Parliament to let Baartman go. It is not insignificant that it was Mandela (not, unsurprisingly, South Africa under apartheid) as president of a new and free South Africa who initiated the process that led to the repatriation of Baartman's body parts to South Africa. Baartman was buried on Women's Day, August 9, 2002.[11]

I have recounted this story in some detail for several reasons: first it situates the African body at various critical intersections in the history of power and control—colonialism, racism, pornography, gender, slavery, and law. Second, the story is worth telling as an act of anamnetic solidarity with Baartman whose real name is lost to us and who died lonely, away from her country and a victim of racial and sexual injustice. Third, this narrative provides a convenient entry point into an analysis of a contemporary situation that is in some respects remarkably similar to that of Baartman. That is the story of our culture's continued fixation with female buttocks as represented in pornography and our popular language.

III

What happened to Baartman represents a typical story of white power (in this mediated through colonialism) over the Black body in modernity. There are several observations to be made about how that power came to be exercised. First, in their encounter with Blacks, Europeans simply doubted the former's humanity. On the notorious "great chain of being"—Blacks were consistently registered as closer to animals.[12] Indeed, the fascination that the body of Baartman provoked was, as we shall see shortly, due to the belief that her being was situated on the borderline (her race was thought to be the missing link) between humanity and the ape.[13] Since Baartman was a "Hottentot" and since the "Hottentot" were regarded throughout the eighteenth and nineteenth centuries as the most primitive form of humanity, they became the central symbol of difference and otherness. The Hottentot woman in particular was seen as carrying (embodying) the physiological markers of that difference in the structure of her genitalia. As Sander L. Gilman has shown, the sexuality of the Hottentot woman was the arena within which European perceptions of difference between Blacks and whites were elaborated.[14]

In these perceptions of difference the otherness of the Hottentot woman is in fact established at two distinct but related levels: her race and her sexuality. In both cases the problem of the other's difference is resolved by reading her body negatively, that is against the white body as the norm. The positing of such a norm assumed that difference could only be understood as abnormality, disordered being or deviation from that which is truly human. This is clear if we recall—and I shall give examples of this later—that African female difference was often characterized speculatively in terms of the possibility of sex between African women and apes. The intention of such speculation was obviously to alienate African women from the sphere of the human. Notice that it is not the suspected (even if negatively) humanity of the subject that delimits its identity but rather its sexuality—the size of its genitals, its alleged excessive libidinal energies, and as a result, its inclination to copulate with animals—that delimits its lack of humanity. What is significant here is how sexual degeneracy represented by the size of the African woman's genitals as well as by her quasi-animal sexuality stood at the same time for racial degeneracy. The "pathology" of her sexuality was racial.[15]

The second observation about how European power came to be exercised on the Black body is that the grounding of human difference in "sexual physiology" (to use Gilman's term again) involved the emergence of a formal process of discursive conceptualization of sexualized otherness across many academic disciplines from Art and Art History to Anatomy, Philosophy, and Medicine. This meant that in the long run the authority of perceptions of difference derived not so much from the regularity with which difference itself was otherwise socially or culturally enunciated as from the fact that there was a widespread attempt in scientific and philosophical discourse to produce an "empirically" based generalized description of difference. With their standard anatomical studies of the buttocks and genitalia of Hottentot women, scientists such as J. J. Virey (1775–1846), Georges Cuvier (1769–1832), Henri de Blainville (1777–1850), A. W. Otto, Johannes Muller, William H. Flower, to name only a few, exemplified the operations of what might be described as the hegemony of a formal science of sexualized otherness; a science that, moreover, shared in the common practice of determining the dubiety of Black humanity through the measurement of skulls, brain size, and facial angles in order to show their supposed proximity to animals.

The third observation about how white power was deployed against the Black body was, ironically, by amplifying the methods of scientific practice in order to accommodate aesthetic and moral norms as criteria for understanding difference as defined by the sexuality of the other. The role that such aesthetic and moral criteria was given in this discourse shows the extent to which scientific inquiry itself was misappropriated or even perverted in order to give racist thought a naturalistic grounding. We are confronted here by a comprehensive methodological racism consisting of three orders of explanation; scientific, aesthetic, and moral whose aims are (for all its methodological pretensions) framed by the need to account for imagined features of difference, that is, features which have no basis in reality.

Clearly that is why thinkers as different as Virey, Georges-Louis Leclerc (Comte de Buffon (1707–1788)), and Havelock Ellis (1859–1939), the latter as late as 1905, could variously subsume Black female sexuality under scientific, moral, and aesthetic paradigms. For Buffon Blacks were prepossessed of an apelike sexual appetite, which for him explained why their women were desirous of coitus with apes. This was considered in part to be a function of climate. Thus the environmentalism which formed the overall context in which race theories were frequently deployed was also invoked to explain not only the supposed effects of climate on the sexuality of Blacks as well as the structure of their genitalia but also, as a consequence, the form and nature of their desire. The suspected sexual promiscuity of Blacks, especially of Black women, was premised on this. Witness the work of J. J. Virey. Although Virey located Black "lascivity" not in the social mode of Black sexuality—as if Blacks are socially, let alone biologically, any more lascivious than whites—but in the materiality of the naked sexual organs themselves, indeed, in their size ("for their sexual organs are much more developed than those of whites") and argued at the same time that only primitives were attracted by such things (i.e. naked genitals), he nevertheless regarded the female buttocks as the key to determining the beauty of a race.[16] Here we have science and aesthetics recruited in a manner that anticipated Havelock Ellis's use of them to explain human difference in terms of buttocks.

Gilman says of Ellis,

> The list of secondary sexual characteristics that Ellis then gives as the signs of a cultured (that is not primitive) perception of the body—the vocabulary of aesthetically pleasing signs—begins with the buttocks. This is, of course, a nineteenth-century fascination with the buttocks as a displacement for the genitalia. Ellis gives it the quality of a higher regard for the beautiful. His discussion of the buttocks ranks the races by size of the female pelvis, a view that began with William Vrolik's in 1826 that a narrow pelvis is a sign of racial superiority and is echoed by R. Verneau's study in 1875 of the form of the pelvis among various races.[17]

This enthrallment with the buttocks and genitalia of Black women as generally represented by the figure of the Hottentot female and through it by Saartjie Baartman herself raises an important question, one which I will frame in terms of the relation between her race and sexuality on the one hand and the sexuality of the white males who paraded her in the streets and museums of Europe, on the other. Interpretations of Baartman's sexual physiology were never purely scientific or aesthetic; they were also guided by a "pornographic" interest in which her race and her genitals coincided as elements of sexual attraction. As Stephen Jay Gould has put, she was not only a Hottentot woman, she was also a Hottentot Venus. Her identity—which is what made her popular in European eyes—was ultimately that of a sexual object and as such she simultaneously provided or rather was forced to provide "vicarious [sexual] pleasure" to white males while at the same time her corporeality marked her "bestial" difference from them.[18] In this later aspect she was reduced to the sum total of her sexual body parts. It was this that was the basis of what amounted to Baartman's sexual exploitation. That she turned to prostitution when she was removed to Paris was simply a continuation of this. In other words, the white men who were quite prepared to sleep with her there were merely fulfilling their racial fantasies. The point here is not that her turning to prostitution was necessarily structured by the forces of desire (although that is quite possible; after all she was still a human being) but rather that her body was "desired" by others not because of who Baartman was but because of *what it represented*—the excessively sexual exotic other.

IV

What I want to argue now is that the fascination with the buttocks that was so endemic in Victorian voyeurism so much so that it came to be represented in novels, works of art, newspapers, and caricatures never really ended but has resurfaced under the cynical regime of pornography and certain expressions of rap music. Because the materials—the pornographic—on which I shall draw for this discussion tend to be banished by conventional thought to the realm of the morally inappropriate, the prohibited and even the abject (this latter understood in Kristeva's sense of the "radically excluded") it is perhaps necessary to be upfront about what I am attempting to do.[19] My aim is not to invoke the pornographic merely for the sake of style or to prove that formally one—as a theologian—can go against the grain in the treatment of certain topics (to implement a transgressive hermeneutic for its own sake). I want rather to do three things.

The first, following Georges Bataille in the second volume of *The Accursed Share* where he deals with the history of eroticism, is to connect thought with its object so that my own analysis of the representations of the Black female body and their relations to desire and the erotic does not proceed abstractly but is in fact predicated upon the actual collective complex (what Bataille calls "concrete integral totality") of the historical experiences of Black bodies. Since what is at stake here are real historical bodies we need to be careful, as indeed Bataille was, not to dissociate the erotic from the intellectual in the name of the social conventions that produce the prohibitions governing our perceptions of sexuality as if (1) thought is necessarily asexual and (2) as if sexual morality is exhaustively a matter of conventional prohibitions. Bataille is, I think, after a hermeneutic that proceeds from recognition of the fact that the world is made up of "prostitutes and saints, scoundrels and men whose generosity is boundless."[20] In such a hermeneutic ". . . talk about eroticism could no more be isolated from the reflection of the universe in the mind than the latter could be isolated from eroticism." Bataille is clear that to seek to make the erotic measure up to thought in this way (and vice versa) is, again, quite different from reducing the erotic to conventional thought since this later inscribes contempt for the erotic.[21]

I do not, of course, want to assimilate the erotic to the pornographic in any unproblematic way here since, as I shall suggest later, the erotic is in some fundamental sense a positive phenomenon whereas pornography is primarily a negative one, that is, one whose true identity is constituted as the failure—again for reasons I shall advance later—of its transposed and always displaced attempt to reiterate the properly erotic. Nevertheless, or perhaps one should say, precisely because of this—and this is the point of my appeal to Bataille—the pornographic is found in the real world in which the sexual and the erotic themselves are not only defined through the social, political, cultural, and economic institutions that control and service the regime of desire but also where they are actualized upon and through human bodies. This is not in any way to valorize pornography— if by that is meant rationalizing it; it is rather to recognize the fact that the possibility of any critical ethical awareness of what is wrong with pornography can only be achieved when we confront head-on both the popular social forms and concrete images through which it reifies and dehumanizes human bodies.

It is said that pornography is a multibillion-dollar industry.[22] If so, several things follow: (1) that it is a structural part of our capitalist culture;[23] (2) that there is somewhere (if not everywhere) in that culture massive consumption of porn; (3) that the expressive content of porn—pictorial representations of naked bodies, so-called adult movies, books, magazines, sex toys, the linguistic mysogynism that accompanies the marketing of pornography, the treatment of women and men that is promoted, and so on—has largely sedimented into our collective unconscious—that is, the social practices and attitudes that it encourages have socialized significant sectors of society into its culture;[24] and, (4) that, therefore, our tacit assumptions about and our conceptions and representations of certain people in our society are sometimes deeply shaped by the power of pornography. Such, I will suggest below, is the case with the way the term booty is now used to described Black female sexuality.

Thus, in the light of this, the second thing that I want to do in invoking the pornographic is to argue that there are some deeply disturbing parallels between the representations of Black female bodies in eighteenth and nineteenth century Europe—especially as typified by the case of Baartman—and their portrayal in pornography today and in certain forms of rap music. The internet is, of course, one place where pornographic images are readily available in large quantities. That is where I shall start. There are many sites that offer "porn." Some claim to do so free of charge and others sell their services. The range of content covered by many of these sites is, indeed, very large: from pictorial displays of naked bodies (soft porn) to sexual images of bestiality, midgets, and the elderly (so-called mature porn), "incest," pregnant women (preggos), teenagers (lolitas) to images of interracial sex, gay and lesbian porn as well as sexual pictures of bisexuals and transgendered persons. Much of the classification of pornographic videos, magazines, and the division of content into various categories reflects the sexual "anatomization" of the female body.

A large amount of the content is conveyed through imagistic abstractions of the genitals or other body parts in terms of their size (monster cocks, tight asses, tight pussies, big or freaky booties, melons, or big boobs) and body shape (plump or fat). At one extreme pornography is dominated by the figure of the freak, the weird and the monstrous, which it not only assimilates to the exotic but which it also interprets as a drive that provokes and measures sexual intensity.[25] Moreover, race and ethnicity represent two further categories into which pornographic content is arranged and classified such that "black" or "ebony," "Asian" and, more generally, "ethnic" encode a semiosis or system of signs of racial "eroticism." With this we come to the heart of what I want to argue. There are any number of sites where race, the size of Black female buttocks—under the abstract notion of "booty"—and the Black female self are constructed through a process of irreducible identification.[26] This is a process whereby what can be known about a person is determined by the mode and selected qualities in terms of which that person is perceived, (re)presented and thus identified. In order to bring this out clearly I briefly draw on psychoanalytic theory, especially that aspect of it which deals with part-object relations. The term part-object is formally associated with the Kleinian school of psychoanalysis but the basic ideas to which it refers can also be found in the work of Freud and Lacan. In psychoanalytic terms, an object is a thing toward which the attention of an instinct is drawn (say hunger to food); that through which it seeks to fulfill itself. It can be a person or a person's body parts—penis, buttocks, or feet. As Laplanche and Pontalis argue this is how part-objects are generally understood in psychoanalysis, that is, as body parts.[27] It is important to stress at this point that part-objects are part-objects precisely because they are not the whole person but only part of a person. Moreover, objects and part-objects can either be real or fantasized. The argument that I want to make is that by encouraging men to focus on "booty" porn promotes a part-object mode of thinking about Black female identity. This can be shown from an analysis of the representation of Black women on certain Internet sites.

Some of the sites where Black women are presented in terms of their "booties" are Big Butt Girls,[28] Big Booty Club;[29] Alldatazz,[30] Ghetto Booty Freak,[31] Duty Booty,[32] Big Butt Mania,[33] Big Booty Gallery,[34] Big Butt,[35] Black Booty College, Black Ghetto Ass, Thick Ebony Bootay, Big Black Mommas, and so on *ad nauseam*.

When taken together with the representations that they signify the names of all these sites are racialized linguistic devices and strategies that characterize Black female bodies as anatomical abstractions. One can best get at this by describing the actual photographic representation of "booty". On all the sites referred to above the images of women are portrayed by manipulating the relationship of the body to the camera, on the one hand, and on the other, to the intended gaze of the viewer. With regard to the first—the relationship of the body to the camera— we are in most cases presented with a series of images of a naked woman (or sometimes of different women) in different postures facing away from the camera. The most common postures are bending down or kneeling, with kneeling being the most favored. In the bending position the torso is parallel to the floor and the knees are slightly curved so that the center of the knee cap is more or less directly pointing at the floor at an angle. The legs are spread open shoulder width. This allows the buttocks to protrude, which, of course, is part of the point the photograph is trying to establish. The other part is to accentuate the size of the buttocks by manipulating the camera itself: zooming out creates a somewhat faded image which gives a simulated sense of distance between the camera and the subject thus decreasing (but only up to a point) the size of the buttocks and zooming in creates proximity thus enlarging the buttocks. The artificial reduction of the size is symbolically important because, in so far as desire is constituted by lack, want, need and incompleteness, and insofar as the object of desire in these images is precisely a *large* "booty," diminishing it creates desire by making the viewer want a larger, close-up view of the object/image. On the other hand, instead of distance, zooming in creates an equally simulated sense of intimacy. Notice how the act of zooming in and out parodies sexual movement. One significant effect of "zooming in" on the subject as described here is the way in which the area of the body from the waist (and sometimes shoulders) up is elided from the frame of the camera lens such that the head and face of the subject are not seen.[36] Again, this allows a close-up view of the buttocks but at the expense of the image of the whole person. The technique of zooming in and out draws the eye of the viewer not just to the dimensions of the buttocks but also to the detail of form, texture, and color of the skin. This is achieved by a sort of "descriptive" realism, which proceeds by manipulating different degrees of lighting both against the surrounding background and the body itself in order to highlight the hues and tones of the latter's skin color.[37]

There are several features of these images that I want to comment upon. First, I have called them "anatomical abstractions" because their creation involves the "part-object" method of isolating the presentation of an individual from all the other "primary" and differentiated qualities—names, faces, sexuality, gender, histories—by which we ordinarily identify selves. The bodies to which these images refer are identifiable by the way in which they (the images) reduce the humanity of their subjects to their "booties." Here "booty" foregrounds the identity of a person from which is then abstracted her sexuality. Booty is presented not as an aesthetic object or one offered for the sake of aesthetic exploration (in much the same way, for example, that one might explore Dega's Nudes) but because it is supposedly "sexy" or sexually desirable.[38] The term "bootylicious," which is now a part of our slang, expresses this. There is in fact a certain line of continuity that runs throughout the history of the presentation of the relationship of the female buttocks to other parts of the female body. Earlier I indicated how J. J. Virey (and after him Havelock Ellis) privileged the buttocks at the expense of the naked vagina as one marker of racial beauty, here what we see is not so much a reversal or contradiction of Virey's position but a refiguring of the buttocks (for they still retain their "beauty") as an intermediate point between the person whose buttocks they are and her vaginal sexual availability toward which they, in fact, gesture. We are, I suggest, still dealing here with the same distinction between primary and secondary sexual zones described in my previous reference to Sander Gilman's discussion of Ellis. In other words, we are still dealing with the fate of Baartman, except, perhaps, that in pornography the zoning of the buttocks and the genitalia is itself purely gestural since, at least in terms of how pornographers imagine sex, such zoning does not mark off an interruptive boundary between the genital zones. Thus "butts" and "asses" are as much sites of sexual intercourse (anal sex) as are vaginas (heterosexual penetration) and mouths (oral sex).

The second feature of these images, and one which provides the most direct aspect of continuity with the story of Baartman, is the extent to which consistently all the images reproduce, extend, and sexualize the language of size. Phrases such as "big booty sistas," "big booty galleries," "big butt girls," "thick ebony bootay" and "big black mommas," to name a few, are used both as names of internet sites as well as descriptions of the content available on those sites. In each case the "erotic" determination of what "booty" is, that is, the source of the powers of its sexual attraction is ultimately its size.[39] It follows from this, it seems to me, that the language of "booty," at least as it functions in pornography, is both quantitative as well as qualitative. In its quantitative aspects it mobilizes the gaze of desire by directing it at the physical dimensions of the female behind in such a way as to effect a sexualization of quantity. This, of course, is in some ways not different from the way the myth of the size of the Black man's penis has functioned in western culture. But this reading of human bodily dimensions in terms of their imagined "erotic" powers posits something like a transsubstantive logic in which the libidinal energies that drive desire magically transform quantity into quality. Using Kantian language again we might say that size is the determinate concept the object of which is a certain part of the body.

However, by constituting sexuality and desire through preoccupation with size, the language of "booty" is analogous to the discourse on the measurement of human bodies that proliferated throughout the eighteenth and nineteenth centuries.[40] It should be remembered that the measurement of skulls and brains as well as genitalia in that discourse foregrounded negative philosophical and moral judgments about the nature of the Black other. In pornography, we are at first offered something that appears like a pictorial affirmation of the female body—the images are supposed to speak for themselves, or rather they are supposed to speak about the beauty of the female body by arousing attraction towards it—but in truth the descriptive and evaluative language that accompanies the presentation of the images under discussion here and the acts depicted in those images often reveal the operations of a misogynistic culture.

The third feature of these images is that they are offered for sale. In that sense the representation of women they involve may correctly be called commodification for both the images and that of which they are images, are commodities. There is thus a parallel between the commodification of Baartman's body and the commodification of Black female bodies in pornography.

The fourth feature is race. I have already made reference to this. But it is important to stress it here for two basic reasons. The first is the consistent association of Black women with large buttocks such that although white women are sometimes depicted as also endowed with "big booty" they tend to be regarded as rather exceptional—not in terms of size but in the fact of having it at all. After all, steatopygia is supposedly a Black condition. There is, in other words, a "naturalization" of both Black bodily features and the manner in which Black women possess even those features that they might have in common with white women.[41] The second aspect of this racialization of Black genitalia is, as we have seen, its grounding in historical white perceptions of otherness so that we would be mistaken to regard its appearance here as merely a transient matter of fashion.

The fifth feature of the images that is worth noting is that they often present their subjects as both nameless and faceless. Of course, Saartjie Baartman had a face. At least that! If one were to be cynical here one might say she had a face, but what was it worth? After all, it was not her face that was an object of such curiosity. It was, to put it bluntly, her "booty." That is why she was called the Hottentot Venus. She did not only possess booty she was it. In other words, given the excessive "asswatching"[42] that her steatopigous condition provoked, she might as well have been faceless. But did she have a name? As I have already indicated, Saartjie Baartman was not her real (i.e. proper) name. It was a name that she was given at her *baptism* in London, a colonial name chosen for her by her masters.

In African culture names are not socially or culturally indifferent; they ground social identity by relating the subject to a history of kinship, familial, and ancestral bonds. Authentic personhood in this context is a function of maintaining those bonds. The fact that Saartjie Baartman was so called because she had been stripped of her indigenous name means that she was—even in her own eyes—without identity, a non-person. She was deprived of any connection with her kinship history.

Similarly, it is arguable, that by putting before us nameless bodies or parts thereof pornography decontextualizes the identities of human subjects. If it seems that I am making too much of this I should like to invoke the support of Emmanuel Levinas who makes both names and faces important to his ethical thought. In his book, *Proper Names* he uses the Nameless as a collective name for victims of injustice.[43]

If names ground social identity then faces refer us back to the concrete persons signified by names. Faces individuate names and names recall faces. Gilles Deleuze and Félix Guattari argue that the face is, among other things, the screen that mirrors our passions, consciousness or subjectivity as well as the operations of language; they argue, in other words, that signification itself is mediated through the differential structures of faciality.[44] To quote them:

> A child, woman, mother, man, father, boss, teacher, police officer does not speak a general language but one whose signifying traits are indexed to specific faciality traits . . . Similarly, the form of subjectivity whether consciousness or passion, would remain absolutely empty if faces did not form the loci of resonance that select the sensed or mental reality and make it conform in advance to a dominant reality.[45]

I leave aside any consideration of the conditions of possibility of faciality as sketched by Deleuze and Guattari (other than perhaps to say that, for them, "the face is produced in humanity")[46] and go, instead, straight to an appropriation of what I think is the ethical import of their argument for my own. Deleuze and Guattari make three important moves. The first is to refuse to essentialize "the face." There is no such thing as "the face" in general. Faces are concrete and they are not prefabricated or ready made. The second move they make is to link the face to the whole body by suggesting that the face represents an "overcoding" of the entire body such that the identity of body parts is really a function of the process of facialization: "When the mouth and nose, but first the eyes, become a holey surface, all the other volumes and cavities of the body follow . . . Hand, breast, stomach, penis and vagina, thigh, leg and foot, all come to be facialized."[47] Clearly, the idea here is to make the face the framework for interpreting other body parts. The argument that I am making is that by encouraging fixation on the female buttocks in a way that completely and literally displaces or evicts the face from the body pornography conceals and takes away the identity of the person represented in the image. This is especially so if we take seriously the obvious point that "the face" is one of the key makers of our bodily identities on which depends our recognition of each other. The human face announces to us the ethics of social responsibility in which the "other" or the Thou confronts us as the other *person*.[48]

The third move, which Deleuze and Guattari make, and one which is rather problematical is to claim that erotomania and fetishism are inscribed in the very process of facialization. Deleuze and Guattari argue two things; that with facialization everything remains sexual and that facialization underwrites erotomania and fetishism. The first of this point can be read positively, for example, in terms of the capacity of the gaze of desire or the erotic for appreciation of the other's face. On the second point they are simply wrong. Erotomania and fetishism occur precisely when body parts are *defaced* and offered as faceless organs;[49] when the reductive representation of faceless female bodies in terms of their body parts is unproblematically located within the signifying structures of our subjectivity.

In other words, erotomania and fetishism take place through the gaze of desire allowing itself to be directed by a *demented* part-objects logic, which "flays, slices, and anatomizes everything in sight, and then proceeds to sew things randomly back together again."[50] This is not helped by the paradoxical arguments of Deleuze and Guattari for bodies without organs on the one hand and, on the other, for a spirituality of facelessness as the destiny of humanity.[51] If Deleuze and Guattari were correct then their privileging of the face would—insofar as erotomania and fetishism are inscribe in it—itself be an abstraction that privileges only one body part and is thus akin to the abstraction in pornography that I am critiquing here.

One cannot talk about how subjects come to be fixated on part-objects without at the same time talking about reification, which in the context of this essay I define as the process through which human bodies or their parts are invested with abstract (sexual) value cut off from their human value. This abstract sexual value regards bodies and their parts as things, fetishes. The value is abstract precisely because it is derived from and focused upon only a part of the whole. It is sexual because it eroticizes the fetish—booty as commodity and commodity as object unconnected with its owner. Thus the fetishization of the body is also the eroticization of the fetish. This opens a huge question, which cannot be explored here: does pornography in any way reiterate the erotic or does it exile it?

V

So far I have attempted to link two seemingly disparate discourses; the story of Saartjie Baartman and the discursive practices that constituted it on the one hand, and, on the other, the representation of the Black female body in contemporary pornography. The reason for attempting to make that link was to suggest that in both cases Black females are historically assigned an identity that is reductively derived from the association of certain of their body parts—the sexual parts—with their subjectivity. In phrases such as "big booty sistas," "big butt girls," "thick ebony bootay' " and "big black mommas" we are not only dealing with modernized versions of the discourse to which Baartman was subjected in her own time but we are also presented with a process of identification whereby "girls," "sistas," and "mommas" are the subjective side of an already privileged physicality defined with primary reference to the genitals which are themselves given priority over other body parts so that they, in fact, come to be ontologically prior.

The point of my argument, as indicated earlier, is that all this should give us pause before we embark on too easy a celebration of either the Black body or of "the black experience of the erotic." This is because as well as being, indeed, a site of the erotic, the Black body in modernity has also been a site of *unforgettable* pain: beginning with the lash of the slave master and the latter's casual rape of Black women, the castration of Black men as a form of social control, the terror of the ever present threat of being lynched under Jim Crow,[52] the gas chamber and the electric chair, to the practice in the Congo under Belgian colonial rule of asking soldiers to cut off the hands of any one who refused to harvest rubber for the state. According to Adam Hochschild, the state officials expected each soldier to give a number of the hands he had cut off.[53]

Pain is inscribed in the very body—individual and collective—through which the Black presence in the modern world is mediated. To claim that the Black body is the site of *unforgettable* pain is not necessarily to demand the essentialization of Black experience of pain—as though (masochism aside) that is in itself desirable—it is rather to assign it a constitutive role (with regard to our place in modernity) in our collective memory. I have suggested in this essay that one aspect of that memory is constituted by a long story of sexual violence against the bodies of Black women. Indeed, the very term "booty" is implicated in such violence for one of its meanings has to do with plundering one's enemy's goods in war or forcibly expropriating his or her property. Furthermore it is associated with piracy. When these meanings are juxtaposed with "booty" (perhaps itself a linguistic corruption of body) understood as "body" and, specifically, as female buttocks, vulva, or vagina the violence that this term carries becomes focused on women. Of course, it does not follow from granting the need and possibility of a memory of the pain of such violence that the only bodily experiences Black people can remember are or ought to be those of pain and not of pleasure. For any adequate account of the Black body in modernity must ultimately also acknowledge the sexual identity of the Black body. This means that, whatever its history of pain, it has not been beyond the capacity to experience erotic joy, because historically, not even slavery itself could abrogate the erotic function of those subject to it—a fact that marked its limits and attested the humanity of the enslaved.[54] Thus, it turns out, there are in fact two sides to the memory of the history of the Black body: pain and pleasure. The coexistence of these two sides in the same body points to a profound ambiguity which problematizes any cheap discursive moves in the direction of the erotic without remembering that the actualization of the erotic was never, as it were, experienced in itself, that is, as an abstract form, but only in so far as it actualized itself on and through a corporeal surface. It is the task of negative erotics as I defined it above to summon us to such a remembrance. In another essay on the Black erotic I shall specifically explore the contours of such a remembrance.

Notes

1. The idea of "negative erotics" plays on Dorothea Olkowski's discussion of the notion of negative desire in Judith Butler's reading of Gilles Deleuze. See Dorothea Oklowski, *Gilles Deleuze and the Ruin of Representation* (Berkeley and Los Angeles: University of California Press, 1999), 40 ff.
2. There are, of course, all sorts of dangers in speaking about "the black body" as though such was simply an immutable given, a monolithic entity or an historically invariant object. Black thought, it seems to me, must come at this by negotiating the gap between the Cartesian notion of body (so influential in modern philosophy) as invariant (as well as divisible from an equally invariant true-self) over time and the poststructuralist idea represented by Foucault and Bourdieu that the body is socially constructed. On these two options see, David Couzens Hoy, "Critical Resistance: Foucault and Bourdieu, in *Perspectives in Embodiment: The Intersection of Nature and Culture*," ed., Gail Weiss and Honi Fern Haber (New York and London: Routledge, 1999).
3. Theodore Adorno, *Negative Dialectics*, trans. E. B. Ashton (New York: Seabury Press, 1973). Adorno's thought on this is rather difficult and extended—seeking as it does to propose a critique of the entire western philosophical tradition—and I am obviously simplifying it here. A historical account (which is also a decent introduction) of the origin of negative dialectics is available in Susan Buck-Morss's *The Origin of Negative Dialectics: Theodor W. Adorno, Walter Benjamin, and the Frankfurt Institute* (New York: The Free Press, 1977). Obviously I am simplifying Adorno's thought on this which is rather difficult and extended.
4. See Stephen Houlgate, ed., *The Hegel Reader* (Oxford: Blackwell Publishers, 1998), 200–201.

5. Michel Foucault, *The Use of Pleasure: The History of Sexuality*, vol. 2, trans. Robert Hurley (New York: Vintage Books, 1990) 53 ff.

6. By Peter Jennings and Todd Brewster, "Word Up: How Merriam-Webster Decides Which Booty Belongs in the Dictionary" at http://abcnews.go.com/sections/wnt/DailyNews/ISOA_Websters020923.html (accessed: 4/18/2003 9:43:23 A.M).

7. Ibid. The italics are mine.

8. Robert B. Baker, " 'Pricks' and 'Chicks': A Plea for 'Persons' " in *Philosophy and Sex*, third edition, Ed. Robert B. Baker, Kathleen J. Wininger, and Fredrick A. Elliston (New York: Prometheus Book, 1998), 281–288.

9. Quoted in Stephen Jay Gould, *The Flamingo's Smile: Reflections in Natural History* (New York-London: W. W. Norton & Company, 1985), 293.

10. Rosemary Wiss, "Lipreading: Remembering Saartjie Baartman," The Australian Journal of Anthropology, 5:1&2 (1994), 16–17. Wiss discussion is an extended analysis of the court case and its political implications.

11. On the reception of Baartman's remains and the ceremonies surrounding her burial see: http://www.safrica.info/ess_info/sa_glance/history/saartjie.htm In honour of Baartman poems have been written e.g. by Diana Ferrus at http://africanamericanstudies.intrasun.tcnj.edu/students/fall2002/baxter2/memorial.htm); and sculptures and films made at http://www.vgallery.co.za/2000article28/vzine.htm.

12. Stephen Jay Gould, *The Flamingo's Smile*, 294–296.

13. This was predicated on the notion of a "great chain of being": A metaphor describing a complete hierarchy of graded perfections and types of being from the highest to the lowest. The highest and most perfect type of being was God. On the human scale the white male was the highest type of humanity. Blacks were consistently placed at the bottom of this hierarchy. That is why the Hottentot were considered to be the missing link between humans and animals.

14. Sander L. Gilman, "Black Bodies, White Bodies: Toward an Iconography of Female Sexuality in Late Nineteenth Century Art, Medicine, and Literature," *Critical Inquiry*, 12:1 (1985), 209–213.

15. Robert Young, *Colonial Desire: Hybridity in Theory, Culture and Race* (London and New York: Routledge, 1995), chapter 4, and passim.

16. The idea of the beauty of the buttocks has some standing in Western art history. In October of 1997 Gallery Titanik in Finland organized an art exhibition entitled 'Sex Snack'n Pop' and included in the exhibition was a section on "Buttocks in the History of Art," which incorporated pieces by some notable painters: the following selected paintings—which all depict buttocks—are basic examples: "The Verdict of Paris" (1530) by Lucas Granach (1472–1553) housed in the Landesmuseum in Germany; (Compare Granach's piece to Peter Paul Rubens' (1577–1640) "The Judgement of Paris" (1639); "Bacchus" (1494) and "David" (1504) by Michelangelo in the Museo Nazionale del Bargello, Firenze; "Odalisque" (1745) Francois Boucher (1703–1770), Louvre, Paris; "Venus at Her Mirror" (1650–1651) by Velásquez kept at the National Gallery in London, and "Allegory of Fertility" (1622) by Jacob Jordaens (1593–1678), Brussels, Musees Royaux des Beaux-Arts. See http://www.ojaniemi.com/bha/, accessed: 4/18/2003 2:39:57 P.M.

17. Ibid., 218–219.
18. Gould, *The Flamingo's Smile* 296–297.
19. Julia Kristeva, *Powers of Horror: An Essay in Abjection*, trans. Leon Roudiez, (New York: Columbia University Press, 1982). In a section on the perverse and the artistic Kristeva writes: "The abject is related to perversion . . . The abject is perverse because it neither gives up nor assumes a prohibition, a rule or a law; but turns them aside, misleads, corrupts; uses them, takes advantage of them, the better to deny them. It kills in the name of life . . ." 15. She goes on to argue that addressing the abject often involves "a crossing over of the dichotomous categories of Pure and Impure, Prohibition and Sin, Morality and Immorality," 16.
20. Georges Bataille, *The Accursed Share: An Essay on General Economy*, Vol. II&III, trans. Robert Hurley (New York: Zone Books, 1991), 24.
21. Ibid.
22. I say it is "said" because, as Emmanuelle Richard's article "The Perils of Covering Porn" makes clear there is no agreement among analysts as to just how much the porn. industry is worth. This is in part due to the "underground" or opaque nature of the industry. Estimates range from $1 billion to $10 billion. See the USC Annenberg Online Journalism Review at http://www. ojr.org/ojr/business/1017866651.php, accessed:4/17/2003 12:45:06 P.M. Richard's article is, among other things, about how the mainstream media reports porn and the uncertainties of obtaining reliable figures on the overall revenues of the porn. industry.
23. On porn and capitalism see, Alan Soble, "Why Do Men Enjoy Pornography?" in Robert B. Baker, *Philosophy and Sex*. Of interest also is Linda Singer's, "Sex and the Logic of Late Capitalism" in the same volume.
    The integral relationship of porn to the structure of the economy is evident from the fact that several major companies benefit from marketing and selling porn. These companies include hotel chains such as Marriott, Hilton, and Westin, which provide X-rated movies in their rooms through LodgeNet and On Command as well as cable and satellite companies like AT&T broadband with its subscription service for its explicit porn channel, The Hot Network. DirecTV, which is owned by General Motors, offered—through the Vivid Entertainment Group—40 million homes in America three adult movie channels before they were bought by Playboy. In addition to this there is the internet itself where various companies compete to advertise and sell links to porn websites. On all this see the useful data posted on the PBS website: http://www.pbs.org/ wgbh/pages/frontline/shows/porn/business/mainstream.html
24. This point is made here without prejudice to the question of whether such practices and attitudes are initially extracted from society and then redefined to serve the ends of porn. or whether they are generated by the porn. industry itself in the first instance. My point here does not logically depend on deciding the question before analysis of that point. This, ultimately, is really a question about the extent to which the availability of porn on such a large scale is a reflection of society's outlook on sex and sexuality or the extent of the power of porn to create a whole subculture and socialize society into it.
25. In her essay, " Pumping Iron with Resistance:Carla Dunlap's Victorious Body," Jacqueline E. Brady speaks about the "sexualization"; and "freakification" of

African female bodies; In *Recovering the Black Female Body: Self-Representations by African American Women*, ed., Michael Bennett and Venessa D. Dickerson (New Jersey: Rutgers University Press, 2001), 262–265.

26. Robert B. Baker, works with the notion of identification in his essay "Pricks" and "Chicks": A Plea for "Persons" already referred to above.

27. J. Laplanche and J.-B. Pontalis, *The Language of Psychoanalysis*, trans. Donald Nicholson-Smith, with an introduction by Daniel Lagache (New York-London: W. W. Norton & Company, 1973). Also, Dylan Evans, *An Introductory Dictionary of Lacanian Pyschoanalysis* (London and New York: Routledge, 1996).

28. At http://www.bigbuttgirls.com/, accessed: 4/7/2003 7:16:12 P.M.

29. At http://www.Bigbootyclub.com/freepeep.htm (accessed: 4/5/2003 7:11: 57 PM)

30. At http://www.ethniccash.com/pre/aa/aam-11/ebony.shtml?fr, accessed: 4/5/2003 6:15:11 P.M.

31. At http://www.ghettobootyfreak.com/topsites/index.html, accessed: 4/8/2003 9:17:50 A.M.

32. At http://www.dutybooty.com/, accessed: 4/8/2003 9:23:48 A.M.

33. At http://www.bigbuttmania.com/maniacs/index.html, accessed: 4/8/2003 9:27:09 A.M.

34. At http://www.assaholicspost.com/, accessed: 4/8/2003 9:41:14 A.M.

35. At http://sexyadulthost.com/users/september/bigbutts/12/, accessed: 4/8/2003 9:44:06 A.M.

36. Interestingly one of the porn websites is actually called "From the Waist Down". See http://www.fromthewaistdown.com/tour_01.html, accessed: 4/8/2003 10:12:36 A.M.

37. What I have described here is obviously one variety of the images. There are, to be sure, many different varieties defined by different body postures and uses of the camera to position them. The range includes images of squatting women, or women standing upright, women lying on their stomachs or kneeling with their chests or breasts touching the floor and their backs slightly arched. It would be absurd to try and apply the same description to all these images. There are, however, certain recurrent features which in different degrees characterize them all: they all face away from the camera, they are all concerned with close-up portrayals of the buttocks, most of the images are especially concerned with the size of "booty" and often, though not always, they involve eliding the face of the subject. Naturally, I have selected for my description those images that best support my argument.

38. I realize, of course, that my reference to Dega's Nudes is not unproblematic since it might be construed as encouraging and promoting precisely that against which I am arguing in this essay, namely demeaning representations of women. Obviously that is not what I am trying to do here.

39. In his discussion of the "mathematically sublime" Kant says "Here it is remarkable that although we have no interest whatever in an object—i.e. its existence is indifferent to us—yet its mere size, even if it is considered as formless, may bring a satisfaction with it that is universally communicable and that consequently involves the consciousness of subjective purposiveness in the use of our cognitive faculty. This is not indeed a satisfaction in the object (because

it may be formless), as in the case of the beautiful, in which the reflective judgment finds itself purposively determined in reference to cognition in general, but [a satisfaction] in the extension of the imagination by itself." See, Immanuel Kant, *Critique of Judgment*, trans., with an Introduction by J.H. Bernard (New York: Hefner Press, 1951), 86.

40. See, Stephen Jay Gould's discussion of this in his *The Mismeasure of Man* (New York: Norton, 1996).

41. Dorid Witt has commented in a different context on the "naturalization" of Black female bodies that it shapes "a collective, even atavistic racial investment in what one might term the 'Hottentot Venus' figuration of black female bodies . . ." See her essay, "Detecting Bodies: BarabaraNeely's Domestic Sleuth and the Trope of the (In)visible Woman" *In Recovering the Black Female Body: Self-Representations by African American Women* referred to earlier.

42. One of the websites dedicated to this is called "Asswatcher" (http://www.pornwithus.com/galleries.php?member = sv2000&site = asswatcher.com&no = 90)

43. Emmanuel Levinas, *Proper Names*, trans. Michael B. Smith (Stanford, California: Stanford University Press, 1996), 119–123 and passim.

44. Gilles Deleuze and Félix Guattari, *A Thousand Plateaus: Capitalism and Schizophrenia*, trans.and foreword by Brian Massumi (London: Athlone Press Ltd, 1988) 167 ff.

45. Ibid., 168

46. Ibid., 170

47. Ibid.

48. Emmanuel Levinas, *Outside the Subject*, trans. Michael B. Smith (Stanford, California: Stanford University Press, 1993), 35 and passim.

49. I have not discussed here the effects of pornographic representations of women on those directly affected by them. There is an interesting discussion on distorted body images in Gail Weiss's essay "The Abject Borders of the Body Image" in Gail Weiss and Honi Fern Haber, eds., *Perspective on Embodiment* . . . To consistently represent others as freaks, abnormal or reducible to their body parts (because these are in fact outlandish, bizarre or spectacular) produces in the other alienated perceptions of her body.

50. Deleuze and Guattari, 171.

51. Ibid.

52. Dwight Hopkins, *Down, Up and Over: Slave Religion and Black Theology*, (Minneapolis: Fortress Press, 2000), 66 ff.

53. See Adam Hochschild, *King Leopold's Ghost: A Story of Greed, Terror and Heroism in Colonial Africa* (New York: Mariner Books, 1999).

54. Bataille, *The Accursed Share*, 138–139.

16

The Black Church and the Curious Body of the Black Homosexual

Victor Anderson

Many people often talk about how silent the Black churches are on sex, sexuality, and homosexuality. I do not think that silent is the right word. They speak constantly about matters of sex and sexuality. And Black Clergy are not particularly shy of talking about homosexuality. As a Black gay academic who is radically estranged from any church at all, I marvel that so many Black gays and lesbians continue to maintain their faith in their churches even as their very lives and bodies are Sunday after Sunday ridiculed, trivialized, and preached against as abominations. In my opinion, there is no body (literally) more contested in Black churches than the curious body of the black homosexual. It is not silence that provokes this short essay. Rather, I want to call attention to the manner in which the Black homosexual has become a curious body in the paradoxical orientation of the Black Church to the public and private spheres that frame its religious and spiritual interests. How is it that Black clergy can be characteristically liberal and progressive on public matters of civil and human rights and conservative or preservative on private matters of marriage, the family, and sex? For purposes of this essay, I will confine my discussion of homosexuality to Black gay men and lesbians. My intent is not to discount the experiences of transgender, bi-sexual, and transsexual members of the Black community. Rather, it is merely a means of maintaining focus on an otherwise insurmountable topic.

To state the problem: when the Black Church is typified as an advocate for the civil and human rights of blacks, they are typically liberal and progressive. Hence, they are seen as being on the frontline of progressive policies for directing social justice. And when they are described as a refuge, Black churches constitute a surrogate world that may tacitly "accept" Black gays and lesbians into their fellowship on the basis of their being silent regarding their sexuality, while their gifts and talents are exploited by the churches in their roles as musicians, choir leaders, ushers, and teachers of youth. Thus, while Black churches tend to be liberal and progressive on matters of civil and human rights, on matters of sexuality in general, as Dr. Robert Franklin shows, the churches are typically conservative in their teaching and preaching. Homosexuality tends to be the test case of this conservativism. Franklin and others whom I discuss in this essay find this divide puzzling and paradoxical. In the end of this essay, I will offer some suggestions that may help transcend the divide.

The survey study conducted by Franklin at the Hampton University Ministers Conference in 1992 indicates that among the 600 participants surveyed on issues surrounding sexuality, Black clergy tended overwhelmingly to be conservative on homosexuality. Of sermons preached on homosexuality 79 percent indicated categorical opposition and 34.6 percent of the clergy regarded HIV/AIDS a divine curse (1997–1979). This is in stark contrast to their typical progressive liberal positions on civil rights in health, education, and housing. Franklin's findings indicate that on sexual practices, but particularly, on homosexuality, Black clergy tend to be overwhelmingly conservative and nonprogressive. He himself tries to reconcile this nonprogressive tendency to what he believes is the characteristic progressive orientation of the Black Churches to social life. Franklin redresses the conservative orientation of the Black clergy under what may be referred to as "preference falsification."

In *Private Truths, Public Lies: The Social Consequences of Preference Falsification*, Timur Kuran explains "Preference falsification [as] the act of misrepresenting one's wants under perceived social pressures" (1995: ix). Although Franklin himself does not evoke this sociological theory, I think that it best characterizes his explanation for the paradoxical attitudes of Black clergy on homosexuality and social justice. According to Franklin, "the church publicly condemns certain behaviors and orientations," while "it privately expresses toleration and acceptance of those involved" (Franklin, 80). Here, the latter clause would be an instance of preference falsification by the former. He goes on to say,

> Most pastors are acquainted with this complexity even as they go on record supporting the conservative values that are perceived as important

for rebuilding the black family. At the same time as they express these views, they seek to exhibit love, mercy, and patience toward those at odds with cherished moral precepts. Just as the love ethic placed Jesus in tension, at times, with legal standards, a similar tension may confront contemporary pastors (80).

This tension is derived from the Black clergy's conservative interests in the Black family. It is also their interest in keeping faith with long standing sexual norms and values that they wish to preserve that lead them to overwhelmingly oppose homosexuality in the church and community.

I appreciate Franklin's puzzlement over the conservative attitudes of the clergy he studied. Both the Black clergy's interests in conserving the Black family and loyalty to their biblical faith are important factors for understanding their moral paradox. Our real problem will be determining which of these interests is most determinative on their attitudes on homosexuality. I have no doubt that religious beliefs about God's commands, the orders of creation, human beings as image bearers of God, biblical holiness, and, of course, sexual sins and abomination all function in the Black clergy's attitudes toward homo-sexuality. Here, theological beliefs operate for ministers as religious reasons for rejecting homosexuality. Franklin sees the divide as the result of a correlation problem in the opinions of the Black clergy, in which case, the clergy's "progressive Christianity" is at odds with their "conservative opinions" on homosexuality. I think of the paradox as resulting from the ministers' attempts to hold competing loyalties between their public convictions on civil rights and their religious beliefs about the morality of homosexuality insofar as they are derived from the ministers' biblical faith. Given their attempts to be faithful both to their religious beliefs and social interests, as they participate in the private and public realms, typically progressive Black Christian clergy may be conservative on the morality of homosexuality, and they may be progressive on civil rights without falling into moral contradic-tion, that is, unless homosexual sexual practices are regarded by them as a matter of civil and human rights.

For example, while taking a progressive attitude toward housing discrimination based on race, Black clergy may argue that the civil right of a person to occupy housing of which he or she meets the minimal economic requirement for ownership but is denied based on race directly insults the humanity of the person. Such a policy violates a basic right of a person regardless of race to move about and associate freely without undue interference. Such a policy calls into question a person's democratic citizenship, and it puts at risk political peace. Therefore, any policy that denigrates the esteem of a person based on race and prohibits the possibility of his or her human fulfillment, in this case, a human right to move about and associate freely, is not only politically and morally wrong—in theological terms, such a policy is regarded as a social sin. Here, then, Black clergy would pursue a progressive disposition toward those programs or policies that aim to correct such injustices in housing and advocate policies that redress the human fulfillment of those discriminated by that policy.

Given the rationale above, a minister may aggressively advocate open housing policies that take no account of a person's being straight or gay to move about and associate freely without undue interference. Failure to do so in this case would bring that minister's morality into contradiction. However, the same minister may not be prepared to advocate the interests of Black gays and lesbians in the private realm of marriage, the family, and sex based on his or her interest in preserving biblical norms and values for regulating marriage, the family, and sex. Black clergy's commitment to biblical moral standards in the private sphere, derived from standards peculiar to their religious traditions, does not constitute any moral contradiction of their public commitments on civil and human rights unless the private is collapsed into the public. Their warrants for not advocating homosexual practices can be developed on biblical and theological grounds, as they pertain to the private sphere of marriage, family, and sex, without violating the civil rights (public interests) of gay and lesbian members of the Black community. Once again, this argument holds only insofar as one buys into the public/private distinction.

Given the public/private distinction, Black clergy may exhibit a paradoxical relation to preserving the public interests of Black gays and lesbians, while in the private realm taking their normative commitments from their understanding of biblical faith norms that regulate marriage, family, and sex. It is not so much, then, that the clergy studied by Franklin are falsifying their preference for the truth in order to gain certain social benefits as it is their holding competing loyalties to their public and private interests. My point is that Franklin sees a correlation problem between Black clergy's progressive disposition on human and civil rights and their conservative attitudes on homosexuality. However, their attitude might not be a fault in correlation but the result of the ministers' attempt to be consistent in their attitudes toward issues of public morality (civil rights, housing, employment, education), while evoking religious and spiritual warrants in support of their conservative interest in the flourishing of the Black family and their nonsupport toward legitimizing homosexuality.

Like Franklin, social critic Michael Eric Dyson has given considerable attention toward understanding the paradoxical position of the Black churches on sexuality in general and homosexuality in particular. However, he takes a strategy different from Franklin's sociological approach. A religious critic by academic training, Dyson offers a genealogical account of the progressive/conservative paradox in the Black churches negotiating their public and private interests. Dyson's essay entitled, "When You Divide Body and Soul, Problems Multiply" is most useful for our purpose. Dyson rightly sees much of the sexual teachings and attitudes of the Black churches as having been derived from dualistic assumptions about the body and soul of early Christian theologians that were disseminated through the white churches to Blacks. This dualism between body (matter) and soul (spirit and eternal) is then reinscribed on Black culture through the Black churches. In their attitudes toward sexuality, Dyson traces the lack of moral leadership by Black churches and clergy on sexual ethics to white sexual distortions that the Black churches inherited from the homophobic practices of slavery. Consequently, the Black churches are complicit in white Manichean sexual theologies in which the body is regarded as evil and the soul worthy of salvation.

By contrast, Dyson argues that in Black religious discourse the Black body is exonerated in ecstatic and ejaculatory forms of worship, preaching, and enthusiasm for social justice. However, he also recognizes that the Black Churches have not developed a sexual theology, much less a theology of homoerotica or homosexuality, that is compatible with its erotic qualities in worship. Rather, the white sexual theologies of the Black churches, Dyson thinks, are at odds with the sexual interests and loves of their members. Again, Dyson traces the homophobic practices of the Black churches to their conceptual dependence on white theology. Therefore, in their legitimate, characteristic attempts to resist "myths of super black sexuality," in which Black sexual appetites were regarded by the slave holding society as unquenchable, Dyson argues that Blacks bought into "the split between mind and body that leads them to confusion about a black Christian theology of Incarnation" (1996: 87).

Dyson sees this dualism at work in the interplay between the Black pulpit, the Black preacher's railings against homosexuality, Sunday after Sunday, and his or her use of gay members to play music and sing songs that will set the stage for his or her delivery and his or her hortatory ejaculations or climax. He suggests that in this ritualized, erotic moment a certain irony occurs. The preacher renders his gay members complicit in acts of self-hatred, while the musical performances of gay members negate the gay bashing sermon just preached. According to Dyson, the Black churches' sexual theologies suggest a fundamental contradiction between their liberationist orientations toward social justice and their refusal to "unlock the oppressive closet for gays and lesbians" (105). He also extends these contradictions to homosexual members themselves who participate in acts of self-hatred in their denials and secrecy while they affirm the homophobia of their churches. Dyson's point is that all of these homophobic practices can be seen as consequences of Blacks' endorsements of a white ideology of heterosexism that is rationalized under a body/soul dualism.

If the Black churches are to be faithful to their essential nature as liberating, prophetic institutions that are fundamentally motivated toward social justice, according to Dyson, the churches must develop a Black theology of homoeroticism. He also calls for Black gays and lesbians to come out of their sexual closets where "they can leave behind as well the destructive erotic habits that threaten their lives" (106). He asks the Black churches to affirm healthy unions between gay and lesbian adults and make certain their solidarity with the "despised members of our society" (107). The despised in this case are not the homeless, prostitutes, or crackheads, but Black gays and lesbians. "Black Christians, who have been despised and oppressed for much of our existence," Dyson argues, "should be wary of extending that oppression to our lesbian sisters and gay brothers" (107). He calls for the Black churches to be centers of sexual healing: to be at the forefront of sexual justice, just as they have been at the forefront of "every major social, political, and moral movement in black culture" (108).

Like Franklin, Dyson also seems puzzled that when it comes to Black homosexuality, the Black clergy and churches appear less than progressive or liberationist. In their identities, he believes that the Black churches are basically oriented toward liberating, prophetic, and avante garde practices. In all civil rights issues, he argues that they are impressive exemplars of social justice when compared to white institutions. Rather, among the many cultural institutions and organizations responsible for the moral well being of the Black community and despite claims to the contrary, Black churches remain a major institution that promotes forms of homophobia that keep Black gays and lesbian silent and make them particular objects of the community's disdain and violence. I think that Dyson's portraiture of the Black Church and clergy and their relation to sexuality greatly distorts the experiences of Black gays and lesbians in the churches. He exhibits a confidence in the Black churches and clergy that, I suggest, many Black gays and lesbians have good reasons to radically call into question.

As with Franklin's answer to the paradox, I also take Dyson's answer to the apparent contradiction between the liberal progressivism of the Black churches on civil rights, race, and poverty and their conservatism on homosexuality to be inadequate. The suggestion that the conservative sexual attitudes and homophobia of the Black Churches can be understood or explained in reference to African Americans' acquiring a self-hating theological body/soul dualism is far too narrow an explanation for understanding the paradox. I have argued in an essay entitled "Deadly Silence: Reflections on Homosexuality and Human Rights" that homophobia is not the unique characteristic of European thought and culture (1998: 192 ff). It develops in complex matrices of cultural experience that are experiential, social, and political. Therefore, homophobia cannot be reduced to any one matrix. It is related to social taboos, associations, and cultural conditions that cultivate both negative and positive effects throughout the culture.

Negatively, homophobic practices may be maintained for the purpose of "deterring" forms of human association, sexual and social, that some in the community, in this case, the Black church and clergy, fear are threats to the moral cohesion of Black culture. Positively, homophobic practices may "insure" the cultivation of moral behavior through socialization in proper sexual practices that the culture deems worthy of promoting such as the Black family. The point is that the homophobia of the Black churches ought not to be explained away simply by appealing to a genealogy of its European transmission. Such an explanation, it seems to me, does not give much credence to the view advocated by Gayraud Wilmore that African American responses to white oppressions is not only reactive to the deformation of Black culture in chattel slavery but is also the proactive effects of Blacks, own initiatives in developing and guiding the moral universe of their culture.

I read Dyson's analysis of homophobia in the Black Church as a reactive consequence of whites' actions on Black cultural life and not a consequence of the Black churches proactive intentions to establish African American cultural practices that are as likely as European ones to produce in the Black community homophobic activities, self-hating practices, and antigay discourses. For Dyson, "The black church has been at the forefront of every major social, political and moral movement in black culture. . . . It has the opportunity to lead again, by focusing the black erotic body in its loving, liberating lens" (108). I hear Dyson asking the Black churches to be centers of sexual healing while maintaining a posture of Black radicalism. However, the question is whether the Black churches can do all that he calls for and remain characteristically Black churches—a powerful, moral force in the community whose family values and sexual teachings are typically biblical and conservative.

As I evaluate both Franklin's and Dyson's discussion on the paradoxical relation of the Black Church on homosexuality, the tension they find in their analyses result from what I see as their having accepted a distorted description of the Black churches under Black radicalism. In *Black Religion and Black Radicalism*, religious historian Gayraud Wilmore early typified the characteristic tendency of Black religion in the United States under Black radicalism. He writes:

> An exceedingly elastic but tenacious thread binds together the contribution and developmental factors of black religion in the United States as one distinctive social phenomenon. It is the thread of what may be called, if properly defined, "black radicalism." Black religion has always concerned itself with the fascination of an incorrigibly religious people with the mystery of God, but it has been equally concerned with the yearning of a despised and subjugated people for freedom—freedom from religious, economic, social and political domination that whites have exercised over blacks since the beginning of the African slave trade. It is this radical thrust of blacks for human liberation expressed in black Christianity and black religion in the United States—from the preacher-led slave revolts to the Black Manifesto of James Forman and the Black Declaration of Independence of the National Committee of Black Churchmen. (1973: x)

From the above quote, it is not so much Wilmore's defining the Black Church to be radical in its disposition toward politics, economy, and society that is problematic, it is when he extends the radical description to religion that homosexuality becomes the test case. The Black churches are consequently either understood as typically liberal and progressive, that is, given a propensity toward social protest and action, or a revolutionary, liberation movement for social change. I suspect that both depictions of the Black Church lie behind both Franklin's and Dyson's puzzlement over the paradoxical disposition of Black clergy on homosexuality. However, I think that there is no greater test than homosexuality that challenges these depictions of the Black Church in ways that racial, civil rights, and gender discourse do not. Typifying Black churches and clergy as characteristically liberal and progressive or radical and liberationist on public morality and religion equally distorts their complexity as human social communities.

The Black Church is complex, but not unusually more complex than other churches. After all, it is a human community. It is an organization of human interests of which some are public and others private. The Black Church exists as a mediating institution among other institutions competing for the loyalties of African Americans and competing for its own legitimacy in the Black community. Moreover, I think it is a mistake to treat it as a sociological collectivity with a widely distributable internal logic as do C. Eric Lincoln and Lawrence H. Mamiya. For these sociologists of Religion, the "Black Church" generically refers to "any black Christian person . . . if he or she is a member of a black congregation" (1990: 1). This description effectively brackets blacks who hold memberships in white denominations such as the United Methodist Church, the Episcopal Church, and the Roman Catholic Church among others. Rather, the Black Church means for them blacks who hold memberships in the seven major "independent, historic, and totally black controlled denominations" represented by the seven major black denominations that claim 80 percent of black church memberships (7).

Lincoln and Mamiya also offer a normative status to the Black Church when they describe it as the guardian of a "black sacred cosmos or the religious world view of African Americans." The Black sacred cosmos is a socially constructed life-world "created [by] [blacks'] own unique and distinctive forms of culture and world views as parallels rather than replications of the culture in which they were involuntary guests"(2). Their talk of a parallel universe, then, is their attempt to see the Black churches an alternative community to white religious institutions. The churches are thematized by incarnational and resurrection triumphantism, universal egalitarianism and freedom, and, in worship, religious immediacy frames black religious experience. They say

> Wherever black people were gathered in significant enough numbers, the distinct quality of a shared Afro-Christian religious world view and faith was felt. Even in predominantly white denominations with a million or more black members like the United Methodist Church and the Roman Catholic Church, the surges and eruptions of the black sacred cosmos were constant and influential. A qualitatively different cultural form of expressing Christianity is found in most black churches, regardless of denomination, to this day (1990–7).

Wherever African Americans locate themselves among various cultural spaces, the Black sacred cosmos is also determinative in those spaces. Whether one locates one's practices in terms of "freedom, justice, equality, and African heritage, and racial parity at all levels of human intercourse," such as occur in "militant, nationalistic, and non-Christian movements," even these cultural spaces owe their success, in Black culture, to their historical links with the Black church. They go on to say that "many aspects of black cultural practices and some major institutions had religious origins; they were given birth and nurtured in the womb of the Black Church" (7).

I have evoked Lincoln and Mamiya's talk of the Black Church as a parallel universe constituted by its own socially constructed sacred cosmos to support a particular argument. Namely, if the Black churches are sustained by their own internal logic, a Black sacred cosmos that is constructed out of their own determination and not merely as a reactive recipient of a white homophobic sexual theology, must we not also infer that their social teachings on homosexuality are also entailed in their own sacred construction of the Black sacred cosmos? Within that Black sacred cosmos, Black clergy have tended toward liberal progressivism in civil rights and other areas of social justice. But on homosexuality, their socially constructed valuations on marriage, the Black family and sex do not differ in any significant way from those of the conservative white religious right. Franklin, Dyson, and others ought not to be surprised by this when the question is: "What are the real interests in the private realm that black clergy seek to fulfill in their conservationist and preservationist dispositions on homosexuality?" Some argue that what is at stake on the Black Church's disposition on homosexuality is their interest in maintaining and supporting the vitality of the Black community through their moral constructions of marriage, the Black family, and sex.

Cheryl J. Sanders a Black Christian ethicist has been most articulate on this point. For Sanders, the task of Black theological reflection and Christian ethics is to support the Black Church as a mediating institution capable of empowering the "Whole Black Community." It ought not to be sidetracked by focusing on isolated pockets of interests groups within the community. For Sanders, adequate moral norms and valuations by the Black Church must be distributable throughout the widest ranges of moral interests within the black community. Insofar as these norms and values are those of Black Christians, they are always particular. They constitute the ethics of a particular community. For her, the Holiness/Pentecostal churches provide adequate resources for directing

Black moral life in ways that promote their progressivism in civil and human rights, while maintaining a conserving agenda in the private realms of marriage, the Black family and sex. Sanders suggests that Black churches have good warrants for supporting progressive policies oriented toward eradicating forms of oppression and discrimination toward persons who seek fulfillment of their civil rights in matters of housing, education, health, and welfare. This is especially the case where such forms of oppression and discrimination are based on race, religion, gender, and sexual orientation. However, in the private realm of marriage, family, and sex, Sanders suggests that the path of biblical holiness empowers the Black churches to protect, enhance, and support the whole Black community. In the private realm, this may require that Black clergy and theologians not affirm homosexual sex or same sex unions in the Black community.

In an essay entitled, "Sexual Orientation and Human Rights Discourse in the African-American Churches," Sanders puts forward a set of moral claims for Black church non-advocacy on homosexual practices. In an important passage, Sanders lays out what she sees as the historic and traditional stance of African American churches on homosexuality. She is worth quoting at length.

> My own assessment of the history and tradition of the African-American churches with respect to this issue in "broad strokes" is so broad that it merits only one stroke—that these churches have generally frowned upon homosexuality on the ground of Scripture. However, since the time of their inception during the eighteenth century, the African-American churches have contributed significantly to the various liberation struggles undertaken by black people in a white racist society, including also the nineteenth-century abolitionist movement and the twentieth-century civil rights movement. While the sexual conduct of gays and lesbians has not been endorsed by most of the African American religious community, the quest for human dignity and civil rights has been viewed as all inclusive. (1998: 178)

The quote readily grabs the two horns of the paradox. On the one hand, there is recognition of the liberal progressive norms relative to all matters of civil and human rights. On the other, there is recognition of the norms regulating the conservative position of the church on homosexuality.

The quote crystallizes Sanders position that in all matters of a person's civil and human rights, regardless of gender, race, or sexual orientation no one ought to be discriminated against for all have a right to equal treatment and access in the public sphere. However, when she turns to the private realm, Sanders says that where their may exist a recognition of homosexuals in the churches— "perhaps most visibly in the music ministries"—the church's typical stance is one of acceptance without advocacy (178). In a side note, she says the fact that Lincoln and Mamiya do not deal with the issue at all in their study shows "a widespread reluctance to draw attention to these concerns" by the Black Church (179).

Sanders offers two rationales for recommending the non-advocacy of homosexuality by African American churches. The first is relatively easy to grab, namely, that if the church seeks to be loyal to grounding its sexual norms in Scripture, then the whole weight of Scripture counts against Church support for Black gays' and lesbians' sexual fulfillment. Hence, the appeal is to Black clergy to be faithful to their spiritual loyalty and commitments in their encounters with Black gay and lesbian members. In judging sexual conduct, one is not warranted in targeting gay and lesbian sexual licenses as being more grievous than those committed by heterosexual members. She also holds that practicing homosexuals ought to be restricted from holding offices in the church as long as abstinence is not their spiritually disciplined way of sexual living.

Sanders is aware that such strictures may hold little weight with Black churches and clergy who have radically mitigated positions on biblical authority and biblical holiness. Nevertheless, appeals to the distinctive sexual teachings of the Pentecostal/Holiness churches provide Sanders with substantive religious and spiritual warrants and reasons for commending Black Church strictures on homosexuality. However, I hold that such appeals to biblical authority and holiness on homosexuality are not likely to be very persuasive on a youth culture growing increasingly alienated from the church—a culture between fifteen to twenty-four years old and most at risk for HIV/AIDS and other STDs due to black church silence and denials on sexuality in general and homosexuality in particular. Furthermore, I do not think that these religious and spiritual reasons are likely to be persuasive on an expanding Black middle class of educated persons whose class privileges open them to ever-widening encounters with worlds of difference that include religious differences on sexuality. Moreover, I doubt that Sanders' religious and spiritual substantive warrants are likely to be highly persuasive for many Black academic theologians who have alienated themselves from such reasons by their critical training in religion and theology.

In the end, however, Sanders does not exclusively appeal to the Bible and biblical holiness to support Black churches non-advocacy of homosexuality. Rather, she makes the homosexual body in the Black community *a curious case of cultural non-generativity* in the private realm of marriage and family. I quote Sanders at length:

> In my opinion, the strongest rational argument that can be offered against same-sex orientation, preference, and conduct—without specific reference to Scripture or revelation—flows from the observation that in the African American community in particular, and also in society at large, the ethic and practice of sexual freedom have seriously undermined the stability of families and their parenting structures during the past three decades. This is not to suggest that gays and lesbians are to blame for the demise of the black family; rather, it is to state that if nobody is willing to support and encourage the formation of covenanted heterosexual monogamous units where the emotional, educational, and economic needs of children and adults can be fulfilled, then the rampant antisocial behavior of adolescents and young adults that has terrorized our neighborhoods and schools will certainly increase. There are many voices in the black community that would celebrate the strengths of the extended family as a support for all our children, but I would argue that if everybody rejects the institution of marriage, so that nobody ever marries anybody, then the extended family will ultimately collapse. Our basic notions of kinship—father, mother, grandmother, grandfather, brother, sister, aunt, uncle, cousin— all presuppose some form of marital relationship in the family tree. In fact, heterosexual marriage is the trunk of the family tree. (182)

I have cited this passage at length for two reasons. First, it illuminates what I take to be the real interest of many Black clergy in not advocating for the sexual freedoms of Black gays and lesbians. Specifically, it is their interest to conserve and preserve the centrality of the Black family in the formation of the Black community and in the legitimating of the Black Church itself. The second reason is that the view expressed above connects well with non-churched Blacks who see homosexuality as a diminishment of the vitality and flourishing of the Black community so desperately in need of heroic models for invigorating its moral strength. *In both cases, black gays and lesbians constitute a curious case of non-generativity.* That is, it is one thing to say as Sanders does that Black gays and lesbians are not to be blamed for the many social crisis that plague Black communities. It is quite another to suggest that their bodily presence in the community does not foster the generative care necessary for providing future generations of

Black children with emotional, educational , and economic necessities that are normatively provided by heterosexual families.

Why do I call this the curious body of the Black homosexual? Looking at social and cultural reality, if we get past stereotyping the poor sissy choir director and organist or the butch-dyke truck driver, we Black gays and lesbians are the Black Church's fathers and mothers, its sisters and brothers, uncles, aunts and cousins. In the Black community, we nurture Black youth as their teachers from pre-school till college. We are Sunday school teachers and preachers, deacons, ushers, and trustees, not just church musicians and choir directors. We do not only play the worship instruments, we also write the hymns and songs that feed Black heterosexual members' souls Sunday after Sunday and throughout the week, even in the darkest hours of their despairs. Seen from social and cultural reality, the Black homosexual's bodily presence both in the Black community and church calls into question the very idea of a "homosexual lifestyle." In both the church and the Black community, the everyday, ordinary existence of Black gays and lesbians at work and play, in family life and in the pews, fosters and nourishes forms of generative care and creativity that keep Black culture and the Black Church themselves open to novelty and creativity. Even in those moments when our Black gay and lesbian bodies sexually express our desires, we keep the Black Church itself sexually honest and we open the church to the worlds of sexual difference that our bodily existence make. We are also fellow believers. This is why many Black gays and lesbians do not leave the churches of their youth. For the very Black churches that tacitly "accept" them without advocating for their sexual loves and practices are also the churches that nurtured their faith. For many, the Black Church is their spiritual home too.

To conclude, I am not puzzled by the paradoxical conservatism of the Black Church on homosexuality. We all seek faithfully to negotiate our commitments toward promoting in the public realm the civil and human rights of all without regard for race, gender, religion, or sexual orientation. We all (including Black gays and lesbians) also seek to be faithful sustainers of norms and values that enrich the private realm of marriage, family, and sex, even if we have disagreement on what those norms and values should be. However, unlike any other mediating institution of civil society and the Black community, the Church is one place where our public and private commitments meet. Sometimes they meet in agreement and sometimes not. So what is to be done with the curious body of the Black homosexual in the Black Church where there exists little agreement on its legitimacy and value? Tacit acceptance by the Church is not ideal, if it requires silence and denial. And creating alternative Black gay and lesbian churches is equally not an ideal answer to the paradox. From my point of view, such a response mirrors sexually the racist social conditions that brought the Black Church into existence in the first place.

The answer lies in the internal logic of the Church itself. It lies in the moral self-realization of the liturgy. The answer lies in the self-realization of the welcome, the passing of the peace, the blessing, the celebration of new life at baptism and in birth. It lies in the moral self-realization of congregational prayer where all present their thanksgiving and needs before a merciful and gracious God. The paradox is transcended in the moral self-realization of the communion table where all are welcomed not because they are straight, gay, lesbian, bi-sexual, transgender, or transsexual, but because all who eat and drink at the table are God's children. The paradox is transcended when the right hand (or left hand) of fellowship extends beyond the two-hour service on Sunday but symbolizes the social reality of our life together in the Black community. Although I am a radically estranged Black gay man from the Black Church now, if I have learned my lessons well enough, these liturgical activities do not only structure our Black worship experiences, they constitute the life of the Church itself.

I am but one Black gay believer and do not pretend to speak for an entire community, although I suspect that my sentiments connect with others when I ask "What do we want of the Black Church?" I do not require it to be an advocate of our sexual freedom. I only ask that it not hate us when we advocate for ourselves sexual liberty. I want it to be a refuge for us as it is for all its other members. In a significant passage, bell hooks best expresses my conviction on the Black Church and homosexuality when she says: "Just as the church can and often does provide a platform encouraging the denigration and ostracization of homosexuals, a liberatory house of God can alternatively be a place where all are welcome—all are recognized as worthy" (2001: 192–193). In the end, the paradox of the Black Church and the curious body of the Black homosexual is reconciled in the moral self-realization of what we all want and need, namely, to be loved and to love one another. To some readers, my conclusion may appear rather "fluffy" as one of my students told me about my theology. It may be. But it's real.

References

Anderson, Victor. "Deadly Silence: Reflection on Homosexuality and Human Rights" in *Sexual Orientation and Human Rights in American religious Discourse*, Saul Olyan and Martha C. Nussbaum, eds. New York: Oxford University Press, 1998: 185–200.

Dyson, Michael Eric. *Race Rules: Navigating the Color Line*. Reading, MA: Addison-Wesley Publishing Company, 1996.

Franklin, Robert M. *Another Day's Journey: Black Churches Confronting the American Crisis*. Minneapolis: Fortress Press, 1997.

hooks, bell. *Salvation: Black People and Love*. New York: William Morrow Publishing Company, 2001.

Kuran, Timur. *Private Truths, Public Lies: The Social Consequences of Preference Falsification*. Cambridge: Harvard University Press, 1995.

Lincoln, C. Eric and Mamiya, Lawrence. *The Black Church in the African American Experience*. Durham, NC: Duke University Press, 1990.

Sanders, Cheryl J. "Sexual Orientation and Human Rights Discourse in the African American Churches" in *Sexual Orientation and Human Rights in American religious Discourse*, Saul Olyan and Martha C. Nussbaum, eds. New York: Oxford University Press, 1998: 178–184.

Wilmore, Gayraurd. *Black Religion and Black Rdaicalism*. Garden, City: NY.: Anchor Press, 1973.

VII

Sociology of Religion

17

Teaching the Body: Sexuality and the Black Church

Alton B. Pollard, III

It was the beginning of my tenure as the pastor of a small African American church in small town New England. I was young then, in my early twenties, and had been invited out to lunch to meet some of the local clergy. The ministers, who came from a number of protestant traditions, enjoyed a distinct and discernible camaraderie as pastors of Black congregations in this blue-collar town.

The luncheon was in fact an orientation session. It was clear from the start that my elder colleagues planned to learn as much as they could about me and provide me with sage advice as well. As we ate they peppered me with questions about my personal interests, marital status, political views, theological education, pastoral experience, and more. At first I was surprised, and then made increasingly uncomfortable by their line of questioning, which bordered on the invasive, couched though it was in pleasantries. Here I was meeting these brethren (there were no women pastors of local churches) for the first time. I could not help but wonder, what had become of the simple act of hospitality that welcomes first the stranger before all else? How would their sizing me up in this way help us more effectively minister to the Black community? What did any of their probings have to do with prophetic leadership for our people?

Their concluding counsel had a chilling effect on me. Almost to a man, they proceeded to ply me with their opinions and pointers on sexual protocol. Clearly, care and precaution in the pursuit of one's "extra-curricular" plans and not right character and conduct, was key. Fraternal counsel was even provided in terms of when and where

I could hold local liaisons. Thankfully, no one went so far as to suggest with whom. That long-ago experience was not the first time I had been exposed to the underside of what in select circles is known as "preacher culture." Nor would it be the last.

My recounting of the above story has everything to do with my insistence in these pages that more pedagogical attention be given to issues of the erotic, to sex and sexuality as well as gender, race, and class in our theological classrooms and in our Black congregations. Looking back, my own disillusionment with the culture of sexual entitlement, so vehemently defended by some clergy (and the practice of which is more common than many of us want to know or care to admit) had everything to do with the very ambivalence and ambiguity, the lure and loathing, I saw embodied in Black Church belief and behavior toward human sexuality at the time. Today, my written response springs from a resolute theological conviction that teaching and preaching on sexuality is integral to the salvific witness of the Black community and the Black Church. While the task of such teaching and preaching is neither obvious nor easy, faith, courage, and scholarship are requisite to its successful implementation. For until and unless the Black faithful are willing to face matters of human sexuality candidly we cannot ever really know who we are, let alone who God is.

Making the Case

This essay is based on the simple proposition that spirituality, sexuality, love, and life are intersecting and interwoven themes in African American culture. In complex respects, the worlds of religious seeking and human loving have always and everywhere been intertwined, grounded in the most intimate hopes and expansive possibilities of the human spirit. I find that to affirm the intricate interrelatedness of this truth is to be compelled to commit to the teaching and preaching of the same.

Notwithstanding the ambivalences and ambiguities inherent in much of institutional Black religious life, the church always has been a principal custodian of the relationships that obtain among gender, sex, and sexuality in the communities of African America. Over the years, teaching and preaching about eros and eroticism or love and care in the Black Christian experience has been limited at best and nonexistent at worst. This is not to say that Black churches did not engage in forms of sexual socialization. They did. However, sexuality was seen as a dangerous subject in the Black Church, seldom to be discussed out in the open—except disapprovingly—and certainly not in the public square.

Today, the prevailing culture in Black churches is still one of silence, repression, denial, miseducation, and misinformation, especially where patterns of patriarchy and sexual oppression are concerned. Yet no one can deny that spirituality and sexuality have always been essential expressions of our communion together as African-descended people and the people of God. There is a critical challenge that awaits those of us who are teachers, students, ministers, and lay women and men; namely, to discover anew how best to help Black religious bodies establish beliefs and behaviors that celebrate and affirm the sacredness of Black embodiment—inclusive of race, gender, social location, sex, and sexuality—that will prove healing and empowering for our collective souls.

Allow me to offer one final point of illustration. In my seventeen years of teaching, eleven in religious studies programs and six in a graduate school of theology, I have attempted to make each course that I have taught increasingly attentive to issues of sex and sexuality as well as race, gender, ethnicity, class, and ecology. I seek to be holistic in my pedagogical theory and method, especially where African American religion and culture are concerned. When it comes to talking about sex in Black faith institutions many of our churches are in real trouble, insecure and inarticulate in matters of human intimacy, and less than certain about who are their kith and kin. A frank new discussion about sexuality and the sacred including women and men, gay and straight, young and old, students and faculty, laity and clergy is urgently needed. This is more than reason enough to teach sexuality and the Black Church.

Defining the Terms

A certain amount of dis-ease and discomfort is inevitable when talking about sex in educational and ecclesial contexts. Not only that, it is essential. The very acknowledgment of our apprehension when asked to discuss something as primary and personal as sex serves as our passport into the world of human vulnerability, interdependence, and possibility. Venturing into the hermeneutical unknown together, we discover that no matter how deeply personal sexuality is for each and every one of us, it is invariably social, political, and public in its implications. A spirit of dialogue and mutual respect and the search for a just and meaningful value system thus pervades and transforms our learning about sex and sexuality from day one.[1]

I begin the course by inviting students to reflect together with me on a number of core concepts, to dispense for the time being with theological certitude and social convention, and to enter instead into the luminous darkness of their own experience. *Sexuality* in everyday terms has to do with our erotic orientation, that is, our attractions to the other sex, the same sex, or to both. Issues of nature and nurture, or intrinsic qualities and social constructions, are its clinical corollary. Are certain meanings intrinsic to our created sexuality? Are sexual meanings created through processes of social interaction? Are attributes of the feminine and the masculine really exclusive to a particular gender? How are these qualities determined? Who determines them? Definitions of *Black sexuality*—the basic dimension of our self-understanding and way of being in the world as Black male and female persons from sex role understandings to affectional orientations, genital activity, and physiological arousal, the capacity for sensuousness and more—help us move through and beyond clinical applications to an equally critical cultural self-awareness and wisdom.

Spirituality is another term that we faithfully and carefully seek to illumine. Not an easy word to define, at the very least spirituality is an affirmation of the human capacity to be self-transcending, relational, and freely committed. It encompasses all of life including our own human sexuality. Spirituality is both a commitment and a lifeway, the growth and response of the human personality to the beauty and benevolence of a liberating and sustaining God. Asceticism, mysticism, the practice of virtue, disciplines, and methods of prayer are counted among its ancillary terms. *Black spirituality* is at once personal, familial, cultural, and communal. It is the response of African-descended children, women and men to the Sacred Presence who lives and loves within us, who calls us by name, and who compels us to liberating and holistic relationships with one another, with all the earth and more. Black spirituality excises the sickness and sin of racism and sexism, heterosexism and homophobia, mitigating factors all in the Black quest for mutuality and wholeness.

The Black Church in the United States is a network of communities of faith, worship, and life born out of and informed by the historic experiences of people of African descent in this land. It has incorporated a host of sexual understandings—for good and ill—into its language and images, singing and preaching, worship and leadership patterns, into its assumptions about power and morality, and even in its definitions of membership. The Black Church is, among its many functions, a sexual community. At the same time, in oppressions affecting us all, children, women, and men, the Black Church has access to liberating and reconciling potentiality, to restoring the ancient covenant of scriptural wisdom (text) and wisdom writ large (context) which upholds the beauty of Black love in all its profoundest meanings. When and where the Black Church and community upholds and models its own virtues of unconditional love and acceptance, and embraces the vast storehouse that is Black spirituality and sexuality, it bears magnificent witness to the common wealth of God on earth.[2]

Yet another example of a concept with radical implications for understanding sexuality is the Zulu word *Ubuntu*, which roughly translated means community, kinship, relatedness.[3] The ancestry of African peoples and its distinctive ethos allows us to share in a collective worldview that does not rigidly or exhaustively separate secular and sacred, ideal and actual, body and spirit, profane and pristine, thought and feeling. Students perceive that the common corpus of the African American experience is but one expression of this seamless garment of destiny that requires us to consider our spirituality and sexuality together. The Black Church has thrived on this sense of African holism, sometimes unconsciously, for generations. In important respects, the call to Black congregations everywhere is a conscious return to the source, to continuously involving spirit sensibilities in the practical affairs of daily life.

Some other terms explored by the students, the full implications of which lie beyond the purview of this discussion, include history, heritage, home, body, gender, race, racism, blackness, whiteness, white supremacy, sex, sexism, patriarchy, chauvinism, machismo, homosexuality, heterosexuality, heterosexism, homophobia, dualism, monism, sensuality, love, God, Jesus, and more.[4] With our initial consideration of these and related concepts the shape of our course on sexuality and the Black Church began to emerge.

The Rudiments of a Course

Few academics or religious leaders considering teaching or preaching on sexuality can claim to be an authority on the subject. My own preliminary work on the subject served to remind me of what has been the case with every course I have developed: there is no substitute for good and substantive cross-disciplinary research, involvement, and collaboration. Neither is it possible to adequately talk about African

American social and religious life without a multi-dimensional analysis. This is especially the case where discussions about sexual and moral values are concerned. Depending on the topic—gender relations, marriage, reproductive rights, celibacy, sexual identity, etc.—the instructor will benefit immensely from methods and insights gained from theology, ethics, Christian education, history of religions, biblical interpretation, pastoral care, homiletics, the physical and social sciences, history, politics, economics, and so on. At the same time, it is wise to know when and where to call upon the expert assistance of others. Indeed, the collective wisdom of us all is indispensable if we are to succeed in the task to which we have been called. What follows next are elements of a course outline for teaching sexuality and the Black Church. While by no means exhaustive it is intended to be adaptable for use in the academy, church, and community.

"I've Come To Take You Home"

On Friday, May 3, 2002, the remains of Saartjie Baartman were returned to South Africa nearly 200 years after her death in Paris, France. Originally from the Eastern Cape, Baartman, also known as Sara, was a member of South Africa's indigenous first people, the Khoisan, who were pejoratively labeled Hottentots by European settlers. Enslaved in the Western Cape capital of Cape Town, Baartman was taken to London and then on to Paris. The principal source of revenue for Baartman's owner was her naked body, put on display for European high society from 1810–1816. Advertised as a biological oddity, Saartjie's anatomy, normative for aboriginal peoples, was used to satisfy white sexual fascinations about African women and to reinforce notions of white supremacy. Saartjies Baartman died at the age of twenty-five, destitute and alone, six thousand miles away from her native land. At the time of Saartjie's death her body was dissected, and her genitalia, brain, and skeleton were preserved. For the next century and a half she remained on display at the Musée de l'Homme in Paris. Thanks to the repatriation efforts of her native South Africa, Saartjie Baartman has finally and at last come home.

The story of Saartijes Baartman, the "Hottentot Venus," is a deeply tragic and moving one. It is at once the story of an everyday woman, a human being who was treated in the most grotesque and inhumane of ways. But hers is also a story that throws into stark relief "the social, political, scientific and philosophical assumptions which transformed one young woman into a representation of savage sexuality and racial inferiority."⁵ The stereotypical caricatures of Baartman are reflective of the sexualization of the Black female body throughout Western history.

The Black male body provided ample evidence as well of an African animality and dark rapaciousness standing in need of white domination (read: exploitation) and control. A tragic example is the little known story of Ota Benga. Benga was a member of the Chirichiri people, called Pygmies by the Europeans, in what was then the Belgian Congo. In 1904 he was placed on exhibit at the St. Louis World's Fair and later moved to the monkey house at the New York Bronx Zoo where he was both housed and kept on permanent display for the public. Despite successful efforts by irate African Americans to put an end to Ota's forced captivity they could not mend his broken heart. Ota eventually took his own life when he was unable to return to his homeland.⁶

The stories of Saartjie, Ota, and other ancestral witnesses help us to look at the historical unfolding of Black self-imaging and self-esteem with a greater appreciation. How can we begin to come home to ourselves, that is, how can we learn to more fully appreciate the height and depth and breadth of who we are as Black people, female and male? It is at this point that I invite students to read about African traditional understandings of gendered and sexual life in order to ask fresh questions of themselves. At the risk of stating the obvious, the African traditional context is no precolonial utopia or panacea; it presents us with repressive tendencies of its own that require resistance and critique. Alternatively, what the African context does afford us is a profound *sense of option* that encourages and evokes deep-rooted and liberating reflection from students in every subsequent class session. To find our way back home, to return to ourselves, to reclaim our embodied existence in culture and in community; this is an altogether worthwhile and spiritual endeavor. (Suggested readings: Ife Amadiume, *Re-inventing Africa: Matriarchy, Religion, and Culture*; Mercy Amba Oduyoye, *The Will to Arise*; Laurenti Magesa, *African Religion*; Jacob Olupona, *African Traditional Religions in Contemporary Society*. Suggested videos: *The Life and Times of Sara Baartman*—"*The Hottentot Venus*"; *Daughters of the Dust*; *Sankofa* [Note: The latter two films well capture transitional themes of rupture and continuity, middle passage and new birth for Africans in the North America context].)

Sacred Texts and Sexuality

It is with considerable self-consciousness and a healthy dose of humility that I venture any suggestions at all when it comes to addressing matters of sexuality and the biblical text. Recognizing my severe limitations as a biblical scholar, I invited my colleague in New Testament and a contributor to this volume, Michael J. Brown, to address my class. Nevertheless, I offer a word or two of reflection here.

The Bible continues to play a formative and foundational role in the self-understanding of the Black faithful, Christian and otherwise. I have learned that a key element in relating the sacred text to sexuality, whether in the classroom or the pulpit, is the willingness to reflect deeply upon our own experiences. It is as important for students to know how they construct the Bible in their understanding of sexuality as to know how the Bible structures their sexual beliefs. Many of the Black faithful, female and male alike, do not think as highly as they ought about the cultural conjunction of sexuality and the sacred. Others still, those whom one biblical scholar names the "unsophisticate," remain literal to the extreme in their reading of the biblical text.[7] Today social-scientific, phenomenological, cultural, literary and other forms of criticism, as well as historical-critical orientations invite us to read the text in the most exciting, interactive, and collaborative of ways. It is incumbent upon we who teach and preach to dare to do likewise, inviting Black believers into meaningful dialogue with the biblical text and more, into lived experience of the *imago Dei*. (Suggested readings: *The Holy Bible* [NRSV]; Randall Bailey, ed., *Yet with a Steady Beat: U.S. Afrocentric Biblical Interpretation*; Cain Hope Felder, ed., *Stony the Road We Trod: African American Biblical Interpretation*; Renita Weems, *Just a Sister Away: A Womanist Vision of Women's Relationships in the Bible*; Vincent Wimbush, ed., *African Americans and the Bible: Sacred Texts and Social Textures*.)

Spirit of the Ancestors

About one quarter of the way through Toni Morrison's novel *Beloved* there is a scene that depicts the beauty and power of African American culture to reveal incarnate truth. Baby Suggs, holy, sings a litany of loving all the pieces that make up the Black body. Deep in the woods, in a wide open clearing she calls Black children, women, and men into sacred being: "we flesh; flesh that weeps, laughs; flesh that dances on bare grass. Yonder they do not love your flesh. They despise it." The scene concludes with Baby Suggs's alternative vision for Black being:

> And O my people, out yonder, hear me, they do not love your neck
> unnoosed and straight. So love your neck; put a hand on it, grace it,
> stroke it and hold it up. And all your inside parts that they'd just as soon
> slop for hogs, you got to love them. The dark, dark liver—love it, love
> it, and the beat and beating heart, love that too. More than eyes or feet.
> More than lungs that have yet to draw free air. More than your life-
> holding womb and your life-giving private parts, hear me now, love
> your heart. For this is the prize.[8]

What Baby Suggs, holy, loving, embracing, healing, is able to accomplish through her preaching, for an extraordinary moment in time, is to prepare a place where amazing grace can be imagined and the dignity of a people restored. Hers is the redemptive struggle to reclaim what enslavement systematically and maliciously intended to eliminate—Black being—mind, body, and soul. Morrison's work, set in the nineteenth century, is an act of resistance to a repeating past fraught with apparitions, incarnations, and remembrances, which continues to haunt Black communities even to this day. At its lyric heart, *Beloved* is a spiritual, a radiantly dark meditation on the transcendent worth of Black bodies. In the words of Nancy Jesser, all the lost ancestors and the lost children must be born(e) into the future, not in the manner of a chain, "but as sutures that hold the body together in the aftermath of violence."[9]

Aside from the fact that *Beloved* is one of my favorite books, its inclusion here is intended to emphasize the importance of the aesthetic imagination in helping us to think about our sexual identity as persons in community. Like religion, sexuality touches us at levels deeper than fact and beyond understanding. Literature, novels, short stories, art, film, dance, and so on help students to imaginatively sort through the mounds of information (theological, theoretical, and scientific) met at the nexus between spirituality and sexuality. In fact, we begin every class session with a meditation in song—spirituals, hymns, gospel, jazz, rhythm and blues, hip-hop, and rap—poetry, fiction, critical commentary, and/or the spoken word. Students in the course have also read to stunning effect Alice Walker's *By the Light of My Father's Smile*, a soaring and unconventional (and quite controversial) story of spiritual and sexual redemption in the twentieth century. Wisdom literature, that is to say, venerable stories of caution and celebration, compassion and critique, abound in African American culture and life. Its collective expressions are oral and written, informal and formal, intuitive and concrete, historical and hip-hop. Whether we have primary responsibility for teaching in the academy, church, or community we dismiss the sharp insights and collective wisdom of our cultural griots to our own peril. (Suggested readings: James Baldwin, *Go Tell it on the Mountain*; John Blassingame, *Slave Community*; Alex Haley, *Roots*; Vincent Harding, *There is a River*; Richard Wright, *Native Son*. Suggested videos: *The Color Purple; One Week; A Raisin in the Sun*.)

Intimacy and Violence

Intimacy means different things to different people and the explanations are especially wide ranging when it comes to talking about sexual intimacy. Such a wide variance of opinion also suggests the need for better information to help instruct us in matters of sexual health. The theological task of "faith seeking understanding" where issues of human intimacy are concerned requires an openness on our part to scientific perspectives into the full range of human sexuality—puberty, adolescence, masturbation, virginity, contraception, conception, celibacy, same gender love, gender differences and similarities, sexual disorders and the like—and the courage to accept that our sexual stereotypes can be challenged by science's purviews without ending in skepticism. At the same time, these scientific descriptions also point beyond themselves to the realm of intense emotions and sexual feelings that they tap.

The etiology of human sexuality thus presents us with a tremendous opportunity in the classroom to increase our understanding of our embodied selves. What is far less certain is whether and to what degree Black churches are also willing to embrace perspectives from the biological and behavioral sciences. For example, problems of alienation and the loss of sexual intimacy between couples are evidenced in all walks of life. People who go to church are not immune from sexual dysfunction and/or dysfunctional relationships, but their faith and belief system may not encourage therapeutic interventions. According to behavioral scientist and sex-therapist June Dobbs-Butts, intimacy is integral to every sphere of life—the spiritual, cultural, familial, intellectual, occupational, cultural, recreational, and so on— with the prototype being the mother–infant bonding relationship.[10] While Dobbs-Butts's intended audience is the medical community, her message also speaks magnificently to persons who make up the helping and healing profession called ministry. "Trust," Dobbs-Butts says, "is the secret behind intimacy."[11] In truth, intimacy is love's exquisite gift to us. It is meant to be shared between partners, in community, and ultimately in God.

If intimacy is about love and trust then violence is about control. Indicative of the violence endemic to modern society, its forms are many including structural, physical, verbal, emotional, psychological, financial, and sexual. Sexual violence, which seems to be increasing exponentially in the Black community, is the continuation of an ancient and pernicious form of antisocial behavior worldwide. The U.S. Department of Justice has estimated that in this country alone one in three women, one in twelve men, and one in six children have been the victims of some form of sexual violence. In 2001, the latest year surveyed, there were 249,000 reported victims of rape, attempted rape, or sexual assault in the United States. Most victims know their assailants. For complex reasons, sex crimes often go unreported. Sexual violence, far more than a women's issue, is a community issue.[12]

Kelly Brown Douglas, in her pioneering work *Sexuality and the Black Church*, well chronicles the history of sexual violence against Black women and men in this land.[13] In the crucible of slavery, relations between African women and men were brutally attacked and sufficiently (but never totally) invalidated by Euro-American culture as to prevent us from fully realizing and achieving our liberation, and doing so together. Women were subjected to the slave owners' bidding, men were torn away from their families, and both were bred like animals. When and where possible relationships were sustained yet burdened in ways painful to recount across the generations.

Four centuries of untold racist-sexual violence have exacted a devastating toll on the African American body and soul. What Brown Douglas essentially argues is that racist white America proved incapable of offering the uprooted of Africa a viable model for being human, sexually, socially, or otherwise. In sum, the responsibility for self-understanding belongs to African Americans, inclusive of our sexuality. The sad and painful truth, however, is that we have internalized the fictitious yet injurious judgments others have made about us and often violated and oppressed our own. Where then can we go to find sanctuary from the nightmares of our own sexual misconduct, brutality, distrust, and fear? Is there a balm in Gilead, is there a safe haven, does refuge and resistance reside in the values and mores of the Black Church? (Suggested readings: June Dobbs-Butts, various essays; Kelly Brown Douglas, *Sexuality and the Black Church*; bell hooks,

Salvation: Black People and Love; Anthony B. Pinn, *Terror and Triumph: The Nature of Black Religion*; Traci West, *Wounds of the Spirit: Black Women, Violence, and Resistance Ethics*; Gail Elizabeth Wyatt, *Stolen Women: Reclaiming Our Sexuality, Taking Back Our Lives*. Suggested videos: *Antwone Fisher*; *Eve's Bayou*; *Soul Food*; *What's Love Got to Do With It*.)

At the Crossroads

There are of course no short or simple answers to the above questions. But one of the most public of secrets in the Black community is that Black churches have perpetuated a cruel sexual ethic of their own, and done so in stark violation of their own best teachings. In recent years, there has been growing public awareness and scrutiny of the sordid and injurious manifestations of sex, sexuality, and gender in the Black religious body. For many people and especially women, the litany of sexual intrigue, exploitation, and oppression strikes a deep and personal chord. Even more tragic still, the sin-sickness of sexism, sexual misconduct, and other forms of malfeasance appear to be undermining the faith, giving rise to a new form of exodus community in the twenty-first century, the Black abandonment of religious institutions out of sheer moral frustration and exhaustion. From the pulpit to the pew we see this painful (and, perhaps, ultimately necessary) drama unfolding, with troubling implications for the future of the African American community, and especially for our youth. Sexually and spiritually, the Black Church is at a dangerous and foreboding crossroads.

The sexual politics of the church has also extended to those whose stories and struggles have everything to do with same-and-both-gender-loving people, to persons infected with HIV/AIDS, to individuals suffering through forms of addiction, who have felt abandoned, betrayed, and denounced by family, friends, and community. The Black Church born of struggle, and whose sacred values so long underscored and upheld the infinite and absolute worth of a people, and whose social legacy is community, solidarity, and freedom, is a church that now struggles to accept many of its own.

As a once disinherited people, African Americans are well familiar with the creeds, customs, and cruelties that worked to impeach our humanity. In today's church and society we continue to contend with no less oppressive realities, powerful prejudices, searing hatreds, social indignities, and moral revulsions, often directed at persons solely or largely for reasons of sexuality or lifestyle. Some in the Black religious community have concluded it is in their best theological interest to participate in religious pogroms and "special rights" polemics against this immoral humanity. I seek to offer a more hopeful and hope-filled perspective. I believe that through worship, community education, counseling, and social activism the message of the church to the world must be "Whosoever will let her or him come." In the spirit of Jesus of Nazareth, and in the best of the Black Church tradition, the divine invitation to wholeness and healing must be extended to "whosoever" (John 3:16). Who is included in this singular word "whosoever"? The "whosoever" of today are the diseased and the dis-eased, the discomforted and the distressed, those who live on the margins of the marginalized, who are the oppressed of the oppressed, the sexually battered and the abused, the homeless and the bereft, the young and the old, who are lesbian and bisexual, transgender and straight. They are our sisters and brothers and partners and friends. And they are very much we ourselves.[14]

A pedagogical note: It is sometimes difficult for students of faith to reflect on these controversial issues relating to sexuality, and to assure them there is no condemnation in the same. On the other hand, some students are less than insightful and empathetic in their responses, yea or nay. In the end, what is of paramount importance in the classroom is not that students adopt the views of the instructor, but that they learn how to wrestle, and wrestle well, with these matters. In no small measure, the greater responsibility for students is to become mature interpreters of what they read, see, and hear as relates to the church, for the sake of the church, and for the sake of us all. (Suggested readings: Alton B. Pollard III and Love Henry Whelchel, Jr., eds. *How Long this Road: Race, Religion, and the Legacy of C. Eric Lincoln*; Marcia Riggs, *Plenty Good Room: Women Versus Male Power in the Black Church*; Emilie M. Townes, *Breaking the Fine Rain of Death: African American Health Issues and a Womanist Ethic of Care.* Suggested videos: *Tavist Smiley Presents: The State of the Black Church.*)

Male and Female

Could you love me in a Bentley?
Could you love me on a bus?
I'll ask 21 questions, and they all about us

—*50 Cent*[15]

An easily overlooked aspect to teaching a class on sexuality and the Black Church is ensuring that just and equitable gender interaction takes place. Some may question the reason why such symmetry is either to be desired or feasible. I have attended lectures, seminars and workshops on gender and/or sexuality, and found incongruity to be at the heart of what caused many an event to be less than advertised. In the case of Black sexuality, it is nothing less than the complete and holistic expression of our embodiment that is at stake in just relationships between Black women and men in our churches and in society. It is vitally important that we, all of us, constantly assess our own words and actions as women and men of understanding and faith in light of the interlocking realities of sexism, homophobia, and racism, as well as other oppressions. It is far too easy and never enough to express glib theoretical concern for the gender and sexual equality of us all; it must be made manifest in our spiritual and social *praxis*.

For Black men, any ethical reflection on sexuality will first have to come to terms with the suffering and oppression women have too often experienced at our hands. For Black women, honest reflection on issues of sexuality must also be willing to highlight positive aspects of the challenge and the conversion possibilities inherent within us all. For heterosexual men and women, there must be genuine acknowledgment of our theological complicity in silencing so many of our own. For same-and-both-gender-loving persons, a willingness to struggle anew with estranged kith and kin must occur if we are to reclaim community. Together, we must all face the challenge of bridging from one generation to the next in order to strengthen our relatedness in God.

In many respects, African America has been reticent to address our own sexual politics so long as the nation seems bent on spotlighting or even blaming us for most of society's ills. Not without good reason, we harbor a deep-seated suspicion and mistrust of larger society. However, movement toward right relatedness within the African American community itself has also been restricted thereby. A less acknowledged obstacle to establishing right relations between Black women and men is the corrosive effect of socioeconomic privilege. Despite our sustaining article of faith in justice and equality for all, new class perceptions prevail. There is room in the hegemonic order for only a few select persons of African descent. Who among us will be in that number? Who are we to blame for our continued marginalization? It is crucial that we carefully, candidly, and without recourse to recrimination, name our problems as male and female and in context.

In mapping the contours of friendship, partnership, marriage, and love along the way, we can then come to a more sophisticated appreciation of how detrimental and inauthentic our accomplishments are in isolation one from another. (Suggested readings: Michael Eric Dyson, *Why I Love Black Women*; bell hooks, *Rock My Soul: Black People and Self-Esteem*; bell hooks and Cornel West, *Breaking Bread: Insurgent Black Intellectual Life*: Johnetta Betsch Cole and Beverly Guy-Sheftall, *Gender Talk: The Struggle for Women's Equality in African American Communities*; Bakari Kitwana, *The Hip Hop Generation: Young Blacks and the Crisis in African American Culture*; Joan Morgan, *When Chickenheads Come Home to Roost*; Mary Pattillo-McCoy, *Black Picket Fences: Privilege and Peril among the Black Middle Class*. Suggested videos: *The Best Man; Love and Basketball; To Sleep with Anger*.)

A Gathering of Men

I mean, I don't know what the fuss is about. I mean, everything in the world loves you. White men love you. They spend so much time worrying about your penis they forget their own. . . . And white women? They chase you all to every corner of the earth, feel for you under every bed. . . . Colored women worry themselves into bad health just trying to hang on to your cuffs. Even little children—white and Black, boys and girls— spend all their childhood eating their hearts out 'cause they think you don't love them. And if that ain't enough, you love yourselves. Nothing in the world loves a Black man more than another Black man. . . . it looks to me like you the envy of the world.

Toni Morrison, *Sula*[16]

The contagion of cultural narcissism and moral turpitude has hardly bypassed the communities of African descent in America. Indeed, scholars and researchers have been painstakingly detailing the deleterious impact of white sociocultural domination on African America for decades. The modern shapers of mainstream mass opinion prefer to paint a more pristine picture of white American culpability, depicting the problems faced by the Black community as implicitly socio-pathic, from the decline of the "nuclear" Black family to the rise in Black juvenile incarceration. Of particular moment is the plight of the African American male, young men and boys most of all. For different reasons, both advocates and adversaries allege that the Black male is under a state of siege, "an endangered species," "vanishing," and "at risk."

It is my conviction, forged out of the crucible of experience that African American males are in a perilous, but far-from-hopeless state. For more than four hundred years we have endeavored, hope against hope, to bear witness to the often magnificent meaning of African manhood in this land. Now the struggle must be taken up as never before. Brutalized and demoralized by the politics of disparity and dis-privilege, it is the case that Black male responses have often erred on the side of the reflexive and self-destructive. Yet, even in the midst of gross societal invalidation, life-affirming resources are ours. The real and tragic truth, as Toni Morrison's *Sula* is quick to remind her best friend's husband, is that many African American men seem to have forgotten just how special they are.

The current maelstrom demands a deeper search for more whole-some ways to be male, especially where the Black Church is concerned. The classroom experience offers men and women—together and apart—the opportunity to examine the roles, attitudes, and identities of men in Black churches. Though a growing body of literature now exists pertaining to various aspects of maleness, few books actually offer a prophetic critique of the forces that have shaped and constrained Black male lives, or provide a textured expression of the hope that lies within men for their ultimate salvation. Making the connection between Black masculinity (Black male experience) and spirituality is one of the more serious challenges facing the contemporary Black church. The basic dis-trust many Black men have for Black religious structures is no accident. Many mobilization efforts in the Black community have also been severely impacted as a result. Given the "manly" silence of Black males when it comes to gender, sexuality, and sex, these and other discussions are requisite before Black men and women can ever fully embark upon that greater insurgent activity called building community. (Suggested readings: Herbert Boyd and Robert L. Allen, eds., *Brotherman*; Devon W. Carbado, ed., *Black Men on Race, Gender, and Sexuality*; Dwight N. Hopkins, *Heart and Head: Black Theology Past, Present and Future*; John Edgar Wideman, *Fatheralong*; Malcolm X, *The Autobiography of Malcolm X*; Sanyika Shakur and Monster Kody Scott, *Monster: The Autobiography of an L.A. Gang Member*. Suggested videos: *A Lesson Before Dying*; *Get on the Bus*; *The Visit*.)

If It Wasn't for the Women

... *she tried to be a book*
but he wouldn't read

she turned herself into a bulb
but he wouldn't let her grow
she decided to become
a woman
and though he still refused
to be a man
she decided it was all
right

—*from "Woman" by Nikki Giovanni*[17]

It is a time-honored phrase: "Women are the backbone of the church." Certainly, for longer than I can remember, this statement has held the status of truism in the African American community. As a refrain, as an aphorism, it embodies unassailable if less than accurate sentiments. Statistically, women are known to account for some 70 percent of the church-going population in African America and are renowned for their support of Black religious activities. As Jacqueline Grant and other womanist scholars have long observed, ecclesial declarations of women as the backbone of the church may sound like the highest form of praise, considering the crucial role of the spinal column in human anatomy. The social, theological, and political reality, however, is that the church and its ordained male leadership emphasize by action if not by word only the first syllable of the word "backbone—*back*."

As an African American male, lifelong member of the church, and sociologist of religion, my participant observation only confirms what countless women experience firsthand—the sorry behavior of many Black men. While many clergy and laity espouse theoretical equality between women and men in the church, real world church practices almost always suggest the opposite. Unofficially, Black Churchwomen have everywhere run the Black Church "almost." But the fact that Black women are not always and everywhere encouraged to move from the backbone to the forefront in terms of official church leadership—administrative positions, heads of boards, pulpits, national offices and so on—despite answering to a higher call—is abhorrent, indefensible, and unjust. Increasing numbers of Black women are not waiting for approval from Black men to assume leadership positions. A case in point is the Rev. Portia Wills Lee, esteemed pastor of the Trinity African Baptist Church in Mableton, Georgia, where my family and I attend. Rev. Lee or "Pastor Lee" as she is affectionately called by members of the church and community is both a true "daughter of thunder" and an ecclesial rarity: a seminary-educated Black female who is the senior pastor of a Baptist congregation in the Deep South. Even phenomenal church leadership by women like Pastor Lee does not disprove the general rule however. The extent to which the culture of gender distrust and enmity continues to germinate and grow in the Black community is real cause for alarm.[18] It is the highest priority that women—and men—expose the reality of gender discrimination and its dehumanizing consequences in Black religious life. Sexism undermines our right relationships with one another and God.

What accounts for the exclusion of African American women from substantive decision-making processes in many of our churches? What accounts for the long-standing and broad-based conspiracy of silence by the men? What is it that makes Black men unable to see the double and triple jeopardy of gender, race, and class faced by Black women? Why has there been such a tacit acceptance on the part of some women of secondary status? Why have so many Black women excelled against all odds? As the course instructor, I do not presume to be the person most competent to address these questions. Students are deeply encouraged to write and speak about these and other questions pertaining to gender role expectations in the Black Church and community for themselves. The goal for students is to be about the business of making the connections among the conditions that oppress, and in so doing, lay claim to a healthy self image and respect for us all. (Suggested readings: Delores C. Carpenter, *A Time for Honor: A Portrait of African American Clergywomen*; Gloria Wade-Gayles, *My Soul Is a Witness*; Cheryl Townsend Gilkes, *If it Wasn't for the Women*; Jacquelyn Grant; *White Women's Christ and Black Women's Jesus: Feminist Christology, Womanist Response*; Vashti McKenzie, *Not Without a Struggle: Leadership Development for African American Women in Ministry*; Sister Souljah, *The Coldest Winter Ever*; Delores Williams, *Sisters in the Wilderness*. Suggested videos: *Waiting to Exhale*; *The Women of Brewster Place*.

Embracing Gayness, Embracing Our Own

> We, African American same-gender-loving people, need to come together. Blow your horn! Call the congregation together so that we may sit down, break bread, and reason among each other. It's time to set our own agenda, locally and nationally. It's time to chart our own course. We are the children of a tenacious lot. We are no strangers to wading/waiting, walking, running or bridging troubled waters.
>
> —Dorinda Henry[19]

The Metropolitan Interdenominational Church is located in Nashville, Tennessee. Situated in a working-class neighborhood, the senior servant is the Rev. Edwin C. Sanders II. The church is not unlike many others in terms of its modest outward appearance. Inside, one finds an unusual African American congregation: one which openly accepts persons from all walks of life into its midst, including persons who are lesbian, gay, bisexual, and transgender. Save for the children of neglect and abuse, these women and men are the most silent and silenced members of our community. Prior to the work of womanists Toinette Eugene and Kelly Brown Douglas, Black religious scholarship had with rare exception been silent on the issue of homosexuality, and human sexuality in general.[20] The church has likewise been silent, unable to find a clear voice where lesbian and gays are concerned, except to express opposition and condemnation. For many Black Church bodies homophobia, the fear and hatred of homosexuals, and heterosexism, heterosexual preference, is palpable and real. It should come as no surprise then that the black heterosexual Christian community fails to accord to same-and-both-gender-loving people equal respect or even to acknowledge their sacred worth.

Lesbian and gay scholars and writers have carefully explicated the enormous price same-and-both-gender-loving women and men pay for the harassment and oppression they face in seminaries and Black churches. For instance, Horace Griffin relates how one group of Black seminarians (supported by heterosexual Black faculty) responded with outrage when the oppression of gays was briefly compared to racial oppression during a theological forum.[21] Invoking the authority of biblical scripture is a strategy frequently employed to invalidate the morality of same-and-both-gender-love. The crushing truth is that the self-image and self-esteem of many lesbians and gays are dealt a multiplicity of blows by their families, churches, community, and larger society. That Black lesbians and gays are made to feel unworthy in what should be the most caring and compassionate of communions opens the door for a host of other problems, from health concerns to issues of fidelity for those who may have spouses.

In her master's honors thesis, Dorinda Henry outlines the beginnings of an emancipatory ethic for the Black Church and its lesbian, gay, bisexual, and (we would add) transgender members. She proposes that same-and-both-gender-loving persons adopt the following pragmatic steps to begin the process of reconnecting, healing, and reconciliation with Black religious bodies: (1) Confront the oppressiveness of Black churches, (2) Come out to our family, friends and the church,

(3) Confront our own self-destructiveness and cease self-effacement, and (4) Educate those whom we care about most—our biological family, church members, and community of origin.[22] Persons who stand in solidarity with lesbian and gay people should also ready themselves to speak out. For same-and-both-gender-loving women and men there is no greater challenge than to change Black Church views and structures that define non-heterosexual relationships as immoral. And, perhaps, no greater reward to claim than to finally and at long last be received as a child of God in one's own family, congregation, and community. (Suggested readings: James Baldwin, *The Evidence of Things Not Seen*; Eric Brandt, *Dangerous Liaisons: Blacks, Gays, and the Struggle for Equality*; Gary David Comstock, *A Whosoever Church*; Delroy Constantine-Simms, *The Greatest Taboo: Homosexuality in Black Communities*. Suggested videos: *All God's Children*; *Tongues Untied*.)

Building Up the Body/Ourselves

Early on in this essay, I defined spirituality as a commitment and a lifeway, a sacred encounter that yields action for living. Students should now be ready to take what lessons they have learned in the classroom and begin to apply them to the vast and varied circumstances of life. Having critically considered a number of pertinent topics and motifs, their responses must now move toward the concrete. If preparation occurs well, students—seminarians, professors, clergy, lay people—should be ready to impart, in various ways, their own communal vision of ways to build up the Black body/ourselves. Every student has had occasion to consider, up close and personal, what happens to a church and world in which the relationship between spirituality and sexuality or the sacred and erotic is deprecated and demeaned. There is in truth an umbilical relationship between the two, and where one is denied the other will be affected. Students can now reflect with greater insight and integrity on issues of trust between women and men, gays and straights, and more. Sexuality can now be taken into the world with an exuberant faith that here also is the arena of divine presence and possiblity.

A principle means by which this affirmation of faith, the building up of the Black body, can go forth is through the preached word. Pastoral care, Christian education, Bible study, liturgy and worship, public advocacy, and community involvements are other avenues to edify the body. In good preaching (and teaching), inspiration is revealed not so much through the sharing of elaborate information, complex sermon design, or sophisticated technology, as helpful as all this most certainly is. Rather, wisdom is manifestly revealed in the preaching moment, when the complex is made simple without oversimplification. The Bible is most instructive in this regard, reminding us that when it comes to effective preaching, "God's foolishness is wiser than human wisdom, and God's weakness is stronger than human strength" (1 Cor. 1:25).

I have heard very few sermons in Black churches that address sexual matters in an open and affirming way. Twenty years ago, after preaching a message on women and equality in the church, I was excoriated from the pulpit by a visiting minister who everyone seemed to know except me. On the whole, the congregation was quite supportive of me—I was after all their new interim pastor![23] For reasons that have been discussed heretofore most heterosexual men and not a few women are reluctant, even loathe, to proclaim a sexually liberating and redemptive word.[24] The present silence only fuels a climate of denial, division, and distraction that may prove to be devastating to future generations of the Black body, no less our own. In an attempt to help us find a way out of our current moral and ethical impasse a cadre of courageous clergy, scattered here and there across the land have begun to emerge, who dare to preach without ceasing, in and through and beyond the storm. The *African American Pulpit* is a good source to find some of these inclusive models of proclamation. James Forbes, Vashti McKenzie, Ella Pearson Mitchell, and Irene Monroe are among the ministers whose sermons on sexuality have graced its pages. Jeremiah Wright is famously known for his collection of published sermons entitled *Good News*, including "Good News for Homosexuals."[25] Ella Pearson Mitchell and Suzan D. Johnson Cook, among others, have published collections of sermons with equally insightful messages on gender equality.[26] Let me here conclude with the wise counsel of James Forbes on preaching sexuality (not limited to HIV/AIDS) for such a time as this.

How to approach the sexuality issues that are linked closely with HIV/AIDS? Remember, you will determine whether people die in agony or in community. Preach only from what you believe, so long as you provide constructive leadership toward ending HIV transmission and caring for those infected and affected. If your current framework prevents you from addressing controversial questions in a way that empowers your congregation to respond to the ravages of this epidemic,

consider entering retreat to seek divine guidance regarding the approach
you should take.[27]

(Suggested readings: The Balm in Gilead, *Though I Stand at the Door
and Knock: Discussions on the Black Church Struggle with
Homosexuality and AIDS*; *A Pastor's Guidebook for HIV/AIDS
Ministry through the Church*; Jeremiah Wright, *Good News: Sermons
of Hope for Today's Families*.)

Appendix: A Love Supreme

This year a group of students from my class took our ruminations fully
to heart. They planned and led a worship service on "Sexuality and the
Black Church." In previous courses, students have done role plays,
mock trials, dramatizations, and other interpretations of sexuality
and spirituality. However, this time students led us into sacramental
worship, an experience that no words can do justice to here. Prepared
for the entire seminary community, its lessons were spiritual, erotic,
humorous, challenging, galvanizing, transcendent, transformative,
intimate, and freeing. The liturgy is appended here in its entirety
(with the students' permission), as an offering and laboratory of the
possible, and as a benediction of love.[28]

Call to Worship (Skit)

They gettin' married tomorra' that's good! Good thang, that baby
bout two years old now.
    Did you notice how them brothahs are always together, always look-
ing at each other during service-Yeah, and you see how they always riding together and he have his kids all the time—Sommum' ain't right.
    I heard deacon (listening) yeah you know—girl, he HIV positive—
    Yeah child! I heard about that girl getting pregnant. It's a shame
fore God! "She ain't but fourteen."
    Well, you heard about Sister Sally and her *girlfriend*. That gal been
livin' there a long time now! You know she ain't never been married!
    Well, I heard Pastor done had it! She said she gonna use the entire
service to talk about sex. Yeah—She gone let some of the seminary students talk about it—yeah, service ought to be off the hook. I hope
everybody stay so that we can at least begin to talk about it.
    It's about time. Well, looka here, I got to do praise and worship so
I'll see you there.

(Musical Interlude)

Litany (Jacquay) Genesis 2:21–24 & and adaptations from *Sexuality and the Black Church* by Kelly Brown Douglas.

Leader: So the Lord God caused a deep sleep to fall upon the man, and he slept; then God took one of the ribs and closed up its place with flesh

Congregation: And the rib that the Lord had taken from the man and God made into woman;

Leader: And Gods creation of man and woman was good. Gods embodied presence in Jesus affirms the testimony of the first chapter of Genesis

Congregation: That all of God's creation was good, including the human body.

Leader: The message of God's embodiment in Jesus is unambiguous: the human body is not a cauldron of evil but, rather, an instrumentally divine presence. It is the medium through which God is made real to humanity, through which God interacts with human history.

Congregation: To accept that Jesus, the first century Jew from Nazareth, is God Incarnate indicates that in Jesus, divinity and humanity are irrevocably united.

All: A sexual discourse of resistance makes clear that there is no longer an excuse for the Black Church behaving in such a way that compromises the humanity or mocks the sexuality of any individual.

Prayer (Tamura)

Scripture (Daphne)

Upon my bed at night I sought him whom my soul loves;
I sought him, but found him not;
I called him, but he gave no answer.
"I will rise now and go about the city,
in the streets and in the squares;
I will seek him whom my soul loves."

Song of Solomon 3:1–2

Song (Lisa)—Redemption Song

The Message—

Pastor—The scripture from Song of Solomon has been taken as religious allegory recounting God's love for Israel and the history of their relationship. It has been interpreted as sacred marriage liturgy. Recent mortuary song theory identifies the song's setting as a funeral repast (or orgies) that affirmed life by setting the power of love against the power of death. In some cases it has simply been taken as a secular love poem. Today it is part of this service as a backdrop to a subject that is very real in the Christian life. Sex is on our minds and today the message is a discourse that will bring the subject to life. You may not agree with the discourse but the point is to resist the desire to keep sex under the covers. Please listen to the conversations.

The following journal submissions were written and read by students in the class "Sexuality and the Black Church."

Michael

A sexual discourse of resistance is the effort to frustrate and disrupt any power structure or system that threatens Black life and wholeness through dialogue. It exposes the power or system that threatens Black life and wholeness and makes it possible to thwart it. It has two central goals: (1) to penetrate the sexual politics of the Black community and (2) to cultivate a life-enhancing approach to Black sexuality within the black community. A sexual discourse of resistance will ultimately change the way we think and act on issues concerning sex and sexuality.[29]

Many predominantly Black churches have traditionally avoided honest discourse about sex due to the belief that such a discussion may give the appearance of condoning evil or promoting sex and thus causing people to "sin." It is time for African Americans to change the way they view sex and sexuality. The Black Church must face the issues concerning sex if it wishes to *save* the people who live in the community. The church must stop avoiding a sexual discourse and jump into the trenches with the rest of society and face the current issues concerning sex in the Black community now. It is imperative that the Black Church leads the way towards sexual honesty and wholeness.

Natasha

Water-walker
When you left
I felt my soul leave my body
The walls closed in and air ceased
When you left

I thought the world was over
and I would never be given the chance
to right the wrong
When you left
I walked through the world
pretending all was well
but trust me, when no one was looking
I turned every corner
hoping, wishing
my air,
my inspiration,
my marrow,
my reason . . .
    would return
but you left
and slowly, I did what all poets do
I died . . .

—Renee Harrison

Michael (written by Tamura Lomax)
In the past, predominantly Black churches have refused to talk openly about sex. Deaths resulting from HIV/AIDS, sexual violence, abortion and hate crimes against gays and lesbians are on the rise in the Black community. Yet, the predominantly Black Church has maintained its silence on these pertinent issues. The Black Church's silence must come to an end on these issues or else their silence will eventually be deemed as consent to some of the aforementioned concerns and African American people will continue to die. Consent to any of the above issues will be detrimental to the Christian faith as a whole because none of the aforementioned concerns are in alignment with God's intent for creation. According to Marjorie Suchocki in *A Fall to Violence*, God's original aim for creation was the well being for *all* of creation.[30] With the growing number of reported deaths within the Black community due to HIV/AIDS, sexual violence, abortion, and hate crimes against gays and lesbians, it is evident that our well being is at stake.

"Mama, I Still Love You."
Twenty years,
Twenty years I've lived in this house,
Winnie the Pooh bedspreads, Barbie dreamhouses, sleepovers,
Sweet sixteen party, the prom, going off to college. . . .

And now Mama says I've got to go.

"GET OUT!" she said, "GET OUT OF MY HOUSE, YOU SINNER!"

What was my great sin?

Using drugs? Drinking? Smoking?

Like most teenagers, I'd tried some of that, but decided it wasn't for me.

Was I a disobedient child?

No, I was rather boring when you get right down to it.

My big mistake was leaving my diary out where my mother could read it.

How would I know she would invade my privacy like that?

Perhaps she thought it was trash and decided to make sure before she threw it out.

Maybe she was looking for answers.

Answers as to why I'd never really had a boyfriend, even though I'd gone to the prom with a "nice boy." He was just a friend, ironically, a friend in the same predicament as I.

You see,

My mother has often wondered why I was never a giggly teenager, talking on the phone all hours of the night about which boy I liked. Why I'd never had a "gentleman caller."

I guess my mother thought I was a late bloomer.

My aunt told her I was just going through an awkward phase and when I went off to college I'd grow out of it.

Twenty years,

And I hadn't grown out of it yet.

And then it happened.

She read my diary. It was an old one from my sweet sixteen years. I had written several entries, rather benign, I thought, about my feelings, my desires, and how it was so hard to be different. How I had to keep silent if I didn't want to be ostracized, taunted, or worse, beaten up.

She called me at school and told me to come home right away. I thought she was sick and I rushed home, driving ninety in a fifty-five.

When I got home, she met me at the door with my diary in hand. She asked for, no, demanded an explanation.

So I gave her one.

I told her that at college I'd finally found a community that accepted me for who I was; that didn't think I was going to hell because I was considered different from the norm. I was finally free and I loved being free.

She recoiled in horror.

She shouted at me that this wouldn't have happened to me if I hadn't gone to that white college. "That's where you get all this nonsense from," she said. Homosexuality is a white thing, according to my mama. God made Adam and Eve, not Adam and Steve!

"Lord, what am I going to tell our family?" Mama cried. "What am I going to tell Pastor?"

I told her, "Tell him I'm full of the love of God, I'm just and honest in all my relationships, and I'm striving to be the person God intended me to be."

She looked at me as if she didn't know me. I guess she didn't. I wasn't her pretty little girl, all dressed up in lace and frills. I was a woman. A woman who loves women.

She couldn't accept it.
Couldn't accept me.
Couldn't love me.
'Cause I'm a sinner.
So she told me, "GET OUT, you SINNER!"
And I'm getting out.

But I still love you, Mama.

Lisa Allen

Michael

The Black Church's approach to human sexuality, as a vessel of sin, focuses solely on genitals and sexual activity. Refusal to promote honest public discourse concerning sexuality betrays our enslaved religious heritage and thus embraces dominant Western European and Euro-American tradition of spiritualistic dualism and pietism. Through a sexual discourse of resistance in the Black Church, African Americans can begin the radical transformation process from traditional and doctrinal enslavement towards the liberation of our sexual selves, our community, and the Black Church as a whole (inclusive of all denominations with majority Black congregations).[31]

Joyce (reading her own piece)

Sexuality in the Black Church

The question posed to the class about how can we broach the subject of sex in the Black Church is a profound one. Not only is the question profound, the dilemma is deep. The topic of sex in the church is a minefield. Sex is not a comfortable subject, generally in mixed company let alone "in church."

Personally, I believe that sex and the church are inseparable. The reality of procreation is part of day-to-day life. The reality of courtship and marriage is true. The reality of male–female, female–female and male–male attraction exists in daily life; and all of this exists in the church. I cannot figure out why sex is a dirty word to church folks. Parishioners gladly announce and warmly embrace the fact when couples marry. Marriage legalizes sex (among other things). That same couple announces they are having a baby. The response is "that's wonderful." The unspoken element here is "we're having sex." So why is it so uncomfortable to talk about sex beyond the context of marriage?

Jacquay

> They Lied
> They lied
> They lied when they said sex is not of God
> and making love is for making babies
> They lied
> When I awake in your arms
> I don't recall making babies
> *Nor* the ancestral or cosmic realm screaming for order
> I just recall feeling alive,
> re-born,
> new,
> and every age that I ever been is wrapped, in that moment
> Why did they lie?
> Renee Harrison

Joyce

I would submit that church folks pretend that sex outside of marriage does not exist. Yet, there are so many obvious facts that speak to the contrary. Single-parent families abound in church. Some of these are created by death and divorce but vast majorities of them are created by sex outside marriage. Teenage pregnancy happens to children in church just like it happens with children who are outside of the church. AIDS is just as prevalent inside the church community as outside. Some of these cases are the result of infected blood transfusions but most result from sexual contact both inside and outside of marriage.

The church community would raise an accusing finger, ignore these issues, and pretend that it is not their problem. That is why it is important to open the door to dialogue about the reality of human sexuality and sex on the church. The children are subliminally bombarded with sex, with everything from Barbie dolls and video games to cartoons. If the parents and church support community won't rise to the challenge of teaching and informing the children then schools, television, radio, videos, and their peers get the call.

I would argue that most pastors are not comfortable raising sexual issues in their congregations for a variety of reasons. However, I would argue further that the environmental climate surrounding the church makes it extremely dangerous to ignore the need for open discussion of these issues. If there is salvation to be had within the Black Church, that salvation cannot come without confronting the reality of sex (on the record and off the record) in the congregation.

Breaking down the barriers to introduce this hot topic will certainly not be easy. Even in our classroom, some of us are uncomfortable with expressing our feelings about sex. Maybe one of the things that we can do as a class is to come up with some suggestions as to how we can approach this minefield in our respective congregations without being blown to pieces.

Aileen

Prayer (by Christopher Neely)

> *"for I am fearfully and wonderfully made.*
> *Wonderful are your works; that I know very well."*

> *Psalm 139:14*

Gracious, loving and creating God,
There is reason to rejoice and praise.
In and by your infinite wisdom and creativity
You have intricately designed humanity and me.
In us you have placed the capacity for us to be sexual beings.
As flesh we may taste, know and love pleasure
Else why would you create us with the magnificent anatomy of
Breasts, mons pubis, labia majora and minora, clitoris and vagina
Prostate, testis, scrotum and penis?
And why should we be made curious enough to taste the
garden tree
So that our eyes are opened, our spirits inspired, and our
curiosity satisfied?
Why do you give us joy and ecstasy through sex and orgasm?
Are you not the one who created us this way?
Sexual attraction, infatuation, love,
Are these not your creation?
If these are not then forgive our weakness and our helplessness.
But if these are your gifts
Then why do we fail to acknowledge them?
Why are we ashamed to talk about them?
And why are we ready to ascribe your work to the devil or evil?
Help us Gracious Lord
To see through every sphere of our being
And to be more appreciative of your wonderful creation.
May we accept these and other good gifts with responsibility.
Ashé. Amen.

Sending Forth—

Notes

1. A special note of appreciation to my teaching associates, Renee Harrison and Nevell Owens, Ph.D. candidates in the Graduate Department of Religion, Emory University.
2. While this essay attends specifically and sociologically to the Black Christian tradition the implications for other faith traditions in the African American community are no less critical.
3. For a broad explication of this term see Michael Battle, *Reconciliation: The Ubuntu Theology of Desmond Tutu* (Cleveland, O H: The Pilgrim Press, 1997).
4. I am indebted to the brief but informative explication of many of these themes in Toinette M. Eugene's excellent article, "While Love Is Unfashionable: Ethical Implications of Black Spirituality and Sexuality," in *Sexuality and the Sacred,*

James B. Nelson and Sandra P. Longfellow, eds. (Louisville, KY: Westminster/ John Knox Press, 1994), 105–114.

5. See the powerful documentary film by Zola Maseko, *The Life and Times of Sara Baartman—"The Hottentot Venus."* New York: First Run/Icarus Films, 1998.

6. Phillips Verner Bradford and Harvey Blume, *Ota Benga—The Pygmy in the Zoo* (New York: St. Martin's Press, 1992).

7. Vincent Wimbush, "Introduction: Reading darkness, Reading scriptures," in *African Americans and the Bible: Sacred texts and Social Textures*, ed. Vincent Wimbush (New York: Continuum, 2000), 11.

8. Toni Morrison, *Beloved* (New York: Alfred A. Knopf, 1987), 88–89.

9. Nancy Jesser, "Violence, Home and Community in Toni Morrison's *Beloved.*" *African American review* 33.2 (Summer 1999), 315–347.

10. June Dobbs-Butts formerly taught a course called "Spirituality and Sexuality" at the Interdenominational Theological Center in Atlanta, GA. See also her essay on "Sex Therapy, Intimacy, and the Role of the Black Physician in the AIDS Era," *Journal of the National Medical Association* 80:8 (1988), 921.

11. Ibid.

12. Monica Coleman, a Professor at Bennett College has done important work in this regard. For the most recent statistical information on sexual violence visit the Rape, Abuse and Incest National Network's website: http://www.rainn.org/statistics.html#mentoo.

13. Kelly Brown Douglas, *Sexuality and the Black Church: A Womanist Perspective* (Maryknoll, N Y: Orbis Books, 1999).

14. For a viable model of "whosoever church" see Gary David Comstock, " 'Whosoever' Is Welcome Here: An Interview with Rev. Edwin C. Sanders II" in *Dangerous Liaisons: Blacks, Gays, and the Struggle for Equality*, ed. Eric Brandt (New York: The New press, 1999), 142–158.

15. 50 Cent, "21 Questions," from the CD compilation *Get Rich or Die Tryin'*. Interscope Records, 2003.

16. Toni Morrison, *Sula* (New York: Alfred A. Knopf, 1973), 89.

17. Nikki Giovanni, *Cotton Candy on a Rainy Day* (New York: William Morrow, 1978), 71.

18. Derrick Bell details the consequences of our divisive behavior in "The Sexual Diversion: The Black Man/Black Woman Debate in Context," in *Black Men on Race, Gender, and Sexuality: A Critical Reader*, ed. Devon W. Carbado (New York: New York University Press, 1999), 237–247.

19. Dorinda Henry, 2002. "Bridge Over Troubled Waters," *Venus*, May, 84.

20. Other religious scholars who have written about and spoken out against Black heterosexism and homophobia include Victor Anderson, Randall Bailey, Michael Eric Dyson, Elias Farajaje-Jones, Dwight Hopkins, and Irene Monroe. See also Toinette M. Eugene, "How Can We Forget? An Ethic of Care for AIDS, the African American Family, and the Black Catholic Church," in *Embracing the Spirit: Womanist Perspectives on Hope, Salvation, and Transformation*, ed. Emilie M. Townes (Maryknoll, NY: Orbis Books, 1998).

21. Horace Griffin, "Their Own Received Them Not: African American Lesbians and Gays in Black Churches," in *The Greatest Taboo: Homosexuality in*

Black Communities, ed. Delroy Constantine-Simms (Los Angeles: Alyson Books, 2000), 110–121.

22. Dorinda Henry, "I, too, Sing Songs of Freedom" (Master's thesis, Emory University, Candler School of Theology, 2000), 28–56.

23. On the subject of sexual inclusion and affirmation in the black church see Alton B. Pollard, III, "Whosoever" http://divinity.library.vanderbilt.edu/kmsi/ Pollardpercent20sermon.htm.

24. Out same-and-both-gender loving clergy, few and far between in mainline black churches, are nevertheless proclaiming the good news in predominantly (but not exclusively) lesbian, gay, bisexual, and transgender churches. For example, in Atlanta, Georgia, Dr. Kathi E. Martin is pastor of God, Self, and Neighbor Ministries.

25. Jeremiah A. Wright, Jr., *Good News: Sermons of Hope for Today's Families* (Valley Forge: Judson Press, 1995).

26. For example, see the three edited volumes by Ella Pearson Mitchell called *Those Preaching Women* (Valley Forge: Judson Press, 1985) as well as *Women: To Preach or not to Preach?* (Valley Forge: Judson Press, 1991) and Suzan D. Johnson Cook and William D. Watley, *Preaching in Two Voices: Sermons on the Women in Jesus' Life* (Valley Forge: Judson Press, 1991). To my knowledge, none of these collections address homosexuality. All of these publications are from Judson Press.

27. James A. Forbes, "Developing Sermons on HIV/AIDS," http://www. balmingilead.org/resources/sermon.asp.

28. Thanks to all my students in "Sexuality and the Black Church" and especially to Aileen Maddox, Lisa Allen, Daphne Anderson, Renee Harrison, Tamura Lomax, Christopher Neely, Jacquay Waller, Natasha Wright, and Joyce Young for allowing me to share your creative spirits with others.

29. Brown Douglas, *Sexuality and the Black Church*, 68–69.

30. Marjorie Hewitt Suchocki, *The Fall to Sin: Original Sin in Relational Theology* (New York: Continuum, 1995), 17.

31. Brown Douglas, *Sexuality and the Black Church*, 121.

18

The Black Church and the Politics of Sexuality

Kelly Brown Douglas

Yes, it does indeed mean something—something unspeakable—to be born, in a white country, an Anglo-Teutonic, antisexual country, black.[1]

It is very important to remember what it means to be born in a Protestant Puritan country, with all the taboos placed on the flesh, and have at the same time in this country such a vivid example of a decent pagan imagination and the sexual liberty with which white people invest Negroes—and then penalize them for. . . . It's a guilt about flesh. In this country the Negro pays for that guilt which white people have about flesh.[2]

"a woman who loves other women, sexually and/or non-sexually. . . . She is committed to survival and wholeness of entire people, male and female.[3]

Recently the Supreme Court handed down two monumental decisions as it relates to human rights. The first involved the University of Michigan's Affirmative Action policies. The second case involved The Texas sodomy law. As we all now know, the Supreme Court handed down its ruling on the Michigan case on June 23, 2003. Though burdened with the ambiguity of a divided court, the June 23, 2003 decision seemed to uphold in principle Affirmative Action policies as a way of achieving diversity. Several days later, the court handed down its decision concerning the sodomy case, the case officially known as Lawrence and Garner v. Texas. This particular case dealt with the Texas Penal Code, commonly referred to as The Homosexual Conduct

Statue. This particular statue criminalizes sexual activity between homosexual persons even if the acts are consensual. The case before the court concerned two men who were arrested after a police officer noticed them engaged in sexual activity in one of the men's bedroom. The court ruled that the Texas penal code was in fact unconstitional and it infringed upon the rights of homosexual persons.

Just as the University of Michigan case has far-reaching ramifications for racial justice in this country, so too does the Texas sodomy case have significant ramifications for sexual justice. Both cases involve issues of political/human rights in regard to certain minorities.

I cite these two cases because not only do they suggest something about the political climate of our nation as it regards civil/human rights, but they are also instructive for understanding the justice politics of the Black Church. It is interesting to note that as vocal as the Black Church community was in regard to the Michigan case, its silence was deafening in terms of the Texas case. At least two major Black Church denominations, the National Baptist Convention and the Progressive National Baptist Convention offered resolutions in support of Affirmative Action. Moreover, various Black clergy offered comments from in and outside of the pulpit about the case and the justice issues involved. Yet, as far as I have been able to determine the Black Church community remained virtually silent in regard to the Texas case. There have been no resolutions as far as I know offered by major Black denominations concerning the justice issues involved in this case. My unscientific polling suggests that not many Black church people were even aware that the Texas case was before the Supreme Court.

These two disparate responses to cases involving human justice are in fact telling when it comes to the Black Church's attitude toward various justice issues, and hence its involvement in what I term the politics of justice. While the Black Church is certainly one of the most enduring and significant Black institutions, it is also one of the most enigmatic. For, it can be in the vanguard for social justice and change, or it can be a stubborn antagonist to social justice and change. More particularly the Black Church has been, and for the most part, continues to be, in the forefront of racial justice concerns. Yet, it has typically been bringing up the rear in regard to issues of gender and or sexual justice.

Indeed, the Black Church is often characterized as stubbornly homophobic. Though recognizing the presence of gay musicians and choirmasters within the church, and vowing to love the homosexual sinner, Black Church people rarely see homosexuality as an acceptable way of life. Far too often they brand homosexuality as an "abomination before the Lord." Homoerotic expressions of sexuality are pronounced "sinful." As one Black Church woman recently said to me, "Why can't we just be clear what is right and what is wrong" (implying that homoerotic behavior is wrong).

While the Black Church community is arguably no more homophobic than the wider Church community or heterosexist society of which it is a part, causal observations do suggest that it is perhaps more unyielding and impassioned than other communities when expressing its anti-gay and anti-lesbian sentiments.[4] Again, making its homophobic convictions appear even more reprehensible is its historic commitment to Black freedom and justice. How is it that a Church community so committed to the politics of racial justice can be so intransigent when it comes to the politics of sexual justice and hence gay and lesbian rights? Why is the Black Church community generally so averse to homoerotic sexuality? Why do Black Church people often regard the homosexual body as a depraved body? What makes Black Church homophobia seem more passionate, trenchant, and relentless than the homophobia present in other communities? These are the questions upon which this paper is focused. There are two primary reasons that make these questions most urgent for me.

First, as one who attempts to do her work from a womanist paradigm, central to my work is a "commitment to the survival and wholeness of entire people." This to me is a mandate to do my theological reflection in such a way that it contributes to the well being and freedom of all Black men and women in particular, and all persons in general. Specifically, the womanist mandate is to name and deconstruct, if you will, those "interlocking systems and structures of oppression"—be they social, political, or ecclesiastical (as well as the theo-ideology which sustains them) in an effort to move toward a place where all people are free from that which would threaten their lives and thwart their wholeness/freedom. It is for this reason that I am compelled to address that which is frequently overlooked in the Black community, the issue of sexual justice.

Second, by reflecting upon the Black Church in relation to issues of sexual justice we can learn something more about the Black Church when it comes to its justice politics in general. Before proceeding, however, let me clarify what precisely is meant when referring to the Black Church.

The Black Church is essentially a disparate grouping of churches that reflect the diversity of the Black community itself. These churches are diversified by origin, denomination, doctrine, worshipping culture, spiritual expression, class, size, and other less obvious factors. This means then that they may be within white denominational structures or independent of them. They can reflect congregational, connectional, and Episcopal systems. They can be urban, suburban, or rural. They range in size from storefronts to mega-churches. They are middle class, working class, and poor. They might reflect highly rapturous or very restrained forms of spiritual expression. Yet, as disparate as Black churches are, they do share a common history and play a unique role in black life, both of which attest to their collective identity as the Black Church.

The Black Church reflects Black people's history of struggle against white racist oppression even as it was born out of that struggle. Moreover, it remains one of the most significant influences upon Black values. It too is a central resource for Black well being—be it physical, emotional, or spiritual well being. W. E. B. Du Bois aptly described the Black Church when he called it both the "religious center" and "social center for black people."[5] Yet, even in recognizing the consistency of the Black Church, it is important also to recognize its variation.

Any discussion of the Black Church in general must appreciate Black churches in particular. For example, while there are prevailing attitudes that characterize the Black Church community, such as the attitudes toward homosexuality, there are also noteworthy exceptions to these attitudes. Thus, while my particular discussion of the Black Church and sexual justice expressly focuses on the prevalent homo- phobic sentiments of the Black Church community, it implicitly acknowledges that there are various and significant Black churches with more liberating and progressive views toward sexual expression. With that said, let me now attempt to answer the question of why the Black Church tends to be so insular when it comes to matters of sexual justice, in spite of its' activism in relation to racial justice. The answer to this question is in fact suggested by James Baldwin's observations, which I cited to open this paper, that it *does* [emphasis mine] "mean something . . . to be born in a white . . . Anglo-Teutonic, anti-sexual country, black"; and that "the Negro pays for that guilt which white people have about the flesh."[6] Baldwin's incisive comments point to an insidiously complex relationship between Christianity and white culture and its impact upon Black lives. It is in understanding this relationship and subsequent impact that we can begin to answer the questions concerning Black Church attitudes toward sexual justice in general and homosexuality in particular. Let me begin by briefly examining the relationship between Christianity and white culture.

Christianity and White Culture

Platonized Christianity

One of Christianity's greatest paradoxes is its attitude toward the human body. Since its origins in a first-century Hellenistic world, Christianity's regard for the body has been enigmatic. Christianity's central confession, God's unique presence in the first century Jew from Nazareth, basically esteems the body as a vessel of divine revelation. The reality of the incarnate God marked as heretical any notion that God was not *en sarki*, that is, a fully embodied presence in Jesus. The divine incarnation seemingly precluded as acceptable to Christianity any belief that reviled the human body/flesh. Yet, there has been a prominent Christian tradition that has denigrated and demonized the body.

In efforts to peaceably exist in the Greco-Roman world in which they were a part, as well as a reflection of the Hellenized Jewish tradition from which they emerged, early Christian thinkers and apologists integrated into their Christian theologies the most prominent Greek philosophies of their day. In so doing, they established within mainstream Christian thought a platonic and stoic influenced, or plastoicized if you will, view toward the body and sexuality. Essentially, the aspects of platonic philosophy combined with stoic ideas to shape certain Christian thinking about the body/sexuality.

Specifically, the platonic belief in the world of forms, that is, the immaterial/True world, as being different and superior to the world of senses, that is, the material/earthly world, coalesced in Christian thought with the stoic regard for reason and disregard for passion. In so doing, a significant strand of Christian thinking adopted a theology that esteemed the immaterial world (which came to be regarded as the world of reason/spirit/soul) while it renounced the immaterial world (regarded as the world of passion/flesh/body). This split between two realms of being eventuated into a body devaluing theology and tradition. Indeed, as this body devaluing theology was appropriated by influential Christian interpreters, a *platonized* Christianity developed.

Platonized Christianity invariably places the body in an antagonistic relationship with the soul. The soul is divinized while the body is demonized. The soul is revered as the key to salvation. The body is condemned as a source of sin. The locus of bodily sin is human passion, that is, sexual pleasure. As we know, a "sacred" disdain for the sexual body pervades the Christian theological tradition. Now before I proceed, let me just say a word as to why I term this a platonized tradition. To be sure, more than platonic influences are involved in the formation of this Christian juxtaposition of the body/soul, not the least of which is a stoic influence as well as carry-overs from Christianity's Jewish heritage. However, I identify this as a platonized tradition because it is platonic dualism that provides the essential foundation for this perspective. For it is the platonic view of reality that places the realm of the soul and that of the body in an antagonistic, as opposed to a more reciprocal, relationship. Platonic notions of the world set into motion dualistic paradigms, that is, they set things which are opposite in relationships of opposition—there is no Eastern ying/yang with platonic views of the world. And so it is the case that platonic dualism is often seen as the root of antagonistic dualistic paradigms. It is for this reason that I identify the soul regarding/body devaluing Christian tradition as a platonized Christianity. To be sure, this can be a point for later discussion. For now, let me go on to suggest that the Apostle Paul is perhaps the earliest and most influential representative of this platonized Christianity.

Consumed with a belief in the imminent end of the world and informed by his platonized understanding of Christianity, Paul viewed sex as an impediment to salvation. He made clear that unrestrained sexual activity, that is, sexual pleasure, was immoral and a sin against the very body. He encouraged faithful Christians to "Flee from sexual immorality" while admonishing them that "he who sins sexually sins against his own body" (I Corinthians 6:18). While he urged his followers to remain unmarried and celibate, he conceded that if they could not refrain from sexual activity they should marry, "for it is better to marry than to burn with passion" (I Corinthians 7:9). Some 300 years later, Paul's views of the body/sex would directly impact one who would have the greatest impact upon Western theological thought, Augustine of Hippo.

Troubled by his own uncontrollable sexual desires, Augustine eventually heeded Paul's words to "make not provision for the flesh, to fulfil the lusts thereof" (Romans 13:14). Beholden to Pauline sexual attitudes, Augustine developed a theology that unambiguously pronounced sex as sin. In it sexual desire was considered nothing less than diablolical and a reflection of humanity's sinful nature. The only "moral" reason to engage in sex was for proceative purposes. To reiterate, Augustine was the major conduit for *platonized* Christianity into Western theological thought. In this regard, he influenced both Catholic and Protestant traditions.

In the American theological scene, platonized Christianity found perhaps its most comfortable home in Evangelical Protestantism—that which Baldwin appropriately calls "Protestant Puritanism." Within this tradition, the measure of one's salvation is the ability to be "converted" from the ways of the world. True piety is marked by "self-denial" and resistance to bodily temptations, such as sexual pleasure. Evangelical clergymen such as Cotton Mather prayed that God would not hold against them their participation in the very activity that produced their children.[7]

It is primarily through Evangelical Protestantism that *platonized* Christianity and white culture come together. As a result of this dubious connection, *platonized* Christianity provided a "sacred canopy" for the white cultural attack upon Black bodies. More insidious, this particular sacred/secular collusion undermined Black peoples' views toward sexuality, including their responses to sexual justice. A closer look at the white cultural assault upon the Black body will help us to recognize Christianity's collusion with white culture and complicity in disrupting Black sexual attitudes.

White Culture and the Black Body

In his *Notes on Virginia* Thomas Jefferson described Black men this way:

> They are more ardent after their female: but love seems with them to be more an eager desire, than a tender delicate mixture of sentiment and sensation. . . . In general, their existence appears to participate more of sensation than reflection. Their love is ardent, but it kindles the senses only, not the imagination.[8]

Jefferson's comments reflect the dominant discourse of white culture in regard to Black people. As a part of its dehumanizing efforts, white culture (that culture which protects and mandates white supremacist notions and practices) depicts Black women and men as hypersexual, lustful, passionate beings. White cultural rhetoric claims that Black people are oversexualized and controlled by their libido. They are, as Jefferson opines, a people governed by passion not reason. Black men are regarded as rapacious predators—"mandigo bucks." Black women are considered promiscuous seductresses, "Jezebels." This sexualized caricature initially provided sufficient justification for the enslavement of Black people. It also vindicated the brutal exigencies of slavery, such as forced breeding. To depict Black men as sexual predators further provided a justification for lynching, castration, and other crimes committed against their bodies. To label Black women Jezebels allowed white men to rape them with impunity. In the illogic of white culture their rape was a result of white men being victimized by their seductive nature.

White culture's unscrupulous eroticization of Black people attests to Michel Foucault's analysis of the relationship between sexuality and power. "How is it that in a society like ours," Foucault asks, "sexuality is not simply a means of reproducing the species, the family, and the individual? Not simply a means to obtain pleasure and enjoyment? How has sexuality come to be considered the privileged place where our deepest 'truth' is read and expressed?"[9] Foucault answers that this occurs because sexuality is integral to power. It is the axis where the human body and reproduction come together. Power is exerted over people through careful manipulation of their bodies, their perceptions of their bodies, and their reproductive capacities.

Foucault most significantly notes the role of sexuality in maintaining power, especially inequitable power. He argues that sexuality is a vehicle through which distinctions can be made between classes and groups of people. To question or malign the sexuality of another invariably reinforces one's claims to superiority as it implies another group's inferiority. An attack upon a people's sexuality becomes important, then, because sexuality involves one's humanity. Therefore, to assail a people's sexuality is to call into question their very humanity. This is what occurred in relation to Black women and men.

Overall, white cultural sexualization of Black people allowed for the Black body to be exploited in ways that benefited white racist society. Most importantly, it legitimated white supremacist ideology. The fact that Black people were deemed ruled by passion was sufficient proof that they were inferior to white people, a people ostensibly ruled by reason. Black people were considered people of the body/flesh, while white people were considered those of the intellect/soul. In this way, blackness became a sign of an "ardent" nature (that is sexual) at the same time that it signaled a lack of intellect. Thomas Jefferson enunciated this when he commented that "[though] their imagination [was] glowing and elevated . . . yet could I find a black man uttered a thought above the level of plain narration."[10] White cultural rhetoric fundamentally supports the social–political, if not ecclesiastical, domination of Black people by white people. It is in appreciating white cultural representations of Black women and men, that we can recognize the compatibility between Christianity and white culture.

White culture asserts that blackness is synonymous with unrestrained sexuality. *Platonized* Christianity asserts that sexuality is a cauldron of evil and opposes the human connection to God. By arguing the "evil-ness" of sexuality, Christianity implicitly provides a theological justification for any claims that a people governed by sexual desires are innately evil and need to be controlled. Christianity, especially when it does not explicitly challenge the sexualized depictions, in effect supports white culture's debasement of Black people. Moreover, it sanctions white domination over them. For as *platonized* Christianity argues that the body/flesh must be controlled by the intellect/soul, it then follows that Black people (people of the body/flesh) must be controlled by white people (people of the intellect/soul).

The inherent compatibility between *platonized* Christianity and white culture made the advent of religious racism in eighteenth- and nineteenth-century America almost certain. Evangelical Protestantism provided ample apologia for the white racist treatment of Black people. *Platonized* Christianity, with its views on sexuality, was the implicit theological foundation for assertions that black people were divinely cursed (i.e., the Hamitic curse) and/or non-human, souless creatures.

Platonized Christianity and white culture are basically de facto allies in dehumanizing an entire race of people. White cultural portrayals of Black people are granted sacred legitimation vis-à-vis *platonized* Christianity. Left to discern is the impact that this conspiratorial relationship has had on Black people, especially their views on sexuality.

The Black Church Response to Sacred Sexualization

Black People and Platonized Christianity

Ironically, at the same time that religious racism began to flourish in America, Black people were most influenced by *platonized* Christianity. During America's eighteenth-century religious revivals a significant population of Black men and women were converted to Evangelical Protestant thought. A people whose African religious heritage suggested the sanctity and goodness of human sexuality, now adopted a religious belief that claimed it wicked and evil. It has been widely documented that in many of the West African traditions from which a large segment of the enslaved population originated, sexuality was seen and celebrated as a sacred gift from God. "Secularity has no life in many African traditions."[11] This means that there is no diminution of the earthly realm, that is, things of the flesh. Every dimension of the world and humanity, according to numerous African religions, is sacred, is of God, and communicates God's presence. This includes sexuality. Again, there was no contradiction between flesh and divinity.[12] This African cosmological understanding had a profound impact on the way in which the enslaved viewed God (about which more will be said later). In large measure then, it was as a result of these eighteenth-century conversions, that *platonized* views toward the human body and thus sexuality were integrated into Black religious thinking, eventually becoming a substantial theological strand within the Black faith tradition.

Black Church people affected by this evangelical tradition tend to affirm the assertions of the Apostle Paul that one should "make no provision for the flesh," but if one must engage in sexual behavior, "it is better to marry than to burn." In general, for that part of the Black faith tradition most influenced by "Protestant Puritan" (i.e., evangelical) thought, the belief that things of the flesh are evil and antithetical to one's salvation is prominent. While such a belief has certainly served a positive function by promoting a certain set of moral values, family stability, self-regard, and perhaps saving Black lives,[13] there can be a more devastating consequence when a *platonized* Christian tradition shapes Black life—a life already put upon by sexualized racist ideology.[14]

Sexuality: A Taboo Issue

What we too often find in relation to Black Church people is, in fact, a twofold sexualized condemnation of their humanity. In this regard, the interaction between white culture and *platonized* Christianity is almost lethal. For at stake, is not simply the sinfulness of the body, but also the vileness of Blackness. This double burden of sin fundamentally forces Black women and men to develop an intransigent attitude toward sexuality, all in an effort at least to sever the tie between it and their blackness. Practically speaking, Black peoples' hope for "social" acceptance and salvation is contingent on one pivotal requirement: a "radical" rejection/denial of sexuality. Such a rejection potentially invalidates white characterizations and assures divine affirmation. With one radical act of sexual denial, Black people can affirm their humanity and redeem their soul.

This sexual rejection/denial is most typically manifest in a refusal to discuss or acknowledge matters of sexuality. Sexuality is treated as a "taboo" issue within the Black Church community, perhaps indicated by the Black Church's silence in regard to the Texas sodomy case. The consequences of this avoiding silence, it's positive value notwithstanding, has perhaps been more deadly than "saving," particularly in more recent history. For instance, it has contributed to the Black Church community's slow response to the HIV/AIDS crisis even though this disease has had an especially devastating impact upon Black life.[15]

Black Church Homophobia

Another form of sexual rejection/denial has been the Black community's tendency to be hypercritical in regard to behaviors considered sexually atypical or abnormal. Such sexual scrupulousness protects Black people from the charge of being "sexually deviant." It is in this way that we must begin to understand the Black Church's politics of sexual justice as it is revealed in its strong homophobic sentiment. Black people's views toward homosexuality must be understood in light of their responses to sexuality in general, particularly as those responses have been refracted through white culture and sanctioned by "Protestant Puritan" thought.

Essentially, in a heterosexist society where non-heterosexual expressions are considered at best abnormal and at worse perverted, Black Church people have found numerous ways to denounce homosexual practices in the black community. For instance, some have asserted that homosexuality itself is incompatible to black life.[16] Various scholars have also gone so far as to pronounce homosexuality a "white thing" based on the erroneous claim that it was not a part of Black people's African heritage, but was introduced to them by Europeans and European Americans during slavery. More impressive, however, have been the Black Church responses to homoerotic behaviors.

Mirroring the wider evangelical tradition, Black Church people tend to view homoerotism as deviant lustful, sinful behavior. As it does not contribute to procreation, it is not considered an "acceptable/moral" form of sexual activity. Making this view even more intractable are appeals to the Bible. Black Church people often invoke biblical authority to substantiate the view that "homosexuality is wrong." Regardless of the misinterpretation involved, with appeals to texts such as Levitcus 18:22, 20:30, Genesis 19:1–9 and Paul's epistle to the

Romans (1:26-27), Black Church people are able to place a sacred canopy over their homoerotic bias.[17] Most significantly, this divinely sanctioned homophobia has provided a profound way to again sever the link between blackness and sexual deviancy. Specifically, Black people are able to affirm the non-heterosexual Black person, while simultaneously denouncing that person's sexual immorality. They often do so with the familiar refrain, "We love the sinner (i.e. the Black person) but hate the sin (i.e. homoerotic behavior)." This distinction between sinner and sin also enables Black churches to welcome homosexuals into the life of the church, if only as accepted sinners. Practically speaking, this means that the non-heterosexual's space is circumscribed within the Black Church. Some have described the gay experience in the Black Church as one of being in an "open closet." "The 'open closet' allows one to be gay as long as they do not flaunt their sexual identity and maintain their proper place."[18] For, those who have not repented of, or been converted from their "sin" may be church musicians or in the pews, but they cannot be pastors and thus in the pulpits.[19]

Ironically, Black Church people's treatment of homosexual women and men mirrors white cultural characterizations of Black women and men. Just as white culture sexualizes the Black community so to subjugate it, the Black Church does the same to the gay and lesbian community. By castigating homosexual persons on the basis of presumed sexual practices, the Black Church has basically made their very humanity contingent upon a specious view of their sexual activity. Similar to Baldwin's observations regarding the relationship between white society and Black people, the Black Church sexualizes the homosexual person and then "penalizes" them for it.[20]

What is important to note overall, however, is that the discussion of sexual justice in general and homophobia in particular within the Black Church is not a simple matter. Black homophobic sentiments do not reflect merely a close-minded sexual bigotry or a simple adherence to Protestant Puritan views toward sexuality. These are sentiments which in part are a response to white cultural sexualization of Black people and the resultant attacks upon the Black body. The rejection of homoerotic sexuality is a way of de-sexualizing blackness. Black homophobia, to some extent, can be understood as a misguided strategy for protecting the integrity of blackness from hypersexual definitions and hence safeguarding Black lives. The obstinate nature of Black Church homophobia can be seen as an almost unavoidable consequence of the congenial relationship between *platonized* Christianity and white culture.

Ultimately, Black women and men are burdened by *both* white incriminations and Christian judgments in regard to their sexuality. The end result is a radical response of sexual denial that commonly fosters sexual silence and sexual bigotry, that is, injustice. In the final analysis, James Baldwin's observations are borne out: it does mean something to be born in a Protestant Puritan country, Black. Left now to discern are the theological implications for the Black Church in an effort to move toward a more just sexual politic.

Toward a New Politics of Sexuality

Even as Christianity's acceptance of dualistic paradigms that condemn sexuality are theologically problematic for a religion that affirms the incarnation, such an adoption is especially troublesome for the Black Church. The Black faith tradition emerged in defiant response to a *platonized* Christian tradition that supported the enslavement and dehumanization of Black people. Because of God's embodied presence in Jesus, the enslaved were able to testify that God was an active and affirming reality in their lives. Moreover, the enslaved proclaimed that they were created in the image of God.

The testimony of the enslaved crafters of the Black faith tradition witnessed to a God who is neither remote nor abstract but one who is personal and intimate. Such testimony was significant as it revealed the enslaved's rejection of white Christian notions that God sanctioned cruel and inhumane treatment of them. It also denied the assertions of religious racism that blackness was a divine curse and thus an affront to God. Central to the enslaved's understanding of a God who cared about them was a fundamental appreciation that Jesus was God incarnate. It was because God was embodied that God could connect with them, responding to their needs. God's embodiment was crucial to any understanding of God's meaning in human history. No doubt because the enslaved inherited and maintained an African religious tradition in which things of the flesh were not associated with evil, they could fully appreciate the fullness of God's revelation in Jesus. Such an appreciation defied any notion that the human body is an impediment to a relationship with God. Indeed, the theology of the enslaved suggests a high regard for the body/flesh as "the very temple of God," as the medium of God's presence in human lives. The enslaved seemingly understood that it was in becoming body/flesh that God has been significantly revealed in human history, in their history. They also perceived that it is only via body/flesh that human beings can reach out to God as well as to one another.

For the Black Church to adhere to a Christian tradition rooted in a repudiation of the body/flesh is for the Black Church to betray its own libratory theological heritage. What's more, for the Black Church to espouse such a *platonized* tradition is for it to affirm the very theological claims that allowed for the compatibility of Christianity and slavery and the persistent disregard for the Black body. *Platonized* Christianity spawned a religiously racist tradition that has served to sanction white supremacist notions of innate Black inferiority. For Black Church people to profess in any way dualistic splits between the body and soul that inherently condemn the sexual body is for them to uphold the very foundation of such a tradition. It is thus important for the Black Church to connect back to its own enslaved religious heritage—one that defied body/soul splits and protected the sanctity of sexuality. In so doing, it must also allow itself to be critiqued by that tradition.

Specifically, the Black Church needs to recognize the parallels between white cultural contempt for them, and their derision of homosexual people. It must deem homophobia as sinful, just as it has deemed racism sinful. But more to the point, the Black Church is compelled to recognize that platonic Christianity spawns and sanctions systems and structures of oppression. It provides the theological framework for dehumanizing ideologies. As it diminishes the significance of God's embodied reality, it allows for the degradation of the bodies of others. This is thus a tradition that must be repudiated if not deemed sinful.

What then does this mean for the Black Church as it functions in the current political climate? It is worth noting that the current political leadership, from the president to the attorney general, is one that embraces and is motivated by what Baldwin called a "Protestant Puritan tradition," that is, a platonized Christian tradition. It is this Christian tradition, which the current leadership unabashedly makes a part of his politic, that allows the current administration to make with such brash certainty distinctions between good people and evil people. It is this same faith-based politic, that allows him to presume upon the Supreme Courts his opinions about fairness, what is right and what is wrong. What the Black Church community must recognize and its leadership must make clear is that the language of faith is not necessarily the language of justice, and may not even be the language of the God they profess. This is what the enslaved understood, thus allowing them to recognize the hypocrisy of their master's piety, reject their master's faith, rebel against their enslavement as they forged their own understandings of God.

It is no doubt that in reclaiming its own non-platonized African religious heritage, a heritage that precipitated the critique of white racism, the Black Church will become more consistent, if not more reliable in its justice politics, not simply as it involves racism, but sexuality as well as other issues. To be sure, not until the Black Church is freed from this platonized Christian tradition, will it be truly liberated from the politics of white cultural domination and oppression. Until such time it will no doubt continue to be at times seduced by this politic and to perpetuate this politic in its stance toward others, such as gay and lesbian persons.

In the end, the issue of sexual justice in the Black Church is a complicated one. Black Church homophobia bespeaks the denigration of Black people by white racist society. It, in many regards, is a sign of Black people's own brokenness and an attempt to be healed. Even still, it is a sin. In this regard, Black Church homophobia can be seen as the sin that sin produced. James Baldwin's observations perhaps puts it best, "the Negro pays for that guilt which white people have about the flesh," and as a result so too do gay and lesbian persons. It is time for the Black Church to truly reclaim its liberating faith tradition. It is time for a new politic of sexual justice in the Black Church.

Notes

1. James Baldwin, "Down At The Cross: Letter from a Region in My Mind," in *The Fire Next Time* (1963; reprint New York: First Vintage International Books, 1993), 30.
2. "Studs Terkel Interview 1961," in *Conversations with James Baldwin*, ed. Fred L. Standley and Louis H. Pratt (Mississippi: University of Mississippi Press, 1989), 8–9.
3. Alice Walker, *In Search of Our Mother's Garden* (New York: Harcourt, Brace, Jovanovich, 1983).
4. For more on the homophobia of the black community in relation to the wider society see Kelly Brown Douglas, *Sexuality and the Black Church: A Womanist Perspective* (Maryknoll, New York: Orbis Book, 1999), 87–88.
5. W. E. B. Du Bois, *Souls of Black Folk* (1903; reprint, New York: Alfred A. Knopf, 1993), 153.
6. See above epigraphs.
7. See Forrest G. Woods discussion of Puritan attitudes toward sexual activity in *the Arrogance of Faith: Christianity and Race in America from the Colonial Era to the Twentieth Century* (New York: Alfred A. Knopf, 1990), see especially 187–196.
8. Thomas Jefferson, *Notes on Virginia in The Life and Selected Writing of Thomas Jefferson*, edited and with an introduction by Adrienne Koch and William Peden (New York: The Modern Library 1998), 239.

9. Foucault quoted in James Miller, *The Passion of Michel Foucault* (New York: Doubleday/Anchor Books, 1993), 293.

10. Thomas Jefferson, *Notes on Virginia*, 240.

11. See Peter Paris, *The Spirituality of African Peoples: The Search for a Common Moral Discourse* (Minneapolis:Fortress Press, 1995), 27.

12. For more on this discussion see Douglas, *Sexuality and The Black Church*, esp. chapter 6.

13. It should be noted that the fear of Black sexuality was pivotal in the lynching of Black people, particularly Black men. given the continuous history of Black men being attacked, maimed, and executed because of presumed sexual activity, the adoption of an ascetic sexuality can become a viable survival tactic.

14. This argument draws upon the analysis I've put forth in an earlier article. In that article I more thoroughly explore the numerous consequences of platonized Christianity on Black lives particularly as it regards Black people's regard for their own body and concept of salvation. See "Black Body/White Soul: The Unsettling Intersection of Race, Sexuality and Christianity" in *Body and Soul:Rethinking Sexuality as Justice-Love*, ed. Marvin Ellison and Sylvia Thorson (Cleveland, Ohio: The Pilgrim Press, 2003).

15. For an in-depth discussion see Douglas, *Sexuality and the Black Church*. Note especially the introduction where this issue is first engaged.

16. See for example the argument made by Black female ethicist Cheryl Sanders in "Christian Ethics and Theology in Womanist Perspective," in *Journal of Religious Thought* 5, no. 2 (Fall 1989), see also Nathan Hare and Julia Hare, *The Endangered Black Family: Coping with the Unisexualization and Coming Extinction of the Black Race* (San Francisco: Black Think Tank, 1984).

17. See a fuller discussion of the use of the bible in supporting Black Church homophobia in Douglas, *Sexuality and the Black Church*, especially chapter 4.

18. For more of this concept of the open-closet see Mindy Thompson Fullilove, M. D. and Robert E. Fullilove, III.Ed.D, "Homosexuality and the African American Church: The Paradox of the 'Open Closet'," at HIVinsite.ucsf.edu.

19. James Baldwin provides a powerful literary depiction of this reality through the protagonist's struggles with his sexuality and spirituality in the novel *Go Tell It on The Mountain*.

20. See epigraph.

Bc. 5/05